# POLITICIANS AND VIRTUOSI

STUDIES PRESENTED TO THE
INTERNATIONAL COMMISSION
FOR THE HISTORY OF
REPRESENTATIVE AND
PARLIAMENTARY INSTITUTIONS

## LXIX

ÉTUDES PRÉSENTÉES À LA
COMMISSION INTERNATIONALE
POUR L'HISTOIRE DES
ASSEMBLÉES D'ÉTATS

Francis Bacon, Viscount St. Albans (1561–1626)
John Vanderbank (c. 1618). *National Portrait Gallery*

# POLITICIANS AND VIRTUOSI

## ESSAYS IN EARLY MODERN HISTORY

H.G. KOENIGSBERGER

THE HAMBLEDON PRESS

LONDON   AND   RONCEVERTE

Published by The Hambledon Press 1986

35 Gloucester Avenue, London NW1 7AX (U.K.)

309 Greenbrier Avenue, Ronceverte WV 24970 (U.S.A.)


ISBN 0 907628 65 6 (Cased)
ISBN 0 907628 66 4 (Paper)

History series 49

*British Library Cataloguing in Publication Data*

Koenigsberger, H.G.
    Politicians and virtuosi: essays in early
    modern history. – (History series; 49)
    1. Europe – History – 476-1492
    2. Europe – History – 1492-1648
    I. Title   II. Series
    940.2'1      D220

*Library of Congress Cataloging in Publication Data*

Koenigsberger, H.G. (Helmut Georg)
    Politicians and virtuosi.

    (History series; 49)
    Includes index.
    1. History, Modern – Addresses, essays, lectures.
    2. History, Modern – Historiography – Addresses,
    essays, lectures. I. Title. II. Series: History series
    (Hambledon Press); v. 49.
D210.K59   1986      940.2'1      85-5588

Printed and bound in Great Britain by
WBC (Printers), Bristol and WBC (Bookbinders), Maesteg

# CONTENTS

# ACKNOWLEDGEMENTS

The articles reprinted here appeared first in the following places and are reprinted by the kind permission of the original publishers.

1    Inaugural Lecture in the Chair of History, University of London at King's College, 1975.

2    *The Journal of Italian History*, vol. 1, no. 1 (1978), 18-49.

3    *Parliaments, Estates and Representation*, vol. 2, pt. 2 (1982), 103-111.

4    *European Studies Review*, vol. 1, no. 1 (1971), 1-22.

5    *Bijdragen en Mededelingen betreffende de Geschiedenis der Nederlanden*, 99, no. 4 (1984), 573-95.

6    *National Consciousness, History and Political Culture in Early Modern Europe*, ed. O. Ranum (Johns Hopkins University Press, Baltimore and London, 1975), 144-72.

7    This chapter appears here for the first time.

8    *The Journal of Interdisciplinary History*, vol. 1, no. 3 (1971), 407-17.

9    *The Diversity of History. Essays in Honour of Sir Herbert Butterfield*, ed. J.H. Elliott and H.G. Koenigsberger (Routledge, London, 1971), 35-78.

10   *Political Symbolism in Modern Europe*, ed. S. Drescher, D. Sabean and A. Sharlin (Transaction Books, New Brunswick and London, 1982), 168-93.

11   *Past and Present*, 83 (1979), 32-56. World Copyright: The Past and Present Society, Corpus Christi College, Oxford, England.

## LIST OF ILLUSTRATIONS

To Emile Lousse, Antonio Marongiu

and the memory of Helen Cam

# Introduction

In the 17th and 18th centuries the term virtuoso meant not only a highly skilful musician but an accomplished person, highly skilful in any of the arts or sciences. The *Shorter Oxford English Dictionary* quotes a remark from 1676, that 'another excellent virtuoso of the same Assembly (the Royal Society), Mr. John Evelyn, hath considerably advanced the History of Fruit and Forest-Trees'. The use of the word, then as now, was not always entirely flattering or approving. In 1677, for instance, it was said of the latitudinarians in the Anglican Church that they 'imagine there were to be virtuosos in religion as well as Philosophy, and that this age made new discoveries of Doctrines as the Astronomers have of the Stars and that new Creeds in Divinity are as necessary as new Systems of the World'.[1] It does not seem as if the word was used for politicians. But Machiavelli spoke of the *virtù* of princes, their ability to handle a political situation to the best advantage.

In these essays I try to explore the conditions in which virtuosi could act in the arts, the sciences and the politics of early modern Europe and I also try to see whether there may not be connections between these different types of 'virtuous' activity. In the last thirty years both political and cultural history has more commonly been seen in terms of economic and social developments. This approach has not produced the universally accepted scientific models which some of its protagonists had hoped for; but it has afforded many new insights into historical processes. In fact, we can no longer do without it. It has become part of every serious historian's equipment. It is not, however, total history; nor should it be, and perhaps least of all in the cultural field. The creative work of artists, musicians, writers, scientists and thinkers of every type was often influenced much more immediately and directly by the institutions and the politics of the society they lived in than by that society's social and economic structure. Similar social structures in early modern society allowed for enormously different types of creative activity. If we are to gain a greater understanding of how this happened we need new types of historical analysis and new sets of correlations, not so much to supersede as to supplement the now classical methods of present historiography.

---

[1] J. Warly, *The Reasoning Apostate: or Modern Latitude-Man Consider'd* . . . (London, 1677), pp. 86–87. Quoted in Margaret C. Jacob, *The Newtonians and the English Revolution 1689–1720*, :Ithaca, 1976), p. 48.

One of the principal methods of this historiography has been to apply the findings, categories and models of the modern social sciences to history. In this book the essays in political history (chapters 1–7) try to show the limitations of this approach and the misconceptions on which it often rests. The models which sociologists, social anthropologists and political scientists have built have usually been generalisations inductively arrived at by observing our contemporary world or, at best, its very recent history. This is of course a perfectly legitimate procedure for these disciplines. But the historians who have tried to use their models have mostly done something rather different. They have tried to impose ready-made models on different societies and conditions. Of course, the historians were usually aware that the social scientists' claim to a universal validity for their models and laws was often exaggerated and they realised that a complete fit of these models for earlier societies was unlikely. But they often found it very difficult to avoid imposing categories on the past which were anachronistic or irrelevant. Thus the debate about the existence of revolutions in early modern Europe was bedevilled from the outset by definitions derived from the experience of modern revolutions, from the French to the Russian or Cuban. Yet the experience of these revolutions and the definitions derived from them were quite alien to the people who made revolutions in the early modern period (see chapters 3 and 7).

The result has often been that historians have either asked the wrong questions or based their questions on wrong assumptions. The two most common assumptions have been, firstly, that early modern societies can be treated as largely self-contained units and that an analysis of these units – England, France, Florence – can give us satisfactory answers to questions such as why revolutions occurred or why absolutism was introduced. Of course, modern social or political units are not really self-contained; but, in order to build their models, social scientists have assumed self-containment and have usually left outside influences to a separate category of exogenous factors. For the early modern period this method tends to distort reality. Most major monarchies of early modern Europe were composite states whose parts had different social structures, different laws and institutions and, sometimes, different religions. Quite often they were not even contiguous but were separated by other countries or by a stretch of sea, and yet the more distant parts were not colonies in the sense in which the Spanish or English settlements in America were colonies. In Europe this composite structure of states meant that not only was tension between centre and periphery an inbuilt pattern of early modern states but that, in the case of actual conflict, the resources which the contestants could command depended on countries, or parts of countries, which were not involved in the causes of the conflict, or only remotely so. This happened for instance in the English civil war of the 1640s in which, for reasons which had little to do with English problems, the Scots were involved and probably turned the military balance in favour of parliament and against the king (see chapter 1).

Because the English civil war was fought when the rest of Europe was busy fighting its own wars, there was little intervention from neighbouring powers. Such non-intervention, however, was unusual. Normally neighbours intervened in a civil war, especially when, as happened so frequently in this period, religion was one of the issues of conflict. This precisely was the pattern during the revolt of the Netherlands (see chapters 3, 4 and 5).

The second common assumption made by historians following the lead of the social scientists has been that equilibrium was the normal condition of early modern society. Any movement, especially any violent or sudden movement, was then interpreted as the introduction of disequilibrium or dysfunction of the society. In other words, historians have been content to adopt a static model when what is wanted is something dynamic. This is, for instance, where reliance on economic models can be misleading. Economists have usually worked with equilibrium models or, when they have used dynamic ones, they have been mostly interested in growth models. But for the historian growth in the economists' sense is only one of many aspects of change and transformation and, especially in the early modern period, often not necessarily the most important one in a dynamic situation. I would argue that early modern society was always in a condition of movement and never in full equilibrium or only for quite short periods at a time (see chapter 7). Marxist historians have only partly avoided the trap of the static model, for they have introduced some curiously static concepts of their own. Their basic concept of feudalism, not as the specific legal-military relationship of the central middle ages which was defined in the laws and customs of the time, but as a *portmanteau* term for any pre-capitalist society in which landownership and political power more or less coincide – this form of labelling imposes a stable pattern on human relationships which were in fact constantly changing. In so far as Marxist historians have built the concept of change into their historiography they have tended towards a moralistic teleology, a kind of social 'whig history'.

On the occasions when social scientists have started with a historical analysis and have tried to employ a dynamic model their results have been much more illuminating for historians. This seems to me particularly the case with K. W. Deutsch's model of medieval unity based on the historical fact of the scarcity of skills in 'underdeveloped' societies and the dynamic effects of the actions of a skilled elite working on an international level (see chapter 8). I have used this model to explain why the break-up of the unified medieval Church became almost inevitable. I have not, however, used this model to posit a reductionist theory of the Reformation; for the model does not encompass the whole human experience of the Reformation, the change in religious sensibilities which profoundly affected not only actual religious beliefs but much of the intellectual, artistic and, arguably, even economic life of nearly half of Europe and most of North America. In shaping this experience, Luther and Calvin undoubtedly played the role of virtuosi.[2]

By contrast, Deutsch's model of the development of nations and nationalism is not nearly as successful because it overemphasises a modern phenomenon, the overwhelming importance of communication. Here again it is important for the historian not to be seduced by a plausible model into monocausal explanations or into reductionism (see chapter 6).

Norbert Elias's theories (see chapter 1) are based on both actual historical analysis and on a dynamic conception of social processes. His concepts of the monopoly mechanism (*Monopolmechanismus*) in international relations and of the royal mechanism (*Königsmechanismus*) in the internal political development of early modern states are, both of them, very useful for the historian. But are they really models or are they only tendencies? They are most clearly visible when one looks through the wrong end of a telescope, so to speak, when one deals in macro-history. But they give no indication of the time scale one should expect in which they might work themselves out, nor of the circumstances in which they will not work at all. The development of French absolutism fits in rather well with Elias's theory of the royal mechanism. But this theory or mechanism tells us nothing about why monarchies failed to become absolute in the Netherlands and in Britain. Much the same problem arises with the theory of the monopoly mechanism, the tendency of political units in competition to expand and swallow up the smaller competitors until one emerges with the monopoly of power. This model certainly illuminates the slow reconstitution of the kingdom of France after the collapse of the Carolingian empire. But it does not explain why so many parts of this empire, even French speaking provinces, remained obstinately outside the French monarchy. And this is, after all, precisely what the medievalist and early modernist historian wants to know.

In cultural history the historiographical position is rather different. Apart from Marxist theories, which have been only partially successful in this field, we have had very few attempts at model building. Nor is this very surprising; for the role of outstanding individuals, the virtuosi, is obviously overwhelmingly important. This is particularly evident in the history of elite culture; perhaps less so in the history of popular culture, although even here I would argue that the popular culture of Europe should not be studied without reference to elite culture. In any case, I do

---

[2] Cf. H. G. Koenigsberger, *Luther: A Profile*, (New York and London, 1973), Introduction.

not believe that the historian of culture, or whole societies and civilisations, should throw in his hand and simply accept the appearance of genius as biologically given and inexplicable. Sociobiology certainly cannot provide any viable explanations in this field; but there are some clear historical patterns. At their simplest one can point to the uncontrovertible fact that medieval Europe was full of brilliant theologians while twentieth-century Europe is full of brilliant scientists and engineers. But this is not the whole story of the distribution of virtuosi among different fields of creative activity, nor is it at all simple to explain how we got from one state to the other. The creative genius of individual virtuosi, of Michelangelo, of Shakespeare, of Beethoven, must ultimately remain opaque. But the clustering of virtuosi in certain times and places, in the Italian Renaissance for instance, and the shift of virtuoso activity from one field to another – from the visual arts to music in Germany in the later 16th century – these are problems which the historian should be able to handle systematically, just as he handles the different types of political institutions.

It is this which I have attempted to do, by looking at both psychological correlations – music and religion, science and religion – and social-political correlations, such as the comparison of cultural activities in early modern courts and cities (see chapters 9–11). I do not claim that these correlations are universally valid models for cultural history. They are deliberately anchored in European history and mostly in the early modern period. They make no claim to be total history or to provide complete explanations for major historical processes, and I remain sceptical about the possibility of complete explanations and models. But I hope my essays will stimulate further discussions and inquiry along some of the lines I have tried to explore.

# Dominium Regale or Dominium Politicum et Regale

# Monarchies and Parliaments in Early Modern Europe

Inaugural lectures, I have been told, should produce something new. The words I have chosen for my title are not new, of course. On the contrary: Sir John Fortescue's two phrases, *dominium regale* and *dominium politicum et regale*, were surely the common currency of Macaulay's fabulous schoolboys; or should have been, anyway. I have used them because they sum up a common English attitude towards our history and towards French and, generally, continental history. According to the distinguished former Chief Justice who wrote his treatise on *The Governance of England* at the end of his long life, in the 1470's, France was ruled as a *dominium regale*. By this he meant an absolute monarchy which for him signified a regime in which the king taxed the common people at will while leaving the nobles exempt. The results, Fortescue maintained, were deplorable, both for the king and for his subjects; for

they drinken water, they eaten apples, with bread right browne made of rye; they eaten no flesh but if it be right seldom a little lard, or of the entrails and hides of beasts slain for the nobles and merchants of the land. They wearen no woollens . . . Their wives and children go barefoot . . . For some of them that were wont to pay to his lord for his tenement, which he hireth by the year, a scute, payeth now to the king over that scute 5 scutes. Wherethrough they be arted by necessity so to watch, labour and grub for their sustenance that their nature is wasted . . . They gone crooked and been feeble, not able to fight nor defend the realm . . . [The king of France had to rely for the defence of his country on Scots, Spaniards and Germans.] Lo, this is the fruit of *ius regale* . . . But blessed be God, this land [England] is ruled under a better law; and therefore the people therof be not in such penurie, nor thereby hurt in their person, but they be wealthy and have all things necessary to the sustenance of nature. Wherefore they been mighty and able to resist the adversaries of this realm, and to beat other realms that do or would do them wrong. Lo this is the fruit of *ius politicum et regale* under which we live.[1]

In other words, the king of England could not tax his subjects without the consent of parliament and therefore he could not overtax them.

---

[1] Sir John Fortescue, *The Governance of England*, C. Plummer, ed. (Oxford, 1885), pp. 114–15. I have modernized the spelling.

England was a constitutional monarchy, and this was the reason for its prosperity, strength and happiness, compared with the unhappy, dark and absolutist countries of the Continent.

It is easy for us to smile at Fortescue. Had he not himself lived through the most decisive defeat this country has ever suffered in a major war, and at the hands of the despised French? And had not Fortescue been involved in some twenty years of civil war in England in which, moreover, he had chosen the losing side? The French, naturally, made the comparison between the two countries rather differently. In 1484, perhaps only ten years after Fortescue wrote *The Governance of England*, they assembled in a States General of their whole huge kingdom, at Tours. The chancellor, Guillaume de Rochefort, opened the assembly in traditional form with an encomium of his country and countrymen:

Nowhere do we read that, even for a single day, our lightness of spirit, over-severe royal orders, the victories of the enemy or, indeed, any misfortunes have ever induced the people of France to break faith with their kings. On the contrary. To defend the king, to uphold his cause, we are wont to take up arms with all our courage and even to die willingly, if fate should so ordain . . . But open the chronicles of foreign nations and we read how often princes are betrayed by their subjects for the least cause . . . Let me just cite in evidence our neighbours, the English. Just look at what happened in that country after the death of King Edward [i.e. Edward IV]. Consider his children, already growing up and gallant, but murdered with impunity and the crown transferred to the murderer by favour of the people.

And if one looked further back, Rochefort continued, hardly two or three of their kings have been left in peace or have come to the throne without a revolution. But our own king, Charles VIII, he concluded, although still a child , had such confidence in his estates that he was now asking the deputies to participate in the government. They were to inform the king of their grievances and to advise him on the good of the kingdom and of their specific provinces.[2]

Later in the stormy course of this assembly, Philippe Pot, a Burgundian deputy, was to argue that it was both the right and the duty of the States General to appoint the king's council during a royal minority, for

history and tradition tell us the kings were originally created by the votes of the sovereign people, and the prince is placed where he is, not that he may pursue his own advantage, but that he may strive unselfishly for the welfare of the nation. [Since the king cannot now himself govern,] the people must resume a power which is their own.[3]

[2] Jehan Masselin, *Journal des États Généraux de France tenus à Tours en 1484* . . . A. Bernier, ed. (Paris, 1835), pp. 37–39. J. Russell Major, *Representative Institutions in Renaissance France 1421–1559*, (Madison, 1960), pp. 72–73.

[3] Major, *ibid.* p. 88.

No English parliament was to make equally far-reaching claims for another 150 years.

Representative institutions and some form of partnership between kings and parliaments were therefore no English monopoly in the fifteenth century. In one form or another, and with varying degrees of authority, they existed in practically every European monarchy, from Poland to Portugal and from Norway to Sicily. Nevertheless, Fortescue's distinction between *dominium regale* and *dominium politicum et regale* was neither imaginary nor foolish. He and his contemporaries were observing a real phenomenon, the tendency of kings to extend their powers, and especially their powers of taxation and legislation, at the expense of the representative institutions of their countries. No doubt the Chief Justice, had he lived, would have taken a gloomy satisfaction at the final outcome of the States General of Tours: the squabbling and manoeuvring of three estates, of the different provinces and of the various princely factions which, together, paralysed the effectiveness of the assembly and allowed the royal government to maintain virtually undiminished its powers over taxation, legislation and policy-making.

For the historian this poses a problem. In the late-medieval partnership between kings and parliaments, throughout Europe, the kings were by far the stronger, although hardly ever the completely dominant partners. *Dominium politicum et regale* was the norm, not the exception. How was it then, that this relatively uniform system of political partnership, uniform, that is, in terms of balance of political power although certainly not of structure – how was it that this system developed in different countries in different directions? had indeed already started to so in the 15th century, when Fortescue made his famous distinctions? By the early 18th century the distinctions had become quite clear. In one group of countries, the parliaments had either abolished the monarchy altogether or had established their clear preponderance in a transformed partnership. This happened in England and Scotland, in the United Provinces of the Netherlands and in Poland.

In a second group the success of the parliaments was more limited, their predominance in the partnership with the monarchy was not as unequivocal as in the first group and their position always remained somewhat precarious. Nevertheless, their power had become or remained formidable. This was the case in Hungary and in some of the German principalities, notably Württemberg, East Friesland and Mecklenburg.

In a third group we may number those countries or provinces of countries – and this latter group is an important one, as we shall see – in which the monarchies defeated their parliaments and either abolished them altogether or simply did not summon them any more, or in which the parliaments survived, but with strictly limited and often gradually diminishing powers, and always as junior partners of the monarchies. In

Spain and Portugal, in Naples, Piedmont and Sardinia the parliaments disappeared altogether, as did the States General of France, the States General of the Spanish Netherlands (Belgium), the Rigsdag of Denmark and the Landtage of several German principalities.

Those parliaments which survived showed a spectrum of varying degrees of authority. At one end were the estates of Bohemia which, after 1620, had virtually lost all effective powers. At the other end there was the Sicilian parliament which in the 17th century compared itself with the English parliament. This was certainly an exaggeration but not entirely beside the mark. In between were the provincial estates of Languedoc, Brittany and Burgundy which preserved considerable powers of taxation and some of the German estates which even controlled their own tax collecting machinery. Other German estates, however, such as those of Bavaria, no longer met in full assemblies but had delegated their powers to a more or less permanent and self-perpetuating committee. Such committees existed also outside Germany. Those of the cortes of Catalonia, the *diputats*, found themselves, in 1640, leading an anti-monarchical revolution.

There are, finally, two important cases which do not easily fit into these three groups. The first is the diet of the Holy Roman Empire, the Reichstag. It does not fit because it came more and more to represent not estates or groups or corporations in the usual European sense but increasingly independent principalities. The second, and very different, case is that of Sweden. Here the centre of power oscillated quite violently, in swings of varying duration, between a relatively absolute monarchy and either the Council of State, representing the high nobility or, in the 18th century, the Riksdag, representing the other estates. This singular history of Sweden is particularly illuminating for some aspects of our problem, and I shall come back to it.

Let me repeat the problem once more: how did this varying distribution of political powers between kings and parliaments arise? Having stated it in this form, i.e. as a search for the reason for the changes in the political structures of European states between the 15th and 18th centuries, we note that certain conclusions will follow immediately. The first and most important is that we are here concerned with the problem of power or, rather, the distribution of power. Now the distribution of power may, at any one moment, rest on consent, and this moment may last some time, perhaps one or two generations. But a change in the distribution of power is not likely to be carried out by consent or certainly not only by consent. Men do not easily give up what they consider vital for the defence of their status when they see this status attacked, as long, that is, as they think they have a chance of successfully defending it. And very often the best defence will appear to be attack. Basically, therefore, the history of the relations between monarchies and parliaments is the story of a struggle for power.

This has often been denied. Many historians have chosen rather to stress the spirit of community in early modern society. They have pointed to the initiative which princes took in summoning assemblies in order to obtain the support of the most powerful groups of their subjects. The key quotation for this argument is the famous address of Henry VIII to the parliament of 1543 in which he stated that

we at no time stand so highly in our estate royal as in the time of Parliament, wherein we as head and you as members are conjoined and knit together into one body politic.[4]

It was very much what Chancellor Rochefort had said at the States General of Tours in 1484, and what countless kings and their chancellors had said in countless addresses to parliaments and assemblies of estates in the latter middle ages. No doubt, it was all very gratifying to the members or deputies, and the analogy of the head and members of an organism for a body politic remained the common currency of political language for centuries. But that does not mean that it necessarily expressed a considered political analysis. What else would a king want to say to his parliament in an opening session or at some other formal occasion? Quarrels would arise soon enough and, sooner or later, they would involve constitutional points and, hence, the problem of power. And this problem of power had to be resolved, sometimes dramatically, by civil war, sometimes slowly, by almost imperceptible pressure; but, one way or another, resolved it had to be, and always by struggle and the exercise or the implicit threat of force, although not necessarily by violence.[5]

The second conclusion which follows from our formulation of the problem is that we should look for answers that go beyond the incidental, the detailed history of each country, even though it does not follow at all that our answer will necessarily be a simple formula applicable to all European countries or that incidentals may not, at times, prove to be very important. It does, however, seem to follow – and this is my third immediate conclusion – that any answer will have to centre on the dynamics of change over a period of time. If this is correct, it will rule

[4] G. R. Elton, ed., *The Tudor Constitution*, (Cambridge, 1960), p. 270. *cf.* also Prof. Elton's somewhat sceptical comments about the authenticity of the passage and his view that Henry VIII muddled what his judges told him, pp. 230 and 257, n. 1.

[5] *Cf.* the formulation by O. Brunner, *Land und Herrschaft*, Publications of the Institut für Geschichtswissenschaft und Archivforschung in Vienna (Vienna, 1943), vol. 1, p. 474; 'But the sovereign and the people confront one another . . . Thus the "country", the "land" in a new sense, opposes the sovereign and finally forms itself into a corporation of the state. At this moment, of course, the old unity of the land is threatened [but did it ever really exist, except for relatively short periods of time? H.G.K.]. The break-up forces the decisive question posed since the 16th century: shall the sovereign or the estates represent in the land? In the first case, the country becomes a privileged corporation; in the second, it becomes the ruler of the land.'

out solutions based on models of equilibrium and disequilibrium or dysfunction in early modern society,[6] and it will relegate to a heuristic device the currently fashionable pattern of historical analysis of *longue durée, conjoncture* and *événements* (long-term conditions, medium-term movements and short-term events).

The blunt truth is that no one has yet come up with an answer to our problem, that is, with anything approaching a satisfactory overall theory.[7] I am not able to do this, either. What I hope to do is, rather, to define some characteristics such a theory must have, some of the elements which must go into its construction, and to indicate how far, in the present state of historical knowledge, it can be composed.

We know a great deal of the history of the parliaments of individual countries. We have had some excellent comparisons of different parliaments in one country, such as those of Germany and of Italy;[8] and we have had some illuminating studies of certain aspects of representative institutions, such as their close connections with the traditions of regionalism and of local loyalties.[9] The only attempt to construct an overall theory has been made by the German historian, Otto Hintze, in two essays, published in 1930 and 1931.[10]

In his first essay, which he called a typology of the constitution of estates in the western world, Hintze distinguishes two ideal types of representative institutions: the bicameral, or two chamber, and the tricamreal, or three-curial system. The two chamber system was most typically represented by England but occurred, in varying forms, in Hungary, Bohemia, Poland, Scandinavia and, generally, the German

---

[6] Robert Forster and J. P. Greene, ed., *Preconditions of Revolution in Early Modern Europe* (Baltimore, 1970), especially the chapters by L. Stone and J. W. Smit.

[7] This is true also for A. R. Myers, *European Parliaments and Estates before 1789*, (London, 1975).

[8] E.g. F. L. Carsten, *Princes and Parliaments from the Fifteenth to the Eighteenth Century*, (Oxford, 1959). G. Oestreich, *Geist und Gestalt des frühmodernen Staates*, (Berlin, 1969); English edition G. Oestreich, *Neostoicism and the Early Modern State*, ed. Brigitta Oestreich and H. G. Koenigsberger, trans. D. McLintock, (Cambridge, 1982). A. Marongiu, *Il Parlamento in Italia nel Medio Evo e nel Età Moderna*, (Milan, 1962); English version by S. J. Woolf, *Medieval Parliaments: A Comparative Study*, (London, 1968).

[9] D. Gerhard, 'Regionalismus und ständisches Wesen als ein Grundthema europäischer Geschichte', Ch. 1 of *Alte und Neute Welt in Vergleichender Geschichtsbetrachtung*, (Göttingen, 1962). For the importance of the corporate element of both European society in general and assemblies of estates in particular, *cf.* E. Lousse, *La société d'ancien régime, Organisation et représentation corporatives*, (Bruges, Louvain, Paris, 1943). On the importance of certain technical aspects of representation *cf.* G. Post, 'Plena Potestas and Consent in Medieval Assemblies', *Traditio, 1* (New York, 1943), and H. G. Koenigsberger, 'The Powers of Deputies in Sixteenth-Century Assemblies', in *Estates and Revolutions*, (Ithaca, 1971).

[10] O. Hintze, 'Typologie der ständischen Verfassungen des Abendlandes', (1930), and 'Weltgeschichtliche Bedingungen der Repräsentativverfassung', (1931), in *Gesammelte Abhandlungen*, vol. 1, G. Oestreich, ed. (Göttingen, 1962). English translation of the 1931 article in *The Historical Essays of Otto Hintze*, Felix Gilbert, ed. (New York, Oxford, 1975).

principalities east of the river Elbe. These were the countries surrounding the old Carolingian Empire in which feudalism did not develop at all or, as in England, did not succeed in breaking down an older regional (shire) organization. In these countries the upper house or chamber developed from the great lay and ecclesiastical magnates who formed the king's council. The lower house was constituted from the rest of the privileged classes. It was in this group of countries, or, at least, in England, Poland and Hungary, that the assemblies triumphed over the monarchy.

The three-curial system, organized as clergy (or prelates), nobles and towns, was most typically represented by France but occurred also in most western German principalities. These were the areas of the Carolingian Empire, the home of feudalism, and from there the system was transferred, with some variations, to the Spanish and South Italian kingdoms. Hintze regarded it as a later and more developed system than the two-chamber system, for here the old magnates–royal council chamber had already disintegrated before the advance of a more effective and professionalized royal administration. In consequence, the monarchies were able to defeat the estates. Hintze saw this defeat and the triumph of absolutism in the 17th and 18th centuries as a temporary phenomenon; for he thought that the 19th and 20th century constitutions of most European monarchies had direct links with the parliamentary traditions of the old regime. The dynamic forces in this development Hintze saw in the 'reception', i.e. introduction, of Roman Law on the Continent at the end of the middle ages and in the early modern period. In his second essay, 'World-historical Conditions of Representative Constitutions', he added to this the rivalries inherent in the European state system and the consequent need for the monarchies to increase their effective power and, therefore, to extend their authority over their estates.

As a typology, Hintze's schema was in many ways perceptive and illuminating even if on occasion he skated rather rapidly over thin ice. Sweden and Denmark, he argued for instance, shifted in the seventeenth century from the two-chamber to the three-curial system. He did not say very clearly why this should have happened and, in fact, it did not really happen in quite this way at all. In both countries the monarchies abolished not only the privileges of the old council of magnates, and did so with the help of the other estates, but they then dispensed with the assemblies of the estates altogether, so that one cannot really say that they changed to a three-curial system. But more important is what Hintze left out of his typology, and this is the one country which does not fit into the schema, even when this schema is interpreted in the loosest possible way. This was the Netherlands. For here was a country, in the heart of the Carolingian Empire, which could boast not only of both two-chamber and three-curial systems in its different provinces, but also of unicameral ones and of all sorts of others, as well as of a States General. Moreover, this country and its institutions eventually split into two, and along lines that bear little relation to Hintze's types. In one of these two countries, the United Provinces of the Netherlands, the estates actually abolished the monarchy altogether; while in the other one, the Spanish Netherlands (Belgium), the monarchy won out over the estates. I shall come back to a consideration of the Netherlands and especially of its States General, and with it to the whole problem of composite assemblies, a problem which Hintze hardly touched on.

Secondly, Hintze's characterization of the reception of Roman Law and of interstate rivalries and war as the dynamic forces in the history of monarchies and parliaments, while valid, is too narrow. They tell us nothing of the dynamism of the English parliament or the Polish diet. Prolonged war, moreover, could just as easily weaken as strengthen monarchies. This happened in both Spain and France during the Thirty Years' War.[11] Clearly we need a wider theory of the dynamics of change for this period of European history.

Such a theory has been provided by the sociologist Norbert Elias in volume II of his book *Über den Prozess der Zivilisation* (*The Process of Civilization* or perhaps just *The Development of Civilization*), first published in 1939.[12] Professor Elias distinguishes three basic mechanisms in the history of Europe from the Middle Ages through the early modern period. The first is derived from the economists' theory of the inevitable formation of monopolies from a situation of free competition through the gradual elimination or absorption of rivals by their more powerful competitors. Professor Elias argues that the same pattern inevitably occurs on a political and territorial plane, and he illustrates his thesis from the history of France after the collapse of the Carolingian Empire. The second mechanism is equally inevitable. It is the depersonalization and institutionalization of the exercise of power which occurs both with the growth of territory under the control of one prince and with the increasing complexity and specialization of society as it develops economically in the course of the middle ages and the following centuries. The third mechanism, which he calls the 'royal mechanism' (*Königsmechanismus*) is the tendency of the monarchy to absorb functions and increase its power because it can balance the different interest groups within the country against each other and gain increasing control over them. The conflicting but complementary interests of all non-monarchical forces within a society will neither allow

[11] For Spain *cf.* I. A. A. Thompson, *War and Government in Spain, 1580–1640, (London, 1976), passim.* For France *cf.* J. Russell Major, 'Henry IV and Guyenne: A Study Concerning the Origins of Royal Absolutism' *French Historical Studies*, IV, 4, 1966, p. 383.

[12] N. Elias, *Über den Prozess der Zivilisation*, Vol. 2, (Basel, 1939). Suhrkamp Taschenbuch, 1977. English edition trans. E. Jephcott, Urizen Books, 1978: *The Civilizing Process: The History of Manners.*

them to combine effectively against the monarchy nor to destroy and absorb each other as they do in the original monopoly mechanism. These last two mechanisms Professor Elias also illustrates from the history of France.

Now I think that this is a very powerful theory of the dynamic forces of European history, more useful to the historian than the Marxist theory of class struggle, because it does not introduce anachronistic nineteenth century definitions of class into earlier periods and because it is free from the teleology and moralization that tends to beset so much of Marxist historiography. Nevertheless, for the historian of early modern Europe it has certain serious limitations. Some of these limitations are clearly recognized by Professor Elias himself; in fact, they follow logically from the nature of his theory. Thus, in the working out of his monopoly mechanism, he insists that the formation of a major state in western Europe was most probable, but that its centre and its frontiers were entirely uncertain.[13] Yet for the historian, with a different point of view and a different set of questions to answer, it cannot be a matter of indifference whether it was the kings of France, originally dukes of Francia, or the dukes of Burgundy or the kings of England who came to form the major dominion in western Europe; nor can it be a matter of indifference as to where the eventual boundaries of their states were to lie. Not only is this a matter of intrinsic concern for the historian, but he must also have a shrewd suspicion that on the outcome of these very specific developments – mere incidentals in the sociologist's theory – would depend a great deal of the future history of the whole of Europe and perhaps even of the whole world.

The same is true for the other two mechanisms of Professor Elias's theory, the tendency towards institutionalization of political and administrative authority and the 'royal mechanism'. These are the ones which interest us particularly in our problem of monarchies and parliaments. The trouble is that they do not tell us enough about particular countries or about the varying developments which we have noted at the outset of this lecture, and they do not give us a time scale which could be determined within a limit of error of even as much as a hundred years. And again, these cannot be matters of indifference to the historian, for they determined much of the political development of Europe during the whole period of medieval and modern history.

But let me be more specific and see how far we can get with the Elias theories, perhaps by combining them with those of Hintze. Evidently, they work rather well in France where the kings could play off against each other the conflicting interests of large and distant provinces and of

[13] *Ibid*, p. 220. 'Only by placing oneself in the past for a moment, and seeing the struggle of many warrior houses, their immediate needs and closest goals – in short, visualizing the total peril of their battles and their social existence – can one understand how probable a monopoly – and supremacy-formation was in this territory, and how uncertain were its centre and boundaries.'

semi-autonomous corporations, especially the three estates.[14] Even in France, however, the victory of absolute monarchy over all other forces was not fully decided by the fifteenth century, when Fortescue thought it was. The civil wars of the second half of the sixteenth century threw the whole question once more into doubt, and it could be argued that the States General was defeated because, in a quite specific situation, that of a prospective Protestant succession to the throne of France, it was captured by the extreme Catholic party. This party, for no reasons of obvious historical necessity, lost the civil war and dragged the States General down in its fall. Even sixty years after these events, the absolute monarchy of Richelieu had to fight once more for survival against the centrifugal forces within the country. The 'royal mechanism' undoubtedly worked; but it was a close run thing. As late as 1650 the institutionalization of the monarchy had developed only just far enough to barely win out. And this was so not least because the States General had been discredited in the 1590s and therefore could not function as an alternative centre of authority and loyalty to the monarchy for the whole country in the way the English parliament could during the English civil war.

The pattern of the 'royal mechanism' can be seen at work in Castile, in Piedmont and in many of the German principalities, and this even though the parliaments in these countries did not suffer from one of the gravest weaknesses of the French States General, the sheer size of the country they represented. Conversely, it is possible to argue that the centrifugal forces inherent in the institutionalization of political powers were likely to overcome the 'royal mechanism' in England, Poland and Württemberg. In these countries, the estates or parliament represented basically one dominant and relatively homogeneous class. In England it was the gentry which had captured the representation of the boroughs as early as the first quarter of the fifteenth century[15] and who, in consequence, dominated the House of Commons. Moreover, the very strength of the medieval English monarchy had broken down much of English regionalism and had greatly weakened or even abolished the autonomy of provincial, urban and ecclisiastical corporations. In this respect, the contrast between the Fronde and the English civil war is particularly illuminating. In France, no single corporation, institution or party could claim to stand for the realm as a whole: not the parlement of Paris, a law court with jurisdiction over only about half of France, not the Prince of Condé, the king's uncle, and his princely friends, not the Cardinal de Retz and his clique and certainly not that curious, popular

---

[14] *Cf.* the excellent summary of these conditions in A. R. Myers, 'The English Parliament and the French Estates-General in the Middle Ages', in *Album Helen Maud Cam*, Vol II, *Studies presented to the International Commission for the History of Representative and Parliamentary Institutions*, XXIV, (Louvain, Paris, 1961).

[15] J. S. Roskell, *The Commons in the Parliament of 1422*, (Manchester, 1954).

but localized movement, the *ormée* of Bordeaux. Only the monarchy stood for the whole realm, however much its representatives, the Spanish queen-mother and her Italian first minister, Cardinal Mazarin, were personally disliked. In England, by contrast, parliament could and did command the loyalties of men of all classes throughout the country so as to encompass a most complex variety of individual and local party motivations. So basic was this loyalty which parliament evoked that even the military dictator, Cromwell, could not do without parliaments.

In Württemberg we have a somewhat similar situation. The nobility had opted out of the state by acknowledging only the emperor, and not the duke, as their sovereign. The prelates had lost their wealth and autonomy in the Reformation. While still attending the meetings of the *Landtage* they had become ducal officials and had become socially integrated with the other families of the *Ehrbarkeit*. The estates were therefore confined to the *Ehrbarkeit*, the members of the leading families of the towns and the officials of the self-governing districts of the duchy. This social homogeneity and consequent unity of interest proved to be a most effective barrier against the 'royal mechanism' and the absolutist policies of the dukes. Württemberg became an outstanding example of a *dominium politicum et regale*.

In Poland, too, the diets were effectively confined to one class, but here it was the nobility and not the towns. The nobles were an overwhelmingly powerful class, making up some ten per cent of the total population and owning by far the greater part of the country's wealth, i.e. its land. Even so, in such a huge and diverse country, divided in language and religion, and with the nobility itself divided into a relatively small group of magnates and a great mass of only moderately wealthy or even quite poor *szlachta*, one would have expected the 'royal mechanism' to work rather well. There are two main reasons why it did not. The first fits in well with Elias's schema. The economic development of Poland and, hence, the division of social functions had not developed sufficiently far to institutionalize royal authority and make it capable of effectively balancing the divergent forces of the country. The other reason, however, was not inherent in the social structure of Poland. It was the conversion of a large section of the *szlachta*, the lower nobility, to one or another form of Protestantism in the sixteenth century. Since this Protestant *szlachta* attacked the higher clergy and the Catholic monarchy, both clergy and monarchy were driven into alliance with the magnates. In 1606–7 this alliance defeated a rebellion of the Protestant *szlachta*, but because of the underdeveloped state of royal institutions, it was the magnates and not the monarchy which reaped the benefit of this victory – the opposite of what had happened in Castile after a similar alliance of monarchy and magnates had defeated the comunero movement in 1520. In Poland the magnates organised the *szlachta* as their clients, first in the provincial diets (dietines) and then in the general diet. Thus they effectively reduced the monarchy to impotence and the country eventually to anarchy.[16]

So far then, and in a general sort of way, Professor Elias's theory works; that is, it works in the sense that its dynamics provide an explanation, even if not a complete explanation, for the victories of either monarchies or parliaments in a number of European countries. This explanation, moreover, fits in quite well with the pattern proposed by Hintze. But what of the other European monarchies and their parliaments?

Up to now we have inquired into the confrontation of always one monarchy and one parliament, acting out their struggles in a closed system, i.e. a system in which outside influences could act as a spur to the monarchies, as Hintze suggested, but in which they did not directly participate in the struggles. This seemed to be a reasonable assumption for England and for Castile and for the German principalities. But it is not a reasonable assumption for France or for Poland. Even for England it is not as appropriate as it looks at first sight, and for most other countries it is downright misleading.

Most states in the early modern period were composite states, including more than one country under the sovereignty of one ruler. These composite states or monarchies could consist of completely separate countries, divided by sea or by other states, such as the dominions of the Habsburg monarchy in Spain, Italy and the Netherlands, those of the Hohenzollern monarchy of Brandenburg-Prussia or, indeed, England and Ireland; or they might be contiguous, such as England and Wales, Piedmont and Savoy, or Poland and Lithuania. With the exception of England and Wales, they would always have kept their separate representative assemblies, as England and Scotland did in the seventeenth century. This was so even where, as in France and the Netherlands, formerly independent countries had been reduced to contiguous provinces. A ruler, therefore, did not normally confront just one parliament but several, and each one of them on quite different terms. These terms depended on the political development of the state or province at the time he acquired it. In practice, this was usually awkward and time consuming. But it did have the advantage that, in case of a dispute with any one of them, he would be able to call on the resources of his other dominions. In all such cases, and they are probably the majority, no theory based on an analysis of the forces acting in a single country can even begin to give us a meaningful answer to our original question, the question of why either monarchy or parliament won its struggle in any particular case. Evidently, the problem has become more complicated.

Now we should expect that a combination of the 'monopoly

---

[16] *Cf.* G. Schramm, *Der polnische Adel und die Reformation 1548–1607*, (Wiesbaden, 1965), *Ch.* IV, sect. 5.

mechanism' and the 'royal mechanism' should supply an answer to this now greatly complicated problem. The monarchy has all the advantages of power deriving from the control of several countries while the parliaments of widely separated countries would be most unlikely to co-operate. Unfortunately, historical experience did not turn out to be as neatly logical as this. Consider the Spanish monarchy, the monarchy *par excellence* of multiple dominions and multiple parliaments. In Castile the confrontation came relatively early and very dramatically, in 1520, when a dispute over taxation between king and cortes escalated into a rebellion of the major cities. Very soon this rebellion turned into a struggle for ultimate power in the country. Both sides were quite clear about this, and hence the decision, the defeat of the towns and therefore the cortes, could never be fully reversed. The situation developed very differently in the peripheral kingdoms of the Spanish monarchy, in Aragon and Catalonia, and in Naples, Sicily and Sardinia. There was, of course, little doubt in anyone's mind of the overwhelming power at the disposal of the ruler. But for this very reason, both sides were anxious to avoid confrontations. The contrast with an only slightly earlier period is illuminating. In the 1460s, John II of Aragon had fought a deadly civil war with the city of Barcelona and with the Catalan nobility for ultimate power in Catalonia, at that time the central part of the multiple kingdom of the kings of Aragon. The war ended in a stalemate, with Barcelona and the cortes maintaining their privileges. But when John II's son, Ferdinand of Aragon, married Isabella of Castile, the monarchy transferred its centre to the larger kingdom, Castile. Catalonia now became a relatively poor and outlying province and the problem of ultimate power seemed to have solved itself without further confrontation. As long as the monarchy was prepared to respect the privileged position of the Catalan ruling groups and made no heavy demands on them, i.e. as long as it did not press its advantage, this state of affairs could go on for a very long time. Much the same happened in the three Italian kingdoms. The parliament of Naples survived until 1642[17] and the parliaments of Sicily and Sardinia continued to be summoned throughout the period of Spanish rule, right into the eighteenth century.[18] They did useful work in defending their countries' privileges and, at least in Sicily, managing to keep down the rate of royal taxation, but they never attempted seriously to challenge royal authority. One might say that the 'monopoly mechanism' had worked in deciding the seat of ultimate power but that the 'royal mechanism', the actual relationship between king and parliaments, had been virtually frozen into immobility.

---

[17] G. d'Agostino, 'Premessa ad una storia del Parlamento Generale del Regno di Napoli durante la dominazione spagnuola', *Atti dell' Accademia di Scienze Morali e Politiche della Società Nazionale di Scienze, Lettere ed Arti in Napoli*, LXXVII, (1966).

[18] Marongiu, *Il Parlamento*, Pt. 2, ch. II and III.

Much the same pattern can be seen in the composite monarchies of Piedmont-Savoy and of France. In the central province of Piedmont the duke carried out a *coup d'état* in 1560 and from then ceased to summon his parliament[19] but he and his successors left the parliaments of the outlying provinces of Saluzzo and Val d'Aosta severely alone. In France, the decline of the States General left the monarchy in a commanding position. But here, too, the assemblies of the estates of the peripheral provinces, especially those of Brittany, Languedoc and Burgundy, maintained their very considerable powers right up to the French Revolution. The most powerful and most absolute monarchy of Europe judged it either not safe or not worthwhile to risk a confrontation with its outlying provinces, nor did the 'royal mechanism' work as an impersonal force in the way that sociological theory suggests that it should.

Even so, could it not be argued that the issue had, for all practical purposes, been decided in favour of the monarchy? Yes, but only if the monarchy was prepared to act as if this had not happened, if it was willing to abdicate the effective exercise of its ultimate powers. For if the monarchy tampered with this frozen balance of forces, the whole issue of power might be raised again, and not necessarily to the advantage of the monarchy. This happened in the case of Catalonia, in 1640. After 150 years of virtually leaving the province alone, the royal government of Madrid tried to force Catalonia to take a more active military and financial part in the Spanish war effort against France, during the Thirty Years' War. The result was a revolt led by the *diputats*, the permanent committee of the Catalan cortes.[20] It lasted for twelve years, precipitated the final and decisive defeats of the Habsburgs in the Thirty Years' War and led directly to the revolt and eventual independence of Portugal from Spain – a surprising and most effective co-operation of two widely separated anti-monarchial movements within a composite monarchy. Perhaps the most dangerous result of all, however, was that it brought a French army to the Ebro. Only the outbreak of a French civil war, the Fronde – from the Spanish point of view a lucky and quite fortuitous event – gave the Spanish monarchy the chance to get the French out of Spain again. The price it had to pay was the re-establishment of the pre-1640 balance with the estates of Catalonia, i.e. *dominium politicum et regale* within an absolute monarchy.

The case of Catalonia highlights yet another and, probably, the most serious complication we have to face in our attempt to construct a theory of the relations between monarchies and parliaments. This is the problem of foreign intervention. It is at this point that we must finally consider the case of the country in which all the elements of the problem

[19] H. G. Koenigsberger, 'The Parliament of Piedmont during the Renaissance', in *Estates and Revolutions*, (Ithaca, 1971).
[20] J. H. Elliott, *The Revolt of the Catalans*, (Cambridge, 1963).

we have discussed so far, as well as several others, came together: the Netherlands.

The Netherlands consisted of a number of originally independent duchies, counties and prince-bishoprics, brought together by inheritance, conquest and purchase, first by a younger branch of the French house of Valois, the dukes of Burgundy, and then by the Austrian house of Habsburg. From 1516 the Habsburgs also ruled Spain and its dependencies and gradually transferred their residence to Spain, permanently so from 1559. The provinces – sometimes called the 17 provinces, but the number really depended on what units one counted – were contiguous and covered only a relatively small area; yet they were very varied. At least four languages were spoken: French, Dutch-Flemish, Frisian and German in various high and low dialects. Flanders, Brabant and Holland were the most highly ubanized areas of Europe outside northern Italy; the other provinces were, to a greater or lesser extent, rural. Flanders, Artois, Brabant and Hainault lay in the very heart of the feudal area of Europe; but in Flanders, at least, the rise of several big cities, Ghent, Bruges and Ypres, had modified feudalism beyond all recognition. In Friesland feudalism had never penetrated at all, among the warlike Frisian cattle breeders, fishermen and coastal traders, and it had penetrated only very partially in Holland and Zeeland, with their trading and fishing towns and their closely knit village communities living below their dykes under the constant threat of death and destruction from the North Sea. Not surprisingly, the provincial assemblies, too, were varied. We find the classic three estates of prelates, nobles and cities in Brabant and Hainault. There were 6, but sometimes up to 18, towns in the assemblies of Holland, each with one vote, while all the nobility together had only one vote and prelates and clergy did not appear at all. In Flanders only the big three cities, Ghent, Bruges and Ypres, formed the assembly, until the dukes, in the 15th century, added the Franc de Bruges, a district between Bruges and the sea which sent representatives of a number of small towns and lower nobility. The rest of the nobility and the clergy were not represented.

The powers of the different provincial assemblies varied as much as their structure, but there is no easy correlation between them. These powers were greatest in Brabant where they were enshrined in a famous charter of 1356, the *Joyeuse Entrée* which every duke had to swear to observe at his 'joyous entry', i.e. his accession.[21] The privileges of Flanders were, formally, not nearly as great as those of Brabant; but the representatives of Bruges and Ghent, with the revolutionary traditions of their formidable weavers' guilds in the background, were powers the dukes could never ignore.

In the course of the fifteenth century, both dukes and provinces had

---

[21] R. van Bragt, 'De Blijde Inkomst van de Hertogen van Brabant Johanna en Wenceslas (3 Januari 1356),' *Anciens Pays et Assemblées d'Etats*, XIII, (Louvain, 1956).

found it convenient to negotiate with each other through the States General, an assembly composed of the representatives of the provincial estates. As early as 1477, after the hated duke, Charles the Bold, had fallen in battle against the Swiss, the States General seized power and set up the first real parliamentary government in European history. Not surprisingly, it did not last, for none of the technical problems of such a form of government had even begun to be thought out. It was especially serious that the States General could not organize an effective defence of the country and that it was forced to cede Burgundy and several provinces of the Netherlands to Louis XI of France. Maximillian of Austria, who married the heiress of Charles the Bold, fought the French successfully and had little difficulty in re-establishing the executive in ducal hands.

In the sixteenth century, the ruler, Charles V, king of Spain and Holy Roman Emperor, always viewed the States General with suspicion but could not do without its consent for the taxes he needed to impose. In the reign of his son, Philip II, the fundamental divergence of the interests of the ruler and his subjects soon came to a head. The Netherlands had become tired of paying for the Habsburg wars with France, of spending their blood and money to conquer Italy for the benefit of the Spaniards, as they put it. At the States General of 1557–58 they reduced the sums the king had demanded from them and they coupled their reduced grant with a number of conditions. The most important were that they would themselves appoint the treasurer for the collection and spending of these taxes and that the king must withdraw the 3,000 Spanish troops he kept in the Netherlands.[22] This last condition was even more important than the take-over of royal taxation (which had precedents in several of the individual provinces, as well as in Catalonia and in some of the German principalities), for it highlighted the growing distrust between the king and his subjects.

The story of what followed, the revolt of the Netherlands, is well known. From the point of view of our original problem, a number of features stand out. In the first place, the Netherlands were an outlying dominion of the Spanish monarchy, like Catalonia or Sicily, but they were much richer and hence, the question of taxation was almost as important for the monarchy as it was in Castile. The relations between king and estates could therefore not be frozen, as in Catalonia and Sicily, nor could the problem of ultimate power be shelved for more than relatively short periods of time. Rather, as in Poland and in the Scandanavian kingdoms, the high nobility competed with the king and his government for influence over the assemblies of estates. Again as in the northern and eastern kingdoms, the two sides, king and high nobility, attempted to form an alliance which would effectively operate

[22] H. G. Koenigsberger, 'The States-General of the Netherlands before the Revolt', in *Estates and Revolutions*.

at the expense of the rest of the country. But, wherever this happened, such an alliance eventually broke down because it left the seat of ultimate power still to be decided. In the Netherlands such an alliance between ruler and magnates had worked, though rather creakily, during the reign of Charles V. Under Philip II it collapsed very rapidly.

The rapidity of this collapse was due largely to the introduction of a new element: religious passion, released by the spread of the ideas of the Reformation and the Counterreformation. It was not that religious passions and motivations were necessarily stronger than social, economic, political or purely personal motivations. The mix between these elements certainly varied from individual to individual. It was rather that religious differences were seen as clearcut, that they tended to span different social groups, and that therefore they tended to subsume all other motivations and intensify them to the point where accommodation with the other side became extremely difficult or, indeed, impossible. It is not surprising, therefore, that the long-term struggles between monarchies and parliaments tended to escalate to dramatic fights for ultimate power precisely during the century or century and a half following the Reformation.

I believe that Professor Elias would argue that the Reformation and the Counter-Reformation were themselves aspects of his *Prozess der Zivilisation* and that they could therefore be integrated in his model of the process of monopoly formation and of the *Königsmechanismus*. This is again a tenable view if one views the course of events from a sufficiently high mountain. But it also fails again to explain the decisive details the historian needs to know. In spite of great efforts by historians since the days of Engels and Max Weber to find unequivocal correlations between the Reformation and economic, social and political developments in Europe, no acceptable overall pattern has emerged. Correlations can be seen on the local level and some very fascinating ones have been established. But they tend to be mutually contradictory. The growth of absolutism, for instance, could be furthered either by the secularization of church property where the Reformation was introduced or by an effective alliance with the old church where it was rejected.

The religious aspect of the constitutional struggles of the sixteenth and seventeenth centuries had one further disturbing result. Once a monarchy and its parliament had become locked in an overt fight for power, there was always the possibility that neighbours would fish in troubled waters and intervene on one side or the other. But when religion became entangled in such conflicts, outside intervention became a virtual certainty. For both sides, fighting now not only for supremacy but, or so at least it seemed to them, for sheer survival, would inevitably call for aid across the frontiers of their state. Conversely, all neighbouring powers would see their own safety and that of their chosen religion threatened by the victory of the side representing the other religion. Thus the revolt of the Netherlands, in origin a civil war with Spain supporting one side, rapidly attracted the intervention of England, France, the Papacy and some of the German states. Even the Ottoman Porte tried to co-ordinate the campaigns of the Moriscos against Spain with those of William of Orange.[23]

The final outcome of this struggle was not predictable by any of our theories or models. Moreover, I think it is inherently unlikely that we could construct a theory which could do this. For, from the point of view of any useful theory, the weight of intervention from outside powers, and even the direction of such interventions, was bound to be arbitrary. It depended not only on the economic and military potential of the intervening states, but on their own international entanglements, shifting alliances and internal problems. In the event, the majority of the nobility and prelates of the Walloon provinces opted for King Philip, driven to this distasteful alliance largely by the fear of the social-religious revolution that had broken out in the great cities of Flanders. They managed to maintain their social privileges and their provincial estates, but they lost ultimate political control over their country to the monarchy in Spain or its appointees. Their frontier with the northern provinces was determined by the outcome of military campaigns which could not be fought without Spain.

The seven northern provinces became independent. There seems to be little doubt that, for all their efforts, this too could not have been done without foreign help. Nevertheless, the internal structure of the new state, the United Provinces of the Netherlands, was largely determined by the social and political forces within these provinces and by the personalities of the leaders of the country. In 1581 the monarchy was abolished and, from then on, sovereign power rested with the estates of the seven provinces and with their delegates in the States General in The Hague. These were appropriately addressed as 'Their High Mightinesses'. In spite of this title, however, the deputies to the States General did not have full powers, like the members of the English parliament, and they could not commit their provinces in really important matters such as taxation and religion. The system worked only because of the political and economic weight carried by the province of Holland which paid more than half of all taxes.[25] Holland itself was ruled by the regent class, an oligarchy of rich and educated families who dominated the politics of the individual cities of Holland and who controlled the great trading companies and the banks.

[23] A. C. Hess, 'The Moriscos: An Ottoman Fifth Column in Sixteenth-Century Spain', *American Historical Review* LXXIV, 1, 1968, p. 19.

[24] Koenigsberger, 'The Powers of Deputies', pp. 199–210.

[25] For a brief summary of the political structure of the United Provinces *cf.* e.g. Charles Wilson, *The Dutch Republic* (New York, Toronto, 1968), or H. H. Rowen, *The Low Countries in Early Modern Times: A Documentary History* (New York, London, 1972).

Here then was a patrician republic or, rather, a confederation of republics in which the church was strictly subordinated to the civil authorities and in which, for largely fortuitous reasons, a high nobility had almost completely disappeared, although a poor country nobility remained important in the political life of the eastern, agrarian provinces of Groningen, Overijssel and Gelderland. The estates did not repeat the mistake of the States General of 1477 of attempting to govern the country without an executive. They therefore invested the Prince of Orange, William the Silent, with considerable executive powers and with the title of stadholder, or governor, of several of the provinces, as well as with the important position of commander-in-chief of the union's armies.

Here was a substitute monarchy, ruling not by the grace of God but by the favour of the estates. William and his descendents were well aware of this distinction and so was the snobbish European court society.[26] Partly through William's exceptional political skill and partly through the imperative demands of the war against Spain, the new executive and the estates co-operated very effectively. But as soon as outside pressures relaxed, during the twelve year truce with Spain, 1609–1621, and after the Peace of Münster, in 1648, when Spain finally recognized Dutch independence, the estates and their subsititute monarchy found themselves engaged in struggles for power – just like any legitimate monarchy and its parliaments and also, of course, like the English substitute monarch, Oliver Cromwell, and his parliaments. And again, as we would now expect, the 'royal mechanism' began to work. Three times determined stadholders defeated their opponents by playing on the divisions between provinces, cities and other privileged groups and, in the first of these bouts, in 1617–19, they played even on the religious divisions within the Calvinist church. Nevertheless, the house of Orange was never remotely strong enough to establish a French-type absolutism. Characteristically, the absence of an adult male heir – always a critical moment even for legitimate monarchies[27] – twice, in 1650 and in 1702, led to the virtual abolition of even the substitute monarchy.

[26] The ultra-aristocratic and snobbish republic of Venice claimed precedence for its diplomats over those of the United Provinces because it included in its territory kingdoms, as against the mere dukedoms and counties of the U.P.

[27] There was, at any time in the early modern period, no more than a 50 per cent chance of an undisputed adult, male succession (*Cf.* H. G. Koenigsberger and George L. Mosse, *Europe in the Sixteenth Century*, London and New York, 1968, p. 249). This statistical fact set severe limits on the working of the 'royal mechanism'. The Hohenzollern rulers of Brandenburg-Prussia were exceptionally lucky in their succession in the early modern period, and they were even more lucky in that three of the four rulers succeeding between 1640 and 1740 possessed more than average intelligence and energy. Hardly any other ruling house in Europe had that amount of good fortune. It goes a long way towards explaining the successful establishment of absolutism in Brandenburg-Prussia, a country whose central and eastern parts were economically and socially not so very different from Poland. Whether this good fortune for the Hohenzollern and their ambitions was equally fortunate for the inhabitants of their country, or for Germany or for Europe is, of course, a different question.

There are many examples of the crucial role played by outside intervention in the struggles between monarchies and parliaments. At the beginning of the 17th century, the estates of Bohemia and of the Austrian duchies won great political and religious victories largely with the help given them by the estates of Hungary. They were all Protestants and they were all subjects of the same ruler, the emperor Rudolph II. Some 15 years later, in 1620, the emperor Ferdinand II reversed this situation by defeating the Austrian and Bohemian estates, but the armies which won his victories were those of an outside power, Bavaria. At the other end of the Empire, the estates of East Friesland successfully defied their rulers throughout the 17th century. Their homogeneous social structure and their political traditions were, no doubt, essential in this struggle. East Friesland was the home of Althusius, the greatest theoretician of the power of the estates in the early modern period. But the decisive force in their protracted struggle was a contingent of Dutch troops stationed permanently by the United Provinces in this strategically important state.[28]

In the 18th century, the estates of Würrtemberg and those of Mecklenburg appealed, on different occasions, to the emperor against the absolutist pretensions of their dukes; and, for reasons which had far more to do with the politics of Vienna than those of Stuttgart or Schwerin, they obtained effective support.

But the most interesting case is the one with which we started this inquiry, England – England, the country *par excellence* of the *dominium politicum et regale*, the country *par excellence* of the closed political system in which, or so it has seemed to many historians, king and parliament could work out their destiny virtually undisturbed by outside influences. When Fortescue wrote, the English parliament was certainly well established; but the issue of ultimate power between parliament and monarchy was far from decided. Many continental assemblies which were later defeated had greater powers in the second half of the 15th century than our parliament. Only in the seventeenth century were the issues decided which gave parliament and, more particularly, the House of Commons, real control over the government of the country: the monopoly over all taxation and its appropriation to the purposes for which it had been voted; free speech, to ensure that parliament could debate all aspects of royal policy; the decisive voice in the appointment of the king's ministers or, at least, insistence on the ministers' responsibility to parliament; the abolition or discontinuance of the ruler's right of veto over parliamentary legislation; and finally the right of parliament to assemble regularly and independently of the king's will and the abolition of his prerogative to dissolve parliament arbitrarily. Nearly all these essential conditions of genuine

---

[28] H. Reimers, *Ostfriesland bis zum Aussterben seines Fürstenhauses*, (Bremen, 1925).

parliamentary government, the sort of government which had existed in the Netherlands since the establishment of the Union of Utrecht, the union of the provinces, in 1579 – these were in England established irrevocably only after the revolution of 1689.[29]

These victories of parliament over the monarchy were, of course, the results of the great struggles of the 17th century and, especially, of the dramatic events connected with the Long Parliament and the civil wars of the 1640s and with the overthrow of James II in 1688. None of these events can be understood in a purely English context. Like most European monarchies, the Stuart monarchy was a composite monarchy, including Scotland, Ireland and Wales, as well as England. Moreover, Great Britain was part of the European state system and subject to foreign intervention, in spite of the Channel and the North Sea. Charles I's attempt to rule without parliament came to grief, in the first place, not in England at all but in Scotland, a classic example of the poor, outlying kingdom in which the 'royal mechanism' had been frozen into virtual immobility. Archbishop Laud's and Charles I's mistake was essentially the same as that of their contemporaries, Philip IV of Spain and his minister Olivares, in the case of Catalonia. From a power-political point of view, Scotland should have been left alone, just as Catalonia should have been left alone. That it was not indicates, in both cases, a distortion of clear political thinking by passion, passion for empire, in the case of Olivares, and passion for religion, in the case of Laud. In both men, this was allied to pedantic and misconceived notions of the nature of royal authority.

It was lucky for Great Britain that France was too much occupied with her war with Spain to interfere in favour of Scotland, her traditional ally, as she was to interfere only a little later in Catalonia. But the Scottish army now interferred in England. It has been pointed out that the initiative which the Long Parliament took against the royal prerogative, in 1640 and 1641, depended heavily on the presence of the Scottish army in England.[30] Later, during the civil war, parliament could hardly have carried on without Scottish military help, nor the king without that of Wales and, to a lesser extent, of Ireland. Both France and the Dutch gave some help to the royal cause; not enough to decide the outcome, since both countries were too heavily engaged in the Thirty Years' War, but enough to cause internal repercussions in the United Provinces. The second round of the great conflict between the house of Orange and the estates of Holland, which came to a head in 1650, started with the estates' objections to Orange support of the house of Stuart.

Even the 'Glorious Revolution' of 1688–89, and the events leading

[29] J. S. Roskell, 'Perspectives in English Parliamentary History', in E. B. Fryde and E. Miller, ed., *Historical Studies of the English Parliament*, Vol. 2, (Cambridge, 1970).

[30] C. Russell, *The Crisis of Parliaments* (Oxford, 1971), pp. 329 ff.

up to it, were not a purely English affair. In the last years of his reign, Charles II managed to rule without parliament. He was able to do this on the basis of the still extensive prerogatives of the crown and with the financial help of Louis XIV. Of course, this help was precarious, but every year that it went on, the position of the monarchy in England grew stronger. The first two years of the reign of James II are a chilling commentary on just how far this process had already gone and how it had become technically possible to 'manage' parliament. One might well speculate about the outcome if James II had not made the mistake of offending the religious susceptibilities of leading Anglican Tories and also if there had not been a conveniently Protestant member of the house of Stuart abroad, able to mobilize the formidable support of the United Provinces of the Netherlands. It was not fortuitous that it should have been a Prince of Orange, the representative of the Dutch parliamentary substitute monarchy who should have become the first truly parliamentary king of England, by virtue of being married to James II's daughter and of having mounted a successful invasion of England. And again, as in 1640, the negative aspect of foreign interference was important. At the critical moment, in the autumn of 1688, Louis XIV was campaigning in the Palatinate and therefore unable to prevent William of Orange from sailing to England. Clearly, at its most critical and dramatic moments, English history cannot be understood in terms of a closed political system.

What conclusions then can we draw? What kind of theory can we construct and what will be the limitations of such a theory? A theory which, we recall, is to answer our original question: how do we account for the relative success or failure of different monarchies and parliaments in their struggle for power? It is best to set out my conclusions schematically so that they can be accepted or refuted and in any case, I hope, debated.

1.  The structure and history of parliaments is evidently related to the social structure of the societies in which they developed. This is trite but basic. The difficulty is that any precise correlation between the social structure and the formal institutions of a society is not at all easy to establish. Hintze's typology attempts to do this but, in the end, produces a picture that, for all its brilliance and comprehensiveness, is both typologically and dynamically inadequate.

2.  Since we are faced with a problem of change, and of change which did not come about by consent, we need a theory of social and political dynamics over a long period, and not a theory of balance and imbalance. We have found that Norbert Elias's three mechanisms, the 'monopoly mechanism', the mechanism of the institutionalization of power, and the 'royal mechanism' go a long way towards providing a useful model of historical dynamics.

3. Nevertheless, Elias's theory, or theories, do not give us sufficiently precise answers. In the first place, they do not give us an adequate time scale. In the second place, having concentrated on the extreme cases of France and England, they do not tell us enough about the intermediate cases. Thus, while the history of Poland can be made to fit very well into Elias's schema, that of Denmark and Sweden cannot. Denmark was a country with a social structure and social dynamics more similar to those of Poland than to those of France. Yet, in 1660, its king carried out a successful *coup d'état* which changed the country from an aristocratic, constitutional and elective monarchy to one of the most effectively absolutist states of Europe. The history of Sweden is even more disconcerting, for here we can observe three very effective royal *coups*, between the beginning of the seventeenth and the end of the eighteenth century. Yet, each time, after a varying number of years, aristocratic, constitutional government was re-established, although not always with the same centres of authority, for in the eighteenth century they shifted from the Riksråd, the magnates' council of state, to the Riksdag, the parliament dominated by the lower nobility. I therefore conclude that the balance between royal and anti-royal forces could be much more evenly matched, and this over a longer period of time, than Elias's one-way mechanisms would suggest. It follows from this that the ultimate decisions cannot always be predicted, or postdicted, by these mechanisms, even when taken in conjunction with an analysis of social structure.

4. The struggle between monarchies and parliaments was rarely fought out in closed political systems. During the later middle ages and during the early modern period, some four or five centuries, most monarchies were composite. Their parliaments were multiple and, in the very common cases of States Generals, they were also composite and, together with the provisional assemblies, they functioned on several levels. We have been able to discern certain functional patterns in the history of the parliaments of small, outlying kingdoms or provinces. These patterns, however, could be vitally affected by unique political decisions, with unpredictable consequences. This happened in Scotland and in Catalonia.

5. The most serious difficulty in the construction of an overall theory is presented by the intervention of outside powers in the struggles between kings and their parliaments. Such intervention would alter the relative strength of the internal forces to an extent which is, I believe, unpredictable, even if we were to use game theory or a computer.

6. The period of the most intense struggle between monarchies and parliaments coincided, on the whole, with the age of religious conflicts. The religious element in this struggle tended to produce
   (a)  strong leadership and cohesion of parties; although the history of the civil wars in France shows that these parties were not necessarily parliamentary or anti–parliamentary parties;
   (b) ' the likelihood of foreign intervention, the internationalization of constitutional conflicts, and hence the almost complete unpredictability of their outcome (*cf.* point 5).

7. The strength of the opposing royal and parliamentary forces could be affected, either over a period of time or at critical moments, by certain specific structural, functional or even fortuitous elements. I will mention only a few:
   (a)  specific powers of procedures of parliaments. For instance, it was important for a parliament to establish the principle of redress of grievances before supply, i.e. a parliament must not agree to grant taxes before the king has met its demands. This was certainly a common opinion in the Netherlands during the sixteenth century. However, the English parliament, although it occasionally used this principle as a tactical device, never established it systematically. Parliaments during both the Tudor and early Stuart periods usually granted the crown's financial demands first and argued about grievances afterwards. Similarly, the problem of the powers of deputies or members of parliaments was ambiguous.[31] English members of parliament enjoyed *plena potestas*, full powers; i.e. they could commit their constituents, without having to refer back to them. The deputies of the Netherlands States General, by contrast, had to refer back practically everything. Yet both established parliamentary government. What this means is that specific powers and procedures were certainly important but that they have always to be considered as elements in complex situations. They are never by themselves either necessary or sufficient causes of the phenomena we are trying to understand.
   (b)  The action of outstanding personalities. We simply cannot write William the Silent, John Pym and Oliver Cromwell out of history.
   (c)  The chance occurrence of undisputed adult male successions. *Coups d'états* with permanent results could be carried out by one ruler, as happened in Piedmont and Denmark. But, in general, the institutionalization of royal power had rarely proceeded far enough before the eighteenth century for the monarchy to avoid a serious setback at every minority or disputed succession. It

---

[31]  Koenigsberger, 'The Power of Deputies', *passim.*

happened in France as late as 1715, after the death of Louis XIV. It would be a reasonable guess to think that it would normally take three successive generations of adult male rulers, i.e. at least two such successions, to establish an unassailable absolutism. With a 50 per cent chance at the death of each ruler, there would be only a 25 per cent chance of this happening twice in succession.

8. And finally, to sum up: we have with the help of other scholars, historians and sociologists constructed a number of theories and models. These models are, I believe, valuable to historical understanding, i.e. to our understanding of the human condition as it changes through time. But we have also run up against the limits of such theories. These limits, I believe, are inherent in the problem we set ourselves to solve. And so we are left to pursue not only theories but also the traditional tasks of the historian: to analyze specific events and chains of events and, not least, to tell the story of events.

1. Elizabeth I is hymned as Venus-Virgo crowned with flowers and attended by the Graces, Muses and other nymphs.

   Illustration to the *April Eclogue* from Edmund Spenser, *Shepheardes Calendar* (London, 1579), f. 11^v.

# 2

# The Italian Parliaments from their Origins to the End of the 18th Century

In the first book of his *Discorsi*, Machiavelli stated his categorical opinion that genuine political life was possible only in cities; for,

> . . . quelle repubbliche dove si è mantenuto il vivere politico ed incorrotto, non sopportano che alcun lor cittadino né viva ad uso di gentiluomo . . . Gentiluomini sono chiamati quelli che oziosi vivono dei proventi delle loro possessioni . . . Questi tali sono perniziosi in ogni repubblica ed in ogni provincia; ma più perniziosi sono quelli che . . . commandono a castella, ed hanno sudditi che ubbidiscono a loro. Di queste . . . sorti d'uomini ne sono pieni il regno di Napoli, terra di Roma, la Romagna e la Lombardia. Di qui nasce che in quelle provincie non è mai stata repubblica, né alcuno vivere politico; perché tali generazioni d'uomini sono al tutto nimici d'ogni civiltà . . . Dove è tanto la materia corrotta, che le leggi non bastano a frenarla, vi bisogna ordinare insieme con quelle maggior forza, la quale è una mano regia, che con la potenza assoluta ed eccessiva ponga freno alla eccessiva ambizione e corruttela dei potenti.[1]

It was an acute observation; but it left out of consideration a most important phenomenon: the existence of parliaments in precisely those parts of Italy which Machiavelli regarded as irretrievably corrupt. We shall come back to the probable reasons why Machiavelli denied a genuine *vivere politico* to countries with representative institutions. He never actually discussed this problem. For the moment, however, it is

---

[1] N. Machiavelli, *Discorsi sopra la prima deca di Tito Livio*, libro primo, cap. 55 '. . . those republics where an uncorrupt political life (*il vivere politico ed incorrotto*) had been maintained will not allow any of their citizens to be gentlemen or to live as gentlemen (*gentiluomini*) . . . Gentlemen is the name given to those who live in idleness from the income of their property . . . These are pernicious in every republic and in every province; but even more pernicious are those who . . . command castles and have subjects who obey them. The kingdom of Naples, the territory of Rome, the Romagna and Lombardy are full of this sort of men. This is the reason why in these countries there has never been a republic nor any political life (*vivere politico*); for this sort of man is altogether hostile to all genuine civil government . . . Where matter is so corrupt that laws are not sufficient restraint, it is necessary to have also a royal authority which, with absolute and indeed excessive force, places a bridle on the excessive ambition and corruption of the powerful'.

sufficient to insist that Italy shared the experience of representative institutions, of what the fifteenth century English jurist and Chief Justice, Sir John Fortescue, called *dominium politicum et regale* (in contrast to *dominium regale*, i.e. royal absolutism), with practically every European country in the latter middle ages and in the early modern period. Indeed, not only did Italy share this experience, it played a large part in initiating and in developing it.

It has been rightly pointed out that there was nothing inevitable or natural about the development of representative institutions or government by consent[2] – at any rate beyond the village or the tribal level. Most larger political societies in human history have tended to be theocratic, imperial and despotic. The European experience was the exception; but the reasons why it was an exception are complex. The various Germanic peoples who set up successor kingdoms on the ruins of the Roman Empire in the west had traditions of mass meetings of free men. These could be either regular annual institutions, such as the March (later May) assemblies of the Franks in Merovingian times, or they could be special meetings, summoned by the king, such as the assemblies of the Longobards in the 7th and 8th centuries, used by the kings, among other matters, to publish royal laws.[3] Such assemblies tended to have two outstanding characteristics. In the first place, they were assemblies of warriors and their primary, although not exclusive, concern was with both advice (*consilium*) and with help (*auxilium*) to their king in his military campaigns.[4] In the second place, they were, from a very early period, dominated by great and powerful men on whose advice and help the king was especially dependent. Both these characteristics were to have an important and continuing influence on the development of representative institutions; but they did not, by themselves, necessarily lead to the development of parliaments. Where political units and the number of free warriors remained small, as for instance in Iceland or in some of the Swiss cantons, such assemblies could persist for centuries, or even into our own times, as effective guardians of the rule of law or even as repositories of sovereignty. Their very success would then prevent the development of genuinely representative institutions; for these latter would simply not be needed.

The second characteristic of the early medieval assemblies, that of being dominated by great and powerful men, was perhaps even more important. Moreover, it was one of the earliest political practices which

[2] B. Tierney, 'Medieval Canon Law and Western Constitutionalism', *Catholic Historical Review*, LII, 1966.

[3] Cf. C. G. Mor, 'Modificazioni strutturali dell'Assemblea nazionale longobarda nel secolo VIII'. *Album Helen Maud Cam*, II (Louvain-Paris, 1961) and bibliographical indications therein.

[4] T. N. Bisson, 'The Military Origins of Medieval Representation', *American Historical Review*, LXXI, 1966.

developed from a functional and traditional to an institutional level. This institutionalisation of the king's need to rely on the advice and help of his greatest followers was closely connected with the development of feudalism, from the later Carolingian period onwards. The feudal contract between the king and his vassal created a system of mutual obligations. For the vassal this meant primarily advice and participation or help in the military campaigns of the king. When the vassal was old or ill, or when he was a cleric or a child, he could not himself fulfil his military obligations and some form of substitute help for the king would have to be found. Almost invariably, this took the form of money. With time, kings found it convenient to ask their vassals not only for military service but also, quite specifically, for money.

For their part, the vassals found that giving advice was a most useful activity for the furtherance of their own interests. Gradually, therefore, the feudal obligation of giving advice came to take on the characteristics of a right which a king's magnates demanded.[5] Here lie the origins of the great assemblies of feudal magnates which the Norman kings and others summoned, from the 11th century onwards. Here also lie the origins of the ambivalent feeling between rulers and such assemblies; for while both kings and their feudal magnates found assemblies useful, their aims did not always coincide and might even be diametrically opposed to each other. Kings naturally wanted the maximum support from their vassals. The vassals, however, might or might not approve of the king's aims and, in any case, would want rewards for services beyond their purely customary obligations. Above all, they would want to safeguard their rights, privileges and properties.

These assemblies of magnates, however, were not parliaments or representative assemblies; for, strictly speaking, they did not represent anything or anybody. Nor did they necessarily develop into parliaments, even when they were summoned with some degree of regularity and when the attendance of the great mass of free warriors had long since become a dim memory. They were, rather, extended versions of the king's council. Or, conversely, the king's council developed as an inner ring of advisers whom the king chose from the larger body of all his magnates and more powerful vassals-in-chief. These developments were not necessarily contradictory.

The concept and practice of actual representation arose from a quite different source. This was the procedure in Roman Law by which persons or corporations were represented in court by agents (*procuratores*) who were invested by their principals with varying degrees of authority to represent their interests. The degree of this authority varied according to the instructions which the agents

---

[5] A. Marongiu, *Il Parlamento in Italia nel Medio Evo e nell'età Moderna*, (Milan, 1962), p. 91 and passim. This book is the basic study of the subject, written mainly from the point of view of a *storia del diritto*. It has an exhaustive bibliography.

received. Under certain circumstances these instructions would amount to full powers (*plena potestas*) to commit their principals to such a course of action or obligation as the agents judged suitable. It was, moreover, a principle of Roman Law that, in cases where several parties were involved in a court action, all would have to be represented in court. The Justinian Code summed up this principle in the words '*quod omnes similiter tangit, ab omnibus comprobetur*' – what concerns all must be approved by all.[6]

These principles and procedures of Roman Law were to prove enormously fruitful. They owed this fruitfulness both to their inherent flexibility and to the specific circumstances of Italy and Europe in the central and later middle ages. The spread of Roman Law in the 12th century coincided with the spread of ecclesiastical corporations and with attempts to organise ecclesiastical institutions over large areas. For this latter purpose the concept of representation proved to be very convenient. It was adopted and spread specifically by the canon lawyers, the men who adapted Roman Law to the needs of the Church. Many of these needs were concerned with communities and corporations, from the separate houses making up an international monastic order, such as the Dominican Order, to the Roman Catholic Church as a whole. By the turn of the 12th and 13th centuries it was held that a general council of the Church 'represented' the whole of the Church and that therefore its canons were binding, even on the pope himself. It was Innocent III, himself a distinguished lawyer and canonist, who first summoned 'representatives' of cathedral chapters and monastic houses to the Fourth Lateran Council, in 1215.

From this it was a relatively easy, and certainly quite logical, step to extend the idea of representation to secular institutions. Significantly, it was Innocent III who summoned representatives with full power from the cities of the Marca d'Ancona to his presence; and it was this pope's legate in Catalonia who seems to have been responsible for the summoning of representatives of the Catalan cities to an assembly (*corts, cortes*) in Lérida, in 1214.[7]

Rulers, of course, had had to consult with the cities of their kingdoms, just as they had had to consult with their principal magnates. The reason was not so much, as has been suggested,[8] because medieval monarchs did not pretend to be infallible – it is unlikely that they were any less conceited in this respect than monarchs of other ages – as because all medieval rulers always needed the support of their most powerful vassals or subjects for their more important enterprises, and

[6] G. Post, 'Roman Law and Early Representation in Spain and Italy, 1150–1250', *Speculum* XVIII, 1943.

[7] For the preceding paragraph cf. *ibid*. and Tierney, 'Medieval Canon Law', *cit*.

[8] G. Dupont-Ferrier, *Ignorances et distractions administratives en France au XIV*ᵉ *et XV*ᵉ *siècles*. Bibliothèque de l'Ecole de Chartres, C. 1939, pp. 154–155; quoted in Marongiu, *Il Parlamento*, p. 476.

especially for their military campaigns. Nor did they possess the administrative machinery to rule their countries without the help of those who could command authority in their own right. With the cities, consultation was likely to be, in the first place, with city magistrates as such, or with the king's own *administrator*, i.e. his own representative of the particular city. The 12th and 13th centuries witnessed the great increase of the numbers, the populousness, the wealth and, above all, the autonomy of the cities of western and southern Europe. With their charters the citizens also gained a sense of corporateness. The legal idea of corporate representation, now in a much wider sense, became therefore a most useful concept which city corporations could use in practice just as conveniently as could ecclesiastical corporations. Rulers, for their part, found the principle useful because by its use they could the more easily obtain the support of these increasingly wealthy and powerful corporations within their kingdoms. Thus it was, characteristically, the emperor Frederick II, that most 'modern' of medieval Italian monarchs, who first summoned representatives of his South-Italian cities to general assemblies.

Equally adaptable was the formula of 'what concerns all must be approved by all'. From a purely technical principle of practical jurisprudence it came to take on the colouring of a fundamental political maxim, embodying the notion of a community of interests within a country and, eventually, the need for conscious consent by the community for its government. As such it was begun to be seen in the 13th century and later, to be specifically developed by Marsilio of Padua, William of Ockam and other great political thinkers of the 14th century.[9]

It took time for these different concepts and practices to develop, to come together and to be accepted by the non-learned. The early history of representative institutions, from the 11th to the first half of the 13th century, is a difficult and controversial subject, not only because of the paucity of the surviving records, but because it raises almost intractable problems of definition. Assemblies were as yet summoned mainly for special occasions, the preparation of an important campaign, the promulgation of a set of laws, the acceptance of a new ruler. Their composition, their representative character and their competence varied widely. It is not always easy to distinguish them from older, purely feudal, types of assemblies, from 'pre-parliaments'.[10] It seems to be agreed, for instance, that the assemblies which Frederick II summoned

---

[9] A. Marongiu, 'Q.o.t., Principe fondamentale de la Démocratie et du Consentement, au XIV$^e$ siècle', *Album Helen Maud Cam* II, cit; A. Marongiu, 'Il principio della democrazia e del consenso (*Quod omnes tangit, ab omnibus approbari debet*) nel XIV secolo', *Studia Gratiana post octava decreti saecularia*, VIII (Bologna, 1962) pp. 555–575.

[10] For details, both of the history of assemblies and of the historiographical controversies, see Marongiu, *Il Parlamento*, cit.

were of this nature. But from the latter part of the 13th century, the assemblies tended to assume a more definite shape, to have more clearly defined competence and to meet at more or less regular intervals. Above all, they became self-conscious *qua* institutions. The idea of representation was now gradually widened to cover not just individual communities or corporations, such as individual cathedral chapters or individual cities, but the totality of such institutions within one country: the estates of the clergy, of the nobility and of the cities and, in some European countries, even the estate of the peasants. It is here that we must seek the reasons for the remarkable diffusion of representative insitutions through the length and breadth fo Christian Europe. They fulfilled a universal need, that of regulating the relations between the ruler of a country and his most powerful subjects, for, by the 13th and 14th centuries, these relations had become much more complex than the simple lord and vassal relationships of the early feudal period in the 9th and 10th centuries. Representative assemblies were able to fulfil this need because they were both conceptually and organisationally adequate to do so. Representation had become thinkable, practical and useful.

Nevertheless, for all its wide diffusion, the institution of representative assemblies did not become universal, and least of all in Italy. The kingdom of Sicily developed a parliament and, when this kingdom was divided at the Straits of Messina, parliament also divided. Some parts of the Papal States had parliaments, although the city of Rome itself and the Roman Campania never enjoyed representative institutions. Parliaments appeared in Piedmont and Montferrat, in the northwest, and in Friuli in the northeast and, finally and late, in Sardinia. But the central core of Italy, Tuscany and most of Lombardy, never had any parliaments before the 19th century.

Tuscany and Lombardy were, of course, the regions *par excellence* of the commune, the city state and, evidently, an independent city had no need of representative institutions. The essence of the commune was, after all, that it could enjoy a *vivere politico*, government by consent, through a general assembly of citizens or through other methods of citizen-participation in government, such as were well-known and tried from the time of the Ancients. But in the 12th and 13th centuries some Italian city republics conquered their neighbouring cities and established territorial states like those of the greater princes. The motivation for such conquests, moreover, was essentially similar to that of the contemporary princes, i.e. the desire to expand the territory from which they could levy troops and taxes or the need to deny such territories and their resources to dangerous rivals.[11] Why then did not representative institutions develop in the contados of Milan, Florence

---

[11] Cf. *Storia d'Italia, supra*, vol. I, p. 416. Also D. Waley, *The Italian City-Republics*, (New York-Toronto, 1969), pp. 111–115.

and Venice? The answer to this question seems to arise from two preoccupations of the communes. The first was their distrust of the feudal nobility. The relationship between the communes and the great nobles in the contado was often an essentially feudal one. At the same time, however, the communes did not have to rely for their government on a council of feudal magnates, as kings had to do. There was therefore no point in summoning the great nobles of the contado, except when their services were needed individually. But more important than the problem of the nobility was that of the subject cities. It could never be in the interests of Florence to summon the representatives of the Tuscan cities together and thus give them a chance to co-operate against herself. The last thing that a city republic would wish for would be the develpment of self-conscious estates in its territory. So strong was this feeling that it seems very likely that it was this which led Machiavelli to deny altogether the possibility of a *vivere politico* outside the city. The anti-estate tradition was so strong that it prevented the development of representative assemblies even in those states which had been transformed from city republics into territorial principalities.

Curiously, it is this absence of representative institutions in the Italian city states which illuminates certain important characteristics of those kingdoms and principalities in which such institutions did develop. It is evident that neither feudal relationships nor the revival of Roman Law and the growth of Canon Law were, by themselves, sufficient to account for the appearance of representative institutions. What was needed, over and above these elements, was a certain feeling of community within a given political structure. Such a feeling of community could depend on geographical facts, as it clearly did in the great island kingdoms of Sicily and Sardinia. But it could also arise from purely historical and relatively recent circumstances, as in the kingdom of Naples or in Friuli and Piedmont. Characteristically, the frontiers of these states remained rather fluid for a long time. The monarchies here played a crucial role in defining both the state and the community; and loyalty to the monarch remained a vital force in this process by constantly reinforcing the feeling of community. It could even override differences in language, as it did in Friuli. Yet, once it had appeared, a feeling of community could persist even apart from the ruler, as it did, for instance, in the different provinces of Piedmont-Savoy.

A feeling of community was precisely what was lacking in the city republics. That is to say, it existed in the cities themselves, but in each as a purely local, civic patriotism. Precisely for this reason it could never be transformed into a wider patriotism. This was not in the interests of the dominant city whose own patriotism had triumphed over that of its rivals. The city centredness of the late medieval chroniclers and historians leaves no doubt on this score.[12] We have chronicles and histories of Florence, but not of Tuscany; yet we have chronicles of both Messina and of Sicily. Machiavelli's attempt to organise a citizen militia in the Florentine contado was misconceived, from this as from many other points of view. As political structures, the city republics were and remained brittle, in constant danger of rebellion from their subject cities. If it was difficult for a king to cut an overmighty subject down to size, it was even more difficult for a dominant city to do this to a subject city. Only Venice managed, in the course of several centuries, to overcome these problems to any considerable degree.

By contrast, those princes who had not started as despots, taking over a city republic, were not bound to identify with the interests of any one of the cities. Their authority, and hence also their favour, extended equally to all subjects and vassals, according to their rank and loyalty. Thus, as has been quite rightly pointed out, one of the purposes of Frederick II in summoning representative assemblies was to demonstrate his greatness and majesty to all his subjects.[13] By the time of the Sicilian Vespers of 1282, the feeling of community in Sicily, coupled with the urgency of the military situation, was strong enough to overcome the original preference of the Sicilian cities for complete independence or even for a league of cities. In the event, an assembly at Palermo which has been called a parliament and which claimed to represent the community of the kingdom offered the crown of the whole kingdom to the king of Aragon.

Sicily is a particularly interesting case because its major cities came very near to the position of autonomous city states; for where this occurred, parliaments could not develop or even continue to exist. The diets of the late-medieval city leagues of Germany never represented a community and never acted in any other capacity than as congresses of ambassadors. In Sicily, the rivalry of Palermo and Messina persisted throughout medieval and early modern times and, on occasion, all but broke down the feeling of a Sicilian community. As late as 1674 Messina actually cut itself off from the rest of the kingdom and called on the French to support its quest for independence – only to find that it had changed one master for another. The kings or their viceroys, for their part, often found it convenient to encourage such rivalries. The interests of the Sicilian, as of all other monarchies were, in fact, highly ambivalent. Representative assemblies were certainly convenient for the monarchies, and a feeling of community could be very useful. Yet there was also a constant temptation for kings to behave like the dominant cities: to play off their subjects against each other and to deal with them individually, by favours or threats. The ability of individual cities to resist the temptation of playing the ruler's game, in this respect, is one of

[12] I wish to thank Dr. Diana Webb for drawing my attention to this point.
[13] Marongiu, *Il Parlamento*, p. 178.

the measures of the degree to which the feeling of community had developed in any particular country; and on this eventually depended much of the likely success or failure of its parliament.

As parliaments developed into regular and clearly defined institutions there grew, together with the feeling for the community of the whole country which parliaments represented, also feelings of solidarity, both of the institutions of parliament itself and of its different parts, the estates. The privileges and rights of the estates, i.e. of the ecclesiastical corporation, of the nobles and of the cities, were regarded as either existing autonomously or as legally derived from grants by the king, the emperor or the pope. In either case, every new ruler at his accession had to swear to observe them. Very early in the history of parliaments it became clear that they were the most effective institutions to preserve and defend these privileges. This followed legally from the fact that the new ruler generally took his oath, either personally or through a representative, in front of the actual assembly. But in practice it was the means which parliaments adopted to defend their privileges, and the persistence with which they pursued such an aim that forms a great part of the substance of the political history of parliaments.[14]

The ruler was not only a part of the community; he was its focal point. The community might even take its very being from him and his house. Nevertheless, he also stood aside from or above the community. The magnates might like to think of him as *primus inter pares*, the first among equals; but that was not generally how medieval kings and princes thought of themselves, either in relation to their barons or, even less, in relation to their clergy and towns. In consequence, the relationship between the ruler and parliament, for all their awareness of the community of interests and traditions that bound them together, was inevitably a relationship that involved the problem of the distribution of power. Now the distribution of power may, at any one moment, rest on consent, and tradition may be regarded as a form of consent. This moment may last some time, perhaps one or two generations. But it is not likely to last much longer. In medieval Italy, as indeed everywhere in Europe, economic conditions and political circumstances changed too rapidly to allow for longer periods of stability. Most commonly, it was royal power which increased. Widening economic resources, more efficient and extensive royal administration, success in foreign wars or the crushing of an internal

[14] Cf. the discussion of the functions of parliaments and estates *ibid.*, Parte Terza; and also in O. Brunner, *Land und Herrschaft*, Veröffentlichungen des Instituts für Geschichtswissenschaft und Archivforschung in Wien, I, (Vienna, 1943); E. Lousse, *La société d'ancien régime. Organisation et représentation corporatives*, Louvain, 1943; D. Gerhard, 'Regionalismus und Ständisches Wesen als ein Grundthema europäischer Geschichte', *Alte und Neue Welt in Vergleichender Geschichtsbetrachtung*, (Göttingen, 1962).

rebellion – all these allowed kings to play increasingly autocratic roles in their relations with their parliaments and to attempt to restrict their competence, especially in the crucial field of taxation. But, conversely, disputed successions, minorities and regencies gave opportunities to ambitious magnates to encroach on the prerogatives of the monarchy, or again, foreign danger and the urgent need for immediate support might force rulers to make concessions to their parliaments. One way or another, the distribution of power in the state would be affected. But a change in the distribution of power is most unlikely to be carried out by consent, or certainly not only by consent. Men do not easily give up what they consider vital for the defence of their status when they see this status attacked – as long, that is, as they think they have a chance of successively defending it. And the best defence is often attack. Basically, therefore, the history of parliaments is the history of the struggle for power between parliaments and monarchy. This struggle for power could go on for very long periods of time before it was finally resolved. The resolution happened sometimes dramatically and sometimes slowly, by almost imperceptible pressure; but, in one form or another, this resolution had to come, and always by struggle and by the exercise of the implicit threat of force, although not necessarily by violence.[15]

It must of course be clearly understood that the parliaments of the middle ages and the early modern period were never democratic in the 19th and 20th century sense. Even where they included an estate of peasants, as they did in Sweden, in some South-German principalities and even in some parts of France, the peasants were thought of precisely as an estate, and always the most lowly of the estates, and never as individuals. None of the Italian parliaments included an estate of the peasants. It followed that, even in the cities, there were no parliamentary elections in the modern sense, although there might occasionally be contests between different interest groups for the important position of a parliamentary deputy. In most cases, however, the city councils simply appointed one or several of their councillors or some other important personage as their deputy, or they reserved this duty to a specific civic official. The struggle between the rulers and their parliaments was therefore always a struggle within the ruling groups.

Nevertheless, the history of the Italian parliaments up to the end of the *ancien régime*, at the close of the 18th century, is not just a series of histories which can be understood in terms of long drawn-out duels between rulers and their estates, i.e. in terms of just the political histories of those Italian states in which parliaments appeared. This aspect was certainly important but, by itself, it will not give us a meaningful story. None of the Italian states formed a closed political

[15] Cf. above, chapter 1.

system. In all of them the outcome of the struggle was decided not only by the changing internal balance of power between rulers and estates but, to at least an equal degree, by outside interference. It is this element of outside interference which makes it difficult to generalise about the history of the Italian parliaments and virtually impossible to construct a model which will fit them all.

Nowhere is this more evident than in the parliaments of the Mezzogiorno and of the great islands. The Sicilian parliament was the earliest secular assembly in Italy, and probably in Europe, for which a truly representative character can be argued. Its real importance, however, began not with the formal assemblies summoned by the despotic Frederick II but with the moment when the kingdom split into two parts, after the Sicilian Vespers of 1282, and when the rulers of each part, both of them foreigners, were fighting for political and even personal survival.

King Peter of Aragon might claim Sicily by inheritance through his wife. But it was a parliament, assembled at Palermo, which effectively tranferred the crown to him, and the Sicilians would never allow Peter or his successors to forget that they had transferred their allegiance voluntarily to the house of Aragon. Peter followed up the parliament of Palermo by summoning another to Catania, later in the year 1282. One would guess from this action that the parliament of Palermo had represented mainly prelates, nobles and cities of the western part of the island, and that the king wanted to make sure of support in the eastern half as well. He summoned a third parliament, in Messina, in the spring of 1283, shortly before leaving his new kingdom. This assembly voted him a money subsidy for his war against the Angevins of Naples. From then on, parliaments became much less frequent, being summoned primarily, although not exclusively, on the occasions of the accession of new kings. Nevertheless, by 1296, when the third Aragonese king of Sicily, Frederick II (III), ascended the throne, the Sicilian parliament had achieved substantial successes. In the field of legistlation, it is true, parliament still did little more than promulgate the king's decrees. It was not yet formulating its own laws. But it had successfully insisted on the re-establishment of the kingdom's privileges and charters from the time of the Norman and Swabian kings, privileges which the Angevin kings had abrogated or ignored; it had obtained a promise from the new king that he would not, like his brother James, abandon Sicily for the sake of other kingdoms; that he would not make war or conclude peace without the consent of his subjects; and, perhaps most important of all, that the king and his agents would be subject to the laws of the kingdom, and that parliament should itself elect a committee of twelve to supervise the administration of justice.[16]

Here was a *vivere politico* in which the leading groups of Sicilian

[16] Marongiu, *Il Parlamento*, pp. 192 ff.

society had exploited the precarious international position of their kings, both to reinforce their specific privileges and to force their ruler to follow, at least in broad lines, the interests of his subjects, of the community, as it was understood in its then necessarily hierarchical character. All this had been achieved by the co-operation of the leading men and corporations in parliament. This was quite clearly understood at the time; for one of the *capitoli* of the parliament of 1296 specifically provided for the annual assembly of parliament and the annual election of the judicial supervisory committee.

The position of parliament was, however, much less strongly established than it must have appeared at the turn of the 13th and 14th centuries. This was, paradoxically, due not to the strength but to the weakness of the monarchy in the succeeding generations. The end of the danger of an Angevin reconquest, after 1302, and a succession of weak kings, minors and women had the effect of dissolving both the tension and the co-operation between the king and parliament. The assembly was summoned only sporadically and became the battleground or, worse, the tool of the noble factions who plunged the country into a succession of civil wars. Fourteenth century Sicily demonstrated what eighteenth century Poland was to demonstrate again in a somewhat different form, viz. that the excessive weakness of the ruler will not necessarily lead to the strength of parliament but only to the triumph of factions and anarchy.

In the last decade of the 14th century, Martin, son of the king of Aragon, and the husband of the Sicilian queen Maria, effectively re-established royal power. This made it possible and, indeed, convenient for father and son, who co-operated in this enterprise, to re-establish the parliament. They used a number of assemblies, especially those summoned to Catania in 1397 and to Syracuse in 1398, to rally the cities and at least a part of the nobility to their side. They did this by involving them in the reorganisation of the royal government, of its army and fortifications, and of the reform of royal officials. It was a clever policy by which the rulers appeared to give away more than they really did. Thus they accepted the request for a royal council of whose twelve members six were to be chosen from the Sicilian cities (but chosen, of course, by the king). In return they were formally allowed to choose also three Catalans and they were quite adamant in rejecting a proposal for a council to be chosen from the prelates, nobles and cities.

The parliament itself was reorganised according to the Catalan-Aragonese model. The structure of the Sicilian parliament had never been rigidly fixed. In general, the nobles and the prelates sat together, as they did in England, since both were summoned in their capacity of holders of fiefs.[17] They were now separated so that the Sicilian parliament took on the appearance of the classic assembly of three

---

[17] C. Calisse, *Storia del Parlamento in Sicilia*, (Torino, 1887), p. 84.

estates, here called *bracci*, after the Aragonese *brazos*. Whether this tripartite division was detrimental to the effectiveness of parliament, as has sometimes been maintained, is by no means certain. More important in the long run and much more detrimental was the introduction of the Catalan practice of allowing the prelates and nobles to be represented by proxies. Our sources do not allow us to dertermine whether this was done deliberately, so as to give the king an opportunity to control the proxy votes, or whether Martin I and his father were simply introducing into Sicily a practice with which they were familiar at home and which, no doubt, they found convenient. Certainly, their introduction of Catalan and Aragonese noble families into the island and their appointment of Catalans to Sicilian bishoprics was a quite deliberate policy. It was a policy which the Aragonese monarchy was to pursue quite systematically also in Naples and Sardinia. In this way the kings could circumvent local privileges reserving offices to natives of the country; for the second generation of this immigrant nobility would be legally natives. Indeed, in Sicilian law even the first generation of immigrants would have full rights if they married Sicilian wives. And yet, being newcomers and viewed with considerable jealousy by the old-established families in a society that was even more ridden by family feuds than was usual in the middle ages, they depended very heavily on the favour of the king and they would therefore be more loyal to him than the native nobility.

Once firmly in the saddle, the new king found he could do without further assemblies of parliament. When Queen Maria died, in 1402, the Sicilians petitioned the king's father in Barcelona that their king should now marry Giovanna of Naples. Not unnaturally, old King Martin rejected such a marriage alliance with the Neapolitan Angevins, the archenemies of the house of Aragon. But, even more significantly, he had already decided on his son's marriage with Bianca of Navarre without bothering to inform the Sicilians or even his son himself. The Sicilians still had their own king, as they had always insisted they should have; but the really important political decisions affecting their kingdom were, from now on, being taken in Spain.[18]

After the death of the elder Martin, in 1412, Sicily lost what remained of her political independence. Ferdinand of Antequera, the new king of Aragon of the Castilian house of Trastamara, ruled Sicily through viceroys. He and his successors rejected all Sicilian requests for a resident king of their own. From now on, Sicily was simply a part, and an outlying and relatively poor and unimportant part, of the large, composite Aragonese-Catalan and, later, Aragonese-Castilian (Spanish) monarchy. The effects of this basic situation on the history of

[18] For this point and for the preceding paragraphs cf. R. Moscati, *Per una storia della Sicilia nell'età dei Martini*, (Messina, 1954), chapter 4; and A. Boscolo, *La Politica Italiana di Martino il Vecchio re d'Aragona*, Padua, 1962, pp. 54–61.

the Sicilian parliament were profound. The right which parliament had won at the end of the 13th century of giving its consent to war or peace became meaningless,; for decisions on such matters were now taken in Barcelona and, later, in Madrid; but never in Palermo. The viceroy was always a foreigner. On the relatively few occasions when a Sicilian was appointed temporarily to this office, he was not even allowed to enjoy the title of viceroy but had to be content with that of president. He and his councillors were always appointed by the king in Spain.

Having firmly established its own position of ultimate power and reserved for itself all the most important political decisions and appointments, the Aragonese monarchy did not repeat the mistakes of the French in the 13th century of riding roughshod over the country's customs and privileges. Having diluted the Sicilian ruling classes with a strong admixture of Spaniards, the monarchy was now content to support the status of these classes in the country. This system proved to be remarkably stable for 300 years. Parliament, the representative of the Sicilian ruling classes, maintained considerable powers. It was generally summoned every three years when it voted the regular donative, also for three years. If the government needed more money it would have to summon extraordinary meetings of parliament, and this was naturally not popular.

This control over taxation was the most important and the most jealously defended privilege of the Sicilian parliament. The government did not always get as much as it wanted; but by careful political management a viceroy could usually get his way. Scipio di Castro, a sixteenth-century writer on political subjects who knew Sicily well, has left us an account of the difficulties which viceroys had to face in handling parliaments.[19] These ranged from the complete rejection or severe scaling down of the viceroy's demands to the attachment of awkward conditions to their donatives. Castro's analysis has often been taken at its face value. Yet a careful reading of Sicilian parliamentary history shows that he over-dramatised the problems which parliaments presented to the Spanish viceroys.[20] A complete rejection of a demand for a donative occurred only twice, in 1478 and in 1591. The earlier event will be discussed later. On the second occasion it was only the *braccio militare*, the nobility which rejected the donative. The viceroy, after an initial period of confusion in face of this most unexpected event, soon found that the other two *bracci* would not support the nobility. Thus he had little difficulty in outmanoeuvring the recalcitrant barons.

[19] S. di Castro, *Avvertimenti al Signor Marc' Antonio Colonna, quando andò ViceRe in Sicilia*, ed. A. Saitta, (Roma, 1950).

[20] H. G. Koenigsberger, 'The Parliament of Sicily and the Spanish Empire', *Estates and Revolutions*, (Ithaca, 1971); also published in *Mélanges Antonio Marongiu*, (Brussels, 1968).

The Sicilian estates were never willing to carry their opposition to the length of armed resistance. The sessions of the three *bracci* were too short and too infrequent to make possible the development of a regular opposition with a clear-cut policy, even if such a thing had been conceivable at the time. What was worse, most barons and prelates were content to be represented by proxies. The *braccio ecclesiastico* consisted of three archbishops, six bishops and 40 or 50 abbots and priors. In the parliament of 1556, which was a perfectly typical one, only nine of these prelates attended in person, and of these only one was a bishop. In the same parliament only 17 of 72 lords attended. From time to time parliament petitioned the king to make those who should attend parliament do so or to restrict the number of proxies any one person could hold to a maximum of two or three.[21] But the king invariably rejected these petitions; for the viceroys found the proxy system which they could largely control much too useful to give up.

The petitions, or *capitoli*, which the parliaments submitted to the king were, in theory, the conditions on which they granted donatives, and much has been made of the contractual nature of the Sicilian laws which were based on these *capitoli*.[22] In practice, however, this mattered very little; for the contract was decidely onesided. The king approved or rejected the *capitoli* as he saw fit, and the collection of the donatives always began long before the king's signature gave the act legal force. The kings and their viceroys were more concerned with practical than with legal considerations. 'Siendo Vuestra Magestad servido dello, juntar el parlamento para dar orden en lo de las gabelas, ó ejecutarlas sin él (i.e. without parliament) conforme á la órden que . . . se me diere,' wrote the viceroy García de Toledo, in 1565.[23] This offhand attitude towards parliaments was entirely typical of the Spaniards. In the long and detailed instructions which the Council of Italy always wrote on behalf of the kings for new viceroys, and in the memoranda which outgoing viceroys or their secretaries wrote for their successors, parliament is either not thought worth mentioning at all or is disposed of with a few conventional remarks. Evidently, neither at the royal court in Spain nor at the viceregal court in Sicily was parliament considered a serious political problem. Nor does a reading of the correspondence of the viceroys (in so far as this has been published or has been read by this writer in the Spanish archives) suggest a different picture. Parliament is, of course, mentioned in this correspondence, but nearly always with the viceregal comment that it will do what can be expected, considering the size and poverty of the

[21] E.g. in 1594. F. Testa, *Capitula Regni Siciliae*, II, (Palermo, 1743), p. 312.

[22] E.g. L. Genuardi, *Parlamento Siciliano*, (Bologna, 1924), pp. LXXIX ff; C. Giardina, 'Le fonti della legislazione Siciliana', *Archivio Storico per la Sicilia*, I, 1935, p. 73.

[23] *Colección de Documentos Inéditos para la Historia de España*, XXX, (Madrid, 1857), p. 25.

kingdom. There could hardly be a greater contrast than that between the correspondence of the viceroys of Sicily and of Margaret of Parma, Philip II's regent of the Netherlands, who never ceased complaining of her difficulties with the estates of Brabant, Flanders and Holland.

There were good reasons for this situation. Not only were the Sicilian ruling classes basically loyal to Spain – there was plenty of testimony to the feeling of loyalty through three centuries of Spanish rule and even beyond it, in the 18th century – but the organisation of the Sicilian parliament allowed any reasonably competent viceroy to manage parliament by attaching the leaders of the *bracci* to himself by skilful use of government favours, and by keeping the majority of the proxy votes in the hands of government officials.[24]

The same was true of the *Deputazione del Regno di Sicilia*. This was a committee of parliament, based on the model of the Catalan *diputacío*, whose business it was to guard against the violation of *capitoli* and privileges and to see that donatives appropriated for a specific purpose, usually defence, were not spent on other matters, notably general government debts; for then the government would come back to parliament for more money for defence. The *Deputazione* dated from the 15th century and was given its final form between 1567 and 1570. But this potentially powerful institution which in Catalonia led the revolt of 1640, which in Friuli shared the actual government of the country with the ruler and which in several German principalities effectively upheld the interests of the estates, became in Sicily largely a governmental agency. The viceroys appointed its members and had to approve its decisions before they became effective.[25] The viceroys were unanimous that the *Deputazione* never presented them with any serious political difficulty.

Nevertheless, the importance of the Sicilian parliament should not be underestimated, even during the viceregal period. The great mass of parliamentary *capitoli* were concerned with matters of detail, with the rights of individual barons and cities and ecclesiastical corporations, or with the maintenance of roads and bridges and ports. On such matters the king was usually perfectly willing to accede to parliamentary requests; and thus the majority of the *capitoli* did, in fact, become law. Nor could the viceroys afford a head-on collision with parliament. In the late autumn of 1478 the then viceroy, Count of Prades, summoned parliament to obtain help for the defence of the island against the Turks. This was the third summons in little over a year. In June 1477, the first

[24] H. G. Koenigsberger, 'The Parliament of Sicily', *cit.* Cf. also Koenigsberger, *The Practice of Empire*, emended edition of *The Government of Sicily under Philip II of Spain*, Ithaca, 1969, ch. VI. 2. and passim. Spanish translation, by G., Soriano, *La Practica del Imperio*, Madrid, 1975. Also V. Titone, 'Il Parlamento Siciliano nell'età moderna', *Mélanges Antonio Marongiu*, cit.

[25] G. Schichilone, 'Origine e ordinamento della Deputazione del Regno di Sicilia', *Archivio Storico per la Sicilia Orientale*, ser. 4, anno III, 1950.

of these parliaments had granted a donative of 90,000 florins for Prades
to help the viceroy of Sardinia against the rebellion of the marquis of
Oristano, in that island. In February–March 1478, a second parliament
granted another donative, this time of 30,000 florins, but coupled with
some severe criticisms of the viceroy's intervention in Sardinia. It seems
that there was so much opposition in the country that this donative was
never actually collected at all. On the third occasion, the viceroy tried
to get a favourable vote by travelling around the country and
persuading the individual towns to grant a donative. He had some
initial success in western Sicily; but soon opposition crystallised under
the leadership of Messina and parliament rejected his demands
altogether. At this critical moment the king, John II, died, and Prades
accepted the face-saving mission of representing the island at the
accession of the new king, Ferdinand the Catholic.[26]

Here was a pattern that now became typical for Sicily. Political
struggles came to be concerned with personalities and not with
questions of ultimate power. If the Sicilian ruling groups did not like a
particular viceroy, they could and did get rid of him; for Madrid would
rather drop a viceroy who had become unpopular than offend the
Sicilian establishment. At the Spanish court every man had enemies,
and thus the Sicilians never had any difficulty in finding highly placed
allies in Madrid. The viceroys ignored this set-up at their peril. In 1609
the marquis of Villena accepted and tried to collect a personal donative
of 60,000 florins, contrary to a long-standing tradition according to
which the viceroys always declined such personal offers. Parliament
took the matter to Madrid and Villena was promptly recalled – without
the 60,000 florins.

If the Sicilian ruling classes had lost ultimate political power and had
been excluded from the most important decision-making processes,
they could and did exert great influence over the government of their
country at all other levels. In the 17th century the nobles won, as of
right, the ability to buy local jurisdiction, the *mero e misto imperio* over
their peasants. Their growing indebtedness, and the curious institution
of the *Deputazione degli Stati* (not to be confused with the *Deputazione
del Regno*) which regulated their debts and mortgage payments and
associated their bourgeois or ecclesiastical creditors and their own
tenants in the maintenance of their social position, created a society
frozen at a low and inefficient level of economic production but which
was, nevertheless, remarkably stable.[27]. In most states of early modern
Europe it was the monarchies which were the most dynamic element in
political society. But in composite states the monarchies were inclined to
leave small outlying kingdoms alone; for the necessarily limited results

[26] R. Starrabba, *Il Conte di Prades e la Sicilia (1477–1479)*, (Palermo, 1872).
[27] G. Tricoli, *La Deputazione degli Stati e la crisi del Baronaggio Siciliano dal XVI al XIX
Secolo*, (Palermo, 1966), Pt. I.

of a more active policy did not usually seem to justify the risk of stirring up trouble by offending the local establishment. The Spanish system in Sicily, moreover, tended to build up alternative centres of authority to the viceroy. The most important of these was the Inquisition; and parliament and the viceroy's ministers, whom he did not appoint himself, all acted as legitimate foci of opposition to the viceroys. No viceroy could escape from this opposition; for, sooner rather than later, government policy was bound to offend some powerful personage or clique. Then the opposition to the viceroy would combine, in or out of parliament, and the government in Madrid would recall the viceroy or refuse to renew his three year term of appointment. When a new viceroy had been sent the game would start all over again, so that contemporaries spoke of '*Sicilia fatal a sus virrreyes*'.

It was, in fact, not so much a system of government by consent as a system of cut-throat politics functioning within tacitly agreed but strict limits. What might happen if the ruler did not observe these limits was shown very clearly by the revolt of Catalonia in 1640, like Sicily an outlying and relatively poor dominion of the composite Spanish monarchy. In Sicily parliament had developed sufficiently strongly before the period of the viceroys to become an integral part of this frozen system. This is the basic reason for the continued effectiveness of the Sicilian parliament; but also for the limitations of this effectiveness. There was a popular saying in Italy, that in Sicily the Spaniards nibbled, in Naples they ate and in Milan they devoured. A part, at least, of the credit for keeping the Spaniards at the nibbling stage in Sicily must go to the Sicilian parliament. But when, in the popular and baronial revolts of 1647 and 1649 the whole basis of Sicilian political society came to be questioned, parliament was simply ignored by all parties.[28]

In the kingdom of Naples, just as in Sicily, the War of the Sicilian Vespers forced the monarchy to summon representative assemblies and to promise a return to the constitutions and privileges of the Swabian period. The parliaments were, moreover, supported by the popes, the feudal suzerains of the kingdom, who demanded that the kings levy no taxation without the consent of the estates. The assembly of 1290 even enacted that parliaments must be summoned twice a year, in March and in September.[29]

But the Angevin kings of Naples were not inclined to make more concessions than they were forced to do by circumstances. They never summoned their parliaments regularly and, in the 14th century, the Neapolitan ruling groups were too severely split between different contenders for the throne to take advantage of the relative weakness of

---

[28] H. G. Koenigsberger, 'The Revolt of Palermo in 1647', *Estates and Revolution*, cit.

[29] E. Gentile, 'Parlamenti generali nel regno di Napoli nel periodo angioino', *Studi in Onore di Riccardo Filangieri* , I, (Naples, 1959).

the monarchy in order to strengthen parliament. As in Siciliy, feudal anarchy did not prove a suitable basis for the effective growth of representative institutions. Compared with the Sicilian parliament, that of Naples, moreover, suffered from the absence of the clergy who were not summoned, probably because of the clerical immunities which the suzerainty and proximity of the popes allowed them to claim.

Owing to successive destructions of the Neapolitan archives, our knowledge of the parliamentary history of the 14th and 15th centuries is very patchy. We are rather better informed for the Spanish period, from the end of the 15th century onwards. It seems at least possible that in the early years of Spanish rule the Neapolitan parliament played a somewhat more important role than it had done during the independence of the kingdom. Ferdinand the Catholic, no doubt aware of the surviving strength of the Angevin and pro-French party among the nobility, seems to have been anxious to placate the opinion of the ruling classes, in and outside parliament. Nevertheless, Naples, like Sicily and Catalonia, had now become an outlying dominion of a multiple monarchy. Here, too, the question of ultimate power had been resolved, and the most important decisions affecting the country were taken in Spain, from now onwards. Again, as in Sicily and Catalonia, this led to a freezing of political life within certain narrow limits. There was, however, this difference: Naples was a much larger country than Sicily and, while it was also basically very poor, its total revenue was also much larger. The pressure from Spain for increasing revenues was therefore inevitably also much greater than in Sicily. In the early decades of the 16th century, the Neapolitan parliament had some success in resisting this pressure. Especially in 1536, while the emperor Charles V was himself visiting Naples, parliament managed to scale down an especially large demand for money. It was an ominous sign, however, that the principal opposition took the form of a personal attack by members of the high nobility on the viceroy, the redoubtable Pedro de Toledo.[30] In the end, Charles V compromised on the financial issue, but firmly upheld his viceroy. Personal attacks against the viceroys continued to occur; but they never took on Sicilian proportions, probably precisely because the Neapolitan parliament remained too weak and because there was no Spanish Inquisition in the kingdom to act as an alternative focus of authority. In the famous movement against the proposed introduction of the Spanish Inquisition, in 1546, parliament (as far as is known) took no part at all. A few years later, in 1522, Toledo himself wrote to Charles V that parliament had granted more money than the economic state of the country justified.

Parliament was not always quite so accommodating; but it no longer had teeth. As in Sicily, the king could approve or reject its *capitoli* as he

[30] G. Coniglio, 'La Società napoletana ai tempi di don Pietro di Toledo', *ibid.* II.

saw fit; only in Naples he seems to have rejected them more often than he accepted them. Even in the matter of the appointment of foreigners to government offices, the Neapolitans were less successful in defending their privileges than the Sicilians. The viceroys controlled the composition of the *Deputazione delle grazie*, the parallel institution to the Sicilian *Deputazione del Regno*. Even more effectively they controlled the proxy votes in parliament. In the course of the 17th century, more and more towns on royal domain were either incorporated by purchase or by usurpation into baronial estates, or they preferred to save the expense of sending deputies to the assemblies and voluntarily allowed themselves to be represented by a local baron. The result was that the city of Naples became more and more dominant in the estate of the towns. But Naples, with its five noble and only one 'popular' seggi, and with its economic life dominated by Genoese merchants and bankers and by the presence of the viceregal courts and all the other institutions of government, was nearly always amenable to viceregal influence.

During the first half of the 17th century, as Spanish financial demands continued to increase, the monarchy sold or abdicated many of its rights in the provinces to the high nobility, but retained for itself an increasingly absolute control over the central government of the kingdom. It was not a happy development for anyone, except the favoured few. Even parliament, meeting in 1639 and 1642, became more insistent than usual in its protests about increasing taxation. Whether it was for this reason or from a general dislike of representative institutions, the viceroy wrote to Madrid in 1643 that the assemblies could only damage the public peace and the king's service. Madrid took the hint, and the parliament of Naples was not summoned again.[31] There is no evidence that, as an institution, it was greatly lamented or that it could have either prevented or led the great revolt of 1647.

It is clear that the history of the parliaments of Sicily and Naples can be understood only in terms of the history of the composite Aragonese-Spanish monarchy of which these kingdoms had become a part. But these parliaments were at least indigenous institutions representing, in some aspects, the community of the kingdom. But in Sardinia, the third of the Aragonese-Spanish kingdoms in Italy, the very institution of parliament was imported from Spain. Until the first quarter of the 14th century, the organisation of Sardinian society had not been feudal

[31] For the preceding paragraphs cf. Marongiu, *Il Parlamento*, pp. 226–433; G. D'Agostino, 'Premessa ad una storia del Parlamento General del Regno di Napoli durante la Dominazione Spagnuola', *Atti dell'Accademia di Scienze Morali e Politiche della Società Nazionale di Scienze, Lettre ed Arti in Napoli*, LXXVII, 1966; F. Caracciolo, *Uffici, Difesa e Corpi rappresentativi nel Mezzogiorno in età Spagnola*, (Reggio Calabria), 1974, ch. 4.

but communal, somewhat like that of Tuscany. There was, in consequence, no social basis for a representative assembly. Moreover, Pisa as overlord over the island, was no more anxious to foster parliaments than any other Italian city republic. The Aragonese conquest of 1323–36 completely changed the situation. By 1335, the king had given 38 great fiefs to his followers and he continued to introduce Catalan and Aragonese nobles into the island. Even some of the cities, and most notably Cagliari, were settled by Catalans, and the native Sardinian population was dispossessed and expelled. The Catalan immigration into Sicily under the Martins was never remotely as extensive as that of Sardinia.

At first the monarchy kept a tight hold over its vassals. They had to reside on their fiefs, were responsible for fortifications and had to perform strictly prescribed military services. They were not allowed to sell or subinfeudate their fiefs, so that no regular feudal hierarchy could develop. This was a system well designed to support the power of an alien monarchy; for the new nobility was entirely dependent for its position on the king. It enabled the monarchy to win out in half a century of civil war with its Sardinian opponents led by the Judges of Arborèa. Yet it was not a system that could be maintained in its original rigidity. Inevitably, the new nobility acquired great powers over the local population, most especially in the form of extensive and profitable rights of local jurisdiction. Their obligation to reside on their fiefs gradually fell into disuse, and many chose to live in Spain rather than on a far-away island – just as many Anglo-Irish landowners preferred to live in England.[32] In Sardinia then, much more definitely than in Sicily or Naples, Aragonese rule meant the imposition of an essentially colonial society on a native population which could not claim, as the Sicilians could, that they had invited the house of Aragon to rule over them by their own free will. The Sardinian parliament was therefore basically the parliament of a colonial ruling class in which the native Sardinians came to participate primarily by force of the medieval custom of extending privileges to social equals and by the gradual merging of the Sardinian and Catalan ruling groups. These facts explain much of the curious and often contradictory history of this institution.

And it was certainly curious. Where all the other Italian parliaments developed gradually, out of various types of feudal assemblies and extended royal councils, the Sardinian parliament was born, Athene-like, a fully-fledged assembly of three estates, with the classic powers of granting taxes and putting forward *capitoli* for royal approval. This happened in the year 1355. It is true that it is not now thought that this single fourteenth-century assembly can be meaningfully regarded as the true beginning of Sardinian parliamentary history; for the next session

[32] A. Boscolo, ed., *Il Feudalesimo in Sardegna*, (Cagliari, 1967); 'Premessa', by Boscolo, pp. 1–24.

did not take place until 1421.[33] But many of its members and, indeed, the Catalan ruling class in Sardinia generally, had personal experience of the workings of the Catalan corts, and they continued from time to time to attend the meetings of the corts on the mainland. Indeed, the corts of Catalonia seem to have regarded themselves as competent to advise the king not only on relations with Sardinia as a conquered kingdom but on important internal Sardinian matters. Thus, in 1366, the Catalan corts petitioned the king to revoke a law, passed in the Sardinian parliament of 1355, excluding from entry into the condition of nobility (*heretats*) anyone coming from a non-noble family. It was the king who defended the autonomy of the kingdom of Sardinia by refusing the petition. It was unreasonable, he argued, that laws approved in the parliament of a kingdom should be revoked outside the parliament of that kingdom.[34]

One may suspect that the king put forward such a fundamental constitutional principle less for its own sake than because he wanted to score a tactical debating point. He was at the same time concerned to counter the Catalans' claim that they should be exempt from customs duties and other taxes in Sardinia,[35] and for this purpose, too, he needed to maintain that Sardinian laws applied to all residents of the island, whatever their original nationality. Certainly, the Aragonese kings showed no desire to summon the Sardinian parliament at all frequently, even after 1421, when the kingdom enjoyed a long period of internal peace.

In spite of their infrequent meetings, however, the Sardinian parliaments made remarkably mature claims for themselves. In 1421 they attempted to insist on the principle of redress of their grievances before they voted on taxes. This was one of the most important principles a parliament had to establish if it was to be successful in its struggle with the monarchy. The 1421 parliament also insisted that the collection of the taxes it had voted be entrusted to a committee of three, one from each *braccio* (or *stamento*, as it was called in Sardinia). This was done in deliberate imitation of the rights of the *diputats* in Catalonia. The parliament of 1446 demanded the right to assemble on its own initiative and the king accepted this demand. It is not entirely easy to be certain of the significance of these events. One historian has recently claimed that the demand was made by, and referred only to, the *stamento militare*, the nobility.[36] Other European parliaments made

---

[33] Marongiu, *Il Parlamento*, pp. 205 ff. and bibliographical references therein, emending his earlier views in *I Parlamenti di Sardegna nella storia e nel diritto pubblico comparato*, (Roma, 1932), pp. 9 ff.

[34] A. Marongiu, 'Le *corts* catalane e la conquista della Sardegna', in *Saggi di storia giuridica e politica sarda*, (Padua, 1975), p. 111.

[35] *Ibid.*, p. 112.

[36] B. Anatra, 'Corona e ceti privilegiati nella Sardegna Spagnola', in B. Anatra, R. Puddu, G. Serri, *Problemi di storia della Sardegna spagnola*, (Cagliari, 1975), p. 21.

similar demands, on occasion, but their monarchies invariably resisted them; for they regarded the right to summon representative assemblies as one of their most important prerogatives. Alfonso the Magnanimous, in spite of his nickname, was neither more magnanimous nor more naive than his fellow monarchs in the matter of power politics, whether external or internal. It seems likely, therefore, that neither side took this proposal very seriously. There is certainly no evidence that parliament ever did assemble on its own initiative.

A similar curious ambivalence, one might almost say an air of unreality, afflicted the session which Ferdinand the Catholic summoned soon after his accession. The country had just emerged from another series of civil wars, the rebellions of the marquis of Oristano, in the 1470s. The viceroy, Ximene Pérez Scrivá, summoned parliament in November 1481 to Oristano and, on various occasions, changed the location of the sessions to Cagliari and Sassari. His principal intention was to get financial help for the defence of the island against the Turks who, in 1480, had frightened all of Italy by their capture of Otranto. Parliament was quite willing to accede to the viceroy's demands; but Pérez, a tactless man of autocratic temperament, became involved in a violent quarrel with the city council of Cagliari. Ferdinand, needing the good will of the island, recalled the viceroy. It seemed as if the Sardinians had found the same pattern of political action as the Sicilians. But appearances were deceptive. Within a year the new viceroy died and the king reappointed Pérez. Such a thing never happened in Sicily to a disgraced viceroy. It would probably have led to a revolution. But Ferdinand did not leave it at that but summoned the parliament of 1481 to Spain. In the autumn of 1484 the parliament of Sardinia met in Córdoba and Seville. It is impossible to believe that the Sicilian or even the much more accommodating Neapolitan parliament would have ever accepted such a summons overseas; but there is no evidence that the Sardinians so much as protested. Evidently, the Sardinian ruling classes still felt themselves to be Spanish.

As if this were not a sufficient show of royal strength, the king now turned the principle of 'no redress of grievances before supply' into its opposite:

Item, ordena la prefata Magestat de voluntat e consentiment dels dits elets que les decretacions provisions comisions e altres actes per Sua Magestat atorgades als estaments del dit Regne . . . estinguen sospeses e fins tant que los dicts de voluntat e consentiment dels dits elets per Sua Magestat fets sien publicats en lo dit regne de Serdenya . . .[37]

---

[37] Processo verbale of last session of the cortes in Seville, 27 October 1484. A. Era, *Il Parlamento Sardo del 1481–1485*, (Milan, 1955), p. 245. Item, His Majesty orders, by his will and with the consent of the said deputies, that decrees, provisions, commissions and other acts granted by His Majesty to the estates of the said kingdom . . . will remain in suspension and suspended until the grants of money of the said estates are published by His Majesty in the said kingdom of Sardinia.

Again, there is no evidence of any protests by parliament. The actual tax agreed to was one of 150,000 lira, payable over ten years. This, at least, was a better deal for parliament than Pérez' original demand for a permanent tax of one ducat per household.[38] Apparently, this almost casual attempt to make the government financially completely independent of parliament was taken no more seriously than parliament's earlier attempt to make itself independent of royal summons. Ferdinand and his viceroys made no other attempt to govern Sardinia without parliament. When the tax granted in 1484 ran out, they summoned a new parliament, in 1494. From 1497 to 1511 a whole series of sessions took place, all in Sardinia, which seem to have been different sessions of a single Parliament. Such a long parliament was also completely outside the experience of all others, either in Italy or in the rest of Europe, during this period.

During the 16th century the constitutional position in Sardinia took on the frozen appearance that it did in Sicily, and it did this for very similar reasons. The Sardinian parliament was summoned normally every nine or ten years. It usually granted the taxes which the government asked for, but like the parliament of Sicily, it probably did keep them lower than they would otherwise have been. For the rest, it concerned itself with the local and, often, individual interests of members of the ruling groups or of the towns and corporations of the island. In the 17th century relations between the viceroys and parliaments became more tense. The Spanish monarchy attempted to squeeze more money out of its Italian dominions to help pay for the mounting costs of local defence and of Spanish intervention in the wars of western Europe. At the same time it was more unwilling than ever to see its actions limited by representative assemblies. The first major clash occurred in 1624–25 when the viceroy Juan Vivas found himself opposed by a large section of the Sardinian nobility, episcopate and the city of Cagliari, and supported by the rival city, Sassari and, significantly, by those members of the nobility usually resident in Spain. Although the viceroy, at one stage, tried to break the opposition by quartering troops from Lombardy in their houses, the conflict was fought out mainly by means of memoranda and complaints sent to the Council of Aragon, in Spain.[39] A further conflict, in 1654–55, involved riots and popular demonstrations, but even more serious was the confrontation of 1665–68. The points at issue went far beyond the government's financial demands and included the question of the appointment of Spaniards to public offices in Sardinia, the nobles' rights

---

[38] F. Loddo-Canepa, 'Alcune istruzioni inedite del 1481 nel quadro della politica di Ferdinando II in Sardegna', *Archivio Storico Sardo*, XXIV, 1954, p. 443. Cf. also A. Era, *Il Parlamento Sardo*, cit. and 'Storia della Sardegna durante il Regno di Ferdinando il Cattolico', II. 'I Parlamenti', *Fernando el Catolico y Italia, V Congreso de Historia de la Corona de Aragon*, Estudios III, (Zaragoza, 1954).

[39] Marongiu, 'Parlamento e lotta politica nel 1624–25', *Saggi di storia . . . sarda*, pp. 203–228.

of jurisdiction, the cities' claim freely to export grain without storing it first in government granaries and, finally, the demand that the crown confirm all previous privileges of parliament. In the course of the dispute which became more acrimonious, both the leader of the noble opposition and the viceroy were assassinated; but in the end the opposition to the crown collapsed and the heads of its executed leaders were displayed on the towers of Cagliari.[40] The last session took place in 1697–99, during which parliament, for the first time, actually reduced the ordinary donative.

In the 18th century there was, at various times, talk of reviving the institution. But the new Piedmontese monarchy to whom the island had been assigned by the Great Powers without consultation (1718–20), showed no interest in such a revival. Not only was the political climate of the age in general, and at the court of Turin in particular, decidedly absolutist, but the Piedmontese deeply distrusted the Sardinians. Even in mid-18th century half the island was still in the hands of owners resident in Spain. It proved more difficult than the diplomats had expected to replace one colonial régime by another.[41]

We have already seen that Friuli was a part of Italy in which a feeling of community developed without the help of compelling geographical or ethnic circumstances, neither of which, in fact, existed. The cohesion of the principality was due to the feudal overlordship of its prince, the patriarch of Aquileia. Since the prince was an ecclesiastic, this was not a dynastic overlordship. The state could therefore not pass to a foreign ruler by inheritance, nor could it be divided among a ruler's sons, as happened so frequently in the lay principalities of Germany during the middle ages. Most important of all, monarchical power tended to become institutionalised relatively early. Here is the key to much of the parliamentary history of Friuli.

From the little that is known of the early history of the parliament of Friuli, it seems to have developed as a regular institution in an entirely orthodox way, out of enlarged council meetings and other *ad hoc* assemblies of notables, towards the end of the 13th century, when the patriarchs needed the military and financial support of their barons, ecclesiastical institutions and towns in their constant wars with their neighbours. It was in these wars that the feeling of the community of the *patria* was born. Soon, parliament spoke of itself as acting *'nomine totius universitatis Foriiulii'*.[42] Its basis was essentially military. Nobles, prelates and towns were summoned according to the *talea militiae*, the list determining the military contributions each had to make in case of war. The actual rate of contribution was fixed, from time time, by parliament,

[40] Anatra, 'Corona e ceti', pp. 111 ff.

[41] For the preceding paragraphs cf. especially Marongiu, *Il Parlamento*, pp. 447–466, and *I Parlamenti di Sardegna*, passim.

[42] See P. S. Leicht, *Parlamento Friulano*, I, (1228–1420), Pt. I, (Bologna, 1917), p. LX.

and the patriarch's own extensive domains were included in this list. Quite rapidly, in the course of the 14th century, parliament established its own procedures and powers; for the constant attacks by Friuli's neighbours and the frequent and often lengthy vacancies of the patriarchate inevitably weakened the position of the monarchy.

Parliament usually met several times a year, sometimes as often as ten times; but each plenary session lasted only for one day. Its main work, however, was done by several committees. Apart from a number of committees appointed for specific purposes, such as legal cases, there were two main committees, called *consigli*. The first, a wider committee, was composed of two ecclesiastics, two barons, eight ministeriales and four deputies of the towns. To these sixteen the patriarch could add appointees of his own. This committee sat for one or two days immediately following on the plenary session and it carried on the latter's work. More and more, however, the actual functions of parliament devolved on a second *consiglio*, consisting of twelve members, two each appointed by the three estates and the remainder by the patriarch. This committee was first elected by each plenary session but, later in the 14th century, it came to be elected always for six months. Thus, in practice, it became a permanent committee. Increasingly, the government of the country was carried on through this *consiglio*. The patriarch was even required to select his own appointees from members of parliament.

Here was a *dominium politicum et regale*, an effective system of co-operation between a monarchy and its representative institutions, that perhaps went further than in any other European country in the fourteenth century. In theory, at least, here was an integration of powers and authority that seemed to resolve the basic power struggle between monarchies and parliaments. The Friuli parliament and its committees took an active part not only in the financial administration of the country but also in its legal life, as court of first instance in cases of feudal law, of conspiracy and rebellion, in civil cases which involved the patriarch and as final court of appeal in nearly all other cases.[43] It even did what the Sicilian parliament only claimed to do, it co-operated with the ruler in decisions on war and peace and in the conclusion of treaties with foreign powers. Nevertheless, the patriarch maintained considerable authority, directly through his own appointments to the *consiglio*, and, indirectly, through his *gastaldi* who presided over the administration of the cities and thus ensured a considerable degree of harmony between the aims of the patriarch and those of the cities and the deputies they sent to parliament. There was some justice in the nostalgic characterisation of pre-Venetian Friuli by a sixteenth century antiquary, count Girolamo di Porcia, as being governed 'più a forma di

---

[43] E. Traversa, *Das Friaulische Parlament*, (Vienna, Leipzig, 1911), pp. 128–131.

repubblica che di principato'.[44]

If there was an element of truth in this view, it was nevertheless much too romantic. The feeling of community, genuine as it was, remained underdeveloped. For all their apparent co-operation, there was no really stable balance in the relations between the patriarch and the estates. Any really energetic patriarch who valued his authority soon found himself in conflict with some or even most of his more powerful barons and larger cities. The most forceful patriarch of the 14th century, John of Moravia, ended by being assassinated, in 1393. The country was rarely at rest, or even reasonably peaceful, among the rivalries of the bigger cities and the feuds and actual fighting of the noble clans.[45] Inevitably, Friuli's neighbours intervened in these feuds for their own purposes, and the Friulians themselves came to rely more and more on outside help. It was the great baronial house of Savorgnan and the city of Cividale who called in the Venetians in their quarrel with the city of Udine and with the patriarch, Luigi di Teck who, in his turn, was supported by the emperor Sigismund. At the critical moment, Sigismund was in no position to give help to his allies. When the Venetian army invaded Friuli, one city after another surrendered. The principality was incorporated as a province into the Republic of St. Mark (1420).

The parliament of Friuli now found itself in roughly the same position with regard to the Venetian Senate as the parliaments of Sicily and Naples with regard to the Spanish monarchy. Or rather, it was in a considerably weaker position. For it was not the parliament of Friuli which had transferred the rule of the country to Venice, as the parliament of Sicily had transferred the rule of its kingdom to the house of Aragon. The Venetians had promised to observe the privileges of the nobles and cities with whom they treated in 1420; but they had made no treaty with the parliament as an institution. Nor had they traditionally any great liking for representative assemblies. Their *luogotenente* took the place of the patriarch and, inevitably, his power, backed by that of the Venetian Senate, was much more formidable. Parliament continued to meet and defend the interests of the province and the privileges of its ruling groups; for evidently Venice found it convenient to have it so. But the old feeling of community had now few sources left to feed it. First Udine and then Cividale effectively opted out of parliament. This institution itself split into assemblies for the province east and west of the river Tagliamento. From about the middle of the 16th century, a separate representation of the rural parts of Friuli, the *corpo della contadinanza*, began to appear. A true *vivere politico* for the whole of Friuli had almost ceased.[46]

[44] *Rom. Patria del Friuli* (1567), quoted in P. S. Leicht, *Breve storia del Friuli*, 3rd ed. (Udine, 1951), p. 180.

[45] *Ibid.*, p. 125.

[46] Leicht, *Parlamento Friulano*, II, Pt. I, (Bologna, 1955), passim; Marongiu, *Il Parlamento, cit..*

The only other Italian state in which an effective parliament developed
was Piedmont. Here at least, it would seem was a case of an
autonomous development, of rulers and their parliaments working out
their constitutional destiny without outside interference or, at most, in
conjunction with the destinies of Savoy, Bresse, Pays de Vaud and the
smaller dominions of the house of Savoy. Here, too, the feeling of
community was evident; for the ruling house was a relative late-comer
among the barons and communes who prided themselves on possessing
rights and privileges older than the house of Savoy and on their
voluntary submission to this house. But these appearances are
deceptive; for in the end, just as with all other Italian parliaments, it was
largely outside forces which determined the history of the Piedmontese
parliament.

The early history of this parliament may well have been connected
with the geographical character of Piedmont. Its Alpine and sub-Alpine
valleys were separated by often impassable mountain ranges. The
counts, travelling from valley to valley, would recruit to their councils
always a certain number of local lords, and it has been suggested that
this was the way in which local estates appeared in the 13th
century.[47] However this may be, there is little evidence that parliament
appeared as a regular institution before the 14th century. But by the
second half of that century its role with relation to the ruler had become
well defined: the granting of taxes and the defence of the country's
privileges.[48] Compared with the rest of northern Italy, Piedmont was
an economically underdeveloped region. Its main source of wealth was
land, and this applied to the monarchy and the communes as much as to
the nobility. The revenues of the monarchy were therefore strictly
limited and tended to diminish as successive dukes alienated parts of
their domain in order to meet specific financial crises. This meant that
the residue of power within the state lay with the other landowners, the
church corporations, the nobles and the communes, i.e. the three
estates. The dukes therefore had no option but to have recourse to
parliament for money grants when they needed these for the
unavoidable wars of the period. Inevitably, their demands led to
political confrontations; for parliament was bound to exploit this
situation for the benefit of those it represented. However, in these
confrontations the dukes enjoyed certain advantages. Not only was it
they who summoned parliament and determined the agenda of its
sessions, but they had rarely to deal with all the estates together.
Although parliament met occasionally as an assembly of the three
estates, this was not the rule. In most assemblies the clergy was absent.
Ducal decrees exempted ecclesiastical land from parliamentary

[47] C. W. Previté Orton, *The Early History of the House of Savoy (1000–1233)*,
(Cambridge, 1912), p. 438.

[48] A. Tallone, *Parlamento Sabaudo*, Pt. I, *Patria Cismontana*, I (Bologna, 1928),
Introduzione; Marongiu, *Il Parlamento*, pp. 195–199, 280–287.

taxation. At the same time, the prelates were well represented in the duke's council. They therefore enjoyed a much more direct influence over the duke's government than they could possibly hope to achieve through parliament. The duke, for his part, could rely on the support of the church which, in the 15th century, had an aggregate income that was more than half as high again as that of the monarchy. Nor did most of the members of the high nobility attend parliament. The Piedmontese barons never formed a coherent and self-conscious estate like the Sicilian *braccio militare*, and the dukes could dispense sufficient political patronage to keep always at least a number of the barons on their side.

In practice, therefore, most parliaments consisted of only a relatively small number of barons and of the deputies of the towns. These deputies were always members of the lower nobility or of the urban patriciate whose wealth was largely in the form of land. Parliament therefore represented and was made up of a relatively homogeneous class, a fact which compensated to a considerable degree for the absence of the greater barons and prelates. In the second half of the fifteenth century this parliamentary class seems to have advanced economically as against other sections of the community. This conclusion would seem to follow from a statistical study of the land registers (*catasti*) of Turin, with supporting statistical evidence from Moncalieri and Chieri. If this is a correct conclusion – and there is no reason to think that these cities were in any way exceptional – then it is not surprising to find that during this period the parliamentary class should have sought to extend its political influence. The country was ruled by a dynasty that was as yet more French than Italian, more Savoyard than Piedmontese. The dukes preferred to reside on the pleasant shores of Lake Geneva, rather than in the sun-baked plain of Piedmont. They tended to give the most important offices of state to Savoyards, and the richest ecclesiastical benefices were usually held by prelates from 'the other side of the mountains'. To the Piedmontese, parliament appeared the most convenient instrument to redress this adverse balance. [49]

They were helped by the specific political constellations of the second half of the 15th century. This was a period of incompetent dukes, of child rulers or of female regents. Members of the ducal house had been given large appanages which greatly reduced the resources of the monarchy and from which, moreover, they intrigued for the control of the regency governments. These were classic conditions for the advance of parliamentary authority, provided parliament was prepared to grasp its opportunities. There were those who appreciated this situation. In 1476, for instance, Luigi Talliandi, an experienced noble

[49] M. C. Daviso, 'Considerazioni intorno ai Tre Stati in Piemonte', *Bollettino storico-bibliografico subalpino*, 1947; H. G. Koenigsberger, 'The Parliament of Piedmont during the Renaissance, 1460–1560', *Estates and Revolutions*, especially pp. 42–51.

politician and great parliamentarian – he represented Ivrea in over thirty sessions of the assembly from 1468 to 1512 – could state categorically that

né il signore da sé è potente ad sostenire una impresa se li Tre Stati non l'adiutano, et sempre le Tre Stati concluderano, deliberano et farano quello che da li principali del paise gli serà persuaso, perché naturalmente le comunità non amano disturbo, spesa, né guerra, neanche le gentilhomini et manco le preti . . .[50]

Talliandi gave this appraisal in the context of advice to the Milanese ambassador on how to manage Piedmontese politics; for he went on to suggest that the duke of Milan should keep some eight or ten of the principal members of parliament well supplied with money and honours, so that they would always persuade parliament to support his interests.

While Talliandi had stressed the importance of parliament in the politics of Piedmont, he had also put his finger on its basic weakness; its tendency to become the tool of the country's neighbours; for, naturally, the French and the Swiss followed the same policy as the Milanese, that of building up their clientage within the parliament. It is important to see this phenomenon in the context of both the accepted public morality of the age and of the political realities of the situation. Many of the Piedmontese nobility owned estates in France or the Milanese. While their first loyalty was undoubtedly to the house of Savoy, yet they still had feudal obligations to the rulers of these countries. Members of the ruling house were themselves usually clients of either France or Milan, and for a time also of Burgundy, and they had their own, private ambitions which were rather less designed for the benefit of the whole community than Talliandi's and his fellow nobles' attempts to keep their small and vulnerable country out of the destructive wars of their more powerful neighbours. Yet these neighbours who supported the pretensions of the Piedmontese estates had no love for parliaments. They used them only for their own purposes. Louis XI once proposed an alliance between himself and the dukes of Savoy and Milan for the express purpose of helping each other against their own subjects.[51] Galeazzo Maria Sforza, although no doubt sympathetic to such a policy, was much too astute to give the French such an excellent pretext for sending troops into Italy.

Some years later, his successor, Lodovico il Moro, advised the regent of Piedmont, Bianca of Montferrat, on how to 'vendicare a se stessa

[50] Tallone, *Parlamento Sabaudo*, V. *Patria Cismontana*, V, (Bologna, 1932), p. 180. 'The prince is not sufficiently strong to carry out an action on his own unless the three estates help him; and the three estates always debate, conclude and do what the most important persons of the country persuade them to do. For, naturally, the towns don't like disturbances, expenses and warfare, nor do the gentlemen and the priests even less . . .'

[51] Letter by the Milanese ambassador to Savoy to Galeazzo Maria Sforza, 22 July 1471, Milan, Archivio di Stato, MS. Savoia, box 484, folder July 1471.

tutto l'arbitrio del governo'. She should not oppose parliament directly, but rather appear to assent to its demands and, 'sapendo obsecundare il tempo, redurà le cose al proposito suo, et questo che sarà operato in li Tre Stati non sarà stato altro che una umbra senza forma . . . '[52] On this particular occasion, in 1490, parliament had propsed that, during a ducal minority, it should elect three Savoyard and three Piedmontese councillors, from each of the three estates. Parliament should also have the right to assemble at least every two years on its own initiative. Unlike Alfonso the Magnanimous, the regent Bianca reacted to this proposal most strongly, using the tactics suggested by Lodovico il Moro most successfully. This reaction is all the more significant as the Piedmontese parliament had normally been summoned much more frequently than once every two years. The question was therefore not that of the frequency of the assemblies, let alone of any attempts by the dukes to rule without parliament altogether, but entirely that of the autonomy of parliament. Talliandi and his friends who put forward the proposals of 1490 are not likely to have thought in terms of establishing parliamentary government in Piedmont, although Talliandi had once been in Burgundian service and undoubtedly knew that some such attempt was made in the Netherlands following the death of Charles the Bold in 1477. It is more likely that he was concerned with the position of the Piedmontese nobility in government and with the autonomy of parliament, especially during regencies. However, these were not causes for which it was possible to rally persistent support in the 15th century, especially as the government of Bianca was willing to appoint some more Piedmontese to high offices of state.[53] After little more than a week the parliamentary offensive collapsed, just as Lodovico had predicted that it would.

But the basic constitutional balance remained much as it had before. In the 16th century, the dukes continued to summon parliament, mainly to obtain financial aid; and parliament, while willing to support the duke's policy and meet reasonable demands, was remarkably successful in keeping down the rate of taxation.[54] If it did not make any further constitutional advances, neither did it retreat. It was Piedmont's neighbours who upset this balance. In 1536, French troops occupied Savoy and about two thirds of Piedmont, while Spanish-Imperial troops from Milan, occupied the remaining third. For 23 years Piedmont ceased to exist as an independent state.

In both occupied zones parliaments continued to function but, inevitably, under very different conditions from formerly. The French

[52] Tallone, *Parlamento Sabaudo, VI, Patria Cismontana,* VI, pp. 12–13.
[53] For a detailed discussion of the relations between Savoyards and Piedmontese cf. L. Marini, *Savoiardi e Piemontesi nello Stato sabaudo,* (Roma, 1962).
[54] Koenigsberger, 'The Parliament of Piedmont', p. 65.

generally respected local Piedmontese privileges. But Piedmont was now simply treated as a French province and its parliament as a provincial assembly, like the assemblies of Dauphiné or Burgundy. Ultimate power had been transferred to the king of France, and all important decisions were taken at his court. The Imperialists behaved even more autocratically, virtually ignoring the estates in their zone and collecting heavy taxes at the point of the pike, regardless of parliamentary votes. As so often happens in such situations, and as had been happening in Friuli, the feeling of community within the country began to dissolve, and the estates and even individual cities tried to gain what advantages they could at the expense of the rest of the country.

In 1559, as part of the treaty of Cateau-Cambrésis between France and Spain, the duke of Savoy, Emmanuel Philibert, returned to a demoralised country at the head of a victorious army. There seems to be little doubt that, from the beginning, he was determined to establish absolute rule. He had been Philip II's governor-general of the Netherlands and his experience there of an intractable and even aggressive States General had not inclined him to look favourably on representative institutions. But, astute politician that he was, he summoned one more parliament. This assembly, a sort of 'khaki parliament' reflecting the country's relief and joy at the end of the foreign occupation, voted what all previous parliaments had consistently refused: a huge salt tax. Once having got this, and therefore the means to pay his troops, Emmanuel Philbert refused to confirm parliament's privileges in the traditional way and, from then on, simply did not summon parliament any more. He repeated this pattern in Savoy and in his other French-speaking provinces, but he left the provincial assemblies of Val d'Aosta and Saluzzo severely alone. They were not worth a possibly dangerous confrontation.

Piedmont, after more than two decades of foreign military occupation, had become morally and materially incapable of resisting the duke's absolutism. He carefully bound the high nobility to himself by giving them court positions and he judiciously refrained from interfering with their exploitation of the peasants on their estates. His own interests as a great landowner in any case coincided with those of the nobility, in this respect. But the country paid a heavy price for the alliance of monarchy and high nobility. Where Charles III's revenue, before the French invasion, had averaged 70,000 to 90,000 ducats per annum, Emmanuel Philibert's was about half a million, often much higher and rarely lower. Even allowing for the rise in prices which occurred during this period, this was a staggering increase. The Venetian ambassadors at the duke's court and other foreign observers left no doubt in their reports about the disastrous effects of this rate of taxation on the prosperity of the country. *Dominium regale* was a heavy burden on a ruler's subjects – as the medieval theorists of parliaments and the proponents of *dominium politicum et regale* had always said it was.[55]

By the beginning of the 18th century, there was little left of the once lively parliamentary traditions of Italy. In the inevitable struggle between rulers and parliaments, the rulers had won out. The parliament of the Marca d'Ancona had changed little since Sixtus V had given it definite form, in 1585. But the 40 or 50 towns and districts represented in this assembly had never exercised anything but very limited powers and had never even begun seriously to challenge the authority of their prince, the pope. The papacy, for its part, was content to let the institution persist because its inclination towards conservatism was, perhaps, even stronger than its inclination towards absolutism. The parliaments of the Marca d'Ancona, it has justly been observed, had no history.[56]

In Friuli the position was little better. Parliament still met once a year and, as before, for a one-day session only; but its role was reduced to giving formal approval to business decided beforehand by the Venetian *luogotenente* and his masters in Venice. Even in the Val d'Aosta, a notoriously independent-minded region, princely absolutism proved irresistible. After 1766, the dukes of Savoy no longer summoned the Valdostano parliament. The parliament of Saluzzo had ceased to function since the end of the 17th century.

The parliament of Sicily, however, was a different matter. In the great crises of the 17th century, the revolt of Palermo, in 1647, and that of Messina, in 1674, it had played no significant role, and the rising of the guilds and populace of Palermo in 1773 was to confirm the irrelevance of the existence of parliament in a social crisis. With its many proxy votes accumulated in only a few hands, with its overwhelming concern for purely provincial, local and individual privileges or advantages, parliament did not give a very impressive appearance to outside observers. Victor Amadeus of Savoy, king of Sicily from 1714 to 1720, called it an ice-cream parliament, since the eating of ice-cream seemed to be the main occupation of its members during the session.[57] After one session, in 1714, Victor Amadeus did not summon parliament again. But neither the Austrian Habsburgs, nor the Neapolitan Bourbons who followed him as rulers of Sicily, could do without it. From the government's point of view there was, indeed, no good reason to dispense with parliament; for it voted most obligingly increasingly large extraordinary donatives. (The ordinary donatives had long since ceased to be matter for debate.) But the tradition of parliamentarism in the country remained very strong. It

[55] Above, chapter 1.
[56] Marongiu, *Il Parlamento*, p. 261.
[57] D. Mack Smith, *A History of Sicily*, II, (London, 1968), p. 266.

was celebrated by assiduous savants, such as Antonio Mongitore and Francesco Serio who collected and published the acts of parliament[58] or by historians, such as G. B. Caruso, who reserved for parliament a principal role in their histories.[59] Above all, it was the institution which represented the traditional structure of Sicilian society and the privileges of its great nobles and prelates. As yet, these privileges were not under serious attack from the other classes of society; for too many of those with property and education were directly or indirectly involved in the maintenance of these privileges.

It was this attitude which a reforming viceroy, the Marquis Domenico Caracciolo, experienced to his cost. Caracciolo had spent ten years as Neapolitan ambassador in Paris (1771–81). He had known d'Alembert and other distinguished philosophers and had frequented the intellectually most fashionable salons. To the mind of this proponent of enlightened absolutism parliament seemed nothing but a bastion of the privileges of those who exploited the country for their private benefit. In 1783, Caracciolo proposed changes in the assessment and collection of taxes and, perhaps rather tactlessly, a change of name, from the venerable parliament to 'congress' and from donative to 'contribution'. The Sicilian ruling classes were outraged. They had allies at court, and Caracciolo found himself outmanoeuvred at the centre of political power[60] – as other would-be reformers of Sicilian institutions had found themselves outmanoeuvred before and were to find themselves outmanoeuvred, right into the 20th century. Only the Napoleonic wars and the direct intervention of the British, the unloved allies of a reluctant king, brought about the transformation of the Sicilian parliamentary system in 1812.

The old Sicilian parliament, the earliest, longest-lived and, in its way, the most successful of the Italian assemblies of estates, ended as it had begun: in foreign war and through the interaction of internal and outside forces; and its end was different from that of all the other Italian parliaments of the old régime, for it was a transformation into a modern representative assembly.

If the eighteenth century parliament of Sicily gives the impression of a backward-looking, archaic survival, intent on defending an equally archaic social and political system, there was in that century another Italian island which experimented with a distinctly modern and, for all its traditionalism, forward-looking type of assembly. This was Corsica. Like Sardinia, Corsica was conquered by the Aragonese, in the 15th century and, quite characteristically, Alfonso the Magnanimous

---

[58] A. Mongitore, *Parlamenti Generali del Regno di Sicilia dall'anno 1446 sino al 1748 . . . ristampati colle addizioni, e note di Francesco Serio e Mongitore,* 2 vols. (Palermo 1749).

[59] G. B. Caruso, *Memorie Istoriche di quanto è accaduto in Sicilia,* (Palermo, 1744).

[60] D. Mack Smith, *A History of Sicily,* II, pp. 318–319.

summoned a Catalan-type parliament of prelates, barons and cities at Bonifacio, in 1420.[61] But in contrast to Sardinia, Aragonese rule did not last in Corsica and, in consequence, feudalism never took root in the island. The Genoese, its rulers throughout most the early modern period, dispossessed the seigneurial families and deprived them of their privileges. A pre-feudal, communal, social organisation therefore survived, and one of its traditions was the election of local chiefs and magistrates by popular local assemblies, called consulte.

This was not, perhaps, so very different from the traditions of some other European village communities in remote, mountainous areas. But in 1729 a rebellion broke out against the Genoese, and its leaders inevitably came to rely on the support of the consulte. This rebellion, dragging on for decades, was however more than a peasants' revolt. It became a struggle of at least a large part of the Corsican community against a 'colonial' power. Its educated leaders were receptive to the most advanced political ideas then current in western Europe. The most successful of these leaders, Pasquale Paoli, was an admirer of Montesquieu whose works he carried about with him. In 1755 Paoli was in a position to summon a consulta of the whole island which called itself a general diet and which proceeded to proclaim a constitution:

La Dieta Generale del Populo di Corsica, Lecitamente Padrone di se medesimo . . . (so ran its preamble) . . . Volendo, riacquistata la sua Libertà, dar forma durevole, e costante al suo governo riduccendoli a constituzione tale, che da essa ne dirivi la felicità della Nazione.[62]

This diet, with its distinctly democratic character, had control over legislation and taxation and it was to assemble every year. It appointed an executive council of which Paoli was president without, however, being a member of the diet. Paoli was appointed for life and had control over the army and foreign affairs – very much in the way in which Montesquieu had written about the position of a constitutional monarch. Where the constitution differed from Montesquieu's precepts of the division of powers was in allowing the president to exercise control over the judiciary. But this was very much within the Corsican tradition.

The diet met regularly until the French effectively took over the island, in 1769. Once again, it was outside intervention, as much as internal developments, which determined the fate of an Italian representative assembly.[63]

[61] Marongiu, *Il Parlamento*, p. 209. Also 'Il regno aragonese di Corsica e la convocazione parlamentare del 1420', in *Saggi di storia giuridica e politica sarda*, (Padova, 1975).

[62] Quoted in D. Carrington, 'The Corsican Constitution of Pasquale Paoli (1755–1769)', *English Historical Review*, LXXXVIII, July 1973, p. 482, n. 1.

[63] For the preceding paragraphs cf. *ibid.*, passim and D. Carrington, 'Pascal Paoli et sa "constitution" (1755–1769)', *Annales Historiques de la Révolution Française*, Oct.–Dec. 1974.

2. Philip II of Spain
Unknown artist, c. 1580. *National Portrait Gallery*

# 3

# Why did the States General of the Netherlands become Revolutionary in the 16th Century?[1]

During the reign of emperor Charles V (1515–1555) the Netherlands were a typical example of that most common of all medieval systems of government, *dominium politicum et regale*.[2] The rulers of the Netherlands needed the consent of their representative assemblies to impose taxation. They had to swear to uphold their provinces' privileges and could legislate only in so far as their ordinances did not break these laws. Over important matters, such as decisions on war and peace, they were expected at least to listen to the advice of their estates. The assemblies of the estates functioned on two levels: in each province, where their respective composition varied considerably, and at the centre, as a States General, composed of delegates of the provincial estates.

On the whole, the system worked well, in a phlegmatic way, at least

---

[1] It is not possible in the framework of this article to give a comprehensive account of the origins and course of the revolt of the Netherlands. This would require a whole book.

[2] The expression is Sir John Fortescue's, from *The Governance of England*, ed. C. Plummer, (Oxford, 1885), pp. 114 ff., where he contrasts it with *dominium regale*, government by a king who can legislate and tax his subjects without having to ask the consent of any representative assemblies. There are no other convenient expressions which express this very real distinction in the late medieval and early modern period. The terms parliamentary government and absolution suggest later systems of government, developed much more definitely in the direction of parliamentary or royal power than anyone would have conceived likely before the middle of the sixteenth century. This is what I wish to demonstrate in this paper. Professor Geoffrey Elton has pointed out to me that Fortescue's terms never caught on in the early modern period. In general this is correct, but perhaps somewhat too categorical. The words political and policie were on occasion used to suggest some sort of constitutional government. For instance the subtitle of Sir Thomas Smith's *De Republica Anglorum* is *The Manner of Government or Policie of the Realm of England*. Or again, in an anonymous pamphlet of 1710, 'The Judgement of Kingdoms and Nations', we read: 'Our kings are political kings', by which the author meant that they were not absolute kings. These examples and a discussion of the Aristotelian origins of the word political in Gerald Stourzh, 'Staatsformenlehre und Fundamentalgesetze . . . im 17 und 18. Jahrhundert', R. Vierhaus, ed., *Herrschaftsverträge, Wahlkapitulationen und Fundamentalgesetze*, (Göttingen, 1977), pp. 294, 327.

as long a both sides, rulers and estates, were willing to make it work. For the estates it served as a very effective safeguard of their rights and privileges and they were convinced that it kept down the excessive taxation from which, they believed, their French neighbours were suffering. The estates could and did make representations about major policy decisions, even though these were not necessarily accepted. Some of the larger provinces, Flanders, Brabant and Holland, even built up their tax collecting machinery and they insisted on the strict appropriation of the taxes they voted. For the ruler it was useful to have the overt support of the most powerful persons and corporations in the country, especially as the Habsburg rulers, from the time of Maximilian onwards, were usually represented by regents and were often at war with their neighbours. Moreover, most sixteenth-century princes, outside the pages of Machiavelli, took their coronation or succession oaths seriously and prided themselves on upholding the law.

*Dominium politicum et regale*, was an admirably flexible and often long-lived system; yet it was ultimately not a stable one. There were many areas of friction between ruler and estates. Even when everything went smoothly, the actions of the States General were desperately slow. The delegates had to refer every proposal back to their provincial estates and in these the delegates of the third estate, in their turn, had to refer back to their city councils. If there were disagreements, this complex process might have to be repeated several times and, in the end, agreement would be held up by the States General's demand of redress of grievances before supply. Exasperated governments, frantic about payment of troops in the face of enemy attacks, tried to take short-cuts. In 1530 the regent, Margaret of Austria, proposed to her nephew, Charles V, that the Estates should not be allowed to make requests before agreeing to the *aide* and that this could be achieved, preferably when the emperor was in the country, by government edict or by special deals and manoeuvres in the separate provinces.[3]

The emperor, at that time in Augsburg, put off a decision on this request. Perhaps he hoped to deal with it when he was next in the Netherlands. It was not that he was squeamish. In 1525 he had suggested to Margaret that she should treat the refractory delegation from Ghent with *douceur*. When, in this way, Ghent had been brought to agree with the other members of Flanders in granting an *aide*, she should inform herself secretly about the ringleaders of the opposition and then arrest and punish them, 'which would be an example to the others and in this way one could manage the people and bring them to

---

[3] 'Articles proposez a l'Empereur . . . de par Madame'. July 1530. Brussels, Bibliothèque Royale. MS. 16068–16072, fo. 136 (copy). The original, in Vienna, contains the emperor's answer as an apostille: Wien, Belgien PA21/2 fo. 509v–510r. I would like to thank Prof. Horst Rabe and Dr. Heide Stratenweith for sending me photocopies of the relevant folios of the Vienna MS.

reason and even get some good (monetary) compensation out of the affair'.[4]

Perhaps this ruler was not so far from Machiavelli after all. Margaret of Austria's style was different from her nephew's and reminds one rather of James I tearing a page out of the House of Commons journal. The prelates of Brabant refused to pay their full quota because they had traditionally paid only one third of it. Margaret thereupon declared that the government officials would collect the full amount. When the chancellor of Brabant refused to seal this act, as being contrary to the *Joyeuse Entrée* (the Brabant charter of liberties) according to which no act could be sealed without the consent of all the estates, Margaret took the seal and sealed the act herself in the presence of all the estates of Brabant.[5]

In the first years of the reign of Philip II, when he himself resided in the Netherlands (1555–59), his relations with the estates deteriorated rapidly. It was not really any one's fault or, at least, not anyone's design. The estates resented the steeply increasing cost of the continuing war with France. This war, they claimed, was being fought and financed by the Netherlands to allow the Spaniards to conquer Italy. Economic depression coupled with famine prices foreshadowed popular revolts. It was necessary to import large quantities of grain from the Baltic and this could only be done for ready cash. There was a cash flow crisis on the Antwerp money market and in 1557 the Netherlands government had to declare a moratorium on its debts.[6]

Here was a classic conjuncture for revolution. Yet it did not happen. Everyone was still anxious to make the old system of *dominium politicum et regale* work. The government summoned the States General and, for once, allowed it to meet in joint session to discuss the financial crisis. On their side, the estates, also for once, gave their deputies full powers.[7] Even so, it took them over a year to arrive at an agreed financial settlement. The States General granted the considerable *aide* of 800,000 florins per year for nine years ('novennial aide') but on condition that their own commissioners should control the collection and expenditure of the money. Moreover, in the course of the rather acrimonious debates over this *aide*, they harshly criticised the king's policies.[8]

It looked as if the States General had made a deliberate attempt to tilt the traditional balance of *dominium politicum et regale* in favour of a form of parliamentary government. This was apparently how Philip II and his

[4] Charles V's answer to a 'Memoire au Seigneur de Praet . . . de la part de Madame'. Toledo 31 Oct. 1525. Brussels Bibl. Roy. MS. 16068 –16072, fo. 155 (copy).

[5] Margaret to Charles V. Malines, 7 July 1528. Brussels, Archives Géherales du Royaume, *Papiers d'Etat et de l'Audience*, 36, fo. 217.

[6] Astrid Friis, 'The Two Crises in the Netherlands in 1557', *Scandinavian Economic History Review*, vol. 1(1), 1953, pp. 199–203.

[7] Brussels. Arch. Gén. *Manuscrits divers* 327, fos. 39–56.

[8] K. J. W. Verhofstad, *De Regering der Nederlanden in de jaren 1555–1559*, (Nijmegen, 1937), pp. 119 ff.

principal adviser in the Netherlands, Antoine Perrenot, later Cardinal Granvelle, interpreted it.[9] In fact, it is very unlikely that the States General had any such intention. They had simply reacted to circumstances in what seemed to be a practical way. Even then, Flanders and Holland refused to accept the receiver-general appointed by the States General because he was a Brabanter. After much bitter debate they would allow him to function only when the regent appointed him in the name of the king and as a royal official.

But Philip and Granvelle were now determined that the States General was a danger to royal power and should never be summoned again. By contrast, those who opposed royal policy, for whatever reasons, came to look upon the summoning of the States General as the first and principal step in the settling of the country's problems. They created a mythology of the eirenic powers and superior wisdom of the States General, just as so many would-be reformers of the Catholic Church had created a mythology of the eirenic powers and wisdom of a general Church council, in the first half of the sixteenth century.[10] This mythology could bridge the incompatible aims of Calvinist preachers and Catholic opponents of the inquisition, of unemployed weavers and capitalist merchants, of bourgeois city councillors and aristocratic landowners. As early as the autumn of 1560 Granvelle was warning the king of the danger of revolution. The immediate reason was the presence in the Netherlands of the hated *tercio* of Spanish troops which the Netherlanders regarded as a deliberate threat to their liberty.[11]

In this view they were probably mistaken; but the king's attempts to keep the *tercio* in the Netherlands as a *force de frappe* against possible French aggression coincided with the organisation of the new bishoprics, the stepping-up of inquisitorial action against heretics and the setting up of the regency government in such a way as to leave effective political power with the king in Madrid. And the king, it was clear, was advised by the Burgundian, Granvelle. If the actions of the States General in 1557–58 had appeared to tilt the balance towards parliamentary government, the king's actions in the years following appeared even more strongly to tilt the balance towards absolute

[9] Cf. F. Rachfahl, *Wilhelm von Oranien*, 1 (Halle, 1906), pp. 556 ff. One would like to know what Duke Emmanuel Philibert of Savoy, Philip's governor-general of the Netherlands at the time, thought of it. When two years later he returned to rule his own Italian dominions he manoeuvred the parliament of Piedmont to grant him sufficient money to pay his soldiers and then ceased to summon the parliament. See H. G. Koenigsberger, 'The Parliament of Piedmont during the Renaissance, 1460–1560', in *Estates and Revolutions* (Ithaca and London, 1971), pp. 74 ff, and above, chapter 2.

[10] One would also like to know more about how far this mythology started as a deliberate ploy by the aristocratic opponents of Granvelle. If it did, it could still build on a much older tradition of respect for the States General.

[11] Granvelle to Philip II, 6 Oct. and 28 Oct. 1560. Ch. Weiss, *Papiers d'Etat du Cardinal de Granvelle*, 6 (Paris, 1844), pp. 183, 197 f.

monarchy. Yet for a while it still looked as if the traditional *dominium politicum et regale* might be preserved. Philip withdrew the *tercio* and he even gave way to the league of the high nobility by withdrawing the unpopular Granvelle.

This was the traditional pattern of Spanish policy, practiced in its outlying dominions, notably in Italy. Here the king would regularly sacrifice his viceroys to the local opposition. Politics were therefore kept on a personal level and the local ruling classes could be kept loyal to the king of Spain. This policy worked well as long as the monarchy did not make unusually heavy financial or political demands on the outlying dominion – and that did not happen in Italy until the 1630s and 1640s. [12] In the Netherlands, however, this 'Italian pattern' did not, and perhaps could not, work. The country was much richer than Sicily or Naples, and the question of taxation was therefore almost as important for the monarchy as it was in Castile. At the same time Philip was not prepared, as his father had been, to employ any of the Netherlands high nobility in the rest of his empire, whereas sometimes, even if reluctantly, he so employed Burgundians, Italians and Catalans. The Netherlands seigneurs, or at least the more ambitious among them, were therefore especially anxious to control policy-making in their own country. They found, however, that they could not do this even when they controlled the Netherlands Council of State. Finally, social unrest and religious passions infected all political problems and made them virtually insoluble by the normal political processes of compromise and postponement.

This became very clear in the spring and summer of 1566. After a near famine winter with universal fears of popular risings, an alliance of Protestant and Catholic lower nobility, the Compromise, forced the regency government in Brussels to suspend the laws against heretics. Religious mass meetings of armed men spread rapidly through much of the Netherlands. Some Protestant nobles were beginning to hire regular troops. In August relatively small groups of Protestants smashed images in churches, with virtually no resistance from the established local authorities.

From Madrid it looked like a revolution. In fact it was nothing of the kind. Amid a welter of pamphlets, no one drafted even the beginnings of a coherent political programme. There was no large-scale popular rising. Those Protestants who took over a very few cities by armed force, seem to have done so defensively, to obtain bargaining counters in case of a government counter-attack. The great seigneurs in the Council of State, indeed the majority of the nobility and patrician town councils, were embarassed and frightened by the revolt and rallied

[12] H. G. Koenigsberger, 'The Parliament of Sicily and the Spanish Empire', in *Estates and Revolutions*, pp. 90 ff.

behind the regent to restore law and order. The States General played no role whatever in these events.

Perhaps this was lucky; for it meant that the myth of the States General remained intact, indeed was enhanced, both for Calvinist revolutionaries and for conservative Catholic aristocrats who disliked the Spaniards. From the monarchy's point of view, this would not have greatly mattered if Philip II had now taken the advice of his sister, the regent Margaret of Parma, and had left well alone. For, with the help of the overwhelmingly conservative 'establishment' of the Netherlands, Margaret had defeated the revolt. *Dominium politicum et regale* had been re-established, and with the *regale* part stronger than ever.

The next initiative, the initiative from which, by opposition, the real revolution of the Netherlands sprang (and with it the transformation of the States General into a revolutionary body) came from the king. Of course, Philip II acted in response to his assessment of the situation in the Netherlands. What he saw were the unsolved long-term problems of finance, government and religious beliefs and the spirit of opposition which had arisen from them. What he did not see was that the first two were largely, and the third at least partly, of the monarchy's own making. What he also did not see, perhaps more forgivably in view of contemporary events in France, was that, for the time being at least, these problems had ceased to be explosive. None of this is very surprising. What is surprising is that, until quite recently, historians have made so little attempt to study in depth just how and why Philip II did make the decision to send the Duke of Alba to the Netherlands and kill off the system of *dominium politicum et regale* altogether and at the very moment when the position of the monarchy in this system was stronger than it had ever been. From David Lagomarsino's forthcoming book[13] it is clear that this decision was anything but a foregone conclusion and that it depended more on the court politics in Madrid than on the actual situation in the Netherlands. Alba's regime effectively abolished all those parts of Netherlands public law which he regarded as getting in the way of absolute royal government. The provincial estates still assembled, as they had done before, but their power to resist the government had virtually disappeared. This was therefore *dominium regale* with a vengeance; but immediately the weaknesses of this system became apparent. The army on which it ultimately rested required vast sums of money. These sums could only be raised by massive and highly unpopular taxation. This situation was a prescription not so much for revolution as for armed rebellion and guerilla war by a determined minority. It was also an invitation to foreign intervention.

---

[13] D. Lagomarsino, *Philip II and the Netherlands, 1559–1573*, (forthcoming). I would like to thank Prof. Lagomarsino for permission to quote this point.

Both happened and, by the summer of 1572, the rebels held most of the provinces of Holland and Zeeland. Now, these events did not, in themselves, make a revolution. In July the estates of Holland assembled in Dordrecht.[14] There were the deputies of the towns and of the nobility. Some of them, like Paulus Buys, the pensionary of Leiden, had represented their cities before. All of them were from the same ruling groups as before and represented town councils in which a few names but nothing much else had changed. Their avowed aim was to re-establish their old rights and privileges of which, as William of Orange put it, 'they had been robbed and despoiled . . . by the Duke of Alba and his followers'.[15] The charters of Holland were deposited in the castle of Gouda and the estates appointed a committee to get hold of and copy them. Orange was recognised as governor of Holland, Zeeland and Utrecht, legitimately appointed by the king. As one of the foremost members of the States General, Orange was also held to have the right to protect the Netherlands against invasion and oppression.[16]

All these resolutions were essentially conservative, aimed at re-establishing the former system of *dominium politicum et regale*. The king's authority was not mentioned. Almost from the first moment, however, the estates of Holland were forced by the logic of their situation, i.e. the need to defend themselves against Alba's counter-offensive, into actions that went far beyond their traditional competence. Quite early on, the estates bound themselves not to treat with the king or any agent of his in matters concerning the 'generality of the estates' without Orange's consent. Most members of the Court of Holland, the supreme court of the province, had fled. Orange, as governor, replaced them on the nomination and with the advice of the Estates.[17] This was an unprecedented interference with the royal prerogative. Most important, as early as the 28 July, they appointed a paid committee of their own members to advise Orange on all matters of government[18] and in October they added a committee to act as 'Commissioners in all matters of war'.[19] Representative assemblies had on many occasions claimed the right to appoint the members of the king's council. They had never previously achieved this ambition anywhere in Europe, or at least never for more than a very short period of time.

Unfortunately, most of the registers of the estates of Holland, our principal source for this topic, are missing for the two years between 1572 and 1574. When they resume, in the late summer of 1574, we find

[14] R. C. Bakhuizen van den Brink, 'Eerste Vergadering der Staten van Holland, 19 July 1572'. *Les Archives du Royaume des Pays-Bas*, 1, (The Hague, 1857), pp. 11–46.
[15] *Ibid.*, p. 34.
[16] *Ibid.*, pp. 22 ff.
[17] *Ibid.*, pp. 14 ff.
[18] *Ibid.*, p. 46.
[19] *Holland Staten Resolutien 1572–74*, pp. 5–6.

the estates of Holland busily setting up committees to supervise or actually charge themselves with the administration of the province and the prosecution of the war. Deputies of the estates sat in Orange's council of state (*raede nevens syne Excellentie*), in the Councils of finance and of admiralty where their job was 'to promote all resolutions, accords, placards and ordinances of His Excellency and of the estates, and to execute them and put them into effect, if necessary even by force'.[20] One-man or two-men committees were sent out to supervise the dykes or the evacuation of the population in areas threatened by enemy troops.[21] A committee of three, one nobleman and two deputies of towns, were given powers to visit the principal cities and exhort their burgomasters and councillors or provide and pay for necessary matters of defence. For this purpose the committee had the right to command all officials, from the Court of Holland to the city magistrates, the citizen guards, the village authorities and the local colonels and captains with their soldiers.[22]

Co-operative as were the estates and hard–working as, no doubt, were its committees, the individual towns often dragged their feet in providing Orange with the necessary financial support. In October 1574 he therefore proposed to the Estates that they should actually take over the whole government of the province.[23] The estates were understandably reluctant to go quite as far as this. In the following year they negotiated with Orange about his position and the powers of the estates and they experimented with different types of councils to advise him and to act as an effective executive branch of government. Two points remained constant in these negotiations and experiments. The first was that the estates intended to keep close control over the executive and a voice in all appointments. The second was that Orange always acknowledged that his own authority derived from the estates, even when the estates invested him with the sovereignty of Holland.[24]

Holland and Zeeland had therefore become parliamentary regimes in which ultimate sovereignty and considerable control over the executive had shifted to the estates. From a medieval perspective, it was a thoroughly revolutionary development for which the only precedent, and one clearly recognised by contemporaries, was the Swiss Cantons. How far this position was from the traditional *dominium politicum et regale* became clear during the peace negotiations at Breda, in the spring of 1575. Philip II's representatives started these negotiations from a strongly regalist position: the king would declare a complete amnesty

---

[20] *Ibid.*, p. 73.

[21] *Ibid.*, pp. 75 ff.

[22] *Ibid.*, pp. 125 ff.

[23] Propositie van wegen syne Excellentie de Staten van Hollandt gedaen', 20 Oct. 1574. *Ibid.*, pp. 176 ff.

[24] *Holland Staten Resolutien 1575*, pp. 311–13, 520–24 and *passim*.

and allow the Protestants to emigrate, but he would not send away his soldiers, for they were his subjects, and he would summon the States General only after peace was re-established to have their advice on such matters as they were normally asked about, but not on anything depending on the king's sovereignty.[25] Against this, the representatives of Holland argued that the States General had the right to deal with all matters whatsoever, to amend or abrogate the king's ordinances, if necessary, and that, in any case, the king had no better advisers than the States General.[26] They were unimpressed by the royalist concession to return to the position obtaining under Charles V. For all their talk about recognising the king's sovereignty, the estates of Holland and Zeeland were clearly not willing to return to the medieval system of *dominium politicum et regale*, but wanted to make the king into a parliamentary ruler like the prince of Orange. Their reasons for this line were twofold: they no longer trusted the king, and without at least a minimum of trust no system of *dominium politicum et regale* could function – as Charles I of England was to learn, to his cost, two generations later. Secondly, the estates of Holland, having tasted power, were clearly liking the taste and were becoming disinclined to give up power again. Their later experience with Anjou and Leicester confirmed them in this view. After 1588 they no longer even imagined they could return to a system of *dominium politicum et regale*.

Not unnaturally, the peace talks of Breda collapsed. A year later, in the summer of 1576, the king's authority in the whole Netherlands collapsed. The events leading to this collapse are well known. The government in Madrid declared its bankruptcy in 1575 and found it could no longer send money to the Netherlands. There the regent, Requesens, died and the unpaid Spanish troops mutinied and started sacking loyal towns. On September 5, 1576, troops of the estates of Brabant arrested the Council of State in Brussels. The estates of Brabant and Hainault then summoned the States General and started peace negotiations with Holland and Zeeland. A purged and reconstituted Council of State, dominated by the Duke of Aerschot and the high nobility of the southern Netherlands, cooperated closely with the States General and concluded peace with Holland and Zeeland in the famous Pacification of Ghent, November 8, 1576.

These were all revolutionary acts to which the king had not given his authority. But the States General and the other members of the Netherlands 'establishment' were not thinking in terms of revolution or of a change of religion, but in terms of getting rid of the hated Spanish troops and of reasserting their ancient privileges, i.e. of re-establishing the medieval system of *dominium politicum et regale*, or, as it was often put, of returning to the government as it had been under the late

[25] *Ibid.*, pp. 161 ff.
[26] *Ibid.*, pp. 169 ff.

emperor Charles V, of glorious memory. It was the ambiguous and ultimately hostile response of the monarchy which made the States General continue on the revolutionary road on which it had started in 1576, just as had happened in Holland and Zeeland after 1572. But the situation was now much more complicated. Neither the king nor Don John of Austria, the new regent or governor-general, were genuinely ready to make *dominium politicum et regale* work. Philip was prepared to make political concessions, even quite far-reaching concessions, such as accepting the Pacification of Ghent, to meet an adverse political situation. But not only was he absolutely firm on the question of religion – he would never accept a German-style *Religionsfrieden* or a French-style edict of toleration – he also interpreted his sovereignty, on the maintenance of which he always insisted, as a basis for the re-establishment of absolutism when the conditions should warrant it. Thus later, when the tide began to run in his favour again, he refused to budge on the Prince of Parma's objections to his use of the phrase 'reduction to obedience' for those cities with whom Parma had made a political deal.[27]

Don John, brought up as a soldier in the absolutist atmosphere of Castile, was still less willing to accept the States General, even in a modestly advisory position, than his brother, the king. To him their revolutionary actions demonstrated their basic disloyalty.[28] After Don John's seizure of the citadel of Namur, 24 July 1577, the States General, for all that the majority would still have preferred an accommodation, could not bring themselves to break with Holland and Zeeland. Orange persuaded them to demand that the Council of State be appointed by themselves, just as the estates of Holland and Zeeland appointed Orange's own council. Inevitably, Don John rejected this demand.[29] The breach was now complete and the States General found themselves in a revolutionary stance.

The logical conclusions of this stance were worked out immediately in the conditions the States General now imposed on the new governor-general, the Archduke Matthias, whom they had chosen themselves – just as, effectively, the estates of Holland and Zeeland had chosen Orange as their governor. In both cases, the claim of acting in the name

---

[27] Farnese to Philip II, 21 Feb. 1579. L. P. Gachard, *Correspondence d'Alexandre Farnèse . . . avec Philippe II*, première partie 1578–79, (Brussels etc. 1853), p. 83. Philip II to Farnese, 12 Sept. 1579. *Ibid.*, p. 120.

[28] Don John to Rodrigo de Mendoza, 19 Feb. 1577. A. Morel-Fatio, *L'Espagne au XVIe et au XVIIe siècle, 2. Lettres de Don Juan d'Autriche*, (Heilbronn, 1878), p. 116. 'Entre los tratos, que ha havido entre estos hombres y mí, me han puesto en tantas ocasiones de perder la paciencia, que aunque he tenido algunas vezes infinitas, otras al fin no he podido y heles atropellado, diciéndoles lo que son y lo que merecen, de manera que de todo punto nos havemos hecho inutiles los unos á los otros'.

[29] L. Delfos, *Die Anfänge der Utrechter Union 1577–1587*. Historische Studien, Verlag Ebering, Heft 375, (Berlin, 1941), pp. 48 f.

of the king was no more than a fig-leaf designed to cover the essential nakedness of revolutionary action. Matthias was required to accept a Council of State chosen by the States General and he was required to act on the advice of the majority of its members. Taxes, decisions on war and peace and all important legislation needed the consent of the States General. The same held for the appointment of provincial governors and of military officers. Tax collection and expenditure was to be in the hands of the States General. This body and the provincial estates could assemble when and for as long as they themselves saw fit.[30]

The speed and logical thoroughness with which this parliamentary regime was set up owed a great deal to the experience of Holland and Zeeland in the previous five years and to Orange's view of what sort of government the Netherlands should now have.[31] It was the first time that anything as revolutionary and ambitious had been attempted in a major European country. It was, in its own way, as different from *dominium politicum et regale* as was absolute monarchy. Moreover, just as the estates of Holland were doing and as the Long Parliament was to do in the English civil war,[32] the States General appointed *ad hoc* committees for specific purposes, such as peace negotiations or negotiations with individual provinces or towns or for trouble-shooting in sensitive areas where a crisis of authority had arisen. This happened for instance in Ghent,[33] and in Hainault.[34]

With very clear ideas of the nature of political power and with a remarkably sophisticated organisation designed to exercise this power, the success or failure of the revolutionary States General would now depend on two conditions: firstly, on the strength of the forces which supported the States General and the king and on their ability to organise these forces effectively; secondly, on the effective outside help which the two sides, the States General and the king, could mobilise. In Holland and Zeeland the forces supporting the estates were remarkably homogeneous, the regent class of the towns, supported by the respectable burghers organised in their guilds and in the *schutterijen*, the citizens' guards. Fishermen, sailors, dock workers, and other labourers whom the *gueux* had sometimes mobilised remained unorganised and were carefully excluded from all further active participation in politics. Attempts by Orange to make the lower classes of Dutch society into politically aware and active supporters of his position were immediately

---

[30] The document is printed in G. Griffiths, *Representative Government in Western Europe in the Sixteenth Century*, (Oxford, 1968), pp. 463–68.

[31] *Calendar of State Papers, Foreign Series*, 12 (London, 1901), pp. 280–84.

[32] Cf. D. H. Pennington, 'The Accounts of the Kingdom 1642–1649', in F. J. Fisher, ed., *Essays in the Economic and Social History of Tudor and Stuart England in Honour of R. H. Tawney*, (Cambridge, 1961), pp. 182–203.

[33] C. H. Th. Bussemaker, *De Afscheiding der Waalsche Gewesten van de generale Unie*, 1, (Haarlem, 1895), pp. 436 f.

[34] *Ibid.*, pp. 440 ff.

countered by the regents.[35] although an alliance between the house of Orange and the lower classes was to remain a persistent feature of Dutch politics.[36] This social homogeneity enabled the estates of Holland and Zeeland to overcome their greatest weakness, their confederal structure and the unwillingness of the cities to give up their cherished autonomy and allow their deputies the necessary powers for taking decisions and carrying on the government of the country.[37] It also allowed the Dutch to neutralise the disruptive political effects of Leicester's governor-generalship. It was, however, from their point of view pure luck that both Elizabeth and, later, Henry IV of France fought their own wars against Philip II, wars which critically weakened Spain's ability at the decisive moment to win its counter-offensive in the Netherlands.

The south, Brabant, Flanders and the Walloon provinces, was very different. The revolutionary actions of the Estates of Brabant and of the States General had been started by the Duke of Aerschot and the high nobility. But very soon it became clear that the strongest supporters of anti-Spanish and revolutionary action were the bourgeois of the cities. In Brussels, in Ghent, in Arras and in Tournai they organised citizen committees, depending on, or with strong representation of, the guilds. As long as the States General were assembled in Brussels the crowd could and did put pressure on them, in the classic way of crowds in capital cities.[38] After the States General fled to Antwerp, early in 1578, they seem to have, at least personally, escaped from such pressure; for the patrician authorities of this city appear to have been as effective in keeping control over their lower classes as the patricians of the towns of Holland.

Elsewhere, however, social antagonisms sharpened. In the spring of 1578 they were given a special twist in Flanders when the Calvinists took over Ghent and began to spread their religious and social revolution throughout the province. These Calvinist revolutionaries were basically not interested in the States General; their social and religious aims were diametrically opposed to those of the Catholic patricians and the nobility.

At the other end of the spectrum, many members of the nobilty and higher clergy were from an early date looking for an accommodation

---

[35] e.g. Orange's reply, 21 May 1575, to the draft articles of government proposed on 18 May 1575, *Holland Staten Resolutien 1575*, pp. 297, 311–13. See also Groen van Prinsterer, *Archives de la Maison de Nassau-Orange*, ser. 1. 5, pp. 271 f.

[36] Orange tried a similar move in the south over the ratification of the Pacification of Ghent, in October 1576, *Ibid.*, pp. 467 ff.

[37] See H. G. Koenigsberger, 'The Power of Deputies in Sixteenth Century Assemblies', in *Estates and Revolutions*, pp. 190–210.

[38] See e.g. G. Griffiths, *William of Hornes, Lord of Hèze and the Revolt of the Netherlands (1576–1580)*. University of California Publications in History. 51. (Berkeley and Los Angeles, 1954), pp. 35 f.

with the king. The tendency of the Catholic revolutionary committees to confiscate church and monastic property confirmed them in this determination, and the even more drastic activities of the Calvinist Ghenters made even convinced Spaniard-haters prefer the king's party. But, unlike the Ghenters, they were not basically hostile to the States General. In the Treaty of Arras, in May 1579, the reconciled provinces stipulated that the acts of the States General up to that point, including the Pacification of Ghent and the acts of the Archduke Matthias, were to be regarded as valid, the foreign troops were to leave, the fortresses were to be handed back to the provinces, and two thirds of the members of the Governor-General's council of state were to be approved by the estates.[39]

Here was clearly a return to a *dominium politicum et regale*, with the balance formally tilted much further to the estates than would have been conceivable in the reign of Charles V. However, Philip II's stubborn insistence on his sovereign prerogatives, Parma's political astuteness and the necessity of continuing the civil war, soon shifted the balance of power back to the monarchy. But the estates had prevented the southern Netherlands from returning to a regime of pure *dominium regale*, a lesson that Joseph II would still have to learn, two hundred years later.

The States General at Antwerp eventually merged with the assembly of the estates forming the Union of Utrecht. The Walloon provinces, Flanders and the greater part of Brabant were lost to Parma's counter offensive. The outside military help which the States General sought from the Duke of Anjou was tainted from the start; for Anjou, while willing to fight Spaniards, was just as unsympathetic to the regime of a revolutionary States General as Philip II himself.

But with the southern provinces the States General also lost both the centres of social and religious revolution and the former Catholic majority. As long as this majority had existed the chances for the survival of the States General were slight. For while religion was only one, and for most people not the most important, reason for revolt, it was the area in which it was most difficult to find a compromise. For the estates of Holland and Zeeland, religion was a sticking point on which they would, in the final analysis, repudiate the authority of the States General if this body were to insist on the re-establishment of the Catholic Church.[40] The political structure that eventually emerged in the north, the seven United Provinces of the Netherlands, could function with the revolutionary system of parliamentary government

---

[39] *Articles de la Paix et Reconciliation faicte en la ville d'Arras le XVIIIe de May XVc LXXIX avec sa majesté par les Provinces d'Arthois, Haynault, Lille Douay et Orchies,* (Douay, 1579). See especially articles 3, 5, 6 and 16.

[40] See for instance the arguments of Marnix in Feb. 1577. Griffiths, *Representative Government,* pp. 448–50.

because this system had achieved a high degree of stability. This stability was to a large extent the result of the economic and financial preponderance of the province of Holland, a preponderance which became effective only after the loss of Flanders and Brabant.[41] The social, political and religious enemies and rivals thus remained outside the union and they could be kept there by effectively organised military and naval power and by superior international diplomacy.

[41] I would like to thank Prof. K. W. Swart for drawing my attention to this point.

# 4

## The Statecraft of Philip II

There has, perhaps, been no personality in modern history, not even Napoleon or Stalin, who has been both as enigmatic and controversial as Philip II of Spain. Neither his own contemporaries nor later historians have been able to agree on his character, his aims or even the degree of success he achieved. Was he a man unable to distinguish between vice and virtue, the murderer of his wife and his son, as William of Orange claimed, a man possessed of no single virtue and exempt from some vices only 'because it is not permitted to human nature to attain perfection even in evil', as the nineteenth-century historian Motley judged?[1] Or did he rule 'with justice and divine zeal . . . wise and thorough in all his actions', as his official court historian, Luis Cabrera de Córdoba, wrote,[2] and did his (alleged) murder of his son by slow poison show his 'sublime and tragic grandeur', as a recent historian would have it?[3] Was he the incarnation of *hispanidad*, the true defender of Catholicism against Protestant and Moslem attacks,[4] or was he, the master of the dreaded Spanish Inquisition, a cruel bigot,[5] and was his ultimate aim, as many of his contemporaries as well as later historians thought, less the welfare of the Church than a universal monarchy, or at least, Spanish political hegemony over Europe?[6]

It is easy enough to discount the more extreme verdicts, coloured, as they are only too evidently, by patriotic, religious or philosophical bias, not to say fanaticism. Yet the problem remains. Such views as those cited above simply will not add up to reveal a convincing middle ground. The problem is evidently locked up in the subject itself and in the evidence we

This article was originally written for the *Revista de Occidente* and published in Spanish translation in t. 36, No. 107, Feb. 1972.

[1] Quoted in J. C. Rule and J. J. Te Paske, *The Character of Philip II*, (Boston, 1963), xvii.

[2] *Ibid.*, xviii.

[3] E. Tormo, 'La Tragedía del Príncipe Don Carlos y la trágica Grandeza de Felipe II', *Boletín de la Real Academia de la Historia*, vol. CXII, (Madrid, 1943), 200.

[4] A. Ballesteros y Beretta, quoted in Rule and Te Paske, *Philip II*, xviii.

[5] J. C. Cadoux, quoted *ibid.*

[6] This latter view is the unargued assumption in L. Dehio, *Gleichgewicht oder Hegemonie*, (Krefeld, 1948), transl. C. Fullman, as *The Precarious Balance*, (New York, 1962).

have about him. At least one of Philip's contemporaries was perceptive enough to see this quite early in the king's career:

It is bad business to try to come to firm conclusions about the minds of kings [wrote the Venetian ambassador to Spain, Marcantonio da Mula, in 1559], both because kings have in their hearts a thousand impenetrable dens and caverns which only God can know, and because he who wishes to penetrate into the hearts of men should look at their actions and he will know their will from their actions, as the tree is known by its fruit. But this king is young; it is only four years that he has been king, and he may easily change with time: for happy or adverse events have nearly always been the great instruments that changed the minds of kings.[7]

There were many, and among them most of the Venetian ambassadors who came after Mula, who thought in the following years that they understood the king, that they were able to probe the dark caverns of his mind. But by 1598 their views were more contradictory than they had been forty years before. Philip himself had given them little help. He never outlined a plan or programme for his reign, nor did any of his ministers, as Gattinara and Guevara may be said to have done for his father. Again, unlike his father, he neither wrote an autobiography (which, at least by implication, would have shown the deeds for which he wished to be remembered), nor did he leave a series of elaborate, confidential and highly political testaments or instructions for his son. Those which he dictated on his death-bed to his confessor stress almost exclusively the precepts of a pious, Christian life.[8] Was Philip's religion then more central to his thinking than it had been to that of Charles V, so that, in the end, at the moment of truth, it came to exclude all other considerations? Such a conclusion seems doubtful, at least on the basis of these instructions. Philip III had been carefully brought up and systematically instructed in statecraft under his father's own eyes.[9] Instructions in politics, Machiavellian and otherwise, and hints about court personalities and how to handle them, such as the emperor had written to his son from the other end of Europe and when he himself was still far from death – such matters were hardly called for, nor fitting for a Christian king who was ceremoniously dying with his son in close attendance.[10]

There are, however, other instructions, not as personal as the emperor's testaments, nor probably written or even drafted by Philip himself, but certainly seen and approved by him. These are the

---

[7] E. Albèri, *Relazioni degli ambasciatori veneti*, ser. I, vol. 3, (Florence, 1853), 395.

[8] L. Cabrera de Córdova, *Felipe Segundo*, vol. IV, (Madrid, 1877), 390–92.

[9] *Ibid.*, 191–204.

[10] *Cf.* the brilliant and perceptive description of Philip II's death by F. Braudel, *La Méditerranée et le monde Méditerranéen à l'époque de Philippe II*, 2nd ed., vol. II, (Paris, 1966), 513.

instructions to viceroys and governors of his dominions, to his generals and to his ministers. They were often called 'secret', which meant primarily that they were not designed as royal propaganda. Those written for the duke of Alcalá, viceroy of Naples, in 1559, are typical of many more throughout the reign:

The first thing you must realise is that the community was not created for the prince but rather that the prince was created for the sake of the community; and you will have to represent our person and act as we would act if we were present. Your principal object and intention must be to work for the community which is in your charge, so that it may live and rest in full security, peace, justice and quiet; to watch so that it may sleep without anxiety; and finally to take heed that you are not accepting this office to be idle or to live at your pleasure, nor for any benefit of your own, but only, as I have said, for the peace and quiet and good of the community.[11]

The viceroy was to make himself both loved and feared, by rewarding the virtuous and punishing the wicked, but he was not to give judgement himself, for he was no lawyer; he was to investigate his officials to uncover corruption and to prevent favouritism to powerful men in the law courts. In short, these and other similar points of advice, some of them identical with those put down by Charles V for the benefit of Philip, were the stock-in-trade of scores of fifteenth- and sixteenth-century moralists and writers of 'mirrors of princes'. The king was undoubtedly aware of this, for he wrote a postscript in his own hand to Alcalá explaining that he had not sent these instructions because he thought that the duke needed them but 'to comply with my obligations'.

The instructions which Philip gave to his brother, Don John of Austria in 1568, are somewhat more personal than those for Alcalá but also do not go beyond the pious platitudes current at most European courts.[12] Don John was to go regularly to mass and confession and always to show the devotion of a good Catholic. He was to speak the truth and keep his promises, for this is the foundation of credit and esteem among men . . . and especially necessary in great personages who hold great public offices, for public security rests on their truthfulness and on their keeping faith'.[13] The prince's personal behaviour should be prudent and decorous, temperate at the table and affable in speech. He and his caballeros were to keep up their military exercises even in winter. With the rather important exception of always speaking the truth, these were precepts which Philip II himself observed quite rigorously.

But of Philip II's personal behaviour, of his application to the duties

[11] British Museum, Additional MS 28 701, fos. 86–91.
[12] British Museum, MS Egerton 329, fos. 231–32 (copy).
[13] *Ibid.*, fo. 231.

of kingship and of his methods of work there has been only one opinion which even most hostile observers and historians have accepted. Everyone knows the picture of the lonely king in his small work-room in the Escurial, poring over reports and maps, annotating minutes in his all but illegible, loopy handwriting – itself almost a visual image of the circles of command and power – endlessly returning back to the writer. These methods of work, the king's unwillingness to attend council meetings and listen to spoken arguments, his slowness in taking decisions, his time-wasting concern over trivia,[14] his unpredictability and his carefully concealed vengefulness, all these characteristics were talked about by his contemporaries and often with surprising openness. Don Luis de Manrique, the king's almoner, wrote to the king himself of the grave discontent caused by his seclusion and his immersion in paper work – quite apart from its bad effects on his health.[15] The duke of Alba had the temerity to say to Philip that he did not wish him to acquire the crown of Portugal, for where, in that case, could the sons of the nobles flee from the king's wrath?[16] The famous remark, that the king's smile and dagger were very close to each other, was known already to Venetian ambassadors long before Cabrera wrote it in his *History*.

Philip had developed his methods of working undoubtedly because, with his reserved temperament, he found them congenial. But, from his point of view, they were also logical and sensible. Two considerations reinforced each other in his mind. The first was his father's repeated warnings against fully trusting any of his ministers[17] and his insistence that Philip should never omit to listen to complaints against his viceroys and governors.[18] The second was Philip's own exalted view of his office and of his duty to God for the just government of the subjects entrusted to his care. Now good government meant the meting out of just rewards and punishments and, closely connected with this obligation, the need to appoint suitable persons to public offices. Punishments of the wicked were handled by

[14] I think that too much solemn moralising has been attached to this habit. Concern over details of dress or the religious services of the troops was probably a form of relaxation for Philip. Why should he not concern himself with such matters if he was interested in them, just as other men did? As to correcting the grammar and spelling of dispatches, this looks very much like a useful way of letting off emotional steam for a man who did not think it consonant with his dignity to do so in any other way. Other busy statesmen, including Winston Churchill, have acted similarly.

[15] British Museum, MS Egerton 330, fos. 4–20.

[16] L. von Ranke, *Die Osmanen und die spanische Monarchie, Sämmtliche Werke*, 3rd ed., vol. 35, (Leipzig, 1877), 129–30.

[17] For instance in the secret instructions for Prince Philip of 6 May 1543. K. Brandi, 'Berichte und Studien zur Geschichte Karls V', vol. XII, *Nachrichten von der Gesellschaft der Wissenschaften*, (Göttingen, Phil.-Hist. Klasse, 1934), 70–96.

[18] Instructions of 18 January 1548. F. de Laiglesia, *Estudios Históricos (1515–1555)*, vol. I, (Madrid, 1918), 114.

the appropriate law courts (or, if necessary, by the king's soldiers); but rewards and appointments, including those to the courts and the armies, were subject to the king's patronage. It followed that the king must personally control patronage. Philip was absolutely clear about this. 'They must depend only on me', he wrote, 'and from me only receive favours for services they have rendered me.'[19] And, at the very end of his reign, he spelt out his reasons in instructions to the president of the Council of Castile: 'In order that he may better fulfil this [i.e. his duties] he should consider and believe that he is not obliged to any person in the world for the position he has attained, but only to the will of Our Lord who was pleased to move the will of His Majesty to choose him [the president] and place him in this ministry for the relief of his conscience and the welfare of these kingdoms.'[20] In other words, Philip would only trust himself, and no one else, to carry out God's will disinterestedly.

But this was hubris: not in the sense that Philip was wrong in thinking that even his most faithful servants had their own axes to grind. They had, and the pervasiveness of the patron–client relationship in this period made it necessary for every minister to gain royal favours for his relatives and clients. It was hubris in the sense that Philip thought he could physically and intellectually cope with the amount of work involved, in making all decisions for himself, and it was hubris in the sense that he believed he could rise above the passions of all other men. In practice, many patronage and even policy decisions were made, and were bound to be made, by the king's ministers and, especially, by the royal secretaries. Petitioners knew this and acted accordingly. The very evils which the king wanted to eliminate by his personal control flourished more balefully because he virtually forced his secretaries to act secretly and therefore irresponsibly. From time to time Philip discovered that he had been made use of; apparently by Juan de Escobedo, certainly by Antonio Pérez. His anger then was boundless. But its result was not to make him question his system of government but only to reinforce his suspicions of all his servants.

This suspicion became almost pathological. It led him to deceive his ministers; for he assured them that he would never listen to slanders against them, yet he encouraged their subordinates to spy and report on them.[21] It led him to encourage quarrels between his ministers and between different public institutions in the hope that he could then the

---

[19] '. . . que de me solo han de depender, y recibir merced por los servicios que me hizieron'. Quoted in C. Giardina, 'Il Supremo Consiglio d'Italia', *Atti della Regia Accademia di Scienze, Lettere e Belle Arti di Palermo*, ser. 3, vol. 19, (Palermo, 1936), 131.

[20] British Museum, MS Egerton 339, fo. 276.

[21] H. G. Koenigsberger, *The Practice of Empire* (emended edition of *The Government of Sicily under Philip II of Spain*), (Ithaca, 1969), 177–78.

more easily control them.[22] The results were administrative chaos, and
at times an almost complete breakdown of government. This happened
in the Netherlands during the regency of Margaret of Parma and in
Andalucia in the years before the revolt of the Moriscos, in 1568.
Philip's suspicions fed the very evils they were meant to exorcise; for
men knew only too well how unreliable the king's favour was and
therefore went to almost any lengths to safeguard their positions. The
vicious intrigues and deadly infighting at the court of Madrid became
proverbial even in a century which had as bitter an experience of life at
royal courts as the sixteenth. The surprise is not that some of Philip's
ministers openly turned against him, as William of Orange did, or
committed secret treasons, as Antonio Pérez did, but that nearly all of
them remained fundamentally loyal. Don John of Austria, Marcantonio
Colonna and Alexander Farnese were perhaps lucky to die just before
their disgrace became public. But Granvelle, Margaret of Parma and
Alba were all publicly disgraced and yet continued faithfully to serve
their merciless master. Even Egmont's personal loyalty to the king
never wavered.

What we have said so far about Philip II's character and methods of
government is well known and relatively easy to document. The
problem of Philip's political aims, however, is much more difficult to
solve; for, as we have seen, neither Philip himself nor any of his ministers
ever wrote out any overall political plan. For this failure there can be only
one reasonable explanation: they had no such plan or programme – quite
certainly not during the first 25 years of the reign. This is not surprising.
Charles V's and Gattinara's universalist plans had clearly failed in the
middle of the sixteenth century. The emperor's abdication seemed to
show his own disillusionment. Philip II inherited most of his father's
dominions in Europe and overseas, but not the imperial title. This fact in
itself had marked one of the emperor's more spectacular failures. Philip
seems to have resented it bitterly; so much so that, uncharacteristically
and rather absurdly even in such a status-conscious age, he claimed
greater nobility for himself than for his father: he, the son of an emperor,
his father, only the son of a king. What then was this vast monarchy of
which he was the ruler? As Philip saw it, it was not one monarchy at all,
but a great many, in each of which he was king or duke, count or lord,
according to the particular laws of that country. Spanish theologians and
lawyers hotly debated the king's and the Spaniards' rights of conquest
and government of the American Indians. The king was prepared to

[22] For instance, among many examples, the quarrels between the viceroys and the
Spanish Inquisition in Sicily (*ibid.*, 161–70); the quarrel between the captain-general of
Granada and the *audiencia* and other public authorities in Andalucia (Koenigsberger,
'Western Europe and the Power of Spain', *New Cambridge Modern History*, III
(Cambridge, 1968), 245–46); or Philip's encouragement, against Granvelle's advice, of
the quarrels among the Netherlands high nobility (Ch. Weiss, *Papiers d'état du cardinal de
Granvelle*, vol. 7, (Paris, 1841), 14).

listen to these views and incorporate them in his legislation for the Indies. But it would have seemed absurd to Philip and his contemporaries to debate the laws and rights of the Sicilians or the Neapolitans, the Flemings or the Franche-Comtois. This attitude did not, of course, inhibit the king from legislating on particular issues, such as the setting up of the bishoprics in the Netherlands (and even this was done on the basis of a papal bull) or the Spanish Inquisition in Milan (in which, incidentally, he was unsuccessful). The different dominions were not even expected to support each other financially, let alone contribute to a common defence treasury, as the viceroy of Sicily, Marcantonio Colonna, suggested,[23] and as the count-duke Olivares was to propse in his Union of Arms during the dark years of the Thirty Years War.[24] Only reluctantly and late would Philip admit mutual obligations of his dominions. To a plea by the Council of Italy in 1589 that Sicily be spared further contributions to causes 'which were not her own' (i.e. the Armada campaign), the king replied that 'except in the most urgent cases it is not the custom to transfer the burdens of one kingdom to another. And since God has entrusted me with so many, since all are in my charge, and since in the defence of one all are preserved it is just that I should call on all.'[25]

In practice, however, Philip's different dominions were neither as independent, nor as equal in his mind, as he thought of them in theory. From the latter part of Charles V's reign the predominance of Spain, and more particularly of Castile, within the Habsburg monarchy had become more and more marked. It was from Castile and the Castilian Indies that the king derived the major part of his revenue. As Philip's reign progressed, as the mines of Potosí sent a steadily increasing stream of silver to Seville, and as the Netherlands, once hopefully described as the king's real Indies, turned into a dangerous monster threatening his authority and devouring his treasure, the predominance of Castile and the Castilians became over-whelming. Members of old Italian families, the Colonna and the Pescara, the Doria and the Spinola, served the king as loyally as the Álvarez de Toledo or the Mendoza, the Guzmán or Enríquez, and they neither thought themselves, nor were they regarded by the king, as inferior to the Spanish grandees. But the Spaniards disliked and distrusted them, were deeply jealous of them, and did not cease their intrigues even against the king's own nephew and best general, Alexander Farnese.

It was a commonplace of sixteenth-century statecraft that men served their king better outside their native country or province. 'Experience has shown', the king wrote in 1578, 'that Castilians are better in offices in

---

[23] Koenigsberger, *The Practice of Empire*, 56–57.

[24] J. H. Elliott, *Imperial Spain*, (London, 1963), 326–28.

[25] Simancas, MS Secreterías Provinciales, legajo 984, consulta of 12 June and Philip's answer of 11 November, 1589.

Andalucia than in Castile, and also the other way round,'[26] and in 1592 the Council of Italy went even further, suggesting that Sicilians served best in Naples and Flanders and the Neapolitans in Sicily.[27] These were precepts based on experience and practical considerations, and up to a point Philip was willing to follow them. But they were neither a theory for equal citizenship in an international empire nor universal guides for practical action. His Majesty was determined never to give a castle to an Italian, said a member of the Council of Italy to an importunate Neapolitan gentleman.[28] Cardinal Granvelle suggested that the king should, as a matter of policy, grant occasional ecclesiastical benefices in Spain to Netherlanders; for there was a suspicion in the Netherlands that Philip regarded only the Spaniards as his legitimate subjects and that he wanted to reduce the Netherlands to the position of his Italian provinces. If he were to appoint the prince of Orange to the viceroyalty of Sicily he would most probably serve His Majesty well in that position.[29]

Granvelle, the Franche-Comtois and son of Charles V's chancellor Nicholas Perrenot, had a clearer conception of the character of an international empire than perhaps any other of Philip's advisers. But he was swimming against the stream. Philip turned both the suggestions down out of hand. Just as the count-duke Olivares was to find, in the 1620s, the Spanish court and the Castilian ruling classes (grandees, royal officials, prelates and soldiers) were determined that, in return for Castilian sacrifices in money and blood, the fruits of empire should be enjoyed by Castilians. By this they understood more especially the Castilian monopoly of the trade with the Indies and the reservation of as many military, administrative and ecclesiastical appointments throughout the king's dominions as local laws and the particular balance of forces would allow. They were aware that they had come to be hated; but what did it matter, as long as Netherlanders and Italians were kept in their place as the natives of America were kept in theirs? It was a waste of time to try to make the Italians love us, wrote a Spaniard (probably the marquis de Ayamonte, governor-general of Milan) to Philip. The only possibility was to make them respect us, both friends and enemies. Once they had lost respect, the situation would be hopeless.[30] On the back of this letter there appears the following note: 'It seems to me that in this [letter] everything is said that can be written from here; and Your Honour [Secretary Mateo Vázquez?] should believe me that the fact that some in authority in this court have in the past treated with the Italians, both by word and letter, has done much damage to the service and reputation of His Majesty. For these Italians, although they are not

[26] British Museum, MS Egerton 2082, fos. 2–3.

[27] Simancas, MS Secretarías Provinciales, legajo 985, consulta of 12 November, 1592.

[28] Albèri, *Relazioni*, ser. I, vol. VI, 415.

[29] Granvelle to Philip II, Brussels, 10 March 1563. Weiss, *Papiers d'État*, vol. 7, 53–55.

[30] Ayamonte (?) to Philip II, Milan, 2 February 1570 (copy). British Museum, Additional MS 28 399, fos. 7–8.

Indians, have to be treated as such, so that they will understand that we are in charge of them and not they in charge of us.'[31] In the Netherlands Vargas, the president of Alba's Council of Troubles, expressed a similar sentiment even more succinctly: 'Non curamus privilegios vestros' (we are not concerned with your privileges).[32]

Philip II, even if he did not say so openly, in effect shared the views of his Castilian subjects. They were the only ones he really trusted, even if one had to expect a certain degree of corruption from them. When Granvelle first arrived in Madrid, in 1579, and submitted to the king details of his ministers' highly profitable deals with the foreign bankers at the expense of the treasury, Philip did not share the cardinal's outrage but pretended the faults had already been remedied.[33] Apart from Philip's inability to understand the details of financial transactions[34] he had been warned by his father that even his most loyal servants would generally try to feather their own nests.[35] It would evidently be unwise to antagonize the Castilians at the behest of a foreigner.

Granvelle was the only non-Spaniard whom Philip II ever admitted into the small circle of his advisers in Madrid who were involved in making important policy decisions. From the beginning there was a strong party intriguing against Granvelle and, gradually, it gained the king's ear. Philip, though he continued to admire the cardinal, seems to have found the old man's dictatorial personality and his uncompromisingly internationalist conception of the Habsburg empire distinctly uncongenial. When in 1586 Granvelle argued, logically and forcefully, that the king should permanently move his capital to Lisbon, the Castilians saw their worst fears realized; but Philip ignored the argument and returned to Madrid and the Escurial.[36]

By this time no one in Europe was any longer in doubt as to the nature of Philip II's monarchy: it had become in Europe what it had always been in the Indies, a Spanish empire. From the 1590s on, the Spaniards themselves began to call it by this name.[37]

Philip II's empire was governed according to some more or less definite maxims. But these constituted attitudes rather than clear-cut principles, opinions rather than well-defined theories.[38] The same was true of Philip's foreign policy. Plans for universal empire, even plans for the political leadership of Europe in the way in which Charles V had

---

[31] *Ibid.*, fo. 9.

[32] P. Geyl, *The Revolt of the Netherlands*, (London, 1958), 102.

[33] M. Philippson, *Ein Ministerium unter Philipp II. Kardinal Granvella am spanischen Hofe (1579–1586)*, (Berlin, 1895), 118–19.

[34] J. Gentil da Silva, 'Philippe II et les problèmes de l'argent', *Annales, Economies, Sociétés, Civilisations*, vol. 14, 1959, 736–37.

[35] Secret instructions of 1543. Brandi, '*Berichte und Studien*', vol. XII, 80 ff.

[36] Philippson, *Ein Ministerium*, 612–14.

[37] I owe this last point to Dr I. A. A. Thompson.

[38] Koenigsberger, *The Practice of Empire*, 50–51.

understood this, simply did not exist in the first two decades of Philip II's
reign. Such plans would undoubtedly have involved war, and Philip
disliked war. On this point all who knew him were agreed. Even in the
one war which he could not avoid, the naval war with the Ottoman
Turks, Philip's policy was determined by strategic, and mainly
defensively strategic, considerations. He entertained no plans for the
reconquest of Constantinople, as his father had done, nor for the
Christian conquest of Africa, as his nephew, King Sebastian of Portugal,
did. Don John's foray into the eastern Mediterranean which led to the
great Christian victory of Lepanto was carried out against Philip's
orders. Characteristically, it was Granvelle who wanted to seize the
opportunity of Turkish involvement in Persia to mount a major Spanish
offensive in the Mediterranean. The king preferred to negotiate a truce
with the Sultan.[39]

There were, inevitably, many at Philip II's court who did not share the
king's preference for peace. The traditions of the European nobility were
essentially militarist. Many men liked war, saw their only chance of
advancement in war, and were unutterably bored by peace.[40] In Spain,
moreover, the old crusading zeal for war against the infidels was still
very much alive and was fed by such signal victories as the relief of Malta,
the defeat of the Morisco rebellion and, above all, the battle of Lepanto.
This zeal could be easily transferred to the fight against the Christian
heretics.[41] From the beginning of Philip's reign, foreign ambassadors
observed the tug-of-war between two attitudes at the king's court, the
peaceful and generally defensive one, propounded mainly by Ruy
Gómez de Silva, prince of Eboli, and his friends, and the more warlike
and aggressive one, embodied by the duke of Alba and his adherents.

But it was precisely different attitudes which Eboli and Alba
represented, not different political principles. Yet such principles
existed, both in the king's own mind and in the minds of his advisers and
courtiers. These principles were twofold, with a third, a somewhat
different principle, arising out of them. The first was the defence of the
king's dominions against attacks from the outside or subversion from
inside. Just as his father had done, Philip saw himself called upon by
God to rule his many kingdoms, and since God assuredly had a purpose
in so calling on him, Philip's first duty was to preserve what God had
given him. Secondly, it was clear to Philip, as it had been to his father
when he answered Luther at the diet of Worms, that he was the scion of
many great Catholic houses and that he must preserve the religion of his

[39] Philippson, *Ein Ministerium*, 104.

[40] For instance, the remarks of the Venetian ambassador, Giovanni Soranzo, in 1565.
Albèri, *Relazioni*, ser. I, vol. V, 116. In fact, the literary evidence for such attitudes is
ubiquitous.

[41] *Cf.* L. van der Essen, 'Croisade contre les hérétiques ou guerre contre des rebelles?'
*Revue d'Histoire Ecclésiastique*, vol. 51, No. 1, 1956, 43–78.

ancestors. As he assured Pius V, in 1566, that 'rather than suffer the least damage to religion and the service of God, I would lose all my states and a hundred lives, if I had them; for I do not propose nor desire to be the ruler of heretics.'[42] The third principle was that of providing equal justice for all his subjects.

These principles remained constant throughout Philip II's reign, and, at least in his own mind, he remained absolutely loyal to them. They fill the pages of his correspondence with his ministers and his governors general; they were reiterated in every royal address to the meetings of the córtes of Castile, though usually with the defence of the Catholic religion first and the preservation of justice second.[43]

But even firm principles are not in themselves policies and aims. Philip's contemporaries knew the king's self-proclaimed principles perfectly well. There remained, however, the vital question of what he meant by them and how he was going to act on them in practice; or, conversely, how far his observable actions could be related to his stated principles. And there also remained the even more difficult question of how the first two principles, those of the defence of the monarchy and of the defence of the Catholic Church and religion, related to each other.

There was, no doubt, an element of rhetoric, certainly of self-justification, in Philip's statement to Pius V. Yet, the evidence of all his actions showed that he meant what he said and that he meant it quite literally. That is to say, the emphasis of the statement is on Philip's own subjects. He was not speaking of the rest of Christendom. The statement itself continues (and this part has not usually been quoted): 'If it should be possible, I will settle the religious problem in these states [i.e. the Netherlands] without taking up arms, for I know that to do so would result in their total destruction; but if everything cannot be remedied as I desire without recourse to arms, I am determined to take them up and to go myself to carry out everything; and neither danger [to myself] nor the ruin of these states, nor of all the others which are left to me, will prevent me from doing what a Christian prince fearing God ought to do in his service, the preservation of the Catholic faith and the honour of the apostolic see.'[44]

Apart from the king's failure to go himself to the Netherlands, it was a remarkably clear view of the future. There were to be moments, notably during the autumn of 1576, after the Pacification of Ghent, when Philip was prepared to withdraw his troops and give up all effective political control over the Netherlands to the States General,

---

[42] Philip II to Requesens, his ambassador in Rome, 12 August 1566. L. Serrano, *Correspondencia Diplomática entre España y la Santa Sede*, vol. I, (Madrid, 1914), 316.

[43] *Cf. Actas de las Córtes de Castilla*, vol. 5¹, (Madrid, 1865), 101–02, for the córtes of 1579. Similar passages in all other volumes.

[44] Serrano, *Correspondencia*, vol. I, 316–7.

reserving for himself little more than nominal sovereignty. But he was immovable on the question of religion and peace negotiations in the Netherlands broke down several times over this point.

In stark contrast to his rigid attitude towards his own subjects he was much more flexible and tolerant in his approach to the heterodoxy of other rulers and their subjects. He refused to publish Pius V's excommunication of Elizabeth I and he drove the English and Scottish Catholics to the depths of despair by his unwillingness seriously to support their many schemes of rebellion. He hindered, rather than supported, the duke of Savoy's plans to attack Geneva and he even intrigued with the Huguenot leader, Henry of Navarre, against the Most Christian King of France. Evidently, Philip II did not consider the existence of heresy outside his dominions in the same light as he considered its existence within them, that is, as obliging him to fight it, if need be to the utter ruin of his own subjects.

But this rather tidy pattern does not exhaust the problem of Philip II's aims and policies. He was not Richelieu. Neither psychologically nor in terms of practical politics did he find it possible to maintain a sharp distinction between the problems of heresy in his own states and in other countries. The royal addresses to the córtes mention regularly not only the maintenance of the Catholic faith in His Majesty's dominions but also the 'state and affairs and welfare of Christendom' as a major concern of the king's policy.[45] Moreover, there was always the danger that heresy might spread into the king's dominions from abroad and threaten both his subjects' eternal salvation and his own authority. If this happened, was there not every reason for the king to intervene in the internal affairs of other countries?

As early in his reign as the summer of 1562, just when France was visibly sliding into a religious civil war, Philip wrote to his sister Margaret of Parma, his regent of the Netherlands, a clear justification for intervention in France and of the problems this involved. Having described the almost desperate state of his finances in Spain he continued:

About the affairs of France there is nothing more to say . . . except that they are causing me as much concern as is to be expected, seeing the way things are going, both in the matter of the service of God and in everything else; and therefore I cannot omit to help the Catholics although the expense is coming at a very bad time . . . for it seems to me certain that neither the service of God, which is the most important service, nor my own and the welfare of my states will allow me to neglect helping the Catholics. I know well that something will be risked in this, but certainly much more will be risked in allowing the heretics to prevail; for if they do, we may be certain that all their endeavours will be directed against me and my states, so that they will be like them (i.e.

[45] E.g. *Actas de las Córtes*, vol. 5$^1$, 100.

also heretical): a result which I will never accept nor overlook, even if it should cost me a hundred lives, if I had them.[46]

If the phrase of the loss of a hundred lives was evidently one of Philip's favourite rhetorical tricks, it was nevertheless an expression of genuine conviction. In his correspondence with his sister, unlike his correspondence with the Pope, Philip was not usually given to propagandistic statements. The letter, in fact, spelt out the rationale of his policy very clearly, both in terms of aims and of the risks and costs involved. It remained the basis for his attitude towards France and England for some twenty years. It frightened both the Huguenots and the English, as it was clearly meant to do and perhaps even more than it was meant to, for Alba's famous march along the eastern frontier of France in 1567 inadvertently precipitated the second French civil war. But, for Spain, French civil wars were by no means universal disasters. They were certainly much better than a genuine *modus vivendi* between the French monarchy and the Huguenots, as Coligny's aggressively anti-Spanish policy of 1572 was to demonstrate. Madrid had good reasons, besides pious satisfaction at the just punishment meted out to heretics, to celebrate the massacre of St Bartholomew with special masses and religious processions.

Up to 1580 the initiative in western Europe, except for the Netherlands, remained with Philip. Both temperamentally and politically, it suited the king to use it very sparingly; but neither France nor England seriously disputed it. Then, quite rapidly, the situation changed completely. Philip brought the long Mediterranean war with the Turks to an end and his armies and navies made good his hereditary claims in Portugal. It was an enormous accession of power and prestige, and it was boosted further by the unprecedentedly large amounts of American silver which were just then beginning to reach Spain and the royal treasury. The foreign ambassadors in Madrid now ceased to write of the king's love of peace. The princes of Europe and their diplomatic advisers were certain that Philip II would continue to use his power as aggressively as he had used it in the acquisition of the Portuguese crown.

Philip himself continued to think in terms of the defence of his own just interests against unjustified and unprovoked aggression. For was not the duke of Anjou invading the Netherlands with a French army and had he not allowed himself to be proclaimed sovereign by Philip's traitorous and heretical subjects? Were not France and England openly supporting Don Antonio, the Portuguese pretender, and were not English pirates, with their queen's evident approval, preying on the

---

[46] Philip II to Margaret of Parma, Madrid, 15 July 1562. L. P. Gachard, *Correspondence de Marguerite d'Autriche, duchesse de Parme, avec Philippe II*, vol. II, (Brussels, 1870), lxii–lxiii.

legitimate and peaceful trade of Philip's Spanish and Portuguese subjects?

In the spring and summer of 1585 the growing tensions in western
Europe reached crisis point. Elizabeth was intervening more and more
actively in the Netherlands. Anjou had died and the Huguenot Henry of
Navarre had become heir presumptive to the French crown. The French
king, Henry III, had proved himself utterly unreliable in the defence of
the Catholic Church. If France and the Netherlands were lost, the blow
not only to Spain but to the Church would be irretrievable. A purely
intellectual attack by the heretics could be countered effectively enough,
by strict censorship and the inquisition. Philip never tired of pointing to
the peace and quiet reigning at the centre of his own monarchy, in
Spain.[47] But the Church was now faced with something much more
formidable: an attack by powerful governments with strong armies and
navies and the attempted political, as well as religious, subversion of the
remaining Catholic countries.

Only the king of Spain was powerful enough to resist these subversive
forces. From now on, the defence of his own interests and the defence of
Christendom not only coincided (as they had in his mind coincided
throughout his reign); they became completely identical. He saw this
defence almost exclusively in military terms. Philip made this clear in his
instructions to the count of Olivares, his ambassador to the new pope,
Sixtus V: 'Your first duty must be to make him understand that such
forces as I have, he is to regard as his own in all matters pertaining to the
help and defence of the Church and of the Holy See, and that I take this
course more to heart than my own affairs because, in truth, none other is
as much mine as this'.[48]

Philip did not, of course, mean that the pope could now command the
Spanish forces, but rather that he now thought it inconceivable that the
pope should want to pursue any other policy than he did himself. The old
dilemma of those who champion a universal cause from the base of a
limited territorial power with its own limited but imperative interests, a
dilemma which Philip had clearly recognized in his letter to Margaret of
Parma in 1562, now seemed to have been resolved by the actions of the
enemies of the universal cause. From now on the universal cause,
Catholic Christendom, and its spiritual head, the pope, had no choice but
to rely absolutely on the king of Spain. Time and again Philip insisted on
this point. Olivares was told to stress the contrast between the strength
of the king's forces and the feebleness of the pope's. Naturally, the
weaker must follow the stronger.[49] Having resolved the dilemma in his

[47] For instance, Philip's instructions to the count of Olivares, his ambassador in
Rome, 14 May 1585. L. von Pastor, *Geschichte der Päpste*, vol. 10, (Freiburg, 1926), 193,
and P. Herre, *Papsttum und Papstwahl im Zeitalter Philipps II*, (Leipzig, 1907), 381–83.
[48] Herre, *Papsttum*, 382, n. 1.
[49] *Ibid.*

own mind, it seemed unreasonable to Philip that the pope should not accept the king's judgement in matters which, however important, were in the end purely tactical. When Sixtus V urged Philip to act against England before he was ready, the king commented sourly: 'It seems that the war in Flanders is not big enough for him and that he does not consider how much it costs.'[50] Even more categorical was his reaction to the pope's claim that secular princes should take no part in ecclesiastical affairs. 'One might reply to him', Philip wrote, 'that this is in effect so. Nevertheless, they [secular princes] have always exercised the right to submit to the popes their counsels and requests about what they should do for the welfare and preservation of Christendom, and the popes have shown great deference to their counsels. In the state of danger in which the Church finds itself today there are many reasons why His Holiness should believe me, admit my observations, and listen to my counsels with the attention and deference which his predecessors have shown mine on similar occasions.'[51]

But if the dilemma had disappeared in Philip's own mind, it had done so only there. To everyone else, and especially to Sixtus V, its two horns were only too menacingly apparent. The pope saw his position as that of the medieval popes menaced by the German emperors, only now the support of France, on which these popes had so often relied, had collapsed.[52] A Spanish victory seemed only one degree less disastrous for the papacy than a Spanish defeat and a victory for the heretics, Elizabeth of England and Henry of Navarre, personalities whom, moreover, Sixtus could not help admiring. Philip demanded that the pope declare Navarre, the relapsed heretic, incapable of succeeding to the French throne, send away his envoy to Rome and excommunicate his Catholic followers. To the king these seemed logical, reasonable and necessary moves to assure the victory of Catholicism in France. To the pope the king's demands were an intolerable interference, not only with the prerogatives and liberties of the papacy but with the pope's essential duties as the spiritual father of all Christians.

After Henry III's death, when the question of the French succession became acute, relations between the king and the pope rapidly deteriorated. While the whole of Italy watched with scandalized fascination (for the various Italian ambassadors to Rome sent gleeful reports to their respective governments), Sixtus V and Philip's ambassador Olivares, argued their diametrically opposed views in increasingly dramatic confrontations. By March 1590, the pope had come to threaten to cut off the ambassador's head and excommunicate the king, while Philip was mobilizing troops in Italy and threatening to withdraw his obedience from the pope.[53] In the end, king and pope

[50] Baron de Hübner, *Sixte-Quint*, nouvelle éd., vol. I, (Paris, 1882), 348.
[51] *Ibid.*, vol. 2, 21–22.
[52] Pastor, *Geschichte der Päpste*, vol. 10, 258.
[53] *Ibid.*, 255–66; Herre, *Papsttum*, 384–408; Hübner, *Sixte-Quint*, vol. 2, 227–341.

needed each other too much and avoided a complete break; but Sixtus's death, in August 1590, did not come a moment too soon from the king's point of view.

So unreasonable and perverse did papal opposition appear to Philip II that he decided to solve this, to his mind, quite unnecessary problem once and for all. 'Does the king want to become pope?'. Sixtus V had on one occasion angrily shouted at Olivares and then added sarcastically: 'In that case we will make him a cardinal first.'[54] Naturally, Philip did not want this. He suffered from, or perhaps enjoyed, none of his great-grandfather Maximilian's romantic daydreams of combining the offices of emperor and pope. But he could make certain that Sixtus V's successors would be men who saw the problems of Catholic Christendom the way he himself did. Three times in less than two years, between 1590 and 1592, Olivares succeeded, by a mixture of promises and pressures, in obtaining the election of popes dedicated to the cause of Spain. The fact that he exceeded Philip's instructions in the ruthlessness of his wire-pulling (though not in the aims to be achieved) did nothing to make his contemporaries doubt that in these conclaves they were witnessing Philip II's imperialism, his quest for a universal monarchy, at its most blatant.[55]

But were they correct? Was it a universal empire that Philip was aiming at when he made popes, sent his invincible armada against England and his tercios into France to prevent, as he said, the succession of a heretic king?.

Even for this most critical part of Philip's reign, the late 1580s and the early 1590s, we have no blue-print, no plan for a universal empire. Not even Granvelle, the most ardent protagonist of Habsburg-Catholic power politics, seems to have had such a plan.[56] There is indeed a good deal of evidence that Philip remained very cautious in his approach to international politics. By sixteenth-century standards he was already elderly and his only surviving son was still a boy and not a very promising one. Philip II was much too experienced a statesman, and too conscious of the impenetrable nature of God's will, to count firmly on the success of such a hazardous undertaking as the 'enterprise of England'. In fact, the invasion of England by the duke of Parma's armies was only one of a number of possible aims of the armada campaign which Philip had in mind. It would have served his purpose if the mere presence of the armada in the English Channel, the threat of invasion, had relieved Portugal, the Azores and the Spanish-American shipping routes from the constant threat of Drake's raids and if it had induced

[54] Hübner, *Sixte-Quint*, vol. 2, 283.
[55] Herre, *Papsttum*, 409–596.
[56] It is possible that this view of Granvelle may have to be qualified in the light of unpublished Granvelle papers of which there exist an enormous number, spread over different European archives.

Elizabeth to treat for peace on the basis of withdrawing her help to the Dutch rebels.[57]

Philip's enemies and even his allies, however, were convinced that he was aiming at conquest. At the very least he could never be trusted. The English naturally thought so, once they became convinced that the armada preparations were directed against them. Henry III of France said drily that he did not believe Philip wanted to conquer England for the benefit of James VI of Scotland, whatever the pope said; for the Spaniards were not monks who could be compelled by papal orders to give up what they had conquered by their arms.[58] The papal nuncio at Madrid remarked that the king was a sage person. 'He says he does not want the property of others, but the chances of the occasion, the *penchant* for domination which is innate in men, unforeseen incidents, (all this) could end in the establishment of a universal monarchy.'[59]

Here was the crucial point: empires are not usually acquired according to a blue-print. Philip did not need a plan, the less so if it should appear that God himself had one. Opportunities of conquest and empire might come Philip's way, and there would be little doubt that such occasions would represent the will of God. His Spanish subjects thought in these terms. The córtes of Castile rejoiced repeatedly in the fact that God had given His Majesty so many kingdoms and they said quite naïvely that they hoped he would acquire many more.[60] In 1579 they argued that, even if the king did not have valid claims to the crown of Portugal, he should acquire it; for the succession of a foreign prince would be damaging to Castile and to the Christian religion.[61] They clearly regarded the two as synonymous. Bernardino de Mendoza, Philip's ambassador, first in England and then in France, went so far as to rejoice in the execution of Mary Queen of Scots, for God would now raise up other instruments for the Triumph of his cause.' And, lest the king to whom Mendoza wrote this should have any doubt as to his meaning, he added: 'So it would seem to be God's obvious design to bestow upon Your Majesty the crowns of these two kingdoms [i.e. England and Scotland].'[62] It seemed an acceptable conclusion even to some English Catholics. On hearing the news of Mary Stuart's death, the exiled William Allen, soon to be created a cardinal, wrote to Philip II signing himself 'Your devoted servant and subject'.[63]

---

[57] *Cf.* the convincing arguments and documentation for such an interpretation adduced recently by I. A. A. Thompson, 'The Appointment of the Duke of Medina Sidonia to the Command of the Spanish Armada', *The Historical Journal*, vol. XII, 2, 1969.

[58] *Calendar of State Papers Venetian*, vol. 8, 170.

[59] Hübner, *Sixte-Quint*, vol. I, 357.

[60] *Córtes*, vol. 8, 282.

[61] *Ibid.*, vol. 5[1], 210.

[62] Quoted in G. Mattingly, *The Defeat of the Spanish Armada*, (London, 1950), 84–85.

[63] *Ibid.*, 74.

In France, Philip's policy of keeping his options open was even clearer. As early as 1586 he instructed Olivares to persuade the pope that France under Navarre would become heretical even if Navarre returned to the Catholic faith. Philip would not expose his own states to this contagion. He would support the French Catholics. There would be civil wars and perhaps the kingdom would be dismembered. United and Catholic, the powerful kingdom of France was of great utility to Christendom; but if it vowed itself to damnation, it would be best to reduce its powers.[64]

Philip's appreciation of the likely course of events was again remarkably acute. The civil wars did break out again and France came perilously near to dismemberment. In the event, Philip played for even higher stakes: the succession to the French throne of his own daughter, Isabella Clara Eugenia. Mendoza argued to his French friends that this succession would no more mean a Spanish domination of France than a Spanish general of an international religious order meant a Spanish domination of that order.[65] The great majority of the French were not deceived; nor is it conceivable that Philip II who, whatever his other limitations, was never naïve in matters of international power politics, did not appreciate the political results which would follow from Isabella's succession to the French throne: the unchallengeable predominance of the house of Austria in Christendom and, even if this was not the intention, the effective predominance of Spain.

To achieve these ends Philip gambled on an ever-increasing flow of treasure from the Indies and staked the economic survival of his subjects, just as he had always said he would. For decades the córtes of Castile had supported the king with ever-increasing grants of money. In February 1589, they still thanked him for his great favour in explaining to them in some detail why he wanted them to grant him a new tax of eight million ducats, the notorious *millones*.[66] But already in the previous year one member had wondered aloud 'whether France, Flanders and England would really be better if Spain were poorer',[67] and by 1593 another *procurador* said sarcastically that, even without His Majesty's armies, 'the rebels in Flanders and France would be well and truly punished since they did not wish to follow our holy faith; for if they wanted to earn damnation, let them.'[68]

From the year of 1593 a regular opposition developed in the Córtes, although it does not usually seem to have included more than twelve *procuradores*. They argued that the king should make an end to the foreign wars, for the burdens fell primarily on those least able to bear them, the

[64] Hübner, *Sixte-Quint*, vol. 2, 159–61.

[65] L. von Ranke, *Französische Geschichte*, vol. 2, (Munich–Leipzig, 1924), 34.

[66] *Córtes*, vol. 10, 435–57.

[67] Quoted in C. Sánchez-Albornoz, *España un enigma histórico*, vol. 2, Buenos Aires, 1956, 346.

[68] *Ibid.*

poor.[69] 'The reason why taxes have been raised without noise', Rodrigo Sanchez Doria of Tordesillas argued in 1595, 'is because they have not fallen on the rich, who are those who have a voice, who speak and who are heard in republics [i.e. states], and the sweetness which they find, that is the blood of the poor . . .'[70]

If Philip had any understanding for such arguments he had no such ready answers for them as he had for the pope's. Let the *corregidors* of the cities consult the theologians as to how the kingdom might be relieved of its burdens and yet the urgent needs of the treasury supplied, he suggested.[71] More and more his arguments in justification of his foreign wars took on a defensive colouring, emphasizing less the good of Christendom and more and more Spain's perilous situation, surrounded as she was by enemies. Was it not better to meet these enemies abroad and keep the wars outside the frontiers of Spain?[72] As so often before and since, the argument of the escalation of potential disasters kept the sceptics in line and served to justify aggressive wars.[73] The córtes, for all their grumbling, never seriously opposed the king's policies.

In the end, Philip's very lack of rigid plans, his insistence on keeping his options open, enabled him to withdraw at least from the French war without feeling that he had betrayed God's cause. The detested Henry of Navarre, it was true, had succeeded to the French throne, but he was now, at least publicly, a Catholic. However distasteful it was, the Holy Father had received him back into the bosom of the Church. France had been saved from the danger of a complete Protestant take-over, and this not least because of Philip's intervention. God's main purpose had surely been fulfilled and the religious danger at least had been banished from the frontiers of Spain. It was time to banish the political dangers for the inexperienced young heir to the throne, at least to the extent that this was in the old king's power. If the treaty of Vervins, signed on 2 May 1598, restored to France all the Spanish conquests of the previous years, Philip never, even in his most private correspondence with his son-in-law, the archduke Albert, hinted that the peace was anything but honourable.[74]

Philip II had undoubtedly failed in his highest aims: in the complete re-conquest of the Netherlands, in the conquest of England and in the acquisition of the French crown, and in any further glories which might have followed from such successes. But there is no evidence that, when he lay on his death-bed, in the summer of 1598, either he or the great majority of his contemporaries thought his reign as a whole had been a failure. The French were elated by the terms of the Peace of Vervins. But these were virtually the same as those of the much-decried Peace of

[69] *Córtes*, vol. 16, 169 ff., 179 ff., 201 ff., 238 and *passim*.
[70] *Ibid.*, vol. 14, 53.    [71] *Ibid.*, vol. 14, 200–02.
[72] *Ibid.*, 223; vol. 15, 444–45.
[73] Cf. I. A. A. Thompson, *op. cit.* 231.
[74] A. E. Imhof, *Der Friede von Vervins 1598*, (Aarau, 1966), 273.

Cateau-Cambrésis, 39 years earlier. In other words, the French had had to run very fast to remain on the same spot and had then claimed this feat as as great victory. This change in attitude was itself a remarkable tribute to the fear inspired by Philip II. For the rest, he had more than fulfilled the purposes he seems to have pursued in the first twenty years of his reign: the successful defence of his dominions and of the Catholic faith of his subjects; the successful defence of the central Mediterranean against the Turks; the adding of Portugal and its empire to his own; a significant and worthy contribution to the reform of the Church and its renewed offensive against the Protestants. If he was apprehensive about the future it was mainly on account of his son's personality.

The true failures of his reign escaped him, as they escaped most, though not all, of his contemporaries. These failures were twofold: the first was the economic exhaustion of Castile together with the hardening of mental attitudes and traditions which set Spain on an imperialist course but, at the same time, undermined her ability to pursue such a course. The second was the inevitable resolution of Philip's basic dilemma, of the pursuit of the universal cause of the Catholic Church from the power basis of his territorial states, into Spanish imperialism and implacable European hostility to this imperialism. The first was the tragedy of Spain; the second was the tragedy of the ideal of the universal Church.

3. Archduke Matthias of Austria and William of Orange taking an oath before the States-General in Brussels, 20 January, 1578.
Engraving by Frans Hogenberg.

# 5

# Orange, Granvelle and Philip II

On the 23rd July 1561, Orange and Egmont wrote their famous first letter to Philip II, denouncing the political role of Cardinal Granvelle and complaining that they were excluded from all important decision-making in the government of the Netherlands.[1] The overt opposition of the Netherlands high nobility to the leading minister of the regency government, a government of which they were themselves members, has traditionally been seen as a milestone in, or even the beginning of, the *voorspel*, the events leading up to the revolt of the Netherlands. Now this is rather curious. There was nothing remarkable about aristocratic factionalism or about complaints about a royal minister, either in the Netherlands or anywhere else in early modern Europe. Complaints against Granvelle himself were not new.[2] Has it not simply been hindsight which has endowed the intrigues against the cardinal with more than incidental importance? Were not the real forces causing the revolt much more fundamental than the ambitions of a handful of near-bankrupt noblemen, most of whom eventually took no part in the revolt? Were not the causes of the revolt rather the social upheavals due to the industrialisation of the Flemish countryside, the distress caused in the big cities by disruption of trade, unemployment and high food prices, the spread of Protestant teaching together with the dislike of religious repression even by those who had every intention of remaining good Catholics, the defence of Netherlands liberties against monarchical autocracy, or simply the assertion of Netherlands nationalism against Spanish imperialism? Or again, if one prefers to use the terminology of the modern social sciences, was it not the dysfunction and final breakdown of a society, rather than the actions of a few individuals, which caused such a massive upheaval as the revolt? These questions, which are really arguments and formulations of causes, do indeed have much validity and the answer to them should be at least a qualified yes.

[1] N. Japikse, *Corrispondentie van Willem den Eerste Prins van Oranje*, (The Hague, 1934), pp. 311–15. Antoine Perrenot did not become Cardinal Granvelle until 1561; but for the sake of convenience I shall refer to him by this title throughout.

[2] M. van Durme, *Antoon Perrenot*, (Brussels, 1953), pp. 158–60. K. J. W. Verhofstad, *De regering der Nederlanden in de jaren 1555–1559*, (Nijmegen, 1937), pp. 45–47.

Here I shall only argue that historical instinct and the need for an orderly and dramatic presentation, which are the immediate reasons for our historiographical tradition about the actions of Orange and Egmont, may still be justified by the historical evidence.[3]

The government of Philip II in the Netherlands, like all early modern governments, depended ultimately on the co-operation of the local elites. At the same time, no popular movement was successful for more than a short time unless it had the support and leadership of this elite. At a time when both criticism of the king's policy and fear of popular revolt were growing,[4] a prolonged breakdown in co-operation between the monarchy and the Netherlands elite was a serious matter. It was so regarded at the time,[5] and it is therefore a legitimate subject for continued historical study.

Historians have given different reasons for the breach between Orange and Granvelle. Was it a basic clash between two opposed political philosophies, or were there more specific reasons, such as the appointment of Margaret of Parma, rather than Christina of Lorraine, as governor-general? Was it the publication of the plan for the new bishoprics or Orange's unapproved marriage with the Lutheran daughter of the hated Maurice of Saxony, or was it, as the German historian Ernst Marx maintained in a famous controversy with Orange's biographer, Felix Rachfahl, that the prince, Egmont and Glajon only became fully aware of Granvelle's domination of the government when they returned to Brussels from their provincial governments in the spring of 1561 and began to attend meetings of the council of state regularly?[6] Was Orange piqued by the regent's renewal of the Antwerp magistrate in the spring of the 1561 without consulting him? For as burgrave of Antwerp, Orange claimed this right and he had indeed been so consulted by the king himself in 1558.[7] Perhaps all these events played their part cumulatively. It is certainly difficult to assign them any clear order of importance. Here I propose rather to try to look

---

[3] In doing this I have had the advantage of using three important but as yet unpublished studies: David Lagomarsino, *Philip II and the Netherlands 1559–1573*; María José Rodríguez-Salgado, *From Spanish Regent to European Ruler: Philip II and the Creation of an Empire–*; and Guy E. Wells, *Antwerp and the Government of Philip II 1555–1567*. I would like to thank all three authors for making their typescripts available to me.

[4] There were riots in Antwerp as early as 1554. G. E. Wells, *Antwerp and the Government of Philip II, cit.*, pp. 49–57. Philip II to duke of Savoy, 2 May 1557, writes of the danger of being caught by a revolt without soldiers or money to put it down. Emmanuele Filiberto duca di Savoia, *I Diarii delle campagne di Fiandra*, ed. E. Brunelli, *Biblioteca della società storica subalpina*, vol. CXII, N.S. 21, (Turin, 1928), pp. 182–83.

[5] Marcantonio Mula, 'Relazione di Filippo II re di Spagna, 23 settembre 1559', in E. Albèri, *Le relazione degli ambasciatori veneti al senato*, ser. 1, vol. 3, (Florence, 1853), p. 401: '. . . e già se ne (i.e. "manifesta sollevazione de popoli") son visti qualche segni nelli Paesi Bassi'.

[6] E. Marx, *Studien zur Geschichte des niederländischen Aufstandes*, (Leipzig, 1902), pp. 167 ff.

[7] *Ibid.*, pp. 174–75.

more closely at the terms in which the struggle between Orange and Granvelle was fought, at Philip II's reaction to it and at its historical implications for the Netherlands and for the Spanish empire.

In the middle ages the internal politics of the states of western Europe were largely determined by the relations between the kings and their most powerful feudal vassals. By the sixteenth century the feudal nobility had finally given up its earlier ambitions to become as independent of the monarchy as possible (as the German princes had done very successfully) and had thrown in their lot with the monarchies. It could be a very profitable alliance. In France and in the Netherlands the rulers used the great nobles as provincial governors.[8] In this position they were held to represent both the king's authority in the province and also the interests of the community of the province at the king's court.[9] Naturally, only members of the greatest families were usually appointed to these posts; for the provincial nobility would not have obeyed someone below their own rank. The governors fulfilled essential functions for the monarchies. Not only did they organise the defence and public security of their provinces, but they acted as the king's all-purpose administrative agents, immediately subject to his commands. They would enforce royal legislation and ordinances without being hampered by all the legal precedents, traditions and *esprit de corps* of the lawyers in the parlements and provincial courts. Since they were appointed for life they were, in their turn, most favourably placed to advance their own and their families' influence by building up clienteles of lesser nobles and of local royal officials. This they did directly through their command of the companies of *gens d'armes*, in France, and of the *bandes d'ordonnance*, in the Netherlands, and indirectly by channelling royal patronage to their followers. They came from a small group of families which were closely linked by intermarriage with each other and, through their younger sons, with the noble families just below their own exalted level. These latter families, in their turn and in the same way, were linked with other lesser noble families. At the top of this social grouping, family connections often extended beyond the frontiers of the state, from the Netherlands especially to France but also to Germany.

In the first half of the sixteenth century the system of provincial

[8] Robert R. Harding, *Anatomy of a Power Elite: The Provincial Governors of Early Modern France*, (New Haven and London, 1978). Paul Rosenfeld, *The Provincial Governors from the Minority of Charles V to the Revolt. Standen en Landen*, vol. XVII, (Louvain and Paris, 1959). There was no exactly similar position in England or Spain. The powers of the lords-lieutenant of the English counties were not nearly as extensive, while Spanish viceroys and governors-general, although having even greater powers, were not appointed for life.

[9] See for instance the typically dual rôle played by the count of Hoochstraten, governor of Holland, in the 1530s. H. G. Koenigsberger, 'Patronage and Bribery during the Reign of Charles V', *Estates and Revolutions*, (Ithaca and London, 1971), pp. 166–75.

governorships had worked well for the monarchies. Charles V, Francis I and Henry II had enjoyed loyal and effective service from their great seigneurs, even when some of their families, such as the Egmont and the Montmorency, were split in their allegiance in the wars between these rulers. For these wars were straightforward dynastic power struggles in which, according to the ethos of the time, a nobleman's honour was fully preserved by loyal service to his own sovereign. Just as importantly, the system worked well because for the monarchies it was an age of expansion: territorial expansion, such as the incorporation of Groningen, Utrecht and Guelders in the Netherlands, which provided provincial governships and a host of lesser positions; and economic expansion, both for the countries as a whole and more particularly for the governments. Increased tax revenues and greatly expanded credit facilities were used to extend government activities, especially warfare, and this meant more rewards for government service.

It was in the nature of these conditions that they could not last. In the 1550s this fact became unhappily apparent. Economic expansion gave way to economic crisis or, at best, to shifts in the patterns of trade, with deeply disturbing social results. Government expenditure, optimistically overstretched for decades by continual warfare, finally outran taxable resources and available credit. Peace when it was finally concluded did not end the international rivalries between the great powers and was not expected to last. It did, however, cut off the prospect of new military commands, for the high nobility and of expanding territorial patronage for the monarchies. The simultaneous injection of religious emotions into politics shattered the simple ethos of loyalty between monarch and ruling elite. These new conditions made the personality of the ruler more important than ever. Where, for whatever immediate cause, confidence in his person collapsed, the whole system of consensus politics between prince and high nobility was also likely to collapse. Different sections of the elite and especially its more ambitious individual members were driven to safeguard their positions and prospects. They could do this by one or both of two methods: by systematically expanding their own local power base far beyond anything they would have deemed necessary previously and by attempting to capture control of the central government. Neither line of policy was, at least initially, regarded as anti-monarchical or as inherently treasonous; both hinged crucially on the control of patronage.

The economic and financial crisis struck the whole of western Europe. Collapse of confidence in the person of the ruler occurred in France, Scotland and in the Netherlands. The phenomenon of such a collapse was not entirely fortuitous. It was always very likely to occur at the moment of a disputed succession or of the succession of a child or a woman and of the setting up of a regency, especially if it was the regency of a woman. There was statistically at least a fifty per cent chance of this happening at the end of any reign,[10] and this was precisely what happened in these three countries. It was these three countries, too, whch slid into civil war and again in all three of them the immediate cause of the civil wars lay in the behaviour of the high nobility.

It looks as if Granvelle was the first person fully to appreciate the nature of the crisis precipitated by Philip II's appointment of Margaret of Parma as regent for the Netherlands. It had been an appointment made very much *faute de mieux*, designed to keep out Christina of Lorraine with her French connections and, even more, Philip's detested and feared cousin, Maximilian of Bohemia. To Granvelle it seemed therefore necessary, above all, to maintain royal authority by himself directly controlling government patronage and, indirectly, by extending his own reputation and influence. Was it Granvelle who suggested to the king the setting up of the famous secret consulta, the inner advisory committee for the regent, consisting of himself, Viglius and Berlaymont, which was designed to by-pass the council of state? It seems at least likely, but while this move was necessarily secret, another was deliberately public. Probably in 1559 and possibly before the setting up of the consulta, Granvelle wrote to Philip: 'Not for anything in the world would I be deemed importunate by Your Majesty, but no less would I wish that my relatives and friends should tax me with undue carelessness in my own case . . . for it is so many years now that I have received any favour (*merced*) . . . Now, forced by necessity and to avoid the opposition of my family and of everybody else who are expectantly waiting to see how Your Majesty will treat me . . . ' he hoped that the king would now show him his favour publicly.[11]

Granvelle's arguments were entirely conventional and must have seemed perfectly reasonable to the king. In any case, he arranged for Granvelle's elevation to the cardinalate and to the archbishopric of Mechlin. Granvelle was pleased to be a cardinal and he accepted the archbishopric although he had doubts about the whole policy of the new bishoprics and although both he himself and his friends in Spain thought he had been rather hard done by to have been made to give up the much richer bishopric of Arras. If he wanted to play a prominent political role in the Netherlands and preserve royal authority, there was no way in which he could have turned down this expensive honour. For the whole scheme, together with the incorporation of the

[10] H. G. Koenigsberger and George L. Mosse, *Europe in the Sixteenth Century*, (London, 1968), p. 249.

[11] Ch. Weiss, *Papiers d'Etat du Cardinal de Granvelle*, vol. V, (Paris, 1844), pp. 657–59.

Brabantine abbeys in the new bishoprics, was designed not only to fight the growing threat of heresy but to increase government influence in the estates of Brabant.[12] At the same time it signalled to everyone that Granvelle was a man of influence with, and trusted by, the king. Having earned the king's patronage, he could therefore be relied upon to dispense patronage in turn to his own clients.

As it turned out, the policy worked rather too well. It gave the impression that Granvelle had more influence with the king than he actually did.

Orange was just as concerned about his clientele as Granvelle. For a while, and because they had been friends, they could arrange to split royal patronage by making deals, 'log rolling'. As late as January 1561 Orange wrote to Granvelle, signifying his pleasure at the king's appointment of the Seigneur de Chasteauroulleau to the position of 'chevalier de la cour de parlement' of Dôle. He went on to agree to give the captaincy of Arguel, which Chasteauroulleau had held, to Granvelle's cousin, the Seigneur Pancras Bonvalot.[13] But by the summer of 1561, whatever degree of trust had been left between the prince and the cardinal had evaporated in hard competition. In their letter to the king of 23rd June Orange and Egmont referred three times to the damage to their *honneur et réputation* and another time to their *honneur et estimation*.[14] Now in the sixteenth century *honneur* and *estimation* referred to the image others had of a man's ability to get his way. In political terms this always included his ability to dispense patronage. Orange and Egmont, just as Granvelle, claimed that 'everyone' was watching and, in their case, mocking. For Egmont was a successful military leader in the king's service, second only to the duke of Alba – and Alba had held the post of viceroy of Naples, and was currently serving as one of the principal shapers of royal policy in the king's own Council of State in Spain. Orange was an independent prince in his own right, like the duke of Savoy, the previous governor-general. His marriage to a princess of the electoral house of Saxony showed his own view of his social-political status and was meant to show it to the world. With the king in Spain and the government of the Netherlands entrusted to an inexperienced and not very intelligent woman – a great change, this, from the formidably intelligent and forceful Mary of Hungary – Orange would expect, and would be expected, to play the leading political role in the country. In modern language neither Egmont nor Orange could afford to play second fiddle to a jumped-up civil servant from Franche-Comté.

[12] Geoffrey Parker, *The Dutch Revolt*, (London, 1977), p. 48, n. 24. I wish to thank Professor Parker for letting me have a photocopy of Granvelle's letter of 12 May 1576 where he specifically makes this point.

[13] L. P. Gachard, *Correspondance de Guillaume le Taciturne*, vol. 2, (Brussels, 1850), pp. 4–6.

[14] See note 1 above.

Over the next two years both sides built up their clienteles. Orange's precise political objectives in this period are notoriously difficult to penetrate[15]; but it looks as if he and his friends were aiming at a position in the Netherlands similar to that enjoyed by the Guises in France during the reign of Francis II. This meant obtaining the decisive voice in decision making in the government and control of both central and local patronage in order to build up irresistible support in the country. In this strategy the provincial governorships were crucial. Mansfeld in Luxembourg was the most blatant in exploiting his position. It was reported that he 'tyrannises the provincial council, signs any requests by his secretary, appropriates fines and browbeats the attorney-general in his chambers'.[16] He sold positions in the town councils for ten gold florins, let off a murderer for 100 *écus* and, horror of horrors, received the Jews in his province.[17] In Hainault Berghes' behaviour was almost equally autocratic. In March 1560 Margaret of Parma had recommended his appointment to the king precisely because he had local influence and could therefore counter-balance the excessive authority of the estates and of the bishop of Cambrai.[18] The appointment turned out to be a great disappointment for the regent. Berghes exercised quasi-dictatorial powers over the clergy yet failed to take effective action against heresy in a province which, because it bordered on France, was particularly exposed to the infiltration of Calvinist preachers.[19]

Orange, as one would expect, acted more subtly and, at the same time, with a surer aim for the acquisition of power. He tried to obtain the nomination as 'First Grandee' of Zeeland, a position which would have made him the sole representative of the nobility in the assembly of a province of which he was the governor.[20] More sinister still, he tried to be appointed *ruward*, or *surintendent*, of Brabant. This position, as Granvelle wrote in alarm to the king, would have made him supreme in a province which the ruler had always taken care to administer without the intervention of a provincial governor.[21]

There is no doubt that Orange and his friends were highly successful in attaching large numbers of the nobility and of government officials to themselves. But inevitably their policy aroused jealousy and

[15] Cf. K. W. Swart, 'Willem van Oranje en de Vestiging van de Macht van de Nederlands Statenvergadering', p. 2. I wish to thank Professor Swart for letting me have a copy of the typescript of his unpublished article.

[16] Rosenfeld, *Provincial Governors*, p. 52.

[17] Morillon to Granvelle, 9 Dec. 1564. Weiss, *Papiers d'Etat*, VII, p. 533.

[18] Margaret to Philip II, 17 March 1561. Gachard, *Correspondance de Marguerite d'Autriche, Duchesse de Parme, avec Philippe II*, vol. I, (Brussels, 1867), p. 148.

[19] Rosenfeld, *Provincial Governors*, p. 51.

[20] *Ibid.* p. 53.

[21] Gachard, 'La chute du cardinal de Granvelle en 1564', *Études et notices historiques concernant l'histoire des Pays-Bas*, (Brussels, 1890), p. 110.

opposition. They failed to win over Berlaymont, although they tried to tempt him with the promise of support for his son's election to the bishopric of Liège[22] – a promise which was in itself a measure of their growing influence in the region. More serious still than their failure with Berlaymont was the resisitance to their overtures by the duke of Aerschot and with him the resistance of the whole huge clan of the Croy and its widespread connections in the Walloon provinces. Margaret and Granvelle gleefully reported to Philip a quarrel which had arisen during a wedding party attended by all the great seigneurs. Aerschot had declared to Egmont that he was not willing to join the league against Granvelle, that they should not lay down the law for him and that, if they did not wish him for a friend as an equal, he did not care, 'for he had as much following of nobles and friends as any of them'.[23]

There is equally no doubt that Granvelle was building up his own party. In the spring of 1562 he wrote to Philip that the seigneurs no longer accepted his invitations for dinner but that he did not really mind and that he invited 'Gentlemen, councillors and even burghers to gain their goodwill in case these (i.e. the seigneurs) should push matters further'.[24] A year later he was still using the same tactics. Many now had their eyes opened to the true nature of the seigneurs' policy, he informed the king, and many of the nobility had excused themselves to him that they could not do what they wished for fear of offending the seigneurs; but he, Granvelle, was entertaining them and keeping his friendship with them. This was the more necessary as Orange did not even bother any more about being *surintendent* of the estates of Brabant because in effect he exercised a great part of the powers of this office anyway and he did this with the help of van Straelen, the Antwerp banker and superintendent of the taxes of the novennial *aide* of 1558.[25] He himself, Granvelle added virtuously, had asked the regent to excuse him from attending the consultas, so as to prevent further jealousy. But it was an empty gesture, and his enemies knew it; for he had arranged that Margaret should continue to consult him privately.[26] It was also well known that Viglius, the president of the privy council through which all patronage business was handled, was a faithful 'cardinalist'.[27]

By the spring of 1563 Granvelle was unequivocally presenting the struggle for the control of patronage and, hence, for power in the

---

[22] Margaret to Philip, 6 Feb. 1563. Weiss, *Papiers d'Etat*, VII, pp. 5–6.

[23] *Ibid.*

[24] Granvelle to Philip, 13 May 1562. *Ibid.* VI, pp. 557–60. '. . . cavalleros, y consejeros y aun burgeses por ganarles la voluntad para en caso que quisiessen estos (i.e. the league of seigneurs) rebolver mas las cosas'.

[25] Granvelle to Philip, 10 March 1563. *Ibid.* VII, pp. 19, 38.

[26] *Ibid.* p. 21.

[27] Van Durme, Antoon Perrenot, p. 177.

Netherlands, as the principal issue between himself and the seigneurs.[28] Soon afterwards he knew of the ultimatum Orange, Egmont and Hoorn had sent to Philip on March 11h, threatening to resign from the council of state – not, significantly, from their provincial governorships – unless the cardinal went. At almost exactly the same time the Edict of Amboise (19 March 1563) granted the French Huguenots at least a limited degree of toleration and, no doubt ominously from Granvelle's point of view, specially favoured the Huguenot nobility. He feared, as yet without giving any evidence, that one of the seigneurs in the Netherlands would make himself leader of the heretics, presumably just as had happened in France.[29] In July he wrote to Philip that the *superintendencia* which Orange was claiming in Brabant would allow him to appoint the margraves of the four principal cities. The margraves were the representatives of the central government for criminal jurisdiction in these cities. If Orange controlled them, Granvelle argued, he would be more powerful than the duke of Brabant (i.e. Philip II or his regent). It was the cardinal's opposition to this aim which was the main reason for the quarrel between them.[30]

In the next letter, on 25th July, Granvelle voiced his fears of the seigneurs' plots with German troops but added, perhaps sincerely, that not all of them knew of the ultimate plans.[31] On the 20th August, in a long, confused and almost hysterical letter to the king, Granvelle concentrated on the demands for the summoning of the States General. What he feared was not the traditional assembly of the deputies of the estates of the different provinces who would listen together to the king's proposals and then deliberate and answer separately, but a joint meeting where all discussed and resolved on the proposals together. This was what they had done in 1558, when the States General had hammered out the conditions of the huge nine-year *aide* together with the then regent, the duke of Savoy. Granvelle had opposed the joint sessions at that time but had been overridden by Savoy. He was particularly angry about the loss of royal authority which, he claimed, had been involved in allowing the States General to administer the nine-year *aide*. Straelen, the commissioner for this tax had become his special *bête noir*.[32] Now Granvelle returned to the charge. Joint meetings would

[28] Granvelle to Philip, 10 March 1563. Weiss, *Papiers d'Etat*, VII, p. 21. 'Y porque veo que se ofenden mucho de que no entren en la consulta, y en renovar el magistrado de las villas, *en lo qual no conviene en ninguna manera que tengan parte, porque seria la ruina de la authoridad de V. M.*, por quitarles el sentimiento que muestran tener de que entrevenga yo en ello, he suplicado á Madama (i.e. the regent, Margaret of Parma) lo que ántes muchas vezes, que consienta que yo me abstenga de las consultas, y que de lo que de mí quisiere ser informada lo haré aparte . . .' My italics.

[29] Granvelle to Philip, 9 May 1563. *Ibid.* pp. 74–75.

[30] *Ibid.* pp. 135–38.

[31] *Ibid.* p. 165.

[32] F. Rachfahl, *Wilhelm von Oranien und der niederländische Aufstand*, vol. 1, (Halle and The Hague, 1906), pp. 553–68. Verhofstad, *De regering*, pp. 116–49. G. E. Wells, *Antwerp*, ch. 3, section C, pp. 168–192; ch. 4, section D, pp. 236, 243.

encourage the estates to put forward demands they would not dare to make singly. By this he meant particularly the question of the new bishoprics and the placards against heresy. If the estates controlled the taxation, the government would lose its credit on the money market and would no longer be able to raise loans on its own authority. The States General, even if it showed good will, would be so slow about raising money on credit that, if there was a rebellion or an invasion, the enemy would have captured half the country before the government could raise any troops and, within a short time, both the country and the Catholic religion would be lost. Orange and Berghes were in league with Straelen and even with some of the associates of Schetz, the king's financial agent in the Netherlands. They wanted to change the constitution so that they could command the state, and the regent, or even the king himself if he came, would have no further say.[33]

But in spite of all these dire predictions Granvelle still raised doubts about the success of Orange's and Berghes' policy with the estates. Would the estates really want to pay for the garrisons and service the king's enormous debts, just because the great lords called the tune?[34] Much of the fault lay with the prelates and their refusal to consent to the *aides* because of the plans to incorporate their abbeys in the new bishoprics. This had made the clergy hated and had exasperated the king, although it was really the fault of others. The abbots had 'allowed themselves to be led like buffaloes without thought of the disastrous results this might have for them'.[35]

In December 1563 the States General met in Brussels. It was a traditional meeting in which the provinces discussed the government proposals separately and not in joint session as in 1558. Granvelle thought it best to stay away, for fear the seigneurs would not come at all if he was there. As it was, he admitted that they were trying hard to get the *aides* accepted; but they were doing this by trying to build up their own following. Orange entertained the deputies of Flanders and Artois, of which Egmont was governor. Egmont entertained those of Orange's provinces of Holland, Zeeland and Utrecht. They gave dinner parties for seventy or eighty persons. The marquis of Berghes claimed that the States General would pay the seven million the king owed the troops, if only they were allowed to negotiate together. 'The estates of Brabant want to be the head', Granvelle commented sourly, and 'the marquis wants to be the cock'. Aerschot had got tired of the festivities and had left. Granvelle thought that the estates and the cities, too, were getting tired of the behaviour of the great lords.[36]

---

[33] Archivo General de Simancas, MS Estado 524, fo. 23–29. I would like to thank Dr Rodríguez-Salgado for making a photocopy of this MS available to me. Weiss, *Papiers d'Etat*, VII, pp. 181–87, leaves out some of the most interesting passages of this letter.
[34] *Ibid.* fo. 24.
[35] Granvelle to Philip, 8 Sept. 1563. Weiss, *Papiers d'Etat*, VII, p. 206.
[36] Granvelle to Philip, 10 Dec. 1563, *Ibid.* pp. 259–65.

The pattern then was this: both Granvelle and the great seigneurs were trying to build up networks of clients among the lower nobility, government officials and town councils so as to have the greatest possible political influence in the Netherlands without, however, formally derogating the powers of the king. Neither side could pursue their policy quite openly. The cardinal could not afford to appear to be building up a private following or even to oppose the seigneurs outright. They were still the king's councillors and, in the Eboli party and especially in the secretary Eraso, they had powerful friends at court. Eraso, moreover, had a kind of secret service in the Netherlands in the persons of two officials in the administrations of the Spanish troops in the Netherlands, Alonso del Canto and Cristóbal de Castellanos, and in the Augustinian friar, Lorenzo de Villavicencio. These three ran a campaign against the cardinal's alleged softness towards heretics, and they had the ear of the king. Later, after Granvelle had left the Netherlands and after Eraso had fallen from favour in Madrid, Villavicencio effortlessly transferred his allegiance to the Alba party and switched his campaign against the seigneurs.[37] These circumstances go far to explain the repulsive tone of Granvelle's letters to the king, his constant disclaimers of his own interests in the control of patronage and his assurances in his own implicit belief in the uprightness of Orange and his friends, followed by innuendos about their personal loyalty and trustworthiness in religious matters. The trick was similar to that used by Shakespeare's Mark Anthony: 'For Brutus is an honourable man', and it was just as effective.[38]

Orange, for his part, had to be equally guarded.[39] Not only must the king not suspect him of claiming loyalties which properly belonged to the ruler, but neither must his own aristocratic allies. While all the provincial governors were trying to build up their clienteles, it looks as if only Orange and Berghes really thought in terms of a Guise-like take-over of the whole government machinery. The constant demand for the summoning of the States General was a part of this policy. Perhaps some of the seigneurs really believed that this body could restore consensus in religion. Certainly they wanted to use it in their political game and thought they could control it. This was what Granvelle and, eventually, Philip II also thought. Hence their attempts to split the league of seigneurs, especially by detaching Egmont from it and their refusal to summon the States General. Certainly, Granvelle's interpretation of Orange's policy in the early and mid 1560s is supported by what we know, much more unambiguously, about the prince's later

[37] For a detailed description of the careers and activities of these three persons see Lagomarsino, *Philip II and the Netherlands, cit.* Pt. II.

[38] Among many examples see Granvelle to Philip, 12 March 1562. Weiss, *Papiers d'Etat*, VI, p. 534, and 22 May 1563, *Ibid.* VII, p. 79.

[39] Rosenfeld, *Provincial Governors*, p. 54, especially n. 225.

policy. The constitutional arrangements which he made for the archduke Matthias in 1577 left effective power with himself and with the States General.[40] In order to dominate the States General Orange consistently built up a party of his own followers in the towns. He did so in Holland after 1572, for instance, by his appointment of Pieter Adriansz van der Werff as burgomaster of Leiden, even though van der Werff did not belong to a patrician family in that city.[41] Once civil war with Don John of Austria broke out, both sides systematically deposed opposing magistrates and had their own followers elected or they simply appointed them.[42]

Orange and Granvelle, then, had a very clear view of the nature of power in the Netherlands and their respective policies were entirely logical. But how successful were they in their attempts to control the towns? Evidently, much work remains to be done on this topic; but such evidence as there is suggests that neither the prince nor the cardinal were very successful. Thanks to the forthcoming book by Dr Guy Wells we know most about Antwerp.

Every spring, half of the city council of 18, the *schepenen*, were renewed, i.e. changed. They were chosen by the regent in her consulta with Viglius, Berlaymont and/or Noircarmes, the margrave of Antwerp and the chancellor of Brabant. The consulta chose from a list of nine candidates proposed by the city council and from another nine proposed by the *wijkmeesters* and *hooftmannen van de porterije*. These were the very respectable, propertied persons who made up the 'third member' of the *breede raad* of Antwerp. On no occasion did the regent impose a candidate from outside this group. Not even the duke of Alba did that. The council could make doubly sure of controlling its own renewal by putting forward unsuitable candidates, unknown and obviously unqualified men, or close relatives of actual councillors. This practice would further restrict the choice of the regent and her consulta.[43] Granvelle and Orange would each therefore be able to attract allies in the Antwerp magistrate. Jan van Schoonhoven, burgomaster in 1564–65, was a cardinalist and so was Hendrik van Berchem, a persecutor of heretics in districts under his private jurisdiction outside Antwerp. The banker van Straelen and the

[40] Cf. above, p. 73. I wish to thank Professor Swart for drawing my attention to some of the documentation supporting this point.

[41] J. C. H. de Pater, *Jan van Hout (1542–1609)*, (The Hague, 1946), p. 34. See also C. Hibben, *Gouda in Revolt* (Utrecht, 1983), pp. 72–76.

[42] C. H. Th. Bussemaker, *De Afscheiding der Waalsche Gewesten van de Generale Unie*, vol. I, (Haarlem, 1895), pp. 240–41. Gachard, *Extrait des Registres des Consaux de Tournay, 1472–1490, 1559–1572, 1580–81*, (Brussels, 1846), pp. 114–16.

[43] Wells, *Antwerp*, pp. 89–94. Strictly speaking, the whole council was changed, but half of the new one had to be selected from the membership of the old.

pensionary Wesenbeke, as is well known, were or came to be
Orangists. But neither Granvelle nor Orange could hope to pack the
Antwerp council with a majority of his own clients or even organise a
solid and reliable voting block. Some of the patrician families
deliberately kept contact with both sides. Much the same happened in
the French civil wars, and it happened probably in most early modern
politics, because preservation of the family and its property was
regarded as more important than the views or even the personal fate of
the family's individual members. The Antwerp council as a whole was
most anxious to avoid committing itself to either side. Its aim was to
preserve the city's privileges and independence, especially its
independent jurisdiction which assured foreign merchants their
personal safety in the city, and to escape too close a scrutiny of their
religious convictions. Such a policy was not the same as that of the
cardinal who wanted a much clearer stand on the placards and the
prosecution of heretics and who tried to get the city to accept the
establishment of the new bishopric of Antwerp, as well as supporting
the government over the *aides* demanded from the estates of Brabant.
The prince of Orange was therefore seen as a useful ally in the blocking
of policies which threatened the basis of Antwerp's trade and
prosperity. But he was also a dangerous ally; for the Antwerp
magistrates could not afford to antagonise the Brussels government and
the king because it relied on them to uphold its privileges and trade
treaties with foreign powers. Even the maintenance of law and order in
the city and the position of the city oligarchy depended in the last resort
on the support of the government. Fairly minor disturbances, such as
those of 1554, demonstrated the helplessness of the council in the face of
a popular movement and its need to rely on the government's soldiers
as a sanction of last resort.[44]

Other towns of the Netherlands may not have been as independent as
Antwerp. The methods of renewal of their magistrates varied, and so
did the influence which either the Brussels government or the
provincial governors could exert. In Hainault the governor and grand
bailli was held to control the renewal of the magistrates of the Hainault
towns.[45] The appointment of Berghes as governor therefore turned out
to be particularly unfortunate for the government.[46] In Flanders,
Egmont, as governor, shared the annual renewal with several other
noble commissioners and, no doubt, had the decisive voice.[47] The
governor of Holland was required to consult with the *schout* in each

[44] *Ibid.* pp. 233–36, 239–41 and *passim.*
[45] Rosenfeld, *Provincial Governors*, p. 23.
[46] Cf. above, p. 103.
[47] Archives Générales du Royaume, Brussels. *Papiers d'Etat et de l'Audience* MS 809³,
folders for 1561–1566. No folio numbers. Rosenfeld, *Provincial Governors*, p. 23.

town.[48] Orange, however, became notorious for his high-handed interference in the renewal of the magistrates.[49]

But for all their efforts, it does not look as if the seigneurs were very successful in making the city councils into their clients. When Granvelle had left the Netherlands, the seigneurs who now dominated the council of state found, just as Granvelle had foreseen, that they could still not persuade the cities to grant the *aides* which were essential to maintain the country's defence. As far as we can tell at present, the town councils remained remarkably impervious to the party-building efforts of either the Brussels government or of the provincial governors, at any rate until the outbreak of open civil war.[50] They pursued their own interests, including their religious preferences, which one could characterised for most of them as a non-persecuting catholicism, and they did not allow themselves to be integrated into the parties in the way this was happening in France.

This does not mean that the towns were not aware that the game was being played for very high stakes. This became apparent as early as 1562 over the question of the Biervleet tolls. Ghent had built a canal to the lower Scheldt estuary and petitioned the government for exemption from the tolls at Biervleet. It was a serious challenge to the commercial supremacy of Antwerp and Granvelle tried to use it deliberately to put pressure on the city to give up its opposition to the establishment of its bishopric. By brilliant diplomacy and great determination, especially on the part of Wesenbeke, Antwerp was able to block this challenge without surrendering in its opposition to the bishopric.[51] But in his dying weeks as Margaret's principal minister Granvelle returned to the charge. The occasion was the embargo on English imports, in November and December of 1563, when he advised the regent to pursue a hard line in order to bring pressure both on the English government and on Antwerp. The city lost its English trade to Emden, but also to Flanders, for the Flemish cloth industry received English semi-manufactured cloths via France, or even more simply from extensive smuggling.[52]

After the embargo lifted, the rivalry between Antwerp and Flanders persisted and now came to involve the great nobles. Egmont supported an attempt by Bruges to have the staple of the Merchant Adventurers moved to Bruges instead of back to Antwerp. The Antwerp council turned to Orange. Somewhat tardily, the prince gave his support. The city won this bout, for the regent was not willing to antagonise Antwerp even more. The city was still much too important for the

---

[48] *Ibid.* p. 24.
[49] *Ibid.* pp. 54–55.
[50] Cf. Wells, *Antwerp*, p. 237.
[51] *Ibid.* pp. 259–65.
[52] *Ibid.* pp. 275–85.

economy of the Netherlands and the finances of Philip's government. But the victory was not due to the prince's intervention, and the city knew it.[53]

Once the common enmity to Granvelle had disappeared, the league of seigneurs was showing evident signs of strain.[54] While they now dominated the council of state, they were not able to win control over government patronage. Apparently to everyone's surprise in Brussels, this control passed to Margaret's Spanish secretary, Armenteros. By the early summer of 1564, Viglius was complaining about it to Granvelle.[55] At the same time the provincial governors were still extending their powers in their provinces. 'Armenteros governs everything now', Viglius wrote to the cardinal in October. In Flanders, especially in Bruges, he continued, there was great opposition to the inquisitor Titelmans. The magistrates of the cities were still ready to maintain the law, but they could no longer be relied upon because 'the authority of the governors, with the connivance of Her Highness (i.e. Margaret), increases so much that everyone seeks to please them or at least not to displease them'.[56]

In these circumstances it was quite logical that the seigneurs' next move was to try to subordinate the council of finance and the privy council to the council of state. If they could achieve this, they would have outflanked both Armenteros and Viglius with the other friends of Granvelle who still remained in the government of the Netherlands. In this move Orange, Egmont and Berghes were united, although we simply do not know whether their ultimate political aims were identical. But more crucial even than this question is another: would their political victory have been enough, or rather, would it have produced a reasonably stable situation?

The struggle between Orange and Granvelle and their respective allies had been a struggle for power within a given political context. Neither side had had any intention of breaking this context or of breaking out of it. The ultimate sovereignty of the king (however this ambiguous term

---

[53] *Ibid.* pp. 299–303.

[54] E.g. Morillon to Granvelle, 1 April 1564. Weiss, *Papiers d'Etat*, VII, p. 452. 'Le conte d'Egmont et le prince d'Orenges se caressent, touttefois l'on s'apperceoit que c'est simulation . . . Les femmes ne se cèdent en rien, et se tiegnent par le bras, incedentes pari passu; et si l'on rencontre une porte estroicte, l'on se serre également ensemble, afin qu'il n'y ayt du devant ou derrièrre . . .' This characteristic comic opera aspect of Netherlands politics before the storm – there are similar scenes in Mozart's *Le nozze di Figaro* and in Verdi's *Falstaff* – had already flowered luxuriously in the grotesque manoeuvres of the courts of Madrid and Brussels to arrange the resignation/dismissal of Granvelle. See Van Durme, *Antoon Perrenot*, pp. 207–18.

[55] Viglius to Granvelle, 12 June 1564. G. Groen van Prinsterer, *Archives ou Correspondance Inédite de la Maison d'Orange-Nassau*, ser. 1, vol. 1, 2nd ed. (Leiden, 1841), pp. 263–65.

[56] *Ibid.* pp. 317–19.

might have been interpreted at the time) had not been called into question, nor had the maintenance of the Catholic religion. Unlike Condé and Coligny, none of the great lords of the Netherlands had proclaimed himself a leader of a Calvinist movement. Their opposition to the new bishoprics and the inquisition was political and emotional but not religious. The Brabantine abbots and the city councils all over the Netherlands who were in the forefront of this opposition were defending their property, their legal rights and their political autonomy. On the other side, Granvelle was certainly worried about the spread of heresy. But he saw the fight against it in terms of political power – and that, precisely, was his quarrel with Orange. 'It is laughable', he wrote to Gonzalo Pérez in 1563, 'to send us depositions made before the inquisitors in Spain so that we should look for heretics here: as if there were not thousands professing heresy to whom we dare not say anything.'[57]

Yet while the contestants accepted the context of the struggle, this context was not stable. Forces which neither Granvelle nor Orange could control broke in on the struggle, swept the contestants aside and radically altered its terms. Both Orange and, much later, Granvelle, managed eventually to return to the struggle, but only after they had accepted the new terms. The forces over which, in the mid-1560s, they had no control were of course the spread of the Protestant movement and Philip II's reaction to this movement. The history of Protestantism in the Netherlands, the formation of the Compromise, the hedge preaching, the conventicles, the image breaking, the alliance between Calvinist nobles and burghers and the formation of the *gueux* as a fighting force – all these are well known, and I will not rehearse them here. The king's policy, however, requires a brief account. Inevitably, this account owes a great debt to the still unpublished work of David Lagomarsino and María Rodríguez-Salgado who, between them and without always agreeing with each other, provide the most detailed and best-documented analysis of the politics of the Spanish court.

The key to an understanding of Philip II's policy is his view of the nature of his empire and of his own position as its ruler. Charles V had failed to have Philip succeed him as emperor, yet Philip thought of his dominions essentially in imperial terms, just as his father had done. He was the ruler of each of them, reigning over them not as king of Spain but as their own prince and by virtue of their own laws of succession. He had sworn to uphold their rights and privileges. If at times he chose to overrule certain of these rights and privileges, it was only in order to defend even greater rights of his subjects: to live under his, Philip's, rule, to which God had entrusted them, and to live within the true Catholic faith, without being led astray from their salvation. Of both

---

[57] 17 June 1563. Weiss, *Papiers d'Etat*, VII, p. 106.

these rights he himself, and no one else, was the judge.[58] When he was still in the Netherlands, after the emperor's abdication, he ruthlessley exploited the financial resources of Castile to carry on the war with France from the Netherlands. The emperor himself, both from Brussels and, later, from Yuste, fully supported and even increased this pressure on Spain.[59] There is every reason to take seriously Philip's *cri de coeur* to Emmanuel Philibert, his regent of the Netherlands, in 1557.

Although I have ordered that my cities in Spain be sold for the defence of the Netherlands (and although I understand very well that they don't believe this), there is nobody in Spain who has got the money to buy these cities, for the whole kingdom is so poor, much poorer than the Netherlands . . . I for my part am doing what I can and will risk my person for them and join the army which is to defend these states and I will give them all the money I have . . . And for all this they thank me here by saying or thinking that I care nothing for them and that I prefer an inch of Spanish earth to a hundred leagues here. All this I cannot but feel strongly and grieve much over it, for it is so much without cause . . .[60]

Yet this hostility which Philip recognised was unavoidable. The supranational policy which the king pursued by force of his inheritance was never likely to be acceptable to subjects who had to pay for it, especially when the king was not among them to distribute royal patronage and personally supervise the administration of their country. England, Scotland and France all experienced deadly faction fights for control of patronage and power during royal minorities and regency governments. All of Philip's dominions, except the one in which he himself resided, were permanently in the position of needing regency governments. In 1559, when Philip had been absent from Spain for six

---

[58] See for instance Philip's reply to a petition of the estates of Brabant, in 1562, against the incorporation of the abbeys in the new bishoprics. The king maintained that, in case of a doubtful interpretation of the *joyeuse entrée*, the decision could not rest with the estates. They should 'plustost considérer et interpréter qu'il n'y ait privilège, quelque fort qu'il soit, qui ne deût cesser pour tel bien que le présent, *cum summa sit ratio quae pro religione facit et salus populi suprema lex est*'. Gachard, *Correspondance de Marguerite d'Autriche*, vo. 2, p. 143.

[59] Rodríguez-Salgado, *Spanish Regent to European Ruler*, ch. 5.

[60] Philip to Savoy, London, 27 May 1557. Archives Générales du Royaume, *Les Archives et les Bibliothèques d'Italie*, vol. 1, *Manuscrits divers 1172*, fo. 225–27. '. . . y aunque he mandado que, para defender esos Estados, porque los tengo en mucho (aunque entiendo muy bien que no lo creen así) me vendan las ciudades que tengo en Espanã, no se halla nadie que tenga dinero, porque todo el Reyno está pobre y harto mas qu'esos Estados . . . yo, de mi parte, lo que puedo hago, qu'es poner con ellos my persona y juntar el exercito, y traer para defension d'esos Estados un todo quanto dinero tengo . . . y esto agrandezánmelo ay de manera que dirán ó pensarán que no los tengo en nada y que quiero mas un palmo de tierra en España que ay cien leguas. Todo esto no puedo dejar de sentirlo mucho y dolerme mucho dello, siendo tan sin causa . . .' Gachard's copy of the original in Turin. Partly quoted in Verhofstad, *De regering*, p. 113, n. 90.

years, that country, too, was on the brink of rebellion. The one point
on which nearly everyone agreed during the 1560s was the need for the
king's return to the Netherlands to solve its problems. The question
was how this could be done. Spain was beset by mortal enemies in the
Mediterranean, enemies who could, or so it was believed, count on the
support of a 'fifth column', the Moriscos in southern and eastern Spain.
In the event, Spain was plunged into civil war, the revolt of the
Moriscos, before the most serious stages of the civil war in the
Netherlands had even begun. Moreover, the regent whom Philip
would have had to leave in Spain, the Infante Don Carlos, was showing
progressively more alarming signs of mental instability. Yet there was
no obviously acceptable alternative to Carlos.

Perhaps a much greater integration of the different parts of Philip's
empire would have resolved at least some of his problems. Granvelle, at
least, seems to have thought so. Quite consistently with his view of the
nature of politics, he urged the king to internationalise his patronage
and give *encomiendas* of the Spanish orders of knighthood to
Netherlanders; for then they would have to support the country from
which they were deriving their income, and their relatives and clients
would be won over with them. Even if only two or three Brabanters
were honoured in this way, the cardinal assured the king, 25,000 would
support him the more willingly in hope of similar advancement. In
Italy, too, some high positions in government or in the military or
naval establishment should be given to some of the principal
Netherlands seigneurs who had shown their prowess in these fields.
Orange himself, for instance, 'would not serve badly (as viceroy) in
Sicily, for he would then be far from Germany and perhaps live with
greater contentment.'[61]

It was an astonishing proposal, coming as it did in March 1563, at the
very height of the cardinal's quarrel with the prince. Granvelle was
certainly quite serious about his idea, for he came back to it in a later
letter,[62] and I do not think he proposed it only to get his most
dangerous opponent out of the Netherlands. Philip also took the
suggestion seriously, but could not see it in the same way. As to the
*encomiendas*, he replied, they were given only to persons who took the
habit (i.e. religious vows) and many did this only to get an *encomienda*.
Besides, there were so many people in Spain who served him and
whom he could not reward except with money, which he needed for
other purposes, or with *encomiendas*; and those who did not get one
became disgruntled. Still, he was considering one for Gosuin de Varick,
governor of Diest, who may have been connected with Orange. As to
positions in Italy, there were very few, mainly viceroyalties. For these,
because of the importance of religion, it was necessary to find someone

---

[61] Granvelle to Philip, 10 March 1563, Weiss, *Papiers d'Etat*, VII pp. 53–55.
[62] Granvelle to Philip, 13 June 1563. *Ibid.*, pp. 156–57.

about whom one could feel absolutely safe, not only about his own religious beliefs but about the way he handled such beliefs. With the prince of Orange one just could not know whether it would work out in the way Granvelle suggested.[63]

Here indeed was the heart of the matter. It was the unreliability of the civil authorities, both of the cities and of the provincial governors, in dealing with heresy which, as Dr. Rodríguez-Salgado has convincingly argued, made the maintenance of the inquisition and the enforcement of the placards in the Netherlands a matter on which Philip would never give way. In Naples and Milan, and even in Galicia in Spain, the civil authorities could be relied upon to the extent that the introduction of the inquisition could be given up in the face of local opposition, or at least postponed indefinitely.[64]

The exchange between Philip and Granvelle showed the central ambiguity at the core of Philip's empire: here was a king who could speak only Spanish fluently, who lived in Spain, who surrounded himself with Spanish advisers and who, for seemingly good reasons, was reluctant to extend his imperial patronage to all his subjects. It did not matter that all his dominions, just as all countries of Europe in the sixteenth century, bitterly resented having non-natives appointed to 'their' offices and that hardly anyone really wanted to have a truly imperial, international administration. The provinces of the Netherlands were notorious sticklers on this point, even against each other. It did not matter that, in fact, very few Spaniards were appointed in the Netherlands and not many more in Italy. It did not matter that Philip's imperial policies, and not least his policies in the Netherlands, often ran counter to the interests of his Spanish subjects. The overwhelming impression which Philip gave to his contemporaries was that he was a Spanish king, ruling a Spanish empire in the interests of the Spaniards.

Nowhere was this clearer than in Philip's policy towards France. When the first civil war broke out, in the early summer of 1562, Philip wanted to support the Catholics. The Netherlands, however, refused to cooperate in a policy of intervention. Granvelle and Margaret of Parma counselled against it. The Order of the Golden Fleece voted unanimously against any military action in France.[65] Philip felt this attitude to be both humiliating towards himself and desperately dangerous for the Netherlands. The reports from Chantonnay, Granvelle's brother and Philip's ambassador in France, became more and more alarming. Thus in January 1563 Chantonnay wrote of talk among members of the French royal council, of how, now that heresy had gained a foothold in France, the Netherlands were ripe to fall. They were disenchanted with the

[63] Philip to Granvelle, 13 June 1563. *Ibid.*, pp. 85–89.
[64] Rodríguez-Salgado, *Spanish Regent to European Ruler*, pp. 481 ff.
[65] Viglius, *Mémoires*, ed. A. Wauters, (Brussels, 1862), pp. 46–47. Gachard, 'La chute', p. 109.

Spaniards and would choose either the king of Bohemia as their ruler or, because Maximilian might not be strong enough to defend them, the king of France himself. Philip would be quite unable to mount a diversionary attack from Italy or from Spain. Once the Netherlands had fallen and its warships had joined with those of France, England could not be held and then Spanish commerce with the Indies could no longer be protected. The duke of Savoy would then no longer be able to deny passage to French troops into Italy and the Milanese would be pleased to throw off the burden of Spanish rule. In all this the French would undoubtedly get help from the Turkish fleet and from the Moors.[66]

No doubt, the French councillors, 'important persons but not principal ones', as Chantonnay characterised them,[67] were whistling in the dark to keep up their courage in the middle of a civil war, or perhaps they were just trying to frighten Philip's ambassador. If so, they were more successful than they could have hoped. Chantonnay reported their views in the classic form of a domino theory where one future disaster inexorably leads to another. But, for all the usual implausibilities of this theory, there were sufficient reasons for Madrid not to take the threat lightly. Philip had distrusted Maximilian ever since his cousin had edged him out of the succession to the Holy Roman Empire. Maximilian was known to have ambitions in the Netherlands and, when one thinks of the later venture by his son, the archduke Matthias, such ambitions were far from impossible. Moreover Alba, to whom Chantonnay addressed his letter, had himself in earlier years argued that the Netherlands were strategically very difficult to defend, especially without the presence of their prince. Philip knew all about this argument. He had himself summarised it for his father in 1544 when Charles V was wondering whether to give the Netherlands or Milan as a dowry for a Habsburg princess marrying the second son of Francis I.[68] Finally, both Charles V's earlier experience and the ineffectiveness of the mismanaged Spanish intervention from Milan in the French civil war underlined the point made by the French councillors about the invulnerability of France from attacks mounted from Italy or from Spain. Without troops in the Netherlands that were under his complete control, which the *bandes d'ordonnance* clearly were not, Philip could neither pursue a credible great-power policy in northwestern Europe nor even assure the safety of a dominion for which he regarded himself just as much responsible as for

---

[66] Chantonnay to Alba, Paris, 16 Jan. 1563. *Archivo Documental Español*, publ. R. Academia de la Historia, V, *Negociaciones con Francia (1563)*, (Madrid, 1952), pp. 33–36.

[67] 'Personas principales, no de los mayores que de los que entran en consejo . . .' *Ibid.*, p. 33.

[68] Philip to Charles V. Valladolid, 13 Jan. 1544. M. Fernández Alvarez, ed., *Corpus Documental de Carlos V*, vol II, (Salamanca, 1975), pp. 306–9. F. Chabod, '¿Milan o las Paises Bajos? Las Discusiones en España sobre la "alternativa" de 1544'. *Carlos V (1500–1558). Homenaje de la Universidad de Granada*, (Granada, 1958), pp. 367–70.

Spain. There was no alternative to co-operation with the Netherlands nobility.[69]

The first implication of the full realisation of this fact was the necessity of throwing Granvelle to the wolves. It is quite likely, as Professor Lagomarsino has argued with a convincing wealth of documentation, that the cardinal's enemies at court, Secretary Eraso and the Eboli parti, egged on by the personal enmity of Simon Renard and the fanaticism of Fray Villavicencio, would in any case have won this round against Granvelle's supporters, Alba and Gonzalo Pérez. They certainly organised the political mechanics of Granvelle's recall from the Netherlands.[70] Yet Philip's action in this case was very much part of a pattern of political behaviour which he followed consistently whenever one of his ministers, viceroys or governors ran up against local opposition that seemed for the moment insuperable. So it was with Margaret of Parma and, later, with her son, Alexander Farnese, with the marquis of Mondéjar in Andalucia, with Antonio Pérez and with the duke of Alba himself. With the viceroys of Sicily the practice became a regular system. Machiavelli had recommended making a show of sacrificing unpopular ministers.[71] In fact it was difficult to avoid doing this where an early modern ruler had to rely on the co-operation of a local elite. The almost universal contemporary lament of the fickleness of princes had much justification, for such fickleness was built into the system of early modern government.

Granvelle had faithfully carried out Philip's policy in the Netherlands. In the process he had become unacceptable to a large section of the local elite. As a result, the country was left virtually undefended against both military and religious attack. There was no way – and here I am again following Dr Rodríguez-Salgado's argument – in which Philip could have continued Granvelle in office. Failing his own return to the

[69] Here I am following Dr Rodríguez-Salgado's interpretation, *From Spanish Regent to European Ruler*, pp. 449 ff and *passim*.

[70] Lagomarsino, *Philip II and the Netherlands*, pt. II.

[71] N. Macchiavelli, *Il principe*, cap. VII. 'E perchè conosceva le rigorosità passate avergli generato qualque odio, per purgare gli animi di quelli popoli, e guadagnarseli in tutto, volle mostrare che se crudeltà alcuna era seguita, non era nata da lui (i.e. Cesare Borgia), ma dall'acerba natura del ministro (i.e. Ramiro d'Orco). E preso sopra questo occasione, lo fece una mattina mettere a Cesena in duo pezzi in su la piazza con un pesso di legno e un coltello sanguinoso a canto. La ferocità del quale spettacolo fece quelli popoli in un tempo rimanere soddisfatti e stupidi'. 'And because he knew that the past cruelties had occasioned some hatred towards himself, and in order to purge the minds of the people of this notion and win them over to himself, he wanted to show that, if there had been any cruelty, it had not come from him (i.e. Cesare Borgia) but from the harshness of his minister (i.e. Ramiro d'Orco). Acting on this conclusion, he had him cut into two pieces and, one morning, placed in the piazza of Cesena, with a piece of wood and a bloodstained knife next to him. The savage spectacle left people at once satisfied and stunned'. With Philip II's ministers the cutting in pieces usually applied to their careers rather than their bodies, although Juan de Escobedo might not have thought so if his assassins had left him any time to reflect on his fate.

Netherlands, he had to come to some sort of terms with those who commanded the local defence forces, the *bandes d'ordonnance*. Since Orange and his friends had always proclaimed their loyalty, both to himself and to the Catholic religion, the king had to hope that this alliance would still maintain his ultimate authority, and that the struggle against heresy would, at least, not be further weakened.

It was a forlorn hope. Psychologically and politically the aims of the players in this game were too contradictory to make genuine cooperation possible. The tragi-comedy of mutual misunderstanding during Egmont's visit to Madrid shows that this fact was not immediately clear to most of the participants but that, on the contrary, there was quite a lot of mutual good will. One may well suspect, however, that Orange at least saw the situation more clearly and was not very surprised by the outcome. The immediate result was stasis, a seizing-up of the political process and a virtual standstill of the administrative machine. Again, this was an inbuilt hazard of early modern regimes, and Philip II's empire, with its geographically separate entities and its ethnic and religious tensions, was particularly prone to it. In Sicily, for instance, stasis was practically a permanent condition; for in the island the viceroy and the civil courts, on the one side, and on the other the Spanish inquisition allied with the proto-Mafia of disgruntled nobles and bandits held each other in an immovable balance. Philip reacted by changing the viceroys every three or six years and otherwise making soothing noises to both sides. Neither party, nor anyone else in Sicily, threatened his sovereign authority or the Catholic religion.[72]

In Spain and in the Netherlands, however, such masterly inactivity was in the long run not possible. In Andalucia stasis developed from the conflicting claims and manoeuvres of the inquisition, the *audiencia*, i.e. the supreme civil court of the province, the archbishop of Granada, his hostile cathedral chapter and the governor of the province, the marquis of Mondéjar. All this manoeuvring took place at the expense of the Morisco population and against the background of Moorish raids across the Straits from North Africa. Philip, anxious both over defence and over the apparent resurgence of Islam among the nominally Christian Moriscos, backed the hard-line religious policy of Cardinal Espinosa against Mondéjar, the *de facto* protector of the Moriscos. To satisfy local interest groups, as well as his personal enemies at court, the king relieved Mondéjar of his responsibilities for the Moriscos and for internal security. The result was an explosion, the rising of the Moriscos against the paralysed civil and military authorities,[73] followed by more than two years of civil war, then the dispersal and, finally, in the early seventeenth century, the expulsion of the Moriscos.

[72] H. G. Koenigsberger, *The Practice of Empire*, (Ithaca, 1969), pp. 161–70.
[73] Cf. K. Garrad, *The Causes of the Second Rebellion of the Alpujarras (1568–71)*, Cambridge Ph.D. thesis.

In the Netherlands stasis overtook the regime when, year after year, the estates of Brabant refused to pay the aide for defence which the government had asked for in 1558; when the provincial governors and the city councils blocked the government's religious policy; and when the noble members of the council of state boycotted that body. Then, just as in Andalucia, the dismissal of the principal minister did not succeed in setting the government machinery in motion again. Here, too, the king's initiative in religious policy then triggered the reaction of forces outside the parties of the political and administrative elites, forces which the stasis had allowed to gather strength. They came into the open in the Compromise, the image breaking and the military actions of the armed *gueux*. This was the tragedy of Philip II's empire. For William of Orange it was an opportunity which he had helped to create but which he had not intended and whose nature became clear to him only with time. If for him the story in the end also turned to tragedy, it was at least a tragedy followed by catharsis: the foundation of a new, independent state, the United Provinces of the Netherlands.

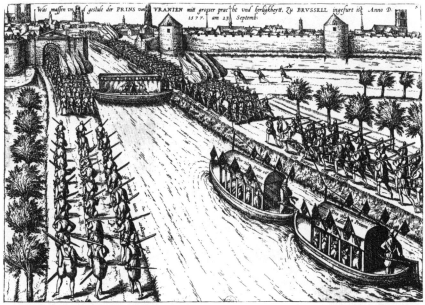

4. Triumphal entry of William of Orange into Brussels, 23 September, 1577. Engraving by Frans Hogenberg.

5. Philip IV of Spain
   Velázquez. *National Gallery*

# 6

# National Consciousness in Early Modern Spain

On September 1, 1947, I was one of a huge crowd assembled in the main square of Salamanca to celebrate the fiesta of the Virgin of the Vega. The medieval silver image of the virgin was carried in solemn procession from the cathedral to the *ayuntamiento*, the town hall, and then a priest preached a sermon for the crowd. Spain, he said, was eternal. Spain had existed long before the national revival of the *caudillo*, Generalissimo Franco. It had existed under the Bourbons and the Habsburgs and before the union of Aragon and Castile by the Catholic Kings, Ferdinand and Isabella. It had existed at the time of the Visigoths and of the Romans and of Tubal (a descendant of Cain and the first to settle in Spain); and it had existed even before that, before the creation of the world itself, in the mind of God.

This proud vision of Spain as a splendid Platonic idea lies at the base of a long tradition of Spanish literature and historiography, and it is closely connected with a favourite theme of Spanish writers, the nature of *hispanidad*, i.e. the essence of Spanishness. Its earliest form was the *laudes Hispaniae* of Orosius in the fifth century and of Saint Isidore of Seville in the seventh, in which Spain is celebrated as the richest, fairest, happiest land, and the cradle of the most valiant heroes and princes[1] – just as a dozen other European countries were similarly celebrated, following a well known classical genre.

With some gaps, this tradition continued through the late Middle Ages. Thus the thirteenth-century canon lawyer, Vincentius Hispanus, countered German claims to the empire by recalling the successful Spanish resistance to Charlemagne's invasion and the slaying of twelve of his paladins. Vincentius clinched a long argument by exclaiming:

Who indeed, Spain, can reckon thy glories? Spain, wealthy in horses, celebrated for food, and shining with gold; steadfast and wise, the envy of all; and skilled in the law and standing high on sublime pillars.[2]

---

[1] R. Menéndez Pidal, *The Spaniards in their History*, trans. W. Starkie (New York, 1966), p. 80.

[2] Quoted in G. Post, 'Two Notes on Nationalism in the Middle Ages', *Traditio*, Vol. 9 (1953), p. 307. See also '"Blessed Lady Spain" – Vincentius Hispanus and Spanish National Imperialism in the Thirteenth Century', *Speculum*, Vol. 29 (1954), pp. 198–209.

In the early-modern period, the style of such *laudes* became more sophisticated but the arguments remained essentially the same. The poet Quevedo, in the early seventeenth century, is not only roused to patriotic fury by the attacks of Joseph Scaliger ('a man of good letters but bad religion') on the Hispano-Roman authors, Quintilian, Lucan, and Seneca,[3] and by the geographer Mercator's deprecatory remarks on the Spanish language,[4] but he praises Spain in the traditional form of the *laudes*:

. . . there is no doubt that Spain, with its temperate climate and its serene sky produces similar effects in [our] humours and dispositions; for it is clear that neither does the cold make us phlegmatic and dull, like the Germans, nor does great heat make us incapable of working, like the Negroes and Indians; for, the one quality being tempered by the other, it produces well-chastened customs.[5]

In Spain, Quevedo continues, there is natural loyalty to the princes, a religious obedience to the laws, and love for generals and captains.[6]

More than three hundred years later, the distinguished twentieth-century writer and scholar, Menéndez Pidal, was still making essentially the same point:

Due to this instinctive influence of Seneca [i.e. of Stoicism], the Spaniard can as readily endure privations as he can withstand the disturbing temptations to greed and self-indulgence, for his innate soberness inclines him towards a certain ethical austerity. This shows itself in the general tenor of his life, with its simplicity, dignity . . . and strong family ties. The Spanish people preserve deep natural qualities unimpaired . . . whereas other races which are more tainted by the luxuries of civilization find themselves constantly threatened by a process of wear and tear which saps their strength.[7]

Since the Middle Ages and the long, drawn-out struggle with the Moors for the control of the Iberian Peninsula, there was a strong religious component to Spanish patriotism. Santiago Matamoros, also known as the apostle St. James and 'the Moor slayer', was the patron saint of the surviving Christians who fought the Moslems from their mountain kingdoms in Asturias, in northern Spain. They called themselves simply Christians; the word *español*, a Spaniard (though not the geographical term Spain) was a thirteenth-century importation from Provence, a convenient appellation invented by foreigners who

[3] F. de Quevedo y Villegas, 'España defendida y los tiempos de ahora' (1609), *Obras completas*, Vol. 1 (Madrid, 1961), p. 489.

[4] *Ibid.*, p. 502.

[5] *Ibid.*, p. 521.

[6] *Ibid.* N.b. Quevedo writes, 'Es natural de España la lealdad . . . ' not 'para los españoles', as one would expect in a more modern writer.

[7] Menéndez Pidal, *The Spaniards*, p. 18.

were also Christians, and only slowly adopted by the Spaniards themselves.[8]

It is almost impossible to overemphasize this religious component in the Spanish concept of nationalism, for one might almost say that it alone provided the moral justification for patriotism. Quevedo clearly felt that it is only God who gives victories and that sin brings defeat and ruin in its train.[9]

We were His militia at Navas de Tolosa [the great Christian victory over the Moors in 1212]. It was God's skill that won in the Cid and the same used Gama, Pacheco and Albuquerque as instruments in the East Indies to deprive the idols of peace. Who but God . . . upheld Cortés so that he might achieve famous deeds of daring whose prize was a whole New World. It was God's voice, which is obeyed by all things, by which Ximénez de Cisneros held back the night in the battle of Oran . . .[10]

Cervantes, the volunteer who was wounded in the battle of Lepanto, thought in similar terms. In the *Exemplary Novels* Spaniards are occasionally mentioned as Spaniards, to distinguish them from Italians or Frenchmen or anyone else. But praiseworthy deeds derived mainly from Christian behaviour, not from the fact of Spanish nationality. In *The Spanish Lady*, for instance, Englishmen are praised for their patriotic and chivalrous behaviour; but the hero of the story is an English Catholic who, with his family, is described as Christian, in contrast to the rest of the English, including their queen, who, as Protestants, presumably could not be regarded as true Christians at all.

Perhaps the finest Spanish literary example of an essentially religious view of patriotism is Calderón's *El Príncipe Constante*. In this play the Infante Don Fernando of Portugal is taken prisoner in battle by the Moorish king of Fez. He is treated chivalrously, and eventually, his nephew, the king of Portugal, makes an agreement to redeem him by giving up Ceuta, which the Portuguese had captured some time before. The prince however refuses to allow the Christians to give up a city over which the cross had stood. All the ill treatment now inflicted on him by the Moors cannot make him change his mind. He dies, but his glorified spirit leads the Christian armies to victory. Calderón speaks highly of Portuguese valor – the crown was worn by the king of Spain when he wrote – but so he does of the valor and chivalry of some of the Moors. The point at issue is, in fact, not national interest nor national honour; it is the cross versus the crescent.

One hundred and thirty years after Calderón wrote *El Príncipe Constante* (1629), Lessing wrote a short classical play, *Philotas*, on a

---

[8] A. Castro, *The Spaniards: An Introduction to Their History*, trans. W. F. King and S. Margaretten (Berkeley, Los Angeles, London, 1971), pp. 10ff.

[9] Quevedo, 'Politica de Dios y Gobiernno de Cristo', *Obras completas*, Vol. 1, p. 683.

[10] Quevedo, 'España defendida', pp. 523ff.

similar theme (1759). Both the similarities and the differences between the two plays are very revealing for the understanding of the concept of nationalism. In Lessing's play, Philotas, a very young prince is taken prisoner by the enemy in the very first skirmish in which he is allowed to participate. Just as Fernando, he is treated chivalrously; and he is told that the son of the king who captured him was also taken prisoner in the same skirmish. The two kings would now exchange their prisoners and make peace. Philotas' country would lose nothing because of his rash action in getting himself captured. Or so it is presented to Philotas. But he snatches up a sword and kills himself so as to give his country the advantage of holding the enemy prince prisoner without having to redeem their own prince. In this play religion is not a factor at all. Philotas talks only of the interest of his father and his country, and he sees this interest in the most stark terms of territorial aggrandizement and glory. He does not discuss any justification of the war, though he takes it for granted that his country is right and the enemy wrong.

The contrast between religious motivation and pure nationalism could hardly be clearer. Calderón undoubtedly accepted Prince Fernando's conduct and motivation as wholly admirable, though the play, written in the middle of the Thirty Years' War, may well have been intended to contain at least an implied criticism of war between Christians. Lessing, writing in the middle of the Seven Years' War, felt much more sceptical about his hero and his motivation, which he can make believable only by constantly stressing his youth or, perhaps, juvenility. The curtain line of the play is spoken by the king whose prisoner Philotas had been and who decides to abdicate: 'In vain we have shed rivers of blood; in vain conquered provinces . . . Do you not think that one can become sick of being king?' If Lessing's play represents nationalism in its purest form, it is also a devastating indictment of its futility and moral emptiness.

According to most writers on the subject of Spanish national feeling, either during the early-modern period or since, the Spaniards avoided this futility precisely because of the religious content of their patriotic emotions. But such a view assumed that Spaniards, properly speaking, were always Christians and Catholics. It is the great merit of the work of the late Americo Castro to have insisted that this is not a tenable assumption. Spanish national consciousness and *hispanidad*, as he pointed out, so far from existing *ab initio* as a Platonic idea, were rather the strictly historical results of the interaction of Christian, Moslem, and Jewish peoples and traditions in the Iberian Peninsula.[11] The characteristically Spanish identification of the state or nation with religion, Castro claimed, 'is a Judeo–Islamic characteristic of Oriental,

---

[11] Americo Castro, *España en su Historia: Cristianos, Moros y Judios* (Buenos Aires, 1948), with subsequent Spanish and English editions. The last is *The Spaniards*, trans. King, *passim*.

not Occidental, civilization'.[12] The first part of this statement, that identification of the nation with religion is a Judeo–Islamic characteristic, is evidently true, and it may well be that this tradition influenced Christian Spain. But it is not true, as Castro was driven to maintain, that other occidental nations, during their formative centuries, in the Middle Ages and the early-modern period, did not identify themselves in religious terms. The French and the French monarchy certainly did.[13] It was a question of degree and of circumstances. Most European states had to assert themselves against other Christian states and hence could not easily identify their cause with that of religion; but they certainly tried to do so when they had the opportunity. Only Spain, however, was a multiracial and multireligious country, which considerably influenced the development of self-identification.[14]

But the problem is more complicated. The Jews not only influenced Christian Spanish customs and attitudes, but the great majority of them were actually absorbed into Christian Spain, a process which certainly left its traces. Since Castro first pointed to the enormously important role of the converted Jews (the *conversos*, sometimes derogatorily called *marranos*) in the literary, theological, legal, and medical life of Spain, the hunt for a *converso* ancestry of the great names of the Spanish Golden Age has become an astonishingly popular and successful sport of historians.[15]

Most of the *conversos*, and even a great many of the Spanish Jews before their expulsion in 1492, thought of themselves as Spaniards. Castro quotes a speech by Don Alonso de Cartagena at the Council of Bâle in 1434. Cartagena, a *converso* who had attained to the position of bishop of Burgos, argued for the right of precedence of Castile over England because:

Spaniards are not wont to prize great wealth, but rather virtue; nor do they measure a man's honour by the store of his money but rather by the quality of his beautiful deeds; wherefore riches are not to be argued in this matter (as the English argued them); for if we should mete out precedences according to riches, Cosimo de' Medici, or some other very rich merchant, mayhap would come before some duke.[16]

But such sentiments hardly marked Spaniards as off 'by an abyss' from the rest of the European nobility, as Castro thought.[17] Cartagena's

---

[12] Castro, *The Spaniards*, p. 15.

[13] J. R. Strayer, 'France: The Holy Land, the Chosen People and the Most Christian King', *Action and Conviction in Early Modern Europe*, ed. T. K. Rabb and J. E. Seigel (Princeton, 1969).

[14] It is possible that a rather similar phenomenon occurred in Russia during the time of the Tatar domination.

[15] See A. Domínguez Ortiz, *Los Judeoconversos en España y América* (Madrid, 1971) and bibliographical indications contained therein.

[16] Castro, *Spaniards*, p. 150.          [17] *Ibid.*, p. 151.

were only a somewhat extreme statement of quite common European aristocratic sentiments. Even Henry IV of France would still refer to Marie de Medici as 'ma grosse banquière', even though by that time the Medici had provided two popes and had become grand dukes. And, of course, he had married her, just as the Castilian aristocrats of Alonso de Cartagena's time had married rich Jewish and *converso* women.

But if the *conversos* thought of themselves as Castilians or Spaniards, as Cartagena evidently did, the great mass of the population, and especially the lower classes, did not accept such an identification at all. They prided themselves on their *limpieza*, their purity of blood, and their descent from Old Christians, untainted by Jewish blood or, later, by the suspicion of heresy. In 1449 there were riots in Toledo against a new tax imposed by the constable of Castile, Alvaro de Luna. The riots turned into pogroms against Jews and *conversos* who were held to be the instigators of the new tax, and the rioters proclaimed a statute requiring purity of blood for holders of all public or private offices in Toledo.[18] From the middle of the sixteenth century, such statutes became common, especially in ecclesiastical institutions.

There was undoubteldy a considerable area in which the emphasis on *limpieza* overlapped with national sentiment in the minds of Spaniards. Nevertheless, the mania for purity of blood, with its strong anti-aristocratic overtones (for it was mainly the upper classes who had intermarried with Jews and *conversos*) was both a restrictive and a divisive force in Spanish society. The Count-Duke Olivares, first minister of Philip IV and a most ardent proponent of the greatness of Castile, certainly interpreted these emotions in this way, largely because he, too, like most of the Spanish high nobility and indeed the royal house itself, had *converso* ancestors.[19]

I have so far attempted to approach the problem of Spanish national sentiment by following the methodology of both the traditional writers of the *laudes Hispaniae*, from St. Isidore to Menéndez Pidal, and also of Americo Castro and his school. They tell us a great deal about Spanish history that is both true and perceptive, even if one does not always agree with their conclusions. There is, however, a fundamental limitation to this approach. By concentrating on a particular tradition, whether as a static characteristic of a national mentality, or as an evolutionary phenomenon, these writers have not accounted for large areas of human emotions and motivations which do not fit easily into the traditions and patterns they describe, regardless of the rich and varied ways in which they have conceived of their patterns. In other

[18] A. A. Sicroff, *Les controverses des statuts de 'pureté de sang' en Espagne du XV^e au XVII^e siècle* (Pris, 1960), pp. 32ff.

[19] J. H. Elliott, 'The Statecraft of Olivares', *The Diversity of History*, ed. J. H. Elliott and H. G. Koenigsberger (London and Ithaca, 1970), pp. 134ff.

words, one can always find instances, and very important ones at that, where the pattern does not fit.

Take the case of the conquistadors in the New World. Here is Menéndez Pidal's characterization:

It is . . . a natural trait in the Spaniard not to allow any calculation of gains and losses to prevail over considerations of another order. Columbus, a foreigner by birth, instead of allowing himself to be carried away by enthusiasm for his enterprise, kept postponing it while he negotiated interminably, and refused to risk the venture until he had secured for himself a dazzling series of profits and rewards. Whereas a host of Spanish explorers, despising material advantage, engaged in perilous exploits for the simple love of adventure, or with only problematic hopes of gain.[20]

Such an interpretation of national attitudes and motives reads strangely in the light of the actual history of the conquests of Mexico and Peru and even of the express views of many of the conquistadors themselves.[21] 'We came here to serve God and also to get rich'. wrote Bernal Diaz, the chronicler of Cortés' expedition.[22] Pizarro, the conqueror of Peru, put it even more brutally, when an ecclesiastic in his band urged him not to rob the Indians but to bring them the Christian faith: 'I have not come for any such reasons. I have come to take away from them their gold'.[23]

No doubt, many of the Spanish conquistadors performed almost incredible feats of daring and were prepared to suffer hardships to the utmost limits of human endurance, and this, it is quite true, often with only problematic hopes of material gain. But does it detract from their personal achievements to wonder why such actions should be regarded as specifically Spanish or how they differed from the hardships endured by the Nansens and Amundsens, the Scotts, the Hillarys and the Tensings, and countless others of different nations and through many ages, who sought personal fame and satisfaction rather than material rewards through the performance of most hazardous quests? There were those, mainly Dominican and Franciscan friars, who genuinely thought of the Spanish conquests as opportunities to spread the word of God among the heathens. They did what they could to protect the Indians from exploitation and they gained the ear of the king of Spain.

[20] Menéndez Pidal, *The Spaniards*, pp. 19ff.
[21] A. Domínguez Ortiz, *The Golden Age of Spain 1516–1659*, trans. J. Casey, (London, 1971), gives a much more sober characterization of the motives of the conquistadors. On p. 289: 'Ambition, the thirst for command, for acquiring nobility and renown, for leaving an honoured name behind – these were the ideals of the Renaissance Spaniard, and he found in the discoveries an opportunity to exploit them to the full'.
[22] Quoted in L. Hanke, *The Spanish Struggle for Justice in the Conquest of America* (Philadelphia, 1949), p. 7.
[23] *Ibid.*

But in practice their efforts and those of the Spanish crown were outweighed by the rapacity of the Spanish settlers. If Spanish culture and the Catholic religion eventually pervaded large areas of the New World, the price paid for this by its original inhabitants was appallingly high. There is a rather horrible irony in finding that at least one of the reasons for the disasters which overtook the Indians was the fact that the Spaniards, who prided themselves so much on their indifference to material wealth, found the Indians' genuine indifference to gold and other possessions not only baffling but downright repellent.[24]

I am not trying to revive the 'black legend' of specifically Spanish cruelty in the New World but simply trying to point to the inadequacy of using mainly literary sources for the understanding of human actions. If Spanish national feelings and the more admirable characteristics of *hispanidad* can be said to have manifested themselves in the conquest of the New World, then those were largely emotions recollected in tranquility, or, rather, in rhetoric after the event, and often, though not always, by those who stayed at home. If the 'empire in which the sun never set' was a source of pride for Spaniards at home, it was not something for which most of them were prepared to make large sacrifices. In 1548, the Córtes of Castile petitioned the king to prohibit the export of Spanish manufactures to the colonies because this export raised prices to the consumer at home. Let the colonists manufacture their own goods from their own materials, they advised.[25]

My critical inquiry into the traditional views of Spanish nationalism is, however, as yet inconclusive. I have demonstrated that national feeling was not as universal and pervasive as has often been claimed. But I cannot, nor do I wish to, deny altogether the existence of national sentiment in Spain in the early-modern period. It should be stressed, however, that attitudes of mind expressed in literature or in the recorded remarks of individuals cannot tell us precisely *how* important such attitudes were and what role they played in the history of a country or a people.

A somewhat different but related problem arises with modern sociological theories of nationalism. Take, for instance, the conceptual framework used by K. W. Deutsch in his book, *Nationalism and Social Communication*.[26] Deutsch proposed a model of a world consisting of highly uneven cluster distributions of human settlement, held together and separated from each other by patterns of transport; barriers

---

[24] L. Hanke, *The First Social Experiments in America* (Cambridge, Massachusetts, 1935), p. 30.

[25] J. Carrera Pujal, *Historia de la Economía Española* (Barcelona, 1943), Vol. 1, pp. 142ff.

[26] K. W. Deutsch, *Nationalism and Social Communication: An Inquiry into the Foundations of Nationality* (New York and London, 1953).

between markets; differences in wealth, language, caste, of class, institutions and the uneven impact of historical events. The techniques of studying these partly overlapping problems have to be provided by all the social sciences, from demography to sociology and from economics to linguistics and history.[27]

So far, this is acceptable. In the process of working out his model, Deutsch makes some illuminating suggestions which are certainly applicable to the history of Spanish national feeling. For instance, the Spanish government's hopes for the assimilation of the *Moriscos*, the Christianized Moors, in the sixteenth century were doomed to failure because of the absence of any real communication between the Old Christians and the *Moriscos*, even when they lived side by side. Or again, there is Deutsch's suggestion – it is little more than that – of the importance for the growth of national feeling of assigning value to people as they are, i.e. whatever their origin and station in life.[28] It has recently been argued that the whole corpus of Spanish Golden Age drama was a sustained and deliberate attempt to shore up the existing social structure by presenting on stage the dignity and sense of honour of members of all classes, of peasants and craftsmen as much as of nobles and princes.[29] But before this interpretation can be accepted, it should be noted that the great playwrights, from Lope de Vega to Tirso de Molina and Calderón, wrote what they thought *should* be, rather than what they thought actually *was*. Calderón's gentlemen officers in *El Alcalde de Zalamea* very evidently do not treat the peasants as if nobles and peasants were all members of a community which could be called a nation. The author needed a *deus ex machina*, the providential appearance of the king, in order to resolve the basically unresolvable class antagonism which he presents. And this his audience would understand, for the only real political emotion which nobles and peasants had in common was their personal loyalty to the king.

In the end, however, the theories of the sociologists, suggestive as they are, do not tell us enough. It looks plausible to analyze the problem of the assimilation of the *Moriscos* in terms of the problem of communication. But as soon as we compare it with that of the assimilation of the *conversos* the inadequacy of the technique becomes apparent. Between *conversos* and Old Christians, there was no communication problem whatever and no easily recognizable distinction, not in language, in social customs, nor in looks – in Spain at least. And yet, the doctrine of *limpieza* was directed both against *Moriscos* and *conversos*. The racialism of the Spanish Old Christians was therefore not primarily, if at all, a problem in social communication,

---

[27] *Ibid.*, p. 161 and *passim*.
[28] *Ibid.*, p. 153.
[29] J. A. Maravall, 'Una interpretación historico-social del teatro barroco', *Cuadernos Hispanoamericanos*, No. 235 (1969).

even in the wide sense which Deutsch uses this term.[30] In other words, a sociological theory developed primarily from the observation of the contemporary scene is found to lack controls when introduced into a situation removed in time.

More serious still, however, is the excessive claim which Deutsch makes for his model. 'The present distribution of sovereign states and blocks of states', he tells us, 'was found necessary in its essential features, though not in its accidents.'[31] Without even venturing into the morass of the taxonomic problems raised by this undefined distinction between essentials and accidents, Deutsch's conclusion simply begs the question for the historian who is studying the early-modern period. Not only is the historian professionally interested in the accidents, but he has the strong suspicion that it may have been precisely what the sociologist would regard as accidents which determined the present distribution of sovereign states. The history of Spain in the early-modern period is very much a case in point, and it is now time to look more closely at this history, and to do so without the teleological preconceptions of either the literateur or the social scientist who has ventured into the territory of the historian.[32]

The history of modern Spain is usually held to start in 1469 with the marriage of Ferdinand and Isabella. This marriage, and the subsequent union of the crowns of Aragon and Castile, has traditionally been seen as an expression of a sense of Spanish nationality which antedated the political union. Some such feeling seems indeed to have existed in

---

[30] It would be possible to argue that this racialism was the result of a much earlier absence of communication in the period during which the separate Jewish, Christian, and Moslem traditions evolved. But such an argument would lead to further formidable problems about the spread of Islam during its expansionist period and also about the ethnic origins of Spanish Jews and Moslems, for none of which the Deutsch model is particularly illuminating.

[31] Deutsch, *Nationalism and Social Communication*, p. 161.

[32] It is only fair to add that at least one stream of recent anthropological thought is moving away from the assumption that an ethnic unit is normally a discrete and homogeneous society. This assumption derived both from the nature of some primitive societies and from the post-Malinowskian methods of studying them. It is an assumption on which many anthropological and sociological generalizations appear to have been based but which, as I have tried to show, is not applicable to Spain. See R. A. LeVine and D. T. Campbell, *Ethnocentrism* (New York, 1972), chap. 7 and *passim*.

I do not, of course, mean to imply a blanket condemnation of social scientists. After I finished writing this paper, Professor Davydd Greenwood, of the Anthropology Department of Cornell University, drew my attention to *El mito del carácter nacional. Meditaciones a contrapelo*, (Madrid, 1970), by the eminent contemporary anthropologist, Julio Caro Baroja. This is an elegant and, often, ironical discussion of Spanish and non-Spanish views of the Spanish 'national character' through modern history. Caro concludes on p. 112: 'En suma, el del carácter nacional es un mito amenazador y peligroso, como lo fueron muchos de la Antigüedad pagana. Pero acaso no tenga la majestad y profundidad de aquéllos'.

intellectual circles at the court of Ferdinand's father, John II of Aragon.[33] The motivation of the chief protagonists, however, was much more practical. John II desperately needed Castilian help to defend his Pyrenees provinces of Cerdagne and Roussillon against French attacks. For this purpose he negotiated with different Castilian factions until he found one which, for its own reasons, was willing to entertain the idea of the Aragonese connection. This was a section of the Castilian high nobility, led by Archbishop Carrillo of Toledo, who supported the succession claims of the Infanta Isabella, sister of King Henry IV, against the King and his daughter, Juana. This was a pure power struggle and its details were sordid. There had been civil wars and, at one stage, the grandees had induced Henry IV to declare that his daughter had been fathered by a certain Beltrán de la Cueva – wrongly, as historians now believe. Isabella's supporters hoped to use the Aragonese alliance for their own purposes and, being the wooed rather than the wooers, were able to impose their own conditions on Ferdinand.[34] Ferdinand and Isabella, being cousins, forged a papal dispensation for their marriage. Because of the expected Castilian help against the French, news of this event was received with great jubilation in Zaragoza and Valencia and even in Palermo (where feelings of Spanish nationalism could not have been prominent); but the Castilians reacted with considerable coldness because they feared the renewal of civil war.[35]

It was not long in coming. Juana married Alfonso V of Portugal, and after Henry IV's death in 1474, both Aragon and Portugal immediately became involved in the renewed Castilian civil war. Alfonso and Juana were eventually defeated and the union of the crowns of Castile and Aragon was confirmed. It was a conclusion with far-reaching implications for the future. But it was not a foregone conclusion, nor was it inherently more national or Spanish than a victory for Juana and Alfonso would have been. Such a victory would have led to the union of the crowns of Castile and Portugal which, in the light of the previous traditions of the Iberian Peninsula, would have been just as natural, national, and Spanish as the actual union of the crowns of Castile and Aragon. It probably would have prevented the involvement of Castile in the Italian policy of Aragon and in the interminable and eventually ruinous wars with France.

If the union of the crowns of Aragon and Castile and the creation of what was called, mainly by foreigners, the kingdom of Spain were not primarily the result of national feeling, neither was much of the

---

[33] J. H. Elliott, *Imperial Spain, 1469–1716* (London, 1963), p. 7, quoting R. B. Tate, *Joan Margarit i Pau, Cardinal-Bishop of Gerona* (Manchester, 1955).

[34] J. Vicens Vives, *Historia crítica de la vida y reinado de Fernando II de Aragon* (Zaragoza, 1962), pp. 242ff, 246ff, and *passim*.

[35] *Ibid.*, p. 263.

subsequent policy of Ferdinand and Isabella. The conquest of Granada certainly appealed to the traditional religious and therefore, one might say, national feeling of Isabella's subjects, and so did the setting up of the Spanish Inquisition and its policy of expelling Jews and persecuting *conversos*.

The Catholic Kings and their successors, moreover, continued King John II's patronage of Spanish historiography. Perhaps it was in this field, in which the feeling for Spanish nationality had already acquired a considerable and respectable tradition, that national awareness was given the strongest boost by the union of the crowns. This national sentiment showed itself particularly in the need felt by Spanish historians to provide their country with antecedents as splendid as those traditionally claimed by the French and the English. Franco, the descendant of Aeneas, for France, and the Trojan Brutus, for Britain, were now matched for Spain by Tubal and even by Hercules himself, not to mention such exotic figures as Osiris. The recent forgeries of Annius of Viterbo provided a particularly rich quarry for the Spaniards.[36] Charles V's court historian, Florián de Ocampo used a large part of his *Crónica general de España* (1544) to recount the pre-Roman history of Spain; in other words, he wrote a nationalistic historical fantasy. Even at the beginning of the seventeenth century, Juan de Mariana, a much more sophisticated historian than Ocampo, did not dare to dispense with the legends of Hercules in his *Historia de España*. The best Spanish historian of the early-modern period, however, Gerónimo Zurita, did not attempt to write a history of Spain at all, but confined himself to the history of Aragon in his *Annales de la corona de Aragón* (1562–80).[37] Spanish Renaissance historiography was therefore essentially a part of the tradition of the *laudes Hispaniae*; and if its critical understanding of Spanish history must be viewed as problematical, at least when compared with the Italian and French historiography of the period, it undoubtedly increased the national self-confidence of educated Spaniards. Apart from this, its effect on Spanish policy-making was practically nil.

Basically, the policies pursued by the Catholic Kings had two aims: the strengthening of the power of the monarchy and the pursuit of dynastic advantages, either through marriage alliances or through wars to conquer and maintain what Ferdinand claimed to be rightfully his. Neither of these aims was specifically inspired by national feeling, though such feeling was not necessarily absent. But even the official rhetoric of the Catholic Kings' diplomacy gives little basis for a

---

[36] R. B. Tate, *Ensayos sobre la Historiografía peninsular de siglo XV* (Madrid, 1970), chap. 1.

[37] See E. Fueter, *Geschichte der neueren Historiographie* (3rd ed.; Munich, 1936), pp. 235ff.

nationalistic interpretation. For example, in 1473 Ferdinand set up Isabella as heiress:

in my said kingdoms of Aragon and Sicily, notwithstanding all laws, fueros, ordinances and customs of these said kingdoms which prohibit the succession of a woman . . . and this not from ambition nor greed nor any excessive affection in which I hold the said princess . . . but rather for the great benefit which the said kingdoms will derive from being united with those of Castile and Leon, and that one prince would be king, lord and governor of them all.[38]

The modern editor of this document comments that 'the great statesman Don Ferdinand prepares the unity of all the medieval kingdoms in order to create the great Spanish nation'.[39] But the document shows nothing of the sort. Not only does it not mention the Spanish nation at all, it expressly includes in the union of crowns, and in the benefits which are supposed to flow from it, the kingdom of Sicily. There is not the slightest hint that this Italian kingdom was in any way different from, or that it should be treated differently from, the Iberian kingdoms. The union which Ferdinand had in mind was a dynastic, not a national, union.

The case of Navarre was very similar.[40] In 1494 the Catholic Kings promised to marry their daughter, Anna, to a son of the king of Navarre. There was to be perpetual peace and an alliance between the countries for the mutual benefit of their respective subjects. But again the name of Spain is conspicuously absent from this document, as is any mention of a common tradition and language of the peoples of Castile and Navarre. As it happened, the marriage alliance was never concluded. In 1512, Ferdinand conquered Navarre by force of arms, again not on the basis of any national argument, but on the basis of the weak dynastic claim of his second wife, Germaine de Foix, and on the even more dubious authority of a papal excommunication of the actual king of Navarre.[41]

In 1504 Isabella died and almost all of the Castilian high nobility threw themselves into the arms of the Burgundian Philip, husband of Isabella's mentally disturbed daughter, rather than support the claims of the 'national' king, Ferdinand. The Castilian grandees correctly calculated that Philip would be easier to handle than the old autocrat from Aragon. Ferdinand was furious, but it is unlikely that he was surprised by the Castilians' lack of national feeling. He expected men to

---

[38] Quoted in F. Gómez de Mercado y de Miguel, *Dogmas Nacionales del Rey Católico* (Madrid, 1953), p. 334.

[39] *Ibid.*, p. 337.

[40] L. Suárez Fernández, *Política Internacional de Isabel la Católica, Estúdio y Documentos* (Valladolid, 1971), Vol. 4, pp. 181–85, 197–99.

[41] R. Б. Merriman, *The Rise of the Spanish Empire* New York, 1918), Vol. 2, pp. 344–47.

act in accordance with more practical motives. This view was manifested in a letter he wrote to Emperor Maximilian in 1496, urging him to make war on France, in which, he said, the German princes would follow the Emperor if he prospered but would join the king of France if the Emperor hesitated.[42] Jumping on the band wagon, or as men put it during the Renaissance, the importance for a prince to have 'reputation', was a well-known phenomenon at the time and one to which judicious politicians attached a great deal more importance than to an abstract idea such as nationalism.

With the succession of Philip of Burgundy in Castile, the union of the crowns of Castile and Aragon was dissolved. Ferdinand acknowledged his son-in-law's succession in public, though privately he declared his agreement to have been obtained by force and hence to be null and void. But Ferdinand now contracted a second marriage, with Germaine de Foix, niece of Louis XII of France, in order to prevent a French attack on his kingdom of Naples, now bereft of Castilian support.[43] The expected son from this union would inherit all the realms of the crown of Aragon, in Spain and Italy. It has been argued that Ferdinand did not want to perpetuate the renewed division of the Spanish kingdoms, but rather intended to place his son by Germaine on the Castilian throne, as well as that of Aragon.[44] This is certainly plausible, though I still think Ferdinand thought more in dynastic than in national terms. Naples remained as important to him as Castile.

This became clear when Philip died and when Queen Germaine's son died immediately after birth. There would now be a Habsburg-Burgundian dynastic claim to both Castile and Aragon. In the meantime, however, the union of the crowns was restored in the person of Ferdinand. For a short time, he left his regent in Castile, Cardinal Ximénez de Cisneros, free to pursue an essentially Castilian national policy, the conquest of the North African coast. It was then that the old cardinal, in the battle of Oran, was credited with having, like Joshua, held back the sun on its course to allow the Christians time to complete their victory. Ferdinand had not actively supported these endeavours; in fact, in 1510 he actually stopped them and switched Castilian resources back into his Italian policy.

It is little wonder that, at Ferdinand's death in 1516, the mutual antagonisms of the different Iberian kingdoms were as virulent as ever. Cardinal Ximénez, regent once again, painted a sombre picture of the mood of the country in his letters to the court of young King Charles in the Netherlands. The men of Navarre, old enemies of the Aragonese,

---

[42] Suárez Fernández, *Política Internacional*, Vol. 4, p. 569.

[43] Treaty of Blois, October 12, 1505. See Baron de Terrateig, *Política en Italia del Rey Católico 1507–1516* (Madrid, 1963), Vol. I, p. 42.

[44] Merriman, *The Rise of the Spanish Empire*, Vol. 2, pp. 329, 332; Elliott, *Imperial Spain*, p. 128.

would rather suffer a Turk than an Aragonese as governor of the fortress of Pamplona.[45] The Cardinal stated that the King's plan to send an Aragonese as his ambassador to Rome should be given up, for the many Castilians resident in Rome would never obey him. The ambassador, he added, should be a Castilian or a Fleming.[46]

As it turned out, the Castilians were not happy about the appointment of Flemings, either – at least, not in their own country. It has generally been held that the revolt of the *comuneros* in 1520 represented primarily a Castilian national movement against a foreign king and his foreign advisers. There was certainly considerable resentment against the Netherlanders in Charles V's court, and there were deliberate and much exaggerated campaigns against their 'carpetbagging', even before they had set foot on Castilian soil.[47] There was also much resentment against Charles V's imperial title, and people said that it was better to be king of Spain than emperor of Germany.[48] Nevertheless, the *comunero* revolt was basically a civil war in which both sides claimed to represent the true interests of Castile. The economic antagonisms were old. The Mesta, the gild of sheep owners, and the merchants of Burgos had grown rich by the export of wool to the Netherlands. They welcomed the Burgundian connection and argued that grazing and the wool trade were 'one of the principal resources [*haziendas*] of these kingdoms, employing a great part of its people and providing them with meat to eat, woolens to clothe themselves, shoes and many other necessities, without which these kingdoms could not survive and on which depend the greater part of the royal revenues . . .'[49] Against this, the cloth manufacturers of Segovia, Toledo, and Valladolid had been arguing for years that the export of raw wool raised the price for the native manufacturer and ruined many poor people who had no other livelihood but weaving; that Flanders and England grew rich by working up Spanish wool into cloth;[50] and that the reason for the drain of money from Spain to other countries was the fact 'that the goods which enter this country cost much, while those which are exported cost little'.[51] Because the monarchy, for financial reasons, had always supported the Mesta and the wool exporters, it is not

---

[45] Ximénez to Diego López de Ayala in Flanders, Madrid, May 12, 1516, in P. Gayangos and V. de la Fuente, *Cartas del Cardenal Don Fray Francisco Jiménez de Cisneros* (Madrid, 1867), p. 129.

[46] Ximénez to Diego López de Ayala in Flanders; Madrid, September 27, 1516, in *ibid.*, p. 158.

[47] *Ibid.*, *passim*; V. de la Fuente, *Cartas de los secretarios del Cardenal D. Fr. Francisco Jiménez de Cisneros durante su regencia en los años de 1516 y 1517* (Madrid, 1875), p. 18 and *passim*. See also J. E. A. Walther, *Die Anfänge Karls V* (Leipzig, 1911), *passim*.

[48] J. Sanches Montes, *Franceses, Protestantes Turcos: Los Españoles ante la Política de Carlos V.* (Madrid, 1951), p. 21, quoting Santa Cruz, *Crónica*.

[49] Memorandum of the Mesta, 1520, quoted in J. Pérez, *La révolution des 'communidades' de Castille (1520–1521)* (Bordeaux, 1970), p. 43, n. 123.

[50] Memorandum by Pedro de Burgos, *ibid.*, pp. 103ff.

[51] Memorandum by Rodrigo de Luján, *ibid.*, pp. 105ff.

surprising to find that Burgos remained royalist during the revolt, while Segovia and Toledo were the centres of the opposition.

The immediate cause of the revolt, however, was financial and political. There was an angry reaction to the government's demand for additional taxes and to its manipulation of the deputies of the Castilian Cortes to obtain consent for these taxes which were to pay for the King's journey to Germany. Though the economic antagonisms and the resentment of the foreign regent, Adrian of Utrecht, were important, the principal issue of the revolt rapidly became a constitutional and a social one: the political powers of the cities *vis-à-vis* the king, and the social and political position of the nobility, in the Cortes, in the cities, and even on their own estates. In these circumstances, the dislike of the Castilian nobles for the Burgundians and their sympathy for the cities were soon overshadowed by their fear for their social and political status. They raised an army and defeated the *comunero* movement and thus restored the authority of their foreign king.[52]

The subjects of the crown of Aragon were no more pleased with this foreign king and his Burgundian retinue than were the Castilians. Their Cortes were even less willing than the Castilian Cortes to pay for Charles V's German policy. But the government made no attempt to force the issue, as it did in Castile; consequently, the Catalans and Aragonese made no attempt to support the *comunero* movement. Common hatred of the foreigner was evidently not enough to produce a nationalistic Spanish policy. The Valencians did indeed have a rebellion of their own, the *Germanía*. But this was a lower class revolt, directed against the *Moriscos* and against the local nobility which protected them as a valuable and cheap labour force. So far from being in sympathy with the *comunero* movement, the *Germanía* loudly proclaimed its royalism. It mattered little. The crown inevitably allied itself with the nobility to suppress it.

During the remainder of Charles V's reign, the Castilian nobility and cities gradually came to accept the foreign king and his imperialist policies.[53] Charles, for his part, learned Castilian and made deliberate efforts to Castilianize himself. The word Castilian, rather than Spanish, is used deliberately, because the Emperor and his government made little effort to unify the Hispanic kingdoms further. Castile was, by far, the largest of his dominions and the one in which, after the *comunero*

---

[52] The fullest modern accounts are in Pérez *La révolution* and S. Haliczer, *The Comuneros of Castile*, (Madison, London, 1981). See also J. A. Maravall, *Las Comunidades de Castilla* (Madrid, 1963).

[53] In 1525, the Venetian ambassador in Spain, Gasparo Contarini, later the famous cardinal and church reformer, still thought that all classes of Spaniards disliked or even hated the emperor and that he reciprocated these sentiments but knew how to dissimulate. E. Albèri, *Relazioni degli ambasciatori veneti*, Series 1, Vol. 2, pp. 44ff.

revolt, the crown had the most authority. Thus the Castilians were granted a monopoly on trade with the New World. While it was possible for the Catalans to engage in this trade by using Castilian cover firms, the same was true for the Genoese and Augsburgers; the non-Castilian Spanish subjects of the Emperor therefore had no advantage over foreigners. Empress Isabella, whom Charles left as regent in Spain during his long absences, was unwilling to leave Castile even to attend the Aragonese Cortes, a procedure which Aragonese law required her to follow.[54] Characteristically, she complained on one occasion that many Castilian grandees and caballeros wished to go to Barcelona to welcome the Emperor, who was expected to arrive there, which she said would lead to 'the export of great sums of money and horses from these kingdoms',[55] i.e. from the kingdoms of the crown of Castile to those of the crown of Aragon!

From Empress Isabella's correspondence with her husband it is possible to see that Charles V's imperial policy was not always what his Castilian subjects would have wished. But the differences were not fundamental. The Castilian grandees were coming to see the advantages of having a ruler who could dispense the patronage of so many countries. Sydney and Beatrice Webb once called the British Empire of the early 1900s 'a vast system of outdoor relief for the British upper classes'. With its viceroyalties and governorships, with its colonelcies and captaincies of an ever-increasing army, with Italian bishoprics for Spanish ecclesiastics and councilorships in ever-proliferating councils in Madrid for educated hidalgos, Charles V's empire was becoming just such a desirable setup for the Castilian upper classes.

Discussions of high policy, in consequence, tended to turn upon the nature of the empire. The debates of 1544 are particularly revealing. After a reasonably successful campaign in France, Charles V concluded the peace of Crépy with Francis I because he had run out of money and because he wished to have his hands free to deal with the German Protestants. An important part of the treaty was a proposed marriage alliance between the houses of Habsburg and Valois, in one of two alternative forms. The first possibility was that Francis I's second son, Charles, duke of Orleans, would marry Emperor Charles V's daughter Mary. The pair would receive the whole of the Netherlands, no less, and Franche Comté as their dowry, to rule with the title of governors until the Emperor's death, when they would get in full sovereignty. The second was that the duke would marry Anna, second daughter of the Emperor's brother, Ferdinand, king of the Romans, and receive as dowry the Duchy of Milan. The Emperor, in Brussels at the time,

[54] J. M. Jover, *Carlos V y los Españoles* (Madrid, 1963), p. 55.
[55] Empress Isabel to Charles V, Madrid, January 20, 1533, in M. del C. Mazario Coleto, *Isabel de Portugal, Emperatriz y Reina de España* (Madrid, 1951), p. 372.

asked his Council of State in Spain to advise which alternative should be followed.

In December 1544, Prince Philip (later Philip II) reported to his father that the Council had been unable to agree.[56] One group of councillors, following the old cardinal-archbishop of Toledo, Juan Pardo y Tavera, took the traditional stance of opposing Castilian involvement in Italy and more especially, in Milan, a province acquired only nine years before, but which had to be defended against the French at a high cost in blood and money. Equally important, the Cardinal was outraged by the very idea that Charles V should give up his hereditary Burgundian lands. The duke of Alba argued the opposite case. The Netherlands were difficult to hold because the supply lines from Spain, either by sea or across the Alps, were highly vulnerable. Without Milan, and hence northern Italy and the Alpine passes, the Netherlands were not really defensible at all. Conversely, Milan was entirely defensible without the Netherlands.

These diametrically opposed views have been characterized quite correctly, as the Castilian and the Catalan-Aragonese traditions in foreign policy, regardless of the fact that Alba was an arch-Castilian.[57] They also represented the views of the traditionalists to whom dynastic loyalties were sacred and of the practical soldiers who made a hard-nosed assessment of the strategic and logistic problems involved in the two alternatives. Some twenty-five years later, Alba himself, as governor-general of the Netherlands, had the correctness of his analysis of 1544 proved to him by events, and this despite his deliberate efforts to prevent just such an eventuality. But neither Alba's nor Tavera's view in 1544 can be regarded as more Spanish than the other.[58]

In the end Charles V predictably decided to give up Milan, rather than his hereditary Burgundian lands, and this certainly for dynastic and emotional, rather than for Castilian national reasons.[59] After all, he

[56] Philip's letter of December 14, 1544 is translated in *Calendar of State Papers Spanish*, Vol. 7, pp. 478–96. Further material and analysis of the discussions can be found in F. Chabod, '¿Milán ó los Países Bajos? Las Discusiones en España sobre la Alternativa de 1544', *Carlos V (1500–1558): Homenaje de la Universidad de Granada* (Granada, 1958), pp. 331–72.

[57] F. Chabod, 'Contrasti interni e dibatti sulla politica generale di Carlo V', *Karl V. Der Kaiser und seine Zeit*, ed. P. Rassow and F. Sehalk (Cologne, 1960), p. 56.

[58] Chabod thought Alba's view 'assai più nazionale proprio dal punto di vista spagnuolo', *ibid.* I doubt whether Alba himself saw it in such a light. It seems to me that Alba thought purely in terms of power and of military necessities for his sovereign. (Alba is perhaps the nearest character in modern European history to the Hagen of the *Nibelungenlied.*) His views were supported by the Italian Ferrante Gonzaga, Charles V's governor of Milan and otherwise no friend of Alba's. Gonzaga had in mind a strategically defensible Italo-Spanish Mediterranean empire. To achieve this he later even suggested an exchange of the Netherlands for Piedmont-Savoy. *Ibid.*, pp. 57ff. At the imperial court Gonzaga's proposals were rejected as being too Italian!

[59] See F. Walser, 'Berichte und Studien zur Geschichte Karls V', Part VI, *Nachrichten von der Gesellschaft der Wissenschaften zu Göttingen* (Phil.-Hist. Klasse), 1932, Hft. 1, pp. 133–43, 167–71.

had never taken much notice of Tavera's repeated criticism of his Italian policy. But much to the relief of the imperial court, the duke of Orleans died, and the question of the first alternative died with him.

With the succession of Philip II in 1555, the Castilian ruling class more readily identified with an imperial policy that was thought of in religious terms but that was pursued in a very practical fashion, and this not least because Philip II himself was much more obviously a Castilian than his father. Officially, the King valued his Italian and Netherlands subjects as highly as the Spaniards. Italians from proud and ancient families, such as the Pescara and Colonna, served Philip loyally, even when they knew that he intrigued against them. Egmont never wavered in his personal loyalty, right up to the steps of the scaffold. Personal loyalty to the sovereign still outweighed national feeling for many of the European nobility, as in earlier times it had done dramatically for Pescara, victor of the battle of Pavia in 1525, who refused to listen when the chancellor of Milan, Girolamo Morone, used nationalistic arguments in an attempt to induce him to change sides and help free Italy from foreign domination.[60] Philip II even admitted that men might serve more effectively outside their own country. But instead of employing Netherlanders and Italians in Castile, as this statement would suggest, it meant that, whenever he could, he appointed Spaniards, or rather Castilians, throughout his empire. Cardinal Granvelle, a Franche-Comtois, suggested, as early as 1563, that the King appoint an occasional Netherlander to a Spanish ecclesiastical benefice, and he urged the King to offer the prince of Orange the viceroyalty of Sicily.[61] This brilliant suggestion does not even seem to have been discussed by the government in Madrid. Philip was evidently unwilling to offend Castilian vested interests and found facile excuses not to act on Granvelle's proposals. Granvelle himself and all the other of Philip's non-Spanish servants in high position – even his own nephew, Alexander Farnese, duke of Parma – found themselves faced with the constant and unremitting hostility and uncooperativeness of the Castilians.

To the rest of the world it became clear quite rapidly that the universalist empire of Charles V had become a Spanish empire. In Spain itself the term did not come to be used until the 1590s.[62] But already in

---

[60] K. Brandi, *Kaiser, Karl V* (Munich, 1937/59), pp. 188ff.

[61] See above, chapter 5.

[62] From the reign of Philip II (1555–98), the phrase 'Roi des Espagnes Catholique' or 'Hispaniarum Rex' begins to appear in diplomatic documents. This is perhaps not surprising as, in view of the prevalent literary and rhetorical tradition, one would expect the Castilians to be claiming to speak to foreigners for the whole of Spain. But I don't think that too much weight should be attached to this convention. Nor was it followed at all consistently. At the very end of the reign, in the Treaty of Vervins, May 2, 1598, Philip II is still styled in the traditional form: 'Roy Catholique, de Castile, de

1579, the córtes of Castile had told the King that he should go ahead and acquire the crown of Portugal, even if he had no valid claims for it, for the succession of a foreign prince would be damaging to Castile and to the Christian religion.[63] The equation of Castilian reason of state with the good of Christendom became even clearer in 1587 when the Córtes argued that they were petitioning the King to lower taxes only so that they could serve him the better:

for with their forces and substance, Your Majesty and your ancestors of glorious memory have conquered and maintained so many kingdoms, and Your Majesty has the obligation to preserve and maintain them and to conquer many others which God might give Your Majesty . . . as is needful for your subjects and vassals and for the Christian religion.[64]

During the last years of Philip II's reign, some doubts began to be raised about the effects of Castilian imperialism on Castile and on the common people who paid the taxes and provided the soldiers. One deputy of the Córtes wondered 'whether France, Flanders and England would really be better if Spain were poorer'.[65] Another detailed the desperate effects of the king's policy on the common people and remarked caustically that 'today there exists no longer a common weal but a common misery for everyone.'[66]

Such voices remained isolated, however. In his addresses to the Córtes the King stressed less and less the good of Christendom, as he had formerly done, and more and more the benefit his subjects derived from his consistent attempts to meet the enemy outside their borders, rather than on their own soil.[67] Such appeals to patriotism and the need to defend the homeland evidently fell on receptive ears, especially after the earl of Essex's raid on Cadiz.

---

Leon, d'Arragon, des deux Siciles, de Hierusalem, de Portugal, de Navarres, des Indes', after which followed the ducal and other non–royal titles. There is not even any attempt here to group the Spanish titles together. J. Dumont, *Corps Universel Diplomatique du Droit des Gens* (The Hague, 1728), Vol. 5, p. 561. Internal documents seem to have followed the traditional style almost invariably: 'Don Phelippe, segundo deste nombre, por la gracia de Dios rey de Castilla, de Leon, de Aragon . . .' (e.g. a statute regulating the election of *regidores* in Toledo, March 17, 1566, quoted in *Privilegios Reales y Viejos Documentos*, Vol. I, Doc. XV (Madrid, 1963).

[63] For a more detailed discussion of this development and of these arguments, see above, chapter 4.

[64] *Actas de las Córtes de Castilla* (Madrid, 1866), Vol. 8, p. 282.

[65] E.g. between 1567 and 1574 some 43,000 men were sent to Italy and the Netherlands. G. Parker, *The Army of Flanders and the Spanish Road 1567–1659* (Cambridge, 1972), p. 42, n. 3, and chap. 1, *passim*.

[66] 'No hay beneficio común, sino mal común, para todos en general.' Rodrigo Sanchez Doria, deputy of Tordesillas, on 26 May, 1595. *Actas de las Córtes*, Vol. 14, pp. 52–59.

[67] *Ibid.*, Vol. 15, pp. 444–45; cf. above chapter 4.

The death of Philip II, the Prudent King who, as many Spaniards and almost the whole of the rest of Europe believed, had aimed at the domination of Europe and the world, was followed by a period of introspection and self-criticism in Spain. The *arbitristas*, who were the spokesmen of this mood, produced acute analyses of the Castilian economy and of Castilian customs and morality. Their proposals were similar to those of their contemporary mercantilist writers in other European countries. They shared a nationalistic concern for the wealth, and hence power, of their own country, with emphasis on the need to protect native industries; to improve transport; to encourage immigrants, especially those with technical skills; and above all, to change the Castilians' dislike for productive economic work. But, apart from the advice to cut government expenditure and to spread the financial burden of supporting the empire over all the dominions of the crown, so as to relieve Castile, they made little attempt at a systematic analysis of the problems of empire and of the role the Spanish monarchy should play in Europe and in the world.

This was equally true of the historians of the time. The old Juan de Mariana, recounting how he had been persuaded to continue his *Historia de España* beyond the end of the War of Granada, rejoiced that the energies of his countrymen had, after 1492, come to be directed toward the conquest of foreign peoples and kingdoms and that 'the name and valor of Spain, known to few and confined within the narrow limits of Spain, was in a short time, and with great glory, spread abroad, not only through Italy and through France and Barbary, but to the very ends of the earth.' It was the conquest of this empire and the resultant greatness of Spain which he was persuaded to describe.[68] In this work at least, Mariana was concerned only with the question of Spanish reputation and he did not even begin to inquire what effects the winning of this reputation might have had on his country and countrymen or on the rest of the world. Even to the spread of Christianity, the usual justification for the Spanish overseas conquests, Mariana allows in all his long work just two sentences: 'God gave them [the American Indians] great benefits and showed them great mercy in delivering them into the power of the Christians . . . Above all, he gave them knowledge of himself, so that they would cease living as savages and live as Christians.' At this point, Mariana seems to have become aware that he might have omitted something in his characterization of the effects of the Spanish conquests, for, as if Las Casas or Vitoria had never discussed the intricacies of this problem, he added quickly, 'They derived greater benefit from being subjected than from continuing in their liberty.'[69]

The Castilian grandees, in whose hands lay the guidance of Spanish

[68] J. de Mariana, *Historia de España*, book 26, chap. 1.
[69] *Ibid.*, chap. 3.

policy during the reign of Philip III, and who not only continued to occupy the Spanish viceroyalties and embassies abroad but now also dominated all the central councils of the government, were not given to such basic analysis either. Brought up in the later, expansionist, years of Philip II's reign, they took three things for granted: that the Spanish monarchy, even if not necessarily aiming at world empire, should still play a predominant role in Europe; that this role was synonymous with the cause of the Catholic Church and, hence, of God himself; and that the Castilian ruling classes should have the running of it. They differed only over tactics. The duke of Lerma – Philip III's *privado*, or principal minister – and the Council of State in Madrid, conscious of the precarious financial position of the monarchy, settled the English and Dutch wars (the latter at least temporarily) and tried in general to keep Spain out of further wars. It was they, however, who took the decision to expel the *Moriscos* from Spain in 1611, a decision that was undoubtedly popular and that did relatively little harm to the economy of Castile, but a great deal to that of Aragon and Valencia.

The Castilian viceroys and governors-general in Italy and the ambassadors in Rome, Venice, Prague, and Brussels felt themselves under no such restraints as Lerma, nor were they restrained by him. By usurpation, bullying, and intrigue they greatly extended Spanish power and influence in Italy and Germany. For two decades, from 1610 to 1630, Spain for the last time dominated the politics of Europe.[70]

The events of those years were wholly disastrous for Spain. To a much greater degree than most contemporaries realized, the Spanish domination of Europe rested on default, on the temporary weakness and disunity of her enemies and, more especially, of France in the twenty years following the assassination of Henry IV in 1610. There were those, such as the count of Gondomar, Spanish ambassador in England, who still felt Spain could be a world empire if only England were conquered, a matter which Gondomar did not regard as exceptionally difficult. The majority of the Council of State who in 1621 debated the question of the resumption of the Dutch war were more restrained. The Dutch had used the Twelve Year Truce (1609–21) to capture the carrying trade of western Europe and the Baltic to Spain. If they continued their piracy and interloping of the Spanish-American trade as they were now doing, then first the Indies would be lost, then the rest of Flanders, the Spanish dominions in Italy, and finally, Spain herself.[71] Here was a clear identification of the national interest, even of the problem of national survival, with the empire. Tactically, the argument used was what I have on other occasions called the argument of the

---

[70] See the brilliant description of this position, especially of the first of these two decades, by H. R. Trevor-Roper, 'Spain and Europe 1598–1621', *New Cambridge Modern History*, Vol. IV, chap. 9.

[71] *Ibid.*, pp. 279–82.

escalation of potential disasters. The strength of this argument is that it is defensive in form (for it is the enemy who is credited with all positive action) but aggressive in intent. It seemed an unanswerable case, and Spain decided on war.[72] Gustavus Adolphus used the same argument to persuade a reluctant but patriotic Riksdag to support the entry of Sweden into the German war a few years later (1628).[73]

Both Castilians and Swedes were to experience the same disillusionment. What looked like the exertion of the national will in the defense of the monarchy's legitimate rights and in the service of God's cause (though, of course, differently interpreted) was seen by the rest of Europe, even by Spain's and Sweden's allies, as naked and aggressive power politics. It was the nemesis of Castile, and it was a shattering demonstration of the weakness of a genuinely Spanish nationalism, as against a Castilian-aristocratic imperialism, that the non-Castilian kingdoms of Spain were no more convinced by the claims of the Spanish monarchy than were non-Spaniards.[74]

Olivares, Philip IV's *privado*, was aware of this problem; at least, he saw it in terms of the need to spread the burden of imperial policy from Castile to the king's other dominions. He also realized that these dominions would only agree to accepting such burdens if they could be made to feel part of the monarchy's cause, i.e. if they could be given a share of the benefits of empire. In a secret memorandum to the king in 1624, Olivares outlined his plan: the laws of Portugal, Aragon, and the Italian kingdoms should be assimilated to those of Castile, but the king should frequently visit these kingdoms to dispense patronage to their inhabitants, who should be given important imperial offices and honours, hitherto reserved to the Castilians. But this was precisely what the Castilian ruling classes would not accept, and Olivares did not even dare to propose his plan openly. In the 1560s, Philip II's failure to implement a similar plan, proposed by Granvelle, for integrating the Spanish empire had left the Spanish government no alternative but Alba's policy of repression, which caused the revolt of the Netherlands. In the 1620s, the failure of Olivares' attempt left him no alternative but the formation of the 'Union of Arms', which caused the revolts of Catalonia and Portugal. The 'Union of Arms' was a scheme for the creation of a reserve army of 140,000 men, for which all the dominions of the Spanish crown were to pay in proportion to their estimated resources. But the non-Castilians disliked this proposal because it infringed on their laws and liberties and because, with some justice, they distrusted the government in Madrid. When the ever-increasing

[72] See H. G. Koenigsberger, *The Habsburgs and Europe 1516–1660* (Ithaca, 1971), pp. 228ff. The argument is now usually called the domino theory.

[73] *Ibid.*, p. 247.

[74] J. H. Elliott, *The Revolt of the Catalans* (Cambridge, 1963), pp. 200–203. See also his 'The Catalan Revolution of 1640', *Estudios de Historia Moderna*, Vol. 4 (1954), pp. 278ff.

demands of the war forced Olivares to be insistent, he set Madrid on a collision course with Catalonia and Portugal. The Catalans and the Portuguese (whose crown had passed to the kings of Spain in 1580) had certain feelings of loyalty to the person of the king. They had none for a Spain which, during the preceding one hundred years, had come to be identified with the imperial ambitions of the Castilian ruling classes. The Portuguese proclaimed their independence in 1640 and were never reconquered. The Catalans, finding themselves too weak for such a course, transferred their allegiance to the king of France, 'as in the time of Charlemagne' (January 1641). Emotionally, it meant little. When the French armies withdrew during the civil wars of the Fronde, the Castilians were able to reconquer Catalonia in 1652. The Catalan upper classes, at least, were relieved. They had found the French even less congenial masters than the Castilians. Madrid did not repeat its former mistakes and restored all Catalan liberties and privileges. But, as subsequent history, right into the present century, was to show, the integration of Catalonia into a Castilian-dominated Spain remained highly problematical.

The history of Spain during the remaining years of the house of Austria, i.e. until the end of the seventeenth century, is a sad one. The decline of Spain, or at least of Castile, observed by contemporary visitors and debated by later historians, is an undeniable fact. It is visible in demography, in economic activity, in national and international politics, and even in literature and painting, for Calderón, Veláquez and Murillo had no successors of comparable stature. Only national consciousness and pride did not decline. In the face of successive disasters, of the defeat and ineffectiveness of Spanish arms, and of the contempt with which Spain came to be treated in the councils of Europe, the Castilian nobility refused to face reality, just as they had refused to face it in the days of their triumph. Alexander Stanhope commented in 1699:

The scarcety of money here is not to be believed but by eye-witnesses, notwithstanding the arrival of so many floats and galleons, supplies not to be expected again in many years, for the last flota went out to India empty, and *ex nihilo nihil fit*. Their army in Catalonia, by the largest account, is not 8000 men, one half of them Germans and Walloons, who are all starving and deserting as fast as they can. When I came first to Spain [in 1690] they had eighteen good men-of-war; these are now reduced to two or three, I know not which. A wise council might find some remedy for most of these defects, but they all hate and are jealous of one another; and if any of them pretends to public spirit to advise anything for the good of the country, the rest fall upon him, nor is he to hope for any support from his Master . . . This is a summary account of the present state of Spain; which, how wretched soever it may seem to others, they are in their own conceit very happy, believing themselves still the greatest nation in the world, and are now as proud and haughty as in the days of Charles the Fifth.[75]

The Castilian temperament always had something of the Quixotic.

It was the hubris of the Castilian ruling class, convinced of the God-ordained justice of their monarch's dynastic power politics, which had led Spain into two centuries of European war. It was the wars which devoured her, even though they were fought mostly beyond her borders. They never created an effective Spanish national feeling. Such a feeling did not appear until the Spaniards found themselves fighting a foreign invader on their own soil, during the Napoleonic wars.

## SUMMARY AND CONCLUSIONS

The history of Spanish national feeling in the early-modern period is complex and ambivalent. The concept of nationalism itself is protean, and the attempts to give it clear definition is not necessarily illuminating, nor perhaps even possible. The rather definite statements which follow are intended to serve primarily as debating points.

1. There was a literary, rhetorical, and historiographical tradition of Spanish nationalism, mainly in the form of *laudes Hispaniae* which went back to Roman times and which was still very much alive in the early-modern period. It did not differ in essentials from similar traditions in other European countries. It is, however, doubtful whether it penetrated much beyond the relatively small literate section of society, and its political effects were slight.

2. There was a strong feeling of religious purpose. It was developed during the centuries when Spain struggled to free herself from Moorish domination, and it came to be identified with a national purpose, even when there was little or no objective basis for such an identification. This sentiment affected all classes of society.

3. The problem of Spanish nationalism, or even of a feeling of Spanish identity, was vastly complicated by the fact that the population of the Iberian Peninsula was multiracial and multireligious. Christians, Moslems, and Jews influenced each other's customs and sensibilities, though the exact degree to which this happened is a matter for controversy. Nearly all baptized Jews (*conversos*) and probably even a majority of the unbaptized Jews seem to have considered themselves Spaniards (n.b. they were literate). This identification was, however, not accepted by large sections of the Old Christians, espcially the lower classes, who developed a strong feeling of racial identity, 'purity of blood'. Nevertheless, successive generations of *conversos* were gradually absorbed in and assimilated to the

---

[75] Alexander Stanhope, British Minister at Madrid, to the Marquis of Normanby, January 6, 1699. *Spain under Charles II, or Extracts from the Correspondence of The Hon. Alexander Stanhope* (London, 1840), pp. 120ff.

Christians. This did not happen to the baptized Moors, the *Moriscos*, and this despite deliberate governmental policy to try to effect such assimilation. The *Moriscos* were eventually expelled from Spain (1611).

4. The word *español*, and the concept of the Spaniards as a nation distinct from other Christian nations, derived from non-Spanish Christians and from the relations of the Spaniards with them. A rather similar phenomenon occurred in other European countries.

5. In Spain, as everywhere else in Europe, there was a strong feeling of xenophobia. This was an old story, voiced very neatly in an anonymous Czech pamphlet of 1325:

> Oh, my God, the foreigner is favoured; the native is trampled upon. The normal and proper thing is for the bear to stay in his forest, the wolf in his cave, the fish in the sea and the German in Germany. In that way the world would have some peace.[76]

Appeals to this feeling were sometimes effective when an actual enemy invasion threatened the homeland, such as Philip II's appeals toward the end of his reign. It was not, however, the same as a feeling of nationalism. It was often, or perhaps even usually, directed against a neighbour in the peninsula. Sometimes, but not invariably, it coincided with differences in language (Castilian, Catalan, Galician, Basque, etc.). It was often institutionalized by custom or law so as to allow only the natives of a province to hold public offices or ecclesiastical benefices. Such customs and laws existed everywhere in Europe, though the degree to which they were enforced varied with time and place.

6. Closely connected with the previous point is the importance of political loyalties. In the Middle Ages these had been largely personal, and this continued to be a most important element in the early-modern period. Only gradually was it supplanted by a feeling of loyalty for an abstraction, such as the state, and then it tended to be for one's local kingdom, rather than for the whole of Spain.

7. The unification of the neighbouring medieval principalities into so-called national monarchies was primarily the result of the dynastic policies of ruling houses. These policies, to a large extent, created the modern nations – a different process from that which gave existing nations political unity, as happened in Germany and Italy in the nineteenth century. This is very evident in the Netherlands and in Switzerland in the early-modern period. It is also evident in the Iberian Peninsula, where dynastic and tactical considerations created Spain by the union of the crowns of Aragon and Castile and

[76] Quoted in S. Harrison Thompson, *Czechoslovakia in European History* (Princeton, 1953). I wish to thank Dr. Kenneth Dillon for drawing my attention to this quotation.

Portugal. To Ferdinand of Aragon the union of the crowns of Aragon, Sicily, and Naples was equally important. Neither a historical determinism, based on the pre-existence of a Spanish nation as a self-conscious political force, nor a sociological determinism, based on a theory of communication, seems to me to offer an acceptable explanation of Spanish history.

8. The Spanish monarchy, from Ferdinand and Isabella to Charles II, was singularly ineffective in promoting either institutional or emotional unity among its Spanish kingdoms. This is not really very surprising. Because the Spanish monarchs ruled non-Spanish countries, notably in Italy and the Netherlands, by hereditary right, they were precluded, largely for psychological reasons, from feeling in national Spanish terms. In effect, they pursued the poltically easiest line, that of deferring to the feelings of the ruling groups of the largest of their kingdoms, Castile.

9. The alliance of the Castilian ruling classes with the dynastic and religious ambitions of the Habsburgs – which began in the reign of Charles V, was consummated in that of Philip II, and was never given up after that – produced a Castilian imperialism that can only very marginally be identified with Spanish nationalism. Genuine Spanish nationalism, as an effective political force, does not seem to have appeared before the Napoleonic Wars in the early nineteenth century.

6. Cardinal Richelieu (1585–1642)
   Philippe de Champaigne. *National Gallery*

# 7

# The Crisis of the 17th Century

## A Farewell?[1]

The study of crises and revolutions is a matter of fashion. The crisis of the 17th century has had a good historiographic run. From Los Angeles to Léningrad and from Copenhagen to Naples, historians have written and debated about it for over twenty years. My impression is that the debate is now beginning to run dry. As so often happens, the questions historians have asked have not been definitively resolved; but they do not seem quite as urgent any more as they once did, and people have begun to ask different questions or, perhaps, the same questions as before, but in a different form and with a different emphasis. Before the matter disappears completely into the limbo of forgotten historiography, like Charles Beard's interpretetation, of the American Revolution, Turner's frontier or Tawney's rising gentry, it may be good to look back and see what it was about, whether it has had more than antiquarian significance and whether we may even perhaps see why this controversy has got stuck and whether that fact – if it is a fact – can tell us something historiographically important.

People living in the middle decades of the seventeenth century were very conscious of living in a time of crisis or revolution. The Venetian ambassador in Madrid in 1648 described the disasters which had befallen the Spanish Monarchy in the last few years: Portugal and Catalonia in open revolt; Andalusia in the grip of corruption owing to the treachery of the duke of Medina Sidonia; the East Indies with Brazil (a country large enough for four kingdoms) lost with Portugal; the West Indies hard pressed by the Dutch; the royal revenues mortgaged, credit extinct, friends become enemies or vacillating neutrals, and the government of the country abandoned to the inexperience of a new favourite. Thus the Spanish Monarchy, so the Venetian concluded with an evident touch of self-satisfaction, resembled that great colossus which for many years had been the wonder of the world and which during an earthquake had collapsed in a few moments while everyone

[1] A somewhat different version of this paper was published in German, 'Die Krise des 17. Jahrhunderts,' *Zeitschrift für Historische Forschung*. The most recent treatment of the whole subject is P. Zagorin, *Rebels and Rulers 1500–1650*, 2 vols. (Cambridge, 1982). Zagorin, however, takes a wider chronological span than the 17th century.

hurried along to enrich himself with the fragments.[2] In histories, memoirs and political pamphlets writers in Italy, France, the Netherlands and England compared the Spanish happenings with similar ones in the whole of Europe.[3] A hundred years later Voltaire, in his *Essai sur les moeurs et l'esprit des nations* extended this viewpoint further with comparisons of events in Morocco, Turkey, India and China.[4]

The modern historiography of this phenomenon of crisis began in 1938 with a small book, *Six Contemporaneous Revolutions* by the Harvard historian Roger B. Merriman, well-known for his splendid four-volume *History of Spain*.[5] Merriman's roughly contemporary revolutions were the English civil war, the Fronde, the revolts in Catalonia, Portugal and Naples and, finally, the fall of the house of Orange in the United Provinces of the Netherlands. Merriman compared his six revolutions with those of 1848; but, in contrast to these, he found no general causes, except in the case of Catalonia and Portugal, and he also found little influence of the revolutions on each other.

Merriman's book aroused little interest at the time. Perhaps, during the Second World War, people were not very interested in revolutions, at least not in the English-speaking countries. When I took up the book, in 1946, it was mainly to add another revolt, that of Palermo of 1647.[6] While I made some comparisons with the English civil war, I did not at that time pursue the theme of revolutions and crises in the seventeenth century. When seven years later Roland Mousnier published his fascinating book on the sixteenth and seventeenth centuries, he characterised the whole seventeenth century as a period of crisis, but at that time he also made no attempt to study the concept of crisis or revolution more deeply.[7]

Such an attempt appeared first in the same year, 1954, but from a different angle, that of economic history. Economic historians generally accepted, at the time, that the great expansion of the European economy in the sixteenth century did not continue through the seventeenth. They knew this mainly from the history of prices. The well-known price rise of the sixteenth century, the so-called price revolution, came to an end in the course of the first three decades of the

    [2] Pietro Basadonna, in Barozzi and Berchet, eds., *Relazioni degli ambasciatori veneti*, ser. 1, vol. II, (Venice, 1860), p. 197.
    [3] G. Parker, 'Introduction', in G. Parker and Lesley M. Smith, eds., *The General Crisis of the Seventeenth Century*, (London, 1978), pp. 1–3.
    [4] Quoted *ibid.*, pp. 3–4.
    [5] R. B. Merriman, *Six Contemporaneous Revolutions*, (Oxford, 1938).
    [6] H. G. Koenigsberger, 'The Revolt of Palermo in 1647', *The Cambridge Historical Journal*, VIII, 3, 1946. Reprinted in somewhat expanded form in H. G. Koenigsberger, *Estates and Revolutions*, (Ithaca and London, 1971), pp. 253–77.
    [7] R. Mousnier, *Les XVIe et XVIIe siècles*, (Paris, 1954).

seventeenth century. War and the very effective Dutch and English competition even produced an economic decline in Germany and Italy. For Spain such a decline was an accepted orthodoxy. On the basis of these assumptions Eric Hobsbawm now tried to sketch a generally valid theory of a crisis of the whole seventeenth century. Using Marxist categories he made the continuing economic, social and political predominance of feudalism responsible for diverting the rising capitalist system from effective production or, at any rate, for limiting such production. The crisis itself then cleared the way for the renewed rise of the capitalist economy in the eighteenth century. According to Hobsbawm this happened because of the growth of the capital cities in the absolutist monarchies, the decline of towns dominated by craft guilds in favour of the capitalist putting-out system, the rise of the slave and plantation economy in the European colonies and, above all, because of the social changes in England which created a large unified market.[8] Hobsbawm, who is a specialist in nineteenth and twentieth century economic and social history, made his foray into the earlier period mainly to start a debate. This object he achieved very successfully, even though his own theory as a whole has not generally been accepted, not even by Marxists. Even for England it is doubtful whether the victory of Parliament over Charles I may be regarded as a victory of capitalism over feudalism. In France and in the dominions of the Spanish Monarchy there can simply be no question of a solution of the crisis, whatever its causes, in favour of capitalism.

The economic historians, however, continued to work out a model of an economic crisis of the seventeenth century based on price and trade statistics. Pierre Chaunu, in his eight-volume work on the Atlantic trade of Seville, showed that, between 1504 and 1650, there were four clearly defined periods in Spain's trade with America. The first expanding phase, during the original conquest and plundering of Central and South America, lasted until about 1550. After some twelve years of sinking prices and contracting trade there was a renewed expansion, based on silver mining, the development of the great colonial agrarian properties, on the African slave trade and on the export of European commodities to the Spanish colonies. This phase lasted until the turn of the century. It was followed by two decades of strongly fluctuating prices and trade figures which then slid into a general decline of both prices and trade. This fourth phase lasted at least until the middle of the seventeenth century, perhaps even to the end. Chaunu related these four phases of the Spanish-American trade, two phases of expansion and two of contraction, first to the whole of the Spanish economy and then to the whole European economy. He had

---

[8] E. J. Hobsbawm, 'The Overall Crisis of the European Economy in the Seventeenth Century', *Past and Present*, 5, May 1954, pp. 33–53 and 6, Nov. 1954, pp. 44–65. Reprinted in T. Aston, *Crisis in Europe 1560–1660*, (London, 1965), pp. 5–58.

found an astonishing correlation of his graphs of Spanish prices with
W. H. Posthumus's price curves for Amsterdam; and Amsterdam's
trade in the seventeenth century of course determined much of the trade
of the whole of Europe.[9]

The theory of a general economic crisis in Europe in the seventeenth
century therefore seemed to be confirmed by Chaunu's immense
statistical investigation. It is true that some of Chaunu's conclusions in
the field of the theory and philosophy of history seemed from the
beginning rather more doubtful. Chaunu had accepted from Braudel
the organisation of historical investigation and writing into *structures,
conjonctures and événements*. If I have understood Braudel correctly – and
I asked him about it in a radio interview on the B.B.C.[10] – he sees his
threefold division as nothing more than a heuristic schema which he has
adopted to show the different speeds of historical development which
go on at the same time. He said that, instead of a threefold division,
there was no inherent reason not to have a fortyfold one; only, it would
be too difficult to handle. For many of Braudel's followers, however,
his threefold division has taken on a quasi-philosophical colouring,
something which seems to be inherent in the nature and structure of
historical development as such. Such a view had the further advantage
that one could either leave out the now despised and old-fashioned
*histoire événementelle* altogether or that one could at least strongly
devalue it. But Chaunu went even further. 'These four fluctuations
exist', he wrote. 'It is possible to arrange everything around them, to
integrate everything in the framework they provide. They allow
everything to be measured, everything to be understood, even what is
qualitative, economic events, indeed just events – in other words,
History.'[11]

This magnificent and also elegantly and subtly worked out theory
would certainly explain the crisis of the seventeenth century. To be fair,
Chaunu does not actually claim to have done this.[12] What he has
claimed is that his long waves (Kondratieffs) are cyclical, the way some
economists have claimed it for the English and American economy in
the nineteenth century. But should one not wonder whether a theory of
long waves in the nineteenth century, a theory which is based on the
statistics of industrial production, would really fit the seventeenth
century for which we have statistics only of prices and of trade? Should
one not also wonder whether Chaunu's *conjonctures* were really cyclical,
i.e. that they are derived from the structure of the economy and not

[9] P. Chaunu, *Séville et l'Atlantique (1504–1650)*, 8 vols., (Paris, 1955–59).

[10] 'Braudel and the Primary Vision', interview of Fernand Braudel by P. Burke and
H. G. Koenigsberger, 13 Nov. 1977. B.B.C. Programme 3.

[11] Chaunu, *Séville et l'Atlantique*, VIII. 2, p. 39.

[12] Chaunu has also not claimed this in a later book where one might have expected it,
*La civilisation de l'Europe classique*, (Paris, 1966).

from quite specific and unique historical events? Chaunu cites the catastrophic decline of the native population in Spanish-America as one of the principal reasons for the economic decline of the Spanish colonies in the seventeenth century. This population decline was the result primarily of the impact of European diseases on the Ameroindians. I do not see how this can be explained by his model of long economic waves. From my point of view, i.e. that of explaining the crisis of the seventeenth century, Chaunu has not eliminated *histoire événementelle* as successfully as he seems to have thought, at any rate twenty years ago.

At the same time, Chaunu's general description of his four phases remained acceptable, and with it the general assumption of the existence of an economic crisis in the seventeenth century. Ruggiero Romano, for instance, continued to work on this assumption but concentrated on the first big international slump, around 1620.[13] He made use of Chaunu's figures among others but he did not base his theory of the crisis primarily on the Atlantic trade nor, as some English economic historians did, on the structural crisis of the older English and Dutch cloth industry which was beaten out of the international markets by newer, lighter and cheaper textiles, the 'new draperies'. Romano saw the key to the crisis in agriculture, for that was, after all, what the vast majority of the population of Europe was still engaged in. Refeudalisation and the decline of agricultural production and productivity, with the consequent fall in the standard of living of the agrarian population, led inevitably to a general economic crisis. The triggers for this crisis were the monetary problems of Baltic and the central European countries and the slump of 1619–16222. Only English and Dutch agriculture did not suffer from the general refeudalisation and therefore England and Holland did not suffer like the rest of Europe from the general economic crisis.

As a first sketch of the complete economic crisis of the seventeenth century Romano's model was brilliant. From our point of view, that of a general and not only an economic crisis, it has the disadvantage that it virtually excludes England, the country *par excellence* of civil war. The discussion of the agrarian crisis, however, has continued and has, for instance, produced a very interesting polemic in *Past & Present* over a number of years.[14] In the process, however, the discussion has widened into a more general one, carried on between Marxists and non-Marxists, about the phases of the European economy, from the crisis of

---

[13] R. Romano, 'Tra cinquecento e seicento', *Rivista storica italiana*, LXXIV, 1962. English translation in Parker and Smith, *The General Crisis*, pp. 165–225.

[14] R. Brenner, 'Agrarian Class Structure and Economic Development in Pre-industrial Europe', *Past and Present*, 70, 1976. 'Symposium: Agrarian Class Structure . . .', by M. M. Postan, J. Hatcher, P. Croot, D. Parker, H. Wunder, *ibid.*, 78, Febr. 1978, pp. 24–55; by E. Le Roy Ladurie, G. Bois, *ibid.*, 79, May 1978, pp. 55–69; by R. Hilton, J. P. Cooper, *ibid.*, 80, Aug. 1978, pp. 3–65. Brennner's reply *ibid.*, 97, Nov. 1982.

feudalism in the later middle ages to the final victory of industrial capitalism.[15]

Parallel with the discussions of the professional economic historians, there developed the discussions of the political and social historians about the actual revolts and revolutions of the seventeenth century. The stimulus and the first attempt to provide a synthesis occurred during the first of the now regular Anglo-Dutch historical conferences, at Oxford in 1959, and it was due to Hugh Trevor-Roper (Lord Dacre). Trevor-Roper's theory or, rather, his model was simple, elegant and comprehensive. The early modern or Renaissance state, by which Trevor-Roper meant the court, the royal officials, the army and the whole system of royal patronage, had grown enormously since the end of the middle ages. This had happened at the expense of the country, i.e. all those who did not directly profit from the growth of the court, as here defined. With the economic crisis of 1620 the contrasts between court and country became more acute until, in one monarchy after another, some incident led to an explosion. This would either lead to a fall of the monarchy, as in England, or the monarchy would be forced into a rationalisation and reorganisation, as in France.[16]

As far as I know, no other historian has accepted Trevor-Roper's model, at least not in the form in which he sketched it. Specialists in the history of different Continental countries pointed out that, while the model might perhaps fit England, it did not other countries.[17] Ernst Kossmann remarked that what happened in the Netherlands around 1650 was a power struggle between the province of Holland, on the one side, and the house of Orange-Nassau, allied with the six remaining provinces, on the other. It was certainly not a struggle between court and country. John Elliott showed that in Spain it was the contrasting interests of the centre and the periphery which led to the revolts but again not a contrast between court and country. He also pointed out that the three (or four) revolutions were very different from each other. In Catalonia the revolt of 1640 started with riots of the lower classes against the Castilian troops quartered on the country, and these riots then drew the leading groups into the struggle with Madrid, but each of them with very different motivations. The Catalan revolt then triggered a revolt in Portugal that was from the beginning led by the high nobility and the clergy. In 1647 popular revolts broke out, first in Naples and then in Palermo. But, in contrast to those of Catalonia and

---

[15] A critical survey which, characteristically, starts with the crisis of the 17th century, by I. Wallerstein, 'Y a-t-il une crise du XVII$^e$ siècle?', *Annales: Economies Sociétés Civilisations*, 34. 2, Febr.–March 1979, pp. 126–44.

[16] H. R. Trevor-Roper, 'The General Crisis of the Seventeenth Century', *Past and Present*, 16, 1959. Reprinted in Aston, *Crisis*, pp. 59–95.

[17] E. Kossmann, in Symposium on Trevor-Roper, 'The General Crisis', *Past and Present*, 18, 1960, pp. 8–11.

Portugal, they were directed not against the king and against Castile but against the vice-regal governments and, even more virulently, against the native nobility.

In France, Trevor-Roper's theory was drawn into a fairly long-standing controversy between the Soviet historian Boris Porchnev and Roland Mousnier and his collaborators. On the basis of French documents in Russian archives – they had been taken there by the Russian ambassador to France during the French Revolution – Porchnev had constructed a Marxist model of the popular risings in France before and during the Fronde. These, he argued, had been class struggles of the peasants against the feudal nobility. The Fronde itself had been a bourgeois revolution *manqué*, in contrast to what he regarded as the successful bourgeois revolution in England.[18] The Mousnier school rejected this model of class struggle and demonstrated that it was frequently the seigneurs themselves who set the peasants against the royal tax collectors. They did this because high royal taxes often made it impossible for the peasants to pay the seigneurs their rents and dues. As a specific answer to Trevor-Roper Mousnier pointed out that the Fronde was not a struggle between court and country but between different groups of nobles and between different groups of royal officials, struggles in which there were continual shifts of front and of alliances.[19]

This first round of the discussion started by Trevor-Roper was published in *Past & Present*. From then on, both the aims and the methodology of the discussion shifted. In the first place, some historians extended the geographical range of the crisis. They discussed the great Cossack rising in the Ukraine, around 1648, the Swiss peasants war of 1653 and the usually rather neglected Irish rebellion of 1641. To these revolts were added some crises which had stopped short of actual explosion, as in Sweden, the Spanish Netherlands and the imperial city of Lübeck.[20] Going back to Voltaire, we heard again about the fall of the Ming Dynasty in China and then even about the messianic movement of Sabbatai Zevi (or Shabbetai Tzevi), in Smyrna in 1665, which perturbed Jewish communities in four continents until the false messiah converted to Islam.[21]

In the second place, there were attempts to build new models, or at least partial models, for the crises. At the same time, the Marxist

[18] B. Porchnev, *Les soulèvements populaires en France de 1623 à 1648*, (Paris, 1963).

[19] R. Mousnier, in Symposium on Trevor-Roper, *cit.*, reprinted in Aston, *Crisis*, pp. 97–104.

[20] D. J. Sturdy, 'La révolte irlandaise (1641–1650)'; P. Janssens, 'L'échec des soulèvements aux Pays-Bas sous Philippe IV (1621–1665)'; G. Livet, 'La guerre des paysans de 1653 en Suisse'; C. Nordmann, 'La crise de la Suède au temps de Christine et de Charles X Gustave (1644–1660)'. All in Colloque de l'Institut d'Histoire de l'Université de Picardie. Chantilly, septembre 1977. *Revue d'histoire diplomatique*, 92, 1978.

[21] Cf. Parker, 'Introduction', *cit.*, p. 17

intrepretation became a great deal more subtle than Porchnev's had been. Thus Rosario Villari, in a critique of both Hobsbawm and Trevor-Roper, directed the attention of historians to the transformation of a section of the European aristocracy in the first half of the seventeenth century. Many members of the high nobility had come to engage in financial speculation, in tax-farming and in making loans to governments. These activities did not make them agents of the development of modern captialism. The revolts of the middle of the seventeenth century had (therefore?) among other characteristics a strongly anti-aristocratic streak and the bourgeoisie affirmed itself, perhaps for the first time, as an autonomous class, although still within the framework of a feudalistic structure of society.[22] Such formulations may result in a mild attack of vertigo; but in his excellent book on the origins of the revolt of Naples Villari has in fact provided a detailed and very acceptable social analysis. What is much more doubtful is whether his analysis would fit anywhere outside the *mezzogiorno*, the Italian south.

Designed from the beginning to be a comprehensive model was Theodore Rabb's elegant and beautifully illustrated *The Struggle for Stability in Early Modern Europe* (1975).[23] It was the first attempt to include cultural events systematically within an overall analysis of the crisis. According to Rabb there was a common psychological attitude in this period which the artists of the Mannerist and Baroque schools shared with the writers, the philosophers, the scientists and the politicians. It was a fear, a king of *Weltangst*, of anarchy. The metaphor of the crisis of mid-seventeenth century gives in fact, a good description of a long illness going through its final, critical stage which is followed by relaxation, calm and classical balance – in short, the acceptance of the authority of the state and of the existing social structure during the century of 1660 to 1760. It was this accepted authority which had been lacking before. The crisis was therefore a crisis of authority. It had started with Savonarola, Machiavelli and Luther and then showed itself with Montaigne and the sceptics, with Descartes starting from absolute doubt and with the whole Copernican-Gallilean revolution in the natural sciences. It was similar in literature. Faust and Don Quixote strive for the unattainable. The tragic heroes of Shakespeare and the comic heroes of Molière have to learn painfully to limit their ambitions. Milton's Satan is damned because he refuses to do this. Rabb sees the whole of the Baroque as an attempt to 'make grandeur and immensity subdue uncertainty'. The uncertainty of the social and political sphere was similar. Rabb enumerates the familiar revolts and, quite properly, points to the increasingly savage and destructive modes of warfare.

[22] R. Villari, 'Rivolte e coscienza rivoluzionaria nel secolo XVII', *Studi storici*, 12.2, 1971, pp. 235–64.
[23] T. K. Rabb, *The Struggle for Stability in Early Modern Europe*, (New York, 1975).

Rabb has worked out his thesis very intelligently, and in book-length it appears a good deal more plausible than in a short summary. Nevertheless, it suffers from misconceptions. Rabb argues, for instance, that the great philosophers and scientists of the century or two before 1660 were all basically pessimists. This is difficult to credit when one reads, for instance, the polemics of Paracelsus or Vesalius with their sublime assurance of their own correctness and the wrong-headedness of everyone else. It is equally difficult to credit of Kepler and Galileo whose self-confidence gave them the courage to challenge the Church. And what was pessimistic about Bacon or Descartes, both convinced that the sum of scientific kowledge was accessible to mankind in one or two generations, provided only that people used their methods of investigation? Incidentally, although Rabb tries to be comprehensive, he says nothing about music, which does not fit very well into his schema and, more surprisingly, he says very little about economic development.

Most historians, however, who tried to construct theories for the crisis of the seventeenth century took over the models of revolution from modern sociology and political science. This led immediately to a controversy over the use of the word revolution. Could the revolts of the seventeenth century properly be called revolutions at all? The word was used at the time, probably in analogy to the revolutions of the planets around the sun in the new Copernican astronomy. This fitted in rather well with a characteristic of the seventeenth century revolution commented on by most historians, the tendency of the revolutionaries to look not ahead, to a rosy future, but backwards, towards a former golden age. Some historians therefore concluded that the revolts of the seventeenth century should really be characterised as counter-revolutions. Others held that a true revolution takes place only when the whole structure of society is overthrown. In that case there was no revolution before the French Revolution, only uprisings and revolts.

If one wants to define the matter in this way, then this conclusion is undoubtedly correct; only, it does not get us much further in our problem. For the people of the seventeenth century the overthrow of a government remained the overthrow of a government. It is really an academic question whether the Netherlanders rebelled against the king of Spain in order, as they officially claimed, to return to a former position of public law or whether, as the Protestant historians of the nineteenth century thought, they were protagonists of modern liberal and national freedom. For most Catholics in the sixteenth and seventeenth centuries, a change of religion was in itself a revolutionary act, for, by experience, it led to a change of regime. To the Spaniards even the Catholic rebels in the Netherlands were conscious or unconscious allies, fellow travellers, of the radical heretics with their doctrines of a necessarily future millennium. In every case they were rebels against the king's rightful authority. The regime which they set in its place, a regime without a legitimate monarchy without an official church, without privileges for the old nobility – this was a regime that was quite revolutionary enough for contemporaries, no matter what the original intentions of the rebels had been.

It was no different in England in the middle of the seventeenth century. Pym and his friends wanted to return to the golden age of Queen Elizabeth. But the authority which they claimed for parliament in the process of this return was quite unprecedented and, hence, in practice revolutionary; and so was the regime of the Rump Parliament and of Cromwell's Protectorate: a regime without legitimate monarchy, without House of Lords, without bishops and an established church, without (one should also add) clerical censorship. This was all highly revolutionary, even if the rest of the social structure of the country remained intact.

At the very least, we are therefore left with the question of the overthrow of a government or a regime. This was the question asked of five historians in a series of conferences at the Johns Hopkins University.[24] Of these five it was especially Lawrence Stone who tried to utilise modern theories of revolution for the English revolution of the seventeenth century. He had previously published a bibliographical article about such theories[25] and he worked out his own views more fully in his book *The Causes of the English Revolution, 1529–1642*, that was to appear a little later.[26] Stone did not take over the modern theories mechanically. His conclusions remain careful and provisional, his models elastic. Basically, he works with three conceptual systems. The first is the Braudelian tripartite framework whose terms he calls preconditions, medium term precipitants and triggers. The preconditions, Braudel's and Chaunu's *structures*, can be completely analysed. For this purpose he uses a second basic concept, that of dysfunction, i.e. what happens when things begin to go wrong, when the individual components of a society or a state are no longer in balance. In England, he thinks, dysfunction started in 1529, with the beginning of the Reformation. After a century of growing dysfunction we arrive at the period of precipitants, *conjonctures*. For this period Stone uses his third basic concept, that of the J-curve or, more accurately, the inverted J-curve, ⌠. This curve illustrates the well-known observation that revolutions do not usually erupt during a long period of a declining standard of living but rather at the end of a period of a rising standard which, for whatever reason, has just begun to

---

[24] R. Forster and J. P. Greene, *Preconditions of Revolution in Early Modern Europe*, (Baltimore and London, 1970).

[25] L. Stone, 'Theories of Revolution', *World Politics*, 18, 1966.

[26] (New York, 1972).

decline. Such a curve may indicate economic conditions but equally political expectations. A reforming regime which ceases to reform, or which does not go as far as people have been led to expect, is more liable to revolution than a consistently repressive regime.

This is all perfectly plausible, and in many respects Stone has illuminated our problem. Nevertheless his conceptual systems create both theoretical and factual difficulties for the early modern historian. One must surely assume that the concept of dysfunction presupposes the concept of function, i.e. the existence of an equilibrium as the normal condition of a society. But if, in England, dysfunction began to appear in 1529 when was there the period of equilibrium, which one would have to assume to have been at least reasonably long to contrast with the hundred years of dysfunction? The fifteenth century, the age of the great defeat in France and of the Wars of Roses? the fourteenth century, with the Black Death, its popular rebellions and the deposition of two kings? In between the disasters there were some relatively short periods of calm and equilibrium. But why should they have any greater claim to be the norm than the rather longer periods of unrest and confusion? I shall come back to this point.

Secondly, when one looks more closely at Stone's precipitants they don't appear all that different from his preconditions. Take Charles I's Scottish war. It was caused, one might almost say it was provoked, by the tactlessness of the king and his minister, Archbishop Laud, in trying to impose the Anglican prayer book in Presbyterian Scotland. The Scots were offended, both in their religious beliefs and in their traditions and rights of autonomy. When the Scots invaded northern England, Charles was forced to summon the English parliament, for the first time in eleven years, in order to get help to counter the Scots. Now are these events as unanalysable as Stone suggests? To me they represent a well-known, even typical pattern. Great Britain was a personal union of kingdoms, a composite monarchy, in which those dominions furthest removed from royal power enjoyed considerable political and religious autonomy. This was the case in all the major European monarchies of the period. It was the exact pattern in Bohemia in 1618 and in Béarn in 1620. In Scotland, as in Bohemia, in Béarn and the autonomous Huguenot cities of southern France, the central monarchies attempted to set aside local privileges and sparked off revolutions. It was the same again in Catalonia in 1640 except that here the quarrel which led to the revolution was not primarily about religion.[27]

What happened in Bohemia, Scotland, southern France, Catalonia and, eventually also in England, was therefore not the result of

[27] Cf. H. G. Koenigsberger, 'Revolutionary Conclusions', *History*, 57, Oct. 1972, pp. 394–98; and Koenigsberger and Stone, 'Early Modern Revolutions: An Exchange', *Journal of Modern History*, 46.1, March 1974, pp. 99–106.

dysfunction. It was also not the result of unfulfilled expectation, i.e. the J-curve. Moreover, the Braudelian tripartite organisation of history does not fit these revolutions very well. Mousnier, in his Johns Hopkins lecture, remarked, both with regard to the Fronde and also more generally, that there was no logical determinism between the conditions for revolutions and the events of the revolutions.[28] Elliott added to this view the observation that in the whole of Europe there existed a very tenacious local patriotism, a loyalty to one's *patria* which was however not identical with the modern nations. The centralising policy of the monarchies constantly offended this feeling and rebellions were therefore a very frequent occurrence. Those of the middle of the seventeenth century were no more unusual, nor more critical, than others, for instance those of the years following 1560.[29]

In so far as they speak of dynamic forces in the political society of the seventeenth century, Mousnier and Elliott lay much greater stress than Stone on the role of the monarchies. The historians of Sweden and Denmark went furthest in this direction. In both these countries, political initiative in the middle of the seventeenth century very clearly lay with the monarchies. It was therefore perfectly logical that a Danish historian, Niels Steensgaard, should work out systematically the role of the monarchy in the seventeenth century. In an article which first appeared in the *Historisk Tidskrift* of 1970 Steensgaard turned the generally accepted interpretation of the economic crisis of the seventeenth century on its head. It was not a crisis of production, as Chaunu, Romano, the Marxists and the critics of the Marxists had all thought, but a crisis of distribution and, in consequence, of demand. The reason for this was the economically central role of the state. In most countries of Europe royal taxes rose much more quickly than total production. By far the largest part of total production was used in daily consumption. Of the relatively small rest, taxes now took an economically paralysing and, moreover, increasing percentage. The state became both the greatest consumer and the greatest employer. This was the essence of absolutism. For Steensgaard then, as for Trevor-Roper, the state is at the centre of the problem. But Steensgaard, as an economic historian, pushed his economic analysis much further and he also concluded that the state or the monarchy did not collapse because of the antagonism of the 'country' but that it overcame the crisis by the development of absolutism. It did so, however, at the expense of economic development. In this way Steensgaard was able to give a good reason for the different development between England and Holland, on the one hand, and most of the rest of Europe, on the other.

[28] R. Mousnier, 'The Fronde', in Forster and Greene, *Preconditions*, pp. 157–58.
[29] J. H. Elliott, 'The Revolts in the Spanish Monarchy', *ibid.*, pp. 109–30. *Idem*, 'Revolution and Continuity in Early Modern Europe', in Parker and Smith, *The General Crisis*, p. 112.

Steensgaard's article is now available in translation in a collective volume edited in 1978 by Geoffrey Parker and Lesley M. Smith.[30] Apart from the article by Romano and others by Elliott, Ivo Schöffer, Lloyd Moote and by Parker himself, the editors also print one which attempts to find a cause for all the crises of the seventeenth century in the whole world, i.e. also for those in the Ukraine and in China. This is a meteorological study by John A. Eddy of the National Center for Atmospheric Research in Boulder, Colorado, 'The "Maunder Minimum" : Sunspots and Climate in the Reign of Louis XIV'. According to the well-documented observations of the sun there were apparently between 1645 and 1715 no, or hardly any, sunspots. This phenomenon is to be explained by a well-known sun-cycle and it resulted in a lowering of the average temperature on earth. This, in its turn, had unfavourable effects on agricultural production. Here, so it is argued, was at any rate one of the 'factors' for the economic crisis of the period and for the widespread popular unrest, caused by inadequate harvests. All this is certainly possible. All the same, the decline of average temperature – and we are talking of no more than one degree centigrade – is not necessarily the same thing as bad weather, and it is the weather, more than average temperature, which matters in harvests. Moreover, the 'Maunder Minimum' began rather late with relation to both the economic and the political crisis. Romano's very well documented crisis occurred some 25 years earlier and the English civil war, the most dramatic of the political crises was, after four years, nearing its end in 1645 when the sunspots stopped. Catalonia and Portugal had declared their independence of Spain five years before. Perhaps where growing and harvest time were short, say in Sweden, Scotland or the Castilian Meseta, a further shortening of this time, caused by climatic changes, may well have been critical. But, except just possibly for Scotland, these were not the centres of revolution. Were the harvests in such a critical stage in the principal centres, in England, in the Ile de France, in Catalonia, Portugal or Naples? It is possible, but it has not yet been demonstrated. In Sicily the revolt of Palermo was certainly triggered off by failed harvests and the harvests remained poor in the island into the 1650s. In the 1670s they were bad again.[31] For Sicily, then, there would certainly appear to be the possibility of a connection between climate, or the weather, and revolt.

It appears, therefore, that the historiographical problem of the crisis of the seventeenth century has reached an impasse. None of the models which have so far been constructed has found general acceptance. With some, as with Steensgaard or the climatologists, one would wish that

[30] *Ibid.*, pp. 26–56.
[31] I would like to thank Dr. Timothy Davies for the information about the Sicilian harvests after 1648.

they would work out their models in more detail. But it does not seem to be happening. This raises the question whether it is possible, or indeed necessary, to construct a comprehensive model at all. I would here like to suggest some considerations which I think have to be kept in mind if one wants to get any further.

Nearly all political and social historians who have studied the problem have started from the assumption that the crisis signified the overthrow or, at the least, a serious disturbance, of a political and social system which was previously at rest or in equilibrium. In this respect it does not matter whether the overthrow is seen as a revolution or a counterrevolution. This, after all, depends largely on the political point of view of the historian. The assumption is equally present with Marxists and with those non-Marxists historians, such as Stone and Lloyd Moote, who attempt to transfer the models of modern political science to the seventeenth century. These models are, as we have seen all static models, constructed in analogy to the economists' static models of balance. All of them, moreover, including the Marxist ones, are heavily dependent on the modern experience of revoutions, from the French Revolution to those of 1848 and 1917, and to Mao Tse Tung and Fidel Castro. These were all revolutions from below, movements in which the non-privileged classes overthrew the political system of the privileged classes. Counterrevolutions in these models are exactly what their name indicates, the re-establishment of the former regime or some variant of the former regime. Revolution and counter-revolution are therefore both seen as struggles of a horizontally divided society. During the actual crisis all other divisions tend to be subsumed in this horizontal division.

It is these assumptions which seem to me to be a basic misunderstanding of the seventeenth century or even of the whole of European history before the second half of the eighteenth century. European society of the *ancien régime* – and I want to use this term of 'old regime' not just for the fifty odd years before the French Revolution but, for the whole of post-feudal history, from about the fourteenth to the eighteenth century – was of course a hierarchical society. The propertied groups, whether organised as monarchies, aristocracies or urban patriciates, were also the ruling groups. All attempts to overthrow this basic organisation of society – and there were really very few – failed either immediately or after a very short time. I think we can all agree about this. But it was only in this respect, its basic organisation and power structure, that European society remained firm. In every other respect the socity of the ancient regime was anything but stable. Its structure was a confusion of mutually hostile groups within the geographically, administratively and ideologically divided ruling classes. Its psychological bonds of group-feeling were on occasion determined by class but much more usually by loyalty to family, profession and estate. Above all, the bonds were frequently vertical, between partron and client, just as in the feudal period they had been between lord and vassal. Property, social influence and political power were much more diffuse and splintered than the modern theories of revolution have recognised. The diffusion and splintering of power was paralleled by a diffusion and splintering of loyalties.[32] It is no accident that the tragedy of divided loyalties has been one of the central themes of European literature from the Nibelung Saga onwards, or even earlier.

The protagonists of sociological analysis in history believe, among other things, that historians should analyse the problem of the sense of criminality in early modern revolutions in order to understand why otherwise law–abiding citizens or subjects feel impelled to commit the criminal act of rebellion.[33] This is certainly an interesting problem; but I believe the question is wrongly formulated. From the point of view of any particular government rebels were of course criminals. That is natural enough, but it doesn't get us very far. For, from their own point of view, this was precisely what the rebels were not. Since the middle ages the right of resistance had been justified, both on moral and on legal grounds. The sixteenth century added to these grounds religious justifications. By definition, those who practiced resistance, i.e. rebellion, for such reasons did not regard themselves as criminals. The followers of Masaniello in Naples who shouted 'long live the king: down with the ministers!' saw themselves as the defenders of the lawful order which, in their opinion, had been broken by the unlawful actions of the king's officials. For Cromwell, for Condé, for the duke of Braganza rebellion was not a question of choice between legality and criminality but between conflicting demands for loyalty. One of the basic reasons why the English parliament won the civil war was because the country, or at any rate the richest and most populous part of the country, accepted its claims for loyalty. In France similar claims by the parlement of Paris were not believed and this disbelief turned out to be one of the greatest weaknesses of the Fronde.

Royalist political theories naturally insisted that the monarchy stood above all factions and that therefore it alone could preserve law and order and the unity of the state. Up to a point this was true enough; but all the same, it was a one–sided and propagandistic description of reality. The monarchy was usually the best organised and the most purposeful force in early modern society and it tried systematically to extend its powers. But, in spite of all its claims, and in contrast with the

[32] Cf. Elliott, 'Revolution and Continuity', p. 117: 'A society grouped into corporations, divided into orders, and linked vertically by powerful ties of kinship and clientage cannot be expected to behave in the same way as a society divided into classes.'

[33] A. Lloyd Moote, 'The Preconditions of Revolution in Early Modern Europe: did they really exist?', in Parker and Smith, *The General Crisis*, p. 144.

modern state, it could command no monopoly of political loyalty. This was the reason why the monarchy inevitably came into conflict with other centres of loyalty in the state, with provinces and cities, with parliaments and estates, with churches and magnates and, finally, with its own tools, the royal officials who were organised in corporations, corporations which could generate as much *esprit de corps* as the self-perpetuating city councils of semi-autonomous towns.

These were the struggles which determined the forms and the tone of the political society of the European countries and, if we accept Steensgaard's analysis, also the dynamics of their economic development. And these were not the only struggles in early modern society. A population subject to periodic famines and murderous epidemics; economic and social upheavals following the fluctuations of population; the rapidly expanding cities with their work forces dependent on the uncertainties of international markets; a country nobility, largely trained for war, whose rental income was subject to violent changes in agricultural prices – all this caused constant movement, an almost unceasing manoeuvring, attack and defence. Popular movements therefore occurred in the countryside and in the towns almost everywhere and almost constantly. Usually the aims of the rioters were practical and local: the price of grain, high taxes, rents or feudal dues and church tithes, often also the depredations and horrors perpetrated by the hated professional soldiers. In Provence, for instance; no fewer than 108 popular movements have been counted for the relatively peaceful period from 1596 to 1635. In the succeeding years of war and rapidly rising taxation, the number of popular movements also rose rapidly and reached 66 in the five years of the Fronde, 1648–53.[34]

It was always possible that such 'respectable' revolts changed into chiliastic-religious and socio-political movements with an immediately widening geographical impact. This would become particularly dangerous to the existing order if individual aristocrats, or even whole groups of the dominant classes, mobilised such movements for their own purposes. In spite of the universal aristocratic disdain of the lower classes, this happened frequently enough, as in the case of Condé and the Parisian populace during the Fronde and in the case of the Catalan nobility in the revolt against Castile. In the latter instance the leading groups could also make use of a strong regional tradition and a deeply felt local patriotism which gave their alliance with a popular movement an air of greater respectability.[35] Since nearly all European monarchies were unions of different states, such conflicts and their intermingling with social movements were a constant danger for any existing regime.

[34] R. Pillorget, *Les mouvements insurrectionnels de Provence entre 1596 et 1715*, (Paris, 1975), p. 988.
[35] Elliott, 'Revolution and Continuity', *cit*. pp. 123–24.

What I have tried to sketch here very briefly is a dynamic model for the European society of the *ancien régime*, or perhaps not so much a model as a characterisation. This, I believe, has shifted the outlines of any possible crisis model for the seventeenth century. We can no longer posit a static order of society or a political regime which is normally in a state of equilibrium and which, under certain circumstances suffers from dysfunction and is then attacked and overthrown from below. On the contrary, normality was unstable, the interaction of constantly shifting dynamic forces of which the strongest and most dynamic was often, although not always, the monarchy. The movement which resulted from this dynamic was neither uniform nor symmetrical. It was, on the contrary, highly complex and changeable and it proceeded often, but again not always, in discrete shifts. Riot and revolution were so to speak built into this dynamic structure and they were psychologically acceptable because of the diffusion of both political power and of the feeling of loyalty. Not until the late seventeenth and the first half of the eighteenth century did the early modern state manage to establish both administratively and psychologically an effective monopoly of power.[36] One could at least argue that, precisely because after this process local revolts were no longer either feasible or useful, the way was now open for the great, national, society-changing revolutions. Perhaps it was this effective state monopoly of political power which made the century from 1660 to 1760 into one of the few long periods of calm and equilibrium? Perhaps it was this characteristic of the century of the enlightenment which misled modern sociologists and political scientists into thinking that equilibrium and stability were the normal conditions of European society?

Now, of course, even with a dynamic model, or a dynamic characterisation, of early modern European history, it is still necessary to explain the occurrence of specific crises or the clustering of crises. It is clear that to do this one has to proceed comparatively and this is also generally recognised although more rarely practised. Wolfgang Reinhard, the only German historian who, to my knowledge, has so far written systematically about this problem, has attempted it.[37] For this purpose he uses the classifications of 'collective behaviour' by the American sociologist Smelser[38] and applies them to the revolts in Naples and Sicily. But, as Reinhard sees quite clearly, Smelser's near-tautological descriptive categories, give no indication of the causes of revolts, let alone of their likely results. For these causes Reinhard constructs a diagram of interrelated conditions and forces within the

---

[36] For an important aspect of this process see G. Oestreich, *Neostoicism and the Early Modern State*, ed. Brigitta Oestreich and H. G. Koenigsberger, (Cambridge, 1982).

[37] W. Reinhard, 'Theorie und Empirie bei der Erforschung frühneuzeitlicher Volksaufstände', in H. Fenske, *Historia Integra*, (Berlin, 1977), pp. 173–200.

[38] N. Smelser, *Theory of Collective Behaviour*, (1963).

early modern state, rather in the manner of the economists before they started using computer models; but he admits that his model is not complete nor closed and that additional (and unpredictable) input will vary it.[39]

It is always assumed, by the Marxists included, that a possible theory of revolution must be constructed for a closed socio-political system, even when one looks at revolutions comparatively. The early modern states were, however, as I have stressed, nearly all of them composite states. With most of them therefore the tension between the metropolitan and the outer states played a particularly important role. Only Elliott has seen this clearly, at any rate for the Spanish monarchy. In fact, as we have seen, it was the same for the Austrian Habsburg monarchy, for Great Britain and even for the United Provinces of the Netherlands where the clash of interests between Holland and the other six provinces often had the decisive influence on the power struggle between the house of Orange-Nassan and the regent class of Holland. I rather suspect that a similar contrast was one of the reasons for the revolt of the Ukraine in the geographically vast and ethnically and politically very diverse kingdom of Poland.

The first consequence of this highly complex condition was that, in a revolutionary situation, both the monarchy and the revolutionaries might expect support from other parts of the composite state, parts in which the economic, social and political conditions might be quite different from those in which these conditions had, in the Braudelian or Stonean progression, led to the outbreak of revolution. Frequently, but not always, this situation gave the monarchy an advantage. In the Spanish monarchy the Catalan revolution was undoubtedly the cause of the outbreak of, but not the deeper reason for, the Portuguese revolution. Masaniello's revolt in Naples seems to have played a similar role in d'Alesi's in Palermo. These pairs of revolutionary movements did not give each other direct help and probably were not in a position to do so, even if they had so desired. By contrast, the Spanish monarchy could call on all its dominions for help. The revolts of Naples and Palermo were only crushed after the appearance of the Spanish fleet. In England, however, Scottish military intervention may well have been decisive for the victory of parliament. The help which the king could draw from Ireland was not equivalent.

The second consequence was that foreign intervention in civil wars was not only encouraged but became virtually unavoidable. This meant that the revolutions of the seventeenth century became entangled with the international power politics of the great states. This happened in France during the Fronde and in Spain during the revolutions of Catalonia and Portugal and, to a certain extent, also in that of Naples –

---

[39]  Reinhard, 'Theorie', p. 197.

just as it had happened in the revolt of Bohemia in 1618–20. England escaped such intervention on an effective scale only because the Continental powers, in the final stages of the Thirty Years War, no longer had the means, or perhaps not the will power, for an effective intervention across the Channel or the North Sea.

All this means that historians may just possibly be able to provide a full analysis of the outbreak of a revolution from the social–political situation of the country in which it occurred, but not of its outcome, its success or failure. The forces which intervene from outside, regardless of whether they are on the side of the revolutionaries or opposed to them, are not fully analysable because they do not depend only on the analysable socio-political forces of the intervening power but on one or more chains of circumstances which compel this power to confront, actively or passively, its own neighbours or even to deal with a revolution within its own frontiers. For precisely this reason France eventually withdrew its help from the Catalans and thus sealed the fate of their revolution.

It seems to me that it is therefore not even theoretically possible to construct a comprehensive theory or model for the revolutions of the seventeenth century. From this proposition it follows further that it is also not possible to construct such a model for the general development of European society in the early modern period. When therefore in the Marxist models the victories of the Dutch estates, in the sixteenth century, and of the English parliament in the seventeenth are seen as both an inevitable and a necessary stage in the development of capitalism, I think that this is not tenable; for these victories can be explained at best approximately from the pre-revolutionary economic, social and political development of Holland and England. A full explanation must take account of the critical interventions/noninterventions of other states and these interventions/noninterventions depended by and large not on the analysable economic and social structure of Holland and England.

This does not mean that therefore the results of revolutions and civil wars are matters of chance. The impossibility of establishing a rigorous casual connection between two groups of facts does not mean that their relationship, or the outcome of this relationship, is a matter of chance. The outbreak of the Catalan revolution in 1640 depended on the social structure of the country as well as on its position in the Spanish monarchy and on the policies of the government in Madrid. The success of the revolution depended, in the last resort, on the military intervention of France, on the available military resources of Castile and again on the continually shifting social struggles in Catalonia itself. None of these changing circumstances between 1640 and 1652, the end of the revolt, was a matter of chance. But all of them and especially their interaction were for contemporaries, and still are for the modern historian, only partially or approximatively analysable.

In the seventeenth century people ascribed the end result to God, but tried nevertheless to act as rationally as possible. For the historian, even if he has to give up the hope of ever constructing a rigorous overall model, it is still imperative to work out partial and approximative models.[40] In the process, narrative history, while not triumphing over analysis, will need to be restored to its rightful place together with all other tools which our historiographical tradition has given us.

[40] Reinhard, *ibid.*, pp. 198ff also suggests that revolts should be seen as part of the accepted culture of European society in the early modern period. Similar views in Y.-M. Bercé, *Révoltes et révolutions dans l'Europe moderne, XVIᵉ–XVIIᵉ siècles*, (Paris, 1980). Cf. also R. Dekker, *Holland in beroering: oproeren in de 17ᵈᵉ en 18ᵈᵉ eeuw*, (Baarn, 1982).

7. Piazza del Popolo, Rome. S. Maria di Monte Santo and S. Maria de' Miracoli (1662-79).
Carlo Rainaldi and Gianlorenzo Bernini.

# 8

# The Unity of the Church and the Reformation

It is a common complaint of social scientists that historians are too often content to study, describe, and analyze specific events, but fail to draw general conclusions from their knowledge. From time to time economists, sociologists, and psychologists have therefore bravely rushed in to remedy these defects of contemporary historiography. Leaving out those interventions which have contributed more to the entertainment than to the enlightenment of historians, it is, ironically, not difficult for these later to detect a certain pattern in the effects of the most intelligent of such interventions: The overall theories propounded by the social scientists in history have usually proved to be unacceptable and untenable, but the methods used, the questions asked, and the insights gained have often turned out to be enormously fruitful. The grandiose historical theories of Marx, Weber, or Keynes have not stood up to detailed historical criticism; but, since Marx, historians can never again ignore the social structure of societies in explaining their politics; since Weber, they can never again ignore the influence of religious beliefs on economic developments; and, since Keynes, they can never again ignore the importance of the technical aspects of monetary systems or happily imagine that all mercantilist writers and statesmen were ignorant or misguided fools.

It looks to me as if Swanson's ingenious theory of the relation between beliefs in the immanence of God in the world and certain types of political regimes may well join this distinguished line of untenable but fruitful theories.[1] I do not think – nor, it seems, do most other professional historians – that it stands up to rigorous historical examination. It may be, however, that for some men there was a psychological connection, conscious or unconscious, between the concepts of immanence and transcendence and their personal experience of certain types of political regime. If so, it may turn out to have been one of the many and complex sources of motivation which determined men's choice of religion during the period of the Reformation.

There remains, however, Swanson's contention that professional

[1] Guy E. Swanson, *Religion and Regime: A Sociological Account of the Reformation* (Ann Arbor, 1967).

historians have failed to point to adequate general causes of the Reformation.[2] While few of us would take serious the more absurd causes which Swanson claims to have encountered in the writings of historians,[3] many of us would probaby admit that we are not entirely happy with the traditional explanations of the Reformation. I therefore want to take this opportunity to propose a new, overall theory of the Reformation, and I am most happy to acknowledge that it was the reading of Swanson's book which induced me to crystalize some ideas that had been floating through my mind for some time past. It is obvious that, in the very short time available, I can do no more than give an outline sketch of my theory. If it should stimulate further discussion, I shall consider that I have succeeded in my aim.

One of the most striking features of the Reformation is the great number and variety of new theological systems which were devised and which found adherents in Europe within a very few years after Luther had first challenged the established Church. Perhaps the most important point that Luther proved between 1517 and 1521, that is between the publication of the ninety-five theses and his defiance of the Emperor and Reichstag in Worms, was that he could get away with such defiance, while John Hus, a hundred years earlier, obviously could not. The moral was not lost on dozens of would-be religious reformers and prophets, each convinced that he held the key to the only, and unique, way of attaining salvation. As important as the incidents of Luther's spiritual development and the details of his theology are for a full understaning of this extraordinary man and of the church he founded *malgré soi*, it is not nearly so clear that these details are as important as they have usually been held to be for an understanding of the cataclysm which so suddenly engulfed the Catholic Church. When so many men were willing to follow so many different religious leaders, the theology of even the most outstanding of them is not likely to explain this phenomenon.

There were, however, two points on which the great majority of the reformers agreed: the central position they assigned to the Bible as the true word of God and their implacable hostility to the old Church and its head, the pope, and to the special position the Church claimed for itself as the intermediary between Christ and man. It is characteristic of this attitude that one of the complaints of the German peasants in 1525 was that the Word of God had not been preached to them unadulterated from Holy Writ. They thought that the authorities had deliberately kept it from the common man because of pride.[4] But such a complaint made sense only when the Bible had become physically available for preaching to, and reading by 'the common man'; and, by and large, this

---

[2] *Ibid.*, 20.
[3] *Ibid.*
[4] Günther Franz, *Quellen zur Geschichte des Bauernkrieges* (München, 1963), 290, 296.

was the case only after the invention of printing. The importance of printing in the phenomenon of the Reformation, while it has always been recognized by historians, has perhaps still been underestimated.[5] The diffusion of the printing press throughout Europe, therefore, gives us a time limit before which a movement such as actually occurred was practically impossible.

From the earliest days of their controversy with Luther, Catholic theologians pointed out that to rely on the Bible as the only religious authority was bound to lead to a multiplicity of religious beliefs. All the magisterial reformers, at least, recognized this danger and tried to guard against it; but, in practice, they were also all willing to risk it, even after they had had to give up all hope of reforming the one, all-embracing Church from the inside, as the Erasmians had urged them to do. Such an attitude was due both to their conviction of their own rightness and to their absolute hostility to Rome. But why was this hostility to Rome so extraordinarily widespread and virulent?

It seems to me that we have looked at the Reformation the wrong way round. We have assumed that the theological and ecclesiastical unity of Catholic Christendom was its natural condition and that, in consequence, the Reformation was a dramatic break in this condition which ran counter to all previous Christian experience and which, in a sense, destroyed the natural order of things. There were, of course, good reasons for such an assumption. It is not easy to ignore more than a thousand years of ecclesiastical history, i.e. the history of the Church since Christianity became the official religion of the Roman Empire. Understandably, many of the reformers themselves could not escape the spell of this great tradition. The Church Universal, it appeared, had allowed itself to be captured by Anti-Christ; but, dreadful as this was, it was no argument against the existence of the Church Universal. Hence the reformers went on hoping against hope that they could re-establish a single church, though, of course, reformed and purified according to their own prescriptions.

But was the long existence of a unified Church really as natural and inevitable as it was assumed to be? In the fifth century, the political and administrative structure of the Roman Empire in the West collapsed. All subsequent attempts to restore the Empire and re-establish the political and administrative unity of Christendom met with, at best, very partial success. For the thousand years of the Middle Ages, Christendom and its institutions remained obstinately divided, and Christians remained distressingly prone to engage in deadly wars with each other. Why was it that only the Church survived as a unified institution?

[5] Cf. Elizabeth L. Eisenstein, 'Some Conjectures about the Impact of Printing on Western Society and Thought', *Journal of Modern History*, XL (1968), 31, 38ff, where the same point is made.

One answer is that, in fact, it did not do so. Throughout the Middle Ages there existed Christian churches in Africa and Asia which were never in communion with Rome at all. More important, a deep schism had developed between the Greek and Roman Churches, and all attempts to re-unite them proved to be abortive. Nevertheless, this schism remained relatively marginal in the religious consciousness of all those who acknowledged the supremacy of Rome. In their experience, the Church had remained a unified institution. The question of why it survived in this form therefore still needs an answer.

In order to find this answer, I propose to make use of a model that, as far as I know, was first proposed by Deutsch in an unjustly neglected article, 'Medieval Unity and the Economic Conditions for an International Civilization'.[6] At the time of writing, during World War II, Deutsch was concerned with the then fashionable proposals for the re-establishment of a medieval type of European unity. He argued that this medieval unity, insofar as it existed, was a function of an economically poor society. The small surpluses of production of any given area would not be wanted in the adjoining area, which was probably producing the same commodities, but rather in much more distant areas. Medieval trade was, therefore, small in volume but covered large distances. In consequence it needed a group of professional merchants who spoke an internationally comprehensible language and, preferably, could carry on their activities under the protection of internationally accepted commercial and legal codes.

What was true of commodities and trade was true of all specialized skills. An example (although not one used by Deutsch) will make this clear. Bell founding was a highly skilled and specialized craft. After a master founder had cast the three or four, or even six or eight, bells for the church of a small town, he would have to move on, for there would be no further work for him in this town nor, very likely, in the neighbouring towns. It was the same with all other skills, from the cathedral builder to the learned scholar, from the forger of fine weapons (remember Wayland's troubles in getting away from his royal employer) to the most proficient wielders of such weapons (remember Siegfried fighting for King Gunther; or, in history and not mythology, the Normans during the eleventh century). Different areas of Europe might advance in certain skills, as Flanders did in the weaving of fine cloth; but no single area of Europe could support all of the skills which European society required. Only the whole of Europe could do this. In the first half of the Middle Ages, from the fifth to the eleventh or twelfth century, Europe was a continent of peasant societies, each clinging tenaciously to its local customs and language. Above this

[6] Karl W. Deutsch, 'Medieval Unity and the Economic Conditions for an International Civilization', *Canadian Journal of Economics and Political Science*, X (1944), 18–35.

mass of the peasantry, with its very rudimentary skills, there was a thin crust of men highly skilled in the production of sophisticated commodities or in the performance of complex services. This upper crust was international in education, attitudes, and often, physical mobility; for this was the only way it could function. The surprising uniformity of the Romanesque style in different parts of Europe is a good indication of this aspect of the cultural unity of western Christendom.

It is in the context of this model that we have to understand the unity of the medieval Church.[7] Functionally speaking, it represented a highly specialized skill, but one that was needed in every part of Christendom, and it had inherited, from Roman times, the traditions and institutions to use these skills most effectively on an international level: the common dogma, the common script and language, the admirably flexible hierarchical organization. This organization had not been directly attacked by the Barbarians in the same way that the political institutions of the Roman Empire had been attacked. Despite strong centrifugal forces during the early centuries of the Middle Ages, the combination of unbroken institutional tradition and of functional necessity enabled the Church to survive as a unified institution and to strengthen further its institutional and theological unity by the skilful development of papal supremacy and canon law.

This, with some slight modification (such as the discussion of the history of the Church) is Deutsch's model. He argues, quite correctly, that the thirteenth century represents the turning point in the history of medieval internationalism; for it was in this century that European internationalism both reached its greatest extent and was beginning to be undermined by resurgent regional forces. In answer to those historians who overstressed the unity of European civilization in the thirteenth century, Deutsch remarks that they 'must have found it difficult to persuade that age to hold still long enough for its portrait'.[8] He sees the break-up of medieval unity mainly in the inability of the international crust of society to assimilate the growing number of new entrants, and he ends his article with a sophisticated and fascinating analysis of the theoretical conditions of linguistic and cultural assimilation. His conclusion is that medieval unity was based 'on a low rate of entry [i.e. into the upper crust], on the scarcity of intercourse, the slowness of economic growth'.[8] When these conditions ceased to hold, that is, from the thirteenth century onwards, medieval unity was bound to disappear.

These conclusions are unexceptionable. However, as a historian, and while still working within the framework of the Deutsch model, I

[7] Deutsch mentions the Church, of course, but he does not expand on its role in his model. For his purposes, there was no particular need to do so.
[8] Deutsch, 'Medieval Unity', 29.

should like to describe the process of break-up somewhat differently. It seems to me more useful to shift the emphasis from the problem of the assimilation of new entrants into the international crust to an analysis of the functional supersession of this crust by other, more regionally based and oriented, crusts. The problem of assimilation is, in fact, only one part of this wider phenomenon. The argument now takes the following form:

The thin international upper crust of medieval Christendom, including the Church, fulfilled its functions most successfully. From the end of the tenth to the beginning of the fourteenth century, Christian Europe grew enormously in population and wealth. By the thirteenth century, its upper, international, civilizing crust had also expanded to its greatest extent and influence. But its very success had undermined the reason for its existence. The different parts of Europe had become sufficiently wealthy to be able to afford more and more of the specialized skills they required. The Gothic style of architecture and art, while still international, shows far greater regional variation than does the Romanesque. A glance at the cathedrals of Salisbury and Chartres will make this point clear. Reading skills had advanced sufficiently for sophisticated vernacular literature to appear, from Italy to England, and from Spain to Scandinavia and Iceland. Scholars still travelled far and wide and attracted an international medley of students to their lecture rooms; but, one after another, kingdoms and even cities began to found their own universities. Soon there would be laws prohibiting students from attending universities outside their rulers' dominions.

The Church was no more immune from the dissolving forces of the growing regionalism of Europe than any other part of the thin international layer we have described. In the eleventh and twelfth centuries it had been considered perfectly natural for Italians, such as Anselm and Lanfranc, to become archbishops of Canterbury, or for an Anglo-Norman cleric to hold the see of Palermo. By the thirteenth century, such an international interchange had become almost inconceivable.[10] The churches in the different kingdoms reserved their ecclesiastical positions more and more for natives of the country, just as was happening in the case of secular offices.

Institutions, and especially institutions with long and venerable histories, will often survive long after they have ceased to fulfil the functions which had made them indispensable in an earlier age. Thus it was with the unified Christian Church. But, with the historian's hindsight at least, it is easy to see the piling up of ominous signs that indicated this could not last forever. Heresies multiplied and became progressively more difficult to suppress because they found wider and

[9] *Ibid.*, 34.
[10] I wish to thank Brian Tierney for drawing my attention to this point.

wider echoes in coherent regions of Europe. Even non-heretical reform movements, such as that of the Brethren of the Common Life, tended to play down the importance of the Church. When the Great Schism set pope against pope, vying in the anathemas they hurled at each other, the Christian powers gleefully took sides for one or the other, and they did this almost entirely for political and not for religious reasons. The conciliar movement of the fifteenth century may be seen as an attempt to restructure the Church so as to allow the growing centrifugal forces in Christendom to play their part while still preserving the overall unity of the Church. The defeat of this movement, and the subsequent concentration of papal energies on Italian power politics, made it virtually impossible for the Church to adapt itself to the changing conditions of European Society.

In the late fifteenth and early sixteenth centuries, the papacy was virtually forced to abandon its remaining control over both the administrative structure and the personnel of the local churches to the great monarchies. The kings of France and Spain, already possessing the right to appoint to the most important ecclesiastical benefices in their kingdoms, claimed the even more fatal powers of the *droit de véréfication* and the *exequatur*, i.e. the right to prevent the publication of any papal brief in their dominions. Even so, the concordats and other arrangements between the popes and the princes did not produce a stable new balance. The Catholic princes of the early sixteenth century, enthusiastically backed by their subjects, including the clergy and the universities, continued their aggression against papal prerogatives and the effective unity of the Church. Ferdinand of Aragon threatened to withdraw all of his kingdoms from obedience to the papacy if the pope should insist on sending a bull of excommunication into the kingdom of Naples.[11] Louis XII of France summoned an anti-papal council at

[11] Ferdinand to Juan de Aragon, Viceroy of Naples, Burgos, 22 May 1508. In Charles Weiss (ed.), *Papiers d'Etats du Cardinal de Granvelle* (Paris, 1841), I, 66–73. The Viceroy had allowed a papal messenger to present a papal bull of excommunication in Naples. Ferdinand was furious: 'De todo lo qual havemos recebido grande alteracion, enojo y sentimiento; y estamos muy maravillados y mal contento de vos [i.e. the Viceroy], viendo de quanta importancia y perjuyzio nuestro, y de nuestras preeminencias y dignidad real, era el auto que fizó el cursor apostólico; . . . porque vos no fizistes tambien de hecho, mandando ahorcar el cursor que vos la presentó? que claro sta, que no solamente en ese reyno, si el papa sabe que en España y França le han de consentir fazer semejante aucto que ese, que le fará por acrecentar su jurisdiction . . . y estamos muy determinado si su santidad no revoca luego el breve, y los autos por virtud dél fechos, de le quitar la obediencia de todos los reynos de la corona de Castilla y Aragon...' 'We have been greatly amazed, angry and moved by all this; and we marvel greatly and are ill content with you (the viceroy), seeing of what importance and prejudice to our preeminence and royal dignity the action of the papal messenger has been; . . . why did you not also take action, ordering the messenger who presented you with the bull to be hanged? For it is obvious that not only in this kingdom (Naples), but also in Spain and France the pope will increase his jurisdiction if such acts are accepted . . . And if His Holiness does not revoke his brief and the actions which have been performed on its

Pisa. The significance, from our point of view, of Henry VIII's withdrawal of obedience from Rome lies precisely in its non-theological and non-religious motivation. Gustavus Vasa broke with Rome in a political manoeuvre directed against his political enemies, the king of Denmark and the archbishop of Uppsala. Even without Luther, the chances of the survival of the unity of the Church were slim.

The model I have sketched is not a rigid historical law.[12] It was not inevitable that the Church should survive the collapse of the Roman Empire in the West and the confusions of the succeeding centuries as a unified oganization. But the structural and functional conditions for such a survival were very favourable, and successive leaders of the Church made the most of these opportunities. By the fourteenth and fifteenth centuries, the functional conditions for the survival of a unified Church had all but disappeared. Given the Church's century-old traditions, it was perhaps not impossible, but certainly psychologically very unlikely, for its leaders to make the necessary profound adjustments that might have saved the unity of the Church. A dedicated and energetic churchman such as Cardinal Ximénez de Cisnéros, could reform his own national church. But, admirable as this undoubtedly was, and useful in helping to defend Spain from the propaganda of the reformers, Ximénez' reforms did little to ease the fatal tension between the claims of papal universalism and political and ecclesiastical regionalism.

Ironically, it was the shock of the actual Reformation which gave the Catholic Church new opportunities for survival as a universal church in at least part of Europe. The Reformation convinced those who still wanted to preserve the old Church that it was necessary to have a thorough reform of its pastoral and educational work, and of its administrative structure and personnel, as well as a clear definition of certain controversial dogmas. Above all, the Reformation convinced many powerful rulers that it was safer to protect the old Church, which was in any case largely under their control, than to unleash the unknown, but evidently powerful, social, political, and moral forces

---

authority, we are determined to withdrdaw obedience to him of all the kingdoms of the crown of Castile and Aragon . . .' The Viceroy is then commanded to arrest the papal messenger, if he should still .be in the kingdom, force him to declare that he never presented the papal breve, and then hang him. The King concluded: 'Pues vedes nuestra intencion y determinacion en eastas cosas, de aqui adelante por cosa del mundo no sufrays que nuestras preeminencias reales sean usurpados por nadie. Porque si el supremo dominio nuestro no defendeys, no ay que defender, y la defension de derecho natural es permitida á todos, y mas pertenece á los reyes, porque de mas de complir ala conservacion de su dignidad y estado real, cumple mucho para que tengan sus reynos en paz y justicia, y di buena governacion.'

[12] Deutsch does not claim this, either. Deutsch, 'Medieval Unity', 10, 30.

which seemed to support the various Reformation movements.[13] Thus, it came about that the old Church found powerful new champions precisely among those princes who had done most to break down it universalism.

The success or failure of any particular brand of the Reformation and the success or failure of maintaining, or re-establishing, the authority of the Church of Rome in any particular country depended on that country's local traditions, political structure and the decisions of powerful personalities. My theory will, I hope, help to explain the causes of the phenomenon of the Reformation, that is, of the break-up of the medieval unity of the Church. It is not, and cannot be, a short-cut through the detailed historical studies which must remain one of the necessary tasks of professional historians.

In brief, my theory of the Reformation is as follows:

1. The unity of the medieval Church was not an inevitable and eternal form necessarily derived from the Church's universalist claims. It was rather the result of quite specific and transitory, although long-term, historical conditions.

2. These conditions were the scarcity of skills and services in an economically poor and underdeveloped European continent between the end of the fifth and the end of the twelfth centuries. The required skills and services had to be supplied by a small upper crust which had to function on an international level if it was to function at all. The Church played a central role in this function, and only the Church had an international organization.

3. From the thirteenth century, the growing prosperity and sophistication of Europe (itself largely the result of the activities of the upper crust) made possible its gradual supersession by regionally based and oriented cultures.[14]

4. Like many well-established institutions, the Church survived for a long time after its functional *raison d'être* had disappeared. Since, however, it failed to adapt itself to the changed world, it was thus bound eventually to collapse.

5. The timing of this collapse was determined by the coincidence of two developments: the increasing political tension between the monarchies and the papacy over the question of the control of the institution of the Church and its personnel in the different countries

---

[13] Swanson, *Religion and Regime*, 232. 'Rapid changes in governmental structure were followed, as our hypothesis would predict, by the acceptance of specific changes in religious doctrine. These observations preclude any argument that the reverse sequence occurred, religious beliefs producing the political novelties of the early Reformation era.' Francis I or Philip II would have found this view puzzling. For them, as for most of their contemporaries, it was axiomatic that changes in religion were followed by political changes. There were numerous examples to support their view.

[14] *Mutatis mutandis*, a similar pattern of development seems to have occurred in the Islamic world during much the same period.

of Europe; and the spread of the printing presses, which made the Bible available to the Christian laity and thus undermined the claim of the Church to act as the indispensable intermediary between God and man.

6. The foregoing makes it clear that, despite the reformers' hopes, none of the Reformation movements could ever be in a position to capture the central bastion of the old Church, as the Cluny movement had done in the eleventh century, nor to take the place of the Catholic Church as the sole universal church of Western Christendom. This fact is independent of the details of the theology of any of the reformers.

7. Once the Reformation had been successfully introduced in some countries, it was bound to engender both religious and political opposition. It was these Counter-Reformation forces which enabled the Catholic Church to reorganize itself and to survive as an international institution throughout half of Europe.

My model is an overall model. It explains why the break-up of the medieval Church was likely to happen and, roughly, when it was likely to happen. Unlike Swanson's model, it does not claim to explain, much less to predict, the course of the Reformation in any single country. This has to remain, as it has always been, the field for detailed and orthodox historical inquiry.

# 9

# Music and Religion in Early Modern European History

. . . and playing with all the dexterousness of the art of Musick, he shewd upon the Pipe, what notes were fit for the herds of Cowes and Oxen, what agreed with the flocks of Goats, what were pleasing to the sheep. The tones for the sheep were soft and sweet, those of the herds were vehement; and for the Goats were sharp and shrill.

Longus, *Daphnis and Chloe*[1]

Sic praedicavit Deus evangelium etiam per musicam . . .

Luther, *Table Talk*, 1528[2]

In the introduction to *The Protestant Ethic and the Spirit of Capitalism*, Max Weber listed music as one of the fields which distinguished European civilization from all others. It was not that the ears of other peoples were musically less sensitive, Weber wrote; perhaps rather the contrary. It was rather that only the Europeans developed a rational harmony and counterpoint, the standardized musical instruments of the modern orchestra and, above all, musical notation, without which both the composition and playing of modern music would have been impossible.[3] Weber did not go beyond this brief paragraph, with its implication that it was the rational element of European music which primarily distinguished its development from that of music in other civilizations. Nor did Weber say very much about this particular problem of the uniqueness – I am deliberately avoiding the word 'superiority' – of European music in his later essay, *The Rational and Sociological Foundations of Music*;[4] yet it is as striking a phenomenon as the uniqueness of modern European capitalism or science. The present essay is not intended to give a complete explanation of this phenomenon. It seeks only to analyse one condition (though, I believe, a very important one) of this peculiar development of music in modern European history. Music, as Weber knew well,[5] was in practically all

[1] Longus, *Daphnis and Chloe*, tr. G. Thornley (1657) (London, 1925), bk. II, p. 102.
[2] Quoted in F. Blume, *Geschichte der evangelischen Kirchenmusik* (2nd ed., Kassel, 1965), p. 7.
[3] M. Weber, 'Die protestantische Ethik und der Geist des Kapitalismus', *Gesammelte Aufsätze zur Religionssoziologie* (Tübingen, 1934), i, 2.
[4] M. Weber, *Die rationalen und soziologischen Grundlagen der Musik* (Munich, 1921).
[5] *Ibid.*, p. 30.

cultures intimately linked with religious worship and ceremonial. It
was so in classical and early Christian Europe, no less than in Asian and
African civilizations. But in Europe the power of religion and religious
sensibility declined, slowly and almost imperceptibly, from the later
Middle Ages and the Renaissance, more and more rapidly, and very
perceptibly, from the end of the seventeenth century.

This growing secularization of European civilization is well known,
and I shall here take it for granted. I shall argue that the extraordinary
development of music in Europe is closely linked with this
phenomenon of secularization. More specifically, I will try to show
that, as religious sensibilities declined, there appeared a new
psychological need in men, a kind of emotional void, and that this need
or void was filled primarily by music. Music found itself rarely in direct
opposition to religion, and when this did happen the initiative came
from the side of certain religious leaders. More normally, it was the
very alliance of religion and music which allowed music to play an
increasingly important and, eventually, even preponderant role in the
European psyche.

The Renaissance was passionately concerned with the relative merits of
different art forms. Sometimes as a kind of intellectual parlour game in
princely courts, more commonly in treatises and other writings with a
high philosophical intent and a sharp social purpose, men (and women)
debated the ideal ranking order of poetry, painting, sculpture and
music, and of the social status of those who practised these arts. The
arguments varied, but among the most common was the power which
works of art exerted on men's minds. For Leonardo, for instance,
painting was, understandably, the supreme art:

Painting will move the senses more readily than poetry . . . [he wrote in his
notebooks]. An artist painted a picture that whoever saw it at once yawned,
and went on doing so as long as he kept his eyes on the picture, which
represented a person who also was yawning. Other artists have represented
acts of wantonness and lust which kindled these passions in the beholders.
Poetry could not do as much. And if you write a description of Gods, such
writings will never be worshipped in the same way as a painting of the deity.
For to the picture many offerings and prayers will incessantly flow, many
generations will flock to it from distant lands and from the eastern seas and
they will ask help from such a painting, but not writing.[6]

Leonardo placed music, too, above poetry because it can produce
'simultaneous harmony', but below painting, because sound does not
last and because the eye is better than the ear.[7]

---

[6] L. da Vinci, *The Literary Works*, ed. J. P. and Irma A. Richter (Oxford, 1939), 2nd
ed., i, 64.
[7] *Ibid.*, pp. 77ff.

The type of argument which Leonardo used is typical for the period, although the conclusions of different writers tended to vary with their professions or predilections, and not all such discussions were necessarily in the form of a competition between the arts. The discussion of music was closely bound up with a persistent literary-philosophical tradition that went back to the Greeks. This tradition had three aspects. The first was the powers ascribed to music and celebrated by historians and poets. Thus music had power to quieten infants, as everyone knew. It had also tamed wild beasts, as Orpheus and Arion had demonstrated. Amphion's lyre had made the very rocks move to form the walls of Thebes, and Asclepiades and many others, like David with his harp, had used music to heal or calm madmen and drunkards.

The second aspect in the discussion of music was the theory of the different types of music and of their respective effects on the listener. Plato had taught that the Dorian and Lydian modes gave men courage and strength, but that most of the other modes had enervating and demoralizing effects. What was worse, such debilitating music was most pleasant to the ear and could insinuate itself into the mind of a virtuous and strong man,

pouring into his soul through the funnel of his ears those sweet and soft and melancholy airs . . . and his whole life is passed in warbling and the delights of song . . . if he carries on the softening and soothing process, in the next stage he begins to melt and waste, until he has wasted away his spirit; and he becomes a feeble warrior.[8]

Any musical innovation, Plato therefore argued, was harmful to the State and should be prohibited; for when the modes of music change, the fundamental laws of the State will change with them.[9]

It seems that not all of Plato's contemporaries agreed with him. He blamed the poets themselves:

They were men of genius, but they had no perception of what is just and lawful in music; raging like Bacchanals and possessed with inordinate delights . . . ignorantly affirming that music has no truth and, whether good or bad, can only be judged rightly by the pleasure of the hearer. And by composing such licentious works, they have inspired the multitude with lawlessness and boldness, and made them fancy that they can judge of themselves about melody and song.[10]

Plato's theory of the difference between good and bad or, rather, moral and immoral music has had, in one form or another, an

[8] Plato, *The Republic*, III, 411. *The Dialogues*, tr. B. Jowett (Oxford and London, 1892), 3rd ed., iii, 99.
[9] *Ibid.*, IV, 424, 112.
[10] Plato, *Laws*, III, 700. *Dialogues*, vol. v, pp. 82–3.

extraordinarily long and successful career and is, perhaps even now, not completely dead; but it celebrated its greatest triumphs in the sixteenth century. How did music have such powers for good or evil?

The answer to this question provides the third aspect of the tradition which the Renaissance inherited, and again it went back to the Greeks; this time, however, to the Pythagorean theory that musical harmony was of the same nature or, at least, that it reflected the mathematical harmony and structure of the universe. In its more than two-thousand-year history, from Pythagoras and Plato to Kepler and Leibniz, this theory took many forms, not least in importance being that of the music or harmony of the spheres.[11] More generally, the exact relationship between musical and cosmic harmony was posited, but left vague, as it was, for instance, in Boethius's enormously influential treatise on music.[12]

During the Middle Ages the theory of the existence of this relationship was never lost: music, together with arithmetic, geometry and astronomy, formed the *quadrivium* in the study of the liberal arts. During the Renaissance the theory received a great impetus through the revival of Neoplatonism. It was naturally, though somewhat uneasily, linked to the tradition of the *laudes musicae*, the praises of the powers of music, and to the Platonic distinctions between moral and immoral music. The so-called musical humanists of the latter half of the sixteenth century faced some difficult practical problems in their attempts to re-create ancient music with all its virtues. In the first place, no one really knew how far the Platonic modes coincided with the modes as they were known in the sixteenth century, and therefore which of them were permissable and which were not. This was not, perhaps, as important as it might seem; for every musical humanist was certain that he himself had the correct interpretation, even if it differed from that of his colleagues. In the second place, modern music did not really display the wonderful effects which the ancients had described or, at least, not in quite the same, very specific, way. The musical humanists thought they saw the logical reason for this shortcoming of modern music in the tendency of contemporary counterpoint to obscure the words of vocal music. They were not concerned with purely instrumental music, partly because there was, as yet, relatively little of it; but, more important, because they (wrongly) thought that

---

[11] Shakespeare, *The Merchant of Venice*, V, i:
           There's not the smallest orb which thou behold'st
           But in his motion like an angel sings,
           Still quiring to the young-eyed cherubins.
[12] Boethius, *De Institutione Musica*, ed. A. Damerini (Florence, 1949), ch. 3, p. 30: 'Sed quorsum istaec [i.e. the powers of music]? Quia non potest dubitari, quin nostrae animae et corporis status eisdem quodammodo proportionibus videatur esse compositus, quibus armonicas modulationes posterior disputatio coniungi copularique monstrabit.'

the ancients had no purely instrumental music. It seemed to them that it was the words, with their impact heightened by music, which were responsible for the famous effects.[13] They therefore felt it necessary to break with the late-medieval polyphonic tradition and to place music strictly into the service of words.

The lengths to which some musical humanists were willing to go in this direction were shown by the French poet Jean-Antoine de Baïf and his friend, the musician Thibault de Courville. These two attempted nothing less than to mould the rather refractory French language into the metrical pattern of Greek and Latin verse and then to set them to music as a '*musique mesurée*' which followed the metre of the verse as closely as possible. It seems that, with the support of the King, Charles IX, they thought they could 'reform' the musical life of France according to Platonic ideals. They hoped to do this through the educative efforts of an academy of poetry and music.[14] Charles IX's letters patent for this academy, in 1570, show clearly the Platonic assumptions about the powerful but ambiguous effects of music:

. . . il importe grandement pour les mœurs des Citoyens d'une Ville [runs the preamble] que la Musique courante et usitée au Pays soit retenue sous certaines loix, dautant que la pluspart des esprits des hommes se conforment et comportent, selon qu'elle est; de façon que où la Musique est désordonnée, là volontiers les mœurs sont dépravez, et où elle est bien ordonnée, là sont les hommes bien morignez.[15]

The Italian musical humanists did not go quite so far. But they were as firmly convinced as the French that it was the words which determined the meaning and effects of music. Girolamo Mei, generally regarded by his contemporaries as the greatest authority on Greek music, was emphatic on this point. It was quite wrong to think that the music of the ancients was meant to delight the ear with its harmony, he wrote to Vincenzo Galilei in 1572; it was rather meant to 'express entirely and powerfully all that speaking intends to express by means of a high-or-low-pitched voice'.[16]

[13] D. P. Walker, 'Musical Humanism in the 16th and Early 17th Centuries', *The Music Review* (1941), vol. 2, pp. 7–13, 111–27, 289–308; vol. 3, pp. 64ff. It is possible, as Dorothy Koenigsberger has suggested to me, that the musical humanists emphasised the importance of the words in singing because their effects were predictable and controllable, whereas those of pure music were not. There were certainly many in the sixteenth century who were afraid of the effects of music and hence sought to subordinate it to the word. But this attitude is clearer with the theologians than the humanists.

[14] D. P. Walker, 'The Aims of Baïf's *Académie de Poésie et de Musique*', *Journal of Renaissance and Baroque Music*, i (1946–7), pp. 91–100.

[15] Quoted in F. Yates, *The French Academies of the Sixteenth Century* (London, 1947), p. 319.

[16] G. Mei, *Letters on Ancient and Modern Music to Vincenzo Galilei*, ed. C. V. Palisca (American Institute of Musicology, 1960), p. 116.

Theologians and religious moralists had long since come to similar conclusions and they had done this for fundamentally similar, though not always equally antiquarian, reasons. Music which delighted the ear was suspect, at least in church; for it would distract the worshipper from the word of God or, worse still, lead his thoughts into worldly, even lustful directions. 'We have introduced an artificial and theatrical music into the church . . .', complained Erasmus. 'Horns, trumpets, pipes vie and sound along constantly with the voices. Amorous and lascivious melodies are heard such as elsewhere accompany only the dances of courtesans and clowns. The people run into the churches as if they were theatres, for the sake of the sensuous charm of the ear'.[17] The English scene was, it seems, particularly bad: 'What else is heard in monasteries, colleges and almost all churches, besides the clamour of voices?'[18] There is, clearly, some awareness here of the powers of music independent of the words set. But Erasmus's main point was a moral one, and he thought of certain melodies as 'amorous and lascivious' because, like so much church music of the time, they were parodies, i.e. they had started life as tunes for popular songs and, even after the words were changed, tended to remind the listener of the original words. As one would expect from Erasmus, he also quoted the ancients and the laws they were supposed to have enacted to prevent music from corrupting the minds of the citizens.[19].

Calvin was even more uneasy about music than Erasmus. Some of his friends may well have condemned music altogether, for Calvin thought it necessary to defend the art. It serves our enjoyment rather than our need, he wrote, but 'it ought not on that account to be judged of no value; still less should it be condemned'.[20] Did not God 'render many things attractive to us, apart from their necessary use?'[21] As long as he could stay on such rational grounds, Calvin seems to have felt safe. Thus he argued that it was God who lightened Saul's melancholy, and not the therapeutic effects of David's harp.[22] Nevertheless, the powers of music were too well attested, and that by the highest authorities: Calvin could not simply write music off as a matter for mere 'enjoyment'. In his Preface to the *Geneva Psalter*, Calvin wrote: 'Car à grand peine y a il en ce monde qui puisse plus tourner ou fléchir çà et là les mœurs des hommes, comme Plato l'a prudemment

[17] Comment on 1 Corinthians i, 14. Quoted in G. Reese, *Music in the Renaissance* (New York, 1954), p. 448.

[18] Quoted in C. A. Miller, 'Erasmus on Music', *Musical Quarterly*, lii, no. 3 (1966), pp. 338–9.

[19] *Ibid.*, p. 348.

[20] J. Calvin, Commentary of Genesis iv, 20, quoted in *The Institutes of the Christian Religion*, tr. F. L. Battles, vol. 2 (Philadelphia, 1960), p. 721, n. 4.

[21] Calvin, *Institutes*, III, x, 721.

[22] H. P. Clive, 'The Calvinist Attitude to Music', *Bibliothèque d'Humanisme et Renaissance*, xix (1957), p. 87.

consyderé. Et de fait, nous experimentons qu'elle a une vertu secrete et quasi incredible à esmouvoir les cueurs en une sorte, ou en l'autre . . .' For while it is true that wicked words pervert good customs, yet 'quand la mélodie est avec, cela transperce beaucoup plus fort le cueur, et entre dedans tellement que comme par un entonnoir le vin est iesté dedans le vaisseau, aussi le venin et la corruption est distillé iusques au profond du cueur, par la melody'.[23] This is pure Plato, even to the metaphor of the funnel. But Calvin's emphasis was on the negative aspect of the power of music. The flute and the tambourin are to be condemned only in their abuse, he said in a sermon on the Book of Job; but this is just what usually happens, 'car il est certain que iamais le tambourin ne sonne pour faire resiouir les hommes, qu'il n'y ait de la vanité, ie ne di point superflue, mais comme brutale, car voilà les hommes qui sont transportez tellement qu'ils ne s'esgayent point d'une ioye moderée...'[24]

It is difficult to escape the impression that Calvin was profoundly uneasy about music, that he was frightened by its dionysiacal powers of giving men joy beyond moderation.[25] It is therefore not surprising that the only music he would allow in divine service was the unaccompanied singing of psalms. The Jews of the Old Testament had admittedly praised the Lord with drums and cymbals and trumpets, but these instrument had performed an educative function, because of the spiritual weakness of the Jews. Since the coming of Christ they were no long needed. And thus Calvin banished musical instruments from his church.[26]

The immediate course of events seemed to justify his decision. Psalm-singing came to be a most powerful, because highly popular, weapon in the spread of Calvinist ideas in western Europe. Its long-term effects on musical life as a whole were a different matter.

The Calvinists spoke slightingly of 'popish music'; but the musical puritanism of the age made itself felt in all denominations. In England, for instance, Bishop Coverdale lamented the profanity of popular music-making:

Would God that our minstrels had none other thing to play upon, neither our ploughmen other things to whistle upon save psalms, hymns and such like godly songs . . . and if women at the rocks and spinning at the wheels had none other songs to pass their time withal than such as Moses' sister sang before them, they should be better occupied than with 'Hey Nonny Nonny', 'Hey Trolley lolly', and such like fantasies.

[23] Quoted *ibid.*, p. 86.

[24] *Ibid.*, p. 93, n. 4.

[25] See also Calvin's Commentary on Genesis iv, 20: 'Damnanda quidem est voluptas, nisi cum Dei timore, et communi humanae societas utilitate sit coniuncta.' Quoted in Clive, 'The Calvinist Attitude to Music', p. 93, n. 4.

[26] *Ibid.*, pp. 90ff.

[27] Preface to the *Goostly Psalms* (1539), quoted in C. Garside, 'Calvin's Preface to the Psalter: A Re-appraisal', *Musical Quarterly*, xxxvii (1951), 572n.

Catholics were less concerned with the iniquities of popular music; but a long line of theologians and church councils condemned over-elaborate and 'lascivious' church music, such as was practised by the Netherlands school of polyphonic composers. It made the words of the liturgy unintelligible, they claimed, and seduced men's minds from attention to the word of God.[28] In the Netherlands the tradition of elaborate polyphony in church music was strong enough to resist the attacks of those who wanted to subordinate music completely to words. But even the tolerant Netherlands Church authorities would not allow their composers to assimilate the chromaticism of contemporary Italian secular music for the sake of heightening the emotional impact of their own religious music. Unwilling to give up their aims completely, some of the Netherlands composers adopted a method of musical notation which involved a double meaning: one, openly apparent, which accorded with the traditional rules of the church modes, and the other, secret or concealed, which was understood only by the initiated.[29]

The deviousness of this method of composition is surprising, even in an age as passionately devoted to allegories, anagrams and hidden meanings as was the Renaissance. Its practitioners appear to have come mainly from those Erasmian circles whose religious orthodoxy was often suspect, but who never chose openly to break with the Catholic Church. It seems unlikely, however, that Erasmus himself would have been pleased with this victory of the power of music over the power of the word.

The orthodox Catholic position was summarized by the decrees of the Council of Trent, in September 1562 and November 1563, prohibiting the use of 'lascivious, impure and profane' music in church,[30] and insisting that the function of church music was not to delight the ears but to strengthen the impact of the words of the liturgy and to incline the hearts of the listeners towards a longing for heavenly harmony and the contemplation of the joys of the blessed.[31] The decrees, however, were silent on detail and left room for different interpretations. Palestrina's splendid unaccompanied masses fulfilled to perfection the demands of the Council of Trent, even in a fairly rigorous interpretation of its decrees. Some churchmen went further. It is told of St Carlo Borromeo that he attracted excellent musicians to Milan by paying them good salaries, but that he insisted on a reformed. music in which the words would be banished from the churches in his

[28] Clive, 'The Calvinist Attitude to Music', pp. 98ff.

[29] E. Lowinsky, *Secret Chromatic Art in the Netherlands Motet*, Columbia University Studies in Musicology, vi (New York, 1946).

[30] *Canones et Decreta Sacrosancti oecumenici et generalis Concilii Tridentini* (Venice, 1564), p. 112.

[31] K. G. Fellerer, 'Church Music and the Council of Trent', *Musical Quarterly*, xxxix (1953), 576.

diocese.[32] But such austerity was far from universal, and the phase of acute musical puritanism in the Catholic Church did not outlast the end of the sixteenth century.

In all this discussion of music during the sixteenth century something seems to be missing. Either, some of the would-be authorities on music are not really very musical, are uneasy about it or even afraid of it, and seem to acknowledge its value only because the ancients did. Perhaps Erasmus, certainly Calvin and many of his followers fit into this category. Or, where they were genuinely sensitive to music, as were presumably the musical humanists and churchmen, such as Borromeo, their thinking was predetermined by Platonic categories of good and bad music, by humanist and theological insistence on the need to subordinate music to words and, by a tradition going back to the early Church Fathers, of hostility towards 'heathenish' instruments in church. Thus they all sought to limit and confine music, to force it into patterns whose origins were philosophical or theological rather than musical, and above all to control the fearful powers of music over men's souls by making it the servant of the much more easily controllable word.

These efforts were never wholly successful. In spite of the continual and often strident demands for its subordination, music constantly tended to escape from all such attempts to harness it to a purely moral purpose. Practising composers and musicians, even at times the ultra-orthodox Palestrina himself, often remained stubbornly impervious to the demands of the moralists, and so did much of the general public. It is inconceivable that the famous school of Flemish contrapuntalists would have retained its fame throughout Europe for generation after generation if their sonorous and complex, but in the eyes of the moralists frivolous, music had not appealed to a wide and influential audience. The moralists themselves sadly recognized that people flocked into the churches to hear music rather than the word of God. Practical musicians, moreover, even when they were also theorists, found it hard to accept the more extreme of the Neoplatonist views. Zarlino, Choirmaster of St Mark's, Venice, as well as author of one of the most famous treatises on music,[33] agreed with the moralists that music should have a moral purpose and that words gave music ultimate force,[34] but he was sceptical about knowing the genuine Greek modes and caustic about 'those who are ignorant of a subject and therefore misrepresent it; as we see with someone who, being unmusical but

[32] G. P. Giussano, *Vita di S. Carlo Borromeo* (Rome, 1610), p. 89. I would like to thank Professor Gordon Griffiths of the University of Washington for drawing my attention to this source.

[33] *Istitutioni Armoniche* (Venice, 1558).

[34] D. P. Walker, 'Musical Humanism', *The Music Review*, ii, 227; iii, 63.

delighting in the study of humane letters, much prefers to hear the words in the cantilena . . . than its harmony; perhaps because he has no ear for it'.[35] This reproof was directed especially against Vincenzo Galilei and Girolamo Mei.

It is clear that there had always been men, and even 'men of genius', who, as Plato had lamented, 'had no perception of what is just and lawful in music',[36] in other words, men for whom music as such was more important than any moral implications it might have. And there were also those whom music affected in this way but who had a bad conscience about it. One of these was St Augustine. 'Yet when it happens to me to be more moved by the singing than by what is sung', he wrote in his *Confessions*, 'I confess myself to have sinned criminally, and then I would rather not have heard the singing'.[37] Augustine's regrets have nothing to do with Platonic notions of moral and immoral music, nor with patristic and later theological and humanist objections to the subordination of words to music. It was the power of music itself, its ability to distract him from the word of God, however clearly heard, which frightened St Augustine. It was the sort of power which Leonardo Da Vinci saw in painting and which many, in the Renaissance, saw in poetry.

Even those who valued the power of words above music might still understand the independent power of music as Augustine understood it. To Ficino, music was a kind of living, moving air which directly affected man's spirit, that corporeal vapour which, it was believed, flowed from the brain through the nervous system.[38]

. . . Musical sound by the movement of the air moves the body [he wrote in his commentaries on Plato's *Timaeus*]; by purified air it excites the aerial spirit which is the bond of body and soul: by emotion it affects the senses and at the same time the soul: by meaning it works on the mind: finally, by the very movement of the subtle air it penetrates strongly: . . . by the conformity of its quality it floods us with wonderful pleasure: by its nature, both spiritual and material, it at once seizes, and claims as its own, man in his entirety.[39]

Since Ficino, as a good Platonist, also believed that musical harmony reflected the mathematical harmony of the universe, he was doubly convinced of its power. Unlike most of the musical humanists of the sixteenth century, Ficino was willing to use music not only, in conjuction with words, for moral purposes, but also as a powerful means for working natural magic. The planets have certain qualities, beneficial

[35]  *Ibid.*, p. 66.
[36]  See above, p. 181.
[37]  St. Augustine, *The Confessions*, tr. J. G. Pilkington (New York, 1943), x, 33, 257.
[38]  D. P. Walker, *Spiritual and Demonic Magic. From Ficino to Campanella*, Studies of the Warburg Institute (London, 1958), xxii, 4.
[39]  Quoted *ibid.*, p. 9.

or dangerous to man. These can be attracted in various ways, but especially by music:

Thus from the tones chosen by the rule of the stars, and then combined in accordance with the stars' mutual correspondences, a sort of common form can be made, and in this a certain celestial virtue will arise. It is indeed very difficult to judge what kind of tones will best fit what kind of stars, and what combinations of tones agree best with what stars and their aspects. But, partly by our own diligence, partly by divine destiny . . . we have been able to accomplish this.[40]

The magical effects which Ficino sought to accomplish were designed only to affect his own mind and, in particular, to effect a proper proportion and balance of the bodily humours and relieve it from excessive melancholy. For Ficino, as for the sixteenth-century humanists, the words of his song held, eventually, a predominant position; for they could influence the mind, whereas music alone, without words, could influence only man's spirit. But it was not the text which gave music its great and sometimes magical power; it was rather the combination of music and words in song; for song affected the whole person, mind and spirit equally.[41] I can see no good reason to doubt that Ficino's musical magic often had the effects which he claimed for it, at least on himself. Whether the causes he posited for these effects were correct is a different matter.

Professor D. P. Walker, on whose work I have relied heavily for the passage on Ficino, suggests that Ficino's astrological singing 'came near to being a religious rite'.[42] The effects which Fincino desired, Professor Walker argues, a Christian would look for in the action of God on man's soul. But if these effects could really be achieved by natural magic, as Ficino claimed, i.e. without the intervention of God and only from the natural powers existing in the universe, then such magic would constitute a real threat to Christianity; for its logical consequence would be atheism or deism.[43]

Natural magic, for all its importance in the intellectual history of the Renaissance and even of the seventeenth century,[44] remained an esoteric cult. But its chief emotional ingredient, music, was accessible to all. Music, moreover, did not need the paraphernalia of magical practices to exert its own, quasi-magical powers. The question was: How far could it be allowed to do so?

The one great theologian of the Renaissance period who gave an unqualified affirmative answer was Luther. 'What a conscience St

[40] Quoted *ibid.*, p. 16.

[41] *Ibid.*, p. 21.

[42] *Ibid.*, p. 20.

[43] *Ibid.*, pp. 83–4.

[44] Cf. A. R. Hall, 'On the Historical Singularity of the Scientific Revolution in the Seventeenth Century', in *The Diversity of History*, pp. 219ff.

Augustine had!' Luther commented on the saint's reference to music in his *Confessions*. 'When he had pleasure in music and was made cheerful by it, he thought he had done wrong and had sinned'. And, he added, with characteristic egocentricity: 'He [Augustine] was a fine, pious man; if he lived in the present time he would be one of us'.[45] It was not the relation of music to the harmony of the universe which was important to Luther; although, as a former student of the traditional *quadrivium*, he certainly knew of this connection. What mattered to Luther was rather the sound of music and its effect on man's mind. Time and again, in his table talk, in his writings and, not least, in his own practice of music in church and home, he comes back to this point: 'One of the most beautiful and magnificent gifts of God is music. Princes should foster it and spend money on it'.[46] Or again: 'The devil is a sad spirit and makes people sad and therefore he does not like gaiety. That is why he flies from music as far as he can, and does not stay when people sing, especially religious songs'.[47]

If religious songs were best, that did not mean that for Luther there was a Platonic distinction between moral and immoral music. On the contrary, since music as such was a gift of God to man, there was no harm in musical parody, the adaptation of secular songs to religious purposes; for why, Luther asked, should the devil have all the best tunes? The famous chorale, *Vom Himmel hoch da komm ich her*, derived from the song *Aus fremden Landen komm ich her* and, even more alarmingly, from *Mit Lust tret ich an diesen Tanz*. The Lutheran hymnal was full of such transformations. Music and the joy it gave men, Luther claimed, were the foretaste of the much greater joys of Heaven; for music was near theology: it made the words come alive.[48] Luther's friend and collaborator, the musician Johannes Walter, set the tone for the long line of *cantors* of the Evangelical Church in a *laus musicae*, published in 1538:

---

[45] Quoted in Clive, *The Calvinist Attitude to Music*, p. 101, n. 1.

[46] M. Luther, *Tischreden* (Weimar, 1912), i, 968.

[47] *Ibid.*, no. 194.

[48] *Ibid.*, no. 968: 'Weil unser Herr Gott in dies Leben, das doch ein lauter Schmeishaus ist, solche edle Gaben geschütt und uns gegeben hat, was wird in jenem ewigen Leben geschehen, da Alles wird aufs Allervollkommenste und Lustigste werden; hie aber ist nur *materia prima*, der Anfang . . . Die Musica ist eine schöne herrliche Gabe Gottes, und nahe der Theologie . . . Die Noten machen den Text lebendig.' Since God has poured into and has given us such noble gifts in this life, which is after all nothing but a shit-house, how will it go in eternal life where everything will happen in the most perfect and cheerful way? For here is only materia prima, the beginning . . . Music is a beautiful, magnificent gift of God, close to theology . . . Music makes the text come alive. A recent historian even suggests that music as a means of communication is possessed, for Luther, both of a theological dimension and of theological power: C. Garside, 'Some Attitudes of the Major Reformers Toward the Role of music in the Liturgy', *McCormick Quarterly*, xxi (1967), 153.

> Sie ist mit der Theologie
> Zugleich von Gott gegeben hie/
> Gott hat die Music fein bedeckt
> in der Theologie versteckt/
> Er hat sie beid im fried geschmückt
> Das kein der andern ehr verrückt/
> Sie sin inn freundschafft nahe verwandt
> Das sie für schwestern wern erkandt/[49]

Theology and music, then, were heavenly sisters and neither would touch the other's honour; there could be no antagonism nor rivalry. In this firm belief generations of Lutheran pastors and *cantors* practised the art and allowed it freely to develop in their churches. It did not occur to them, as it did not occur to Walter and Luther, that one of the heavenly sisters would suffer an all but fatal decline in her appeal and that, without overt antagonism or rivalry, this decline would leave the other sister in a commanding position over men's hearts.

It did not occur to Luther; Zwingli, however, knew it well and feared it, even in his own time. A fine musician himself and able to perform on quite a variety of musical instruments, Zwingli would allow no singing in church at all. Had not the prophet Amos said: 'Take thou away from me the noise of thy songs; for I will not hear the melody of thy viols?'[v. 23] And what would he not have said today to all the singing and dancing, and to the choristers who come to the altar in their silken shirts?[50] In practice, music in church led to vanity and hypocrisy, for not one in a hundred could understand the mumblings of the singing nuns.[51]

Such criticism of music in church was traditional enough. But Zwingli went much further. Prayer was valuable only when said with complete concentration on its meaning. This was difficult enough, even under the most favourable circumstances, for 'when one prays, mouth and mind are not long on the same track'. Zwingli then drew the apparently inescapable conclusion: 'much less so mind and song'.[52] The power of music over men's minds was too great to allow it to compete with the word of God in church.[53] Unlike Calvin, Zwingli believed

---

[49] J. Walter, *Lob und Preis der Löblichen Kunst Musica 1538* (Kassel, 1938).
> God has given it together with theology
> God has skilfully hidden music in theology
> He has adorned them both in peace
> So that one cannot encroach on the other's honour
> They are bound in friendship
> So that they are recognised as sisters.

[50] H. Reimann, *Huldrych Zwingli – der Musiker* (Neujahrsblatt der Allgemeinen Musikgesellschaft Zürich, 1960), cxliv, 16.

[51] *Ibid.*

[52] C. Garside, *Zwingli and the Arts* (New Haven and London, 1966), p. 49.

[53] *Ibid.*, p. 49.

that it really was David's music, and not God's intervention, which had freed Saul, at least temporarily, from the visitations of the Devil.[54] but since God had nowhere actually commanded the use of music in his service, Zwingli could come to only one conclusion: music must be banished completely from church and become a purely secular art.

It is possible that Zwingli's thinking on church music continued to develop and that he might have reintroduced a reformed song into his Church if he had not been killed at Kappel.[55] In actual fact, however, singing ceased in those Swiss churches which were most directly influenced by Zwingli's teaching, and in Zürich and Berne the organs of the churches were destroyed or sold[56] – it is claimed, with the approval of the congregations.[57] Not until 1598 was singing of a very simple kind allowed again in the services of the Reformed Church in Zürich. There has never been a clearer, nor a more devastating, acknowledgment of the power of music in its ambivalent relations with religion.

It is not surprising that Switzerland played little part in the great triumphs of music in the eighteenth and nineteenth centuries. Probably until the end of the seventeenth century and, quite likely, well beyond it, church music formed the bulk of all music that was composed and played. Cut off church music, and the chances were that secular music would be stunted too. That, at least, seems to have been the feeling of many in the sixteenth and seventeenth centuries as they contemplated the austere services of the Calvinists and the even bleaker ones of the Zwinglians and of those Anabaptists who rejected or restricted church music. In England there appeared a voluminous and spirited defence of music, at the turn of the sixteenth century, ranging from Shakespeare's famous thrust against

> The man that hath no music in himself,
> Nor is not moved with concord of sweet sounds,
> Is fit for treasons, stratagems and spoils,[58]

to the crude but forceful verse of Samuel Rowley:

> The dulcet tongue of musicke made the stones
> To move, irrational beasts and birds to dance.
> And last the trumpet's musicke shall awake the dead,
> And clothes their naked bones in coats of flesh

[54] *Ibid.*, p. 67.

[55] Reimann, *Zwingli – der Musiker*, pp. 17ff.

[56] W. Blankenburg, 'Die Kirchenmusik in den reformierten Gebieten', Blume, *Geschichte der evangelischen Kirchenmusik*, p. 344.

[57] Garside, *Zwingli and the Arts*, pp. 61ff.

[58] Shakespeare, *The Merchant of Venice*, v, 1.

> T'appeare in that high house of parliament,
> When those that gnash their teeth at musicke's sound
> Shall make that place where musicke ne'er was found.[59]

A generation later, with the tide of puritanism running more strongly than ever, the battle was still continuing. Sir Thomas Browne was still convinced of the existence of the harmony of the spheres which,

> though they give no sound unto the ear, yet to the understanding they strike a note most full of harmony. Whosoever is harmonically composed delights in harmony; which makes me distrust the symmetry of those heads which declaim against all Church-Musick. For myself . . . I embrace it: for even that vulgar and Tavern-Musick, which makes one man merry, another mad, strikes in me a deep fit of devotion, and a profound contemplation of the first Composer.[60]

Leonardo da Vinci had seen that painting has an enormous psychological power, a numinous power – or a demonic one, as the Calvinist iconoclasts thought. Music has this power to an even greater degree, and there had always been musicians, writers and listeners who had recognized this. Yet during the Renaissance for many the clear recognition of this phenomenon was obscured by a too one-sided evaluation of the relationship between words and music, and its discussion was side-tracked into the arid, and eventually meaningless, attempt to resurrect the Platonic distinctions between moral and immoral music. But by 1600, outside those areas strongly influenced by Zwingli and Calvin, music was emerging triumphantly from the attacks of the musical moralists, both secular and clerical. In Venice, where the *capella* of St Mark's depended on the secular authorities, puritanism in music was never looked upon with any greater favour than any other type of puritanism. The Netherlander Willaert had introduced the use of multiple choirs in St Mark's, and his successors accompanied these with organ, trombones and strings. Towards the end of the sixteenth century, Andrea and Giovanni Gabrieli composed church and secular music, indifferently, and with a richness of texture that matched contemporary Venetian painting. This, it seems, was the way in which the painters saw it. In his *Marriage of Cana*, now in the Louvre, Veronese painted a group of musicians in the very centre of his composition and immediately below the figure of Christ: they were Titian playing a string bass, Tintoretto and Veronese himself playing viols, and Bassano playing the flute. Here were music and painting at the feet of Christ, without the intervention of the word except in so far as the painting told the well-known Biblical story. This was indeed a

---

[59] Quoted in J. Hutton, 'Some English Poems in Praise of Music', *English Miscellany* (Rome, 1951), ed. M. Praz, ii, 41.

[60] Sir Thomas Browne, *Religio Medici*, II, ix; also quoted in W. Mellers, *Music and Society*, 2nd ed. (London, 1950), pp. 104f.

different conception of the role of music (and painting) from that of
Baïf or Borromeo.

In the seventeenth century some theorists, such as Mersenne,
continued to argue as the sixteenth-century humanists had done. But,
effectively, musical puritanism was being transformed by being
channelled into opera, the invention of Vincenzo Galilei and his circle.
For in opera the primacy of words over music, which they had so
earnestly striven for, could be happily combined with the rich
sonorities of Venetian instrumental music and the intricate part writing
and emotional subtleties of the madrigalists. In Catholic church music
the precepts of the Council of Trent were gradually forgotten. By 1628
Orazio Benevoli was commissioned to write, for the consecration of
the new Cathedral of Salzburg, a mass for twelve separate choirs and
fifty-three voices. As in every other form of Baroque art, the total effect
of a complete and complex work on the senses and sensibilities of the
beholder or listener came to be regarded as more important than the
effects or values of any of its parts.

Such an attitude may also help to explain the rapidly growing
popularity of different forms of religious or spiritual music – *geistliche
Musik* – as distinct from traditional church and liturgical music. Their
origins were varied. *Laude spirituali* (spiritual songs), for instance, were
popular already in the sixteenth century, and their Catholic publishers
were as liberal as Luther in parodying secular songs.[61] St Filippo Neri,
in the second half of the sixteenth century, introduced music as a
devotional exercise into his oratory in Rome and, at first, with all the
musical puritanism of the Counter-Reformation. But, precisely because
such music was not part of a regular church service, it rapidly
developed considerable freedom. Thus was launched oratorio on its
immensely successful career, culminating in the sustained popular
apotheosis of Handel's *Messiah* in England, and leading to the
philologically absurd but culturally quite logical genre of secular
oratorio in the twentieth century. Thus also developed spiritual
concerts, organ introductions to church services, motets and cantatas.
The dividing-line between these free forms of religious music and
liturgical or church music properly speaking was by no means always
clear nor rigidly observed. In the Lutheran Church it was hardly made
at all; in the Catholic Church it varied with place and time. But
everywhere this religious music developed according to purely musical
rules and tastes, with barely a curtsy towards the rigid rules which
sixteenth-century theologians and humanists had wanted to impose
upon it. The brilliant orchestration of secular and courtly dance suites
with their concertante solo instruments, the emotional and dramatic
effects of Italian opera with its *da capo* arias and its coloratura singing –
in short, all the splendours of secular Baroque music – were easily

[61] G. Reese, *Music in the Renaissance*, p. 453.

adapted to religious purposes, either by being given a slightly solemn or sentimental tinge or, more commonly, by simply being supplied with appropriate religious texts. Large sections of the European public, especially the educated classes, seem to have wanted to take their religion with a large admixture of music and, what is more, with the most dramatic, exciting and affecting music that was being composed. So strong was this longing that even the Calvinist and Zwinglian parts of Europe could not resit it. *Geistliche Abendmusiken*, religious musical evenings, spread from the Netherlands throughout northern Germany and became immensely popular. Zürich itself, the city which had abolished church music altogether, found that it could not do without 'music in church'.[62]

From about the middle of the seventeenth century some theoreticians of music began to emancipate the art from moral and theological values. For the Italian, Marco Sacchi, music was to be performed no longer *ad maiorem Dei gloriam*, but *ad maiorem musicae artis gloriam*. It was not an altogether original notion: Plato had been enraged by those who thought that music could 'only be judged rightly by the pleasure of the hearer'.[63] Naturally, it had not been a fashionable idea among Renaissance Neoplatonists. But by the early eighteenth century there was a whole school of music theoreticians in Germany who saw the end and justification of music in the pleasure it gave the listener.[64] More important, however, from our point of view, than the emancipation of music as an art was the fact that for most musicians and theoreticians it continued to be linked in some way with religion and with the essential nature of the universe. For instance, Andreas Werckmeister, writing about 1700, saw music as 'a tool of the Holy Ghost by which He awakens all sorts of pious and elevating emotions in the human heart'.[65] It was as if man had his divine image of himself presented to him by music, Werckmeister argued, for music represented the order which God had created.[66]

This type of simplified Neoplatonism dominated also the prevalent French school of musical aesthetics which saw music as an essentially imitative art, able to reproduce in the listener specific emotional and even visual effects existing in the outside world. This theory of imitation worked well enough for painting and poetry. It could still be reasonably applied to songs and opera. But what effects did a symphony or sonata reproduce? The solution to this difficulty seemed to lie again in the old Pythagorean and Neoplatonic theory of a world

[62] Reimann, *Zwingli – der Musiker*, p. 19.

[63] Cf. above, p. 181.

[64] P. Bernary, *Die deutsche Kompositionslehre des 18. Jahrhunderts* (Leipzig, 1955), p. 37.

[65] Quoted in H. Goldschmidt, *Die Musikästhetik des 18. Jahrhunderts und ihre Beziehungen zu seinem Kunstschaffen* (Zürich and Leipzig, 1915), p. 53.

[66] *Ibid.*

harmony based on numbers which, in some way, was mirrored by music.[67] Leibniz put it succinctly: 'Musica est exercitium arithmeticae occultum nescientes se numerare animi' (music is a concealed practice of mathematics of a soul not consciously calculating).[68]

It is against the background of these shifting attitudes towards music that we have to see the towering and enigmatic figure of Johann Sebastian Bach. Not entirely surprisingly, the interpretation of Bach's own attitude towards music has become highly controversial in the last twenty years.[69] There is, of course, no question of Bach's deep religious convictions. But it does seem that it was music itself which was the centre of his religious convictions and which largely determined their form. He was hostile to the Pietists because of their puritanical attitude towards music, and not for theological reasons. Or, rather, music itself was part of his theology. Here Bach was undoubtedly within the Lutheran tradition, but it is clear that music's twin sister, theology, had already suffered a marked eclipse. As in the case of Sir Thomas Browne, it was music itself, and not necessarily or specifically church music, which was man's *laudatio Dei* and *recreatio cordis*.

Thus Bach could accept, as some modern scholars believe, the Leibnizian Neoplatonic view of the relation of music to a fundamental world order and even incorporate a highly complex and esoteric number symbolism in some of his compositions.[70] More important still, it enabled him to compose, without apparent qualms of conscience, music for Catholic church services and, most significant of all, to transform much of his own immense output of secular music into church cantatas, oratorios and even parts of the *St Matthew Passion*, and all this on a scale greater than anyone realized until quite recently. It is not necessary to suppose that Bach's thinking about music was completely consistent throughout his life. If nothing else, the last variation of the *Goldberg Variations*, with themes from the popular song

[67] J. Écorcheville, *De Lulli à Rameau 1690–1730. L'Esthétique Musicale* (Paris, 1906), p. 31.

[68] Quoted in H. H. Dräger, 'Musik-Ästhetik', *Musik in Geschichte und Gegenwart*, ed. F. Blume (Kassel, 1961), ix, col. 1,012.

[69] See, for instance, out of an enormous literature, G. Herz, 'Bach's Religion', *Journal of Renaissance and Baroque Music*, i (1946–7); W. Blankenburg, 'Bach, geistlich und weltlich', *Musik und Kirche*, xx (1950), and 'Das Parodieverfahen Bachs', *ibid.*, xxxii (1962); F. Smend, *Luther und Bach* (Berlin, 1947); F. Blume, 'Bach, Johann Sebastian', *Musik in Geschichte und Gegenwart* (Kassel, 1949–51), i, and 'Umrisse eines neuen Bach-Bildes', *Musica*, xvi (1962), controverted by A. Dürr, 'Zum Wandel des Bach-Bildes', *Musik und Kirche*, xxxii (1962), and answered by Blume, *ibid.* For an attempt at a completely Pythagorean interpretation of Bach see P. T. Barford, 'The Concept of Bach', *Music Review*, xxiii (1962). The most recent attempt at an orthodox interpretation that I have seen is J. Widmann, 'Johann Sebastian Bach. Musik zwischen Gott und Gemeinde', *Musik und Kirche*, xxxviii (1968). See also Blume, *Kirchenmusik*, pp. 168–213.

[70] Smend, *Luther und Bach*, pp. 16–20; Blankenburg, 'Bach, geistlich und weltlich', pp. 41ff.

Kraut und Rüben
Die haben mich vertrieben

(Cabbage and turnips
Have driven me from home)

should warn us against an altogether too solemn interpretation of Bach's attitude towards his greatest works. It seems perhaps most sensible to assume (for we cannot prove it conclusively) that Bach saw no essential difference between secular and church music. For Bach, I believe, all music was sacred, the *Brandenburg Concertos* as much as the organ preludes, the Catholic Magnificat as much as the Protestant cantatas, the coloratura aria 'Prepare thyself, Zion' as much as the chorale 'Oh Haupt voll Blut und Wunden'. If Descartes's God was the great artificer, worshipped most appropriately through mathematics, Bach's God was the great creator of harmony, worshipped most fittingly through music. The metaphors and analogies involved in both beliefs were not as far apart as has often been thought.

In the course of the eighteenth century the last remnants of philosophical and religious puritanism disappeared from musical thought. 'To enjoy music fully, we must completely lose ourselves in it', wrote Rameau.[71] It was just this power of music to make the listener lose himself in it which had terrified Plato and his Renaissance disciples. Worse still, from the traditional point of view: Rameau thought that words might actually get in the way of a proper understanding and appreciation of music.

We must not think but let ourselves be carried away by the feeling which the music inspires [he urges, and then adds (in what I take to be a somewhat ironic bow towards the fashionable philosophy of the age):] As for reason, everybody possesses it nowadays; we have just discovered it in the bosom of nature itself. We have even proved that instinct constantly recalls it to us . . . When reason and instinct are reconciled, there will be no higher appeal.[72]

If music could be reconciled with reason it could also, *a fortiori*, still be reconciled with religion. Music, as we have seen, has a numinous power, like painting, and it has this perhaps to an even greater degree. It is this fact which caused the analogy between the two arts to break down in the eighteenth century. As the strength and fervour of traditional religious beliefs declined, the quality of religious painting began to decline too; for it was, in the end, bound to the artist's (and perhaps also his patron's) convictions in this matter. With some few exceptions, notably in the work of Tiepolo and Blake and, arguably, Goya, the eighteenth and nineteenth centuries produced very little great

---

[71] 'Observations sur notre instinct pour la musique et sur son principe' (1734), quoted and translated by S. Morgenstern, *Composers on Music* (New York, 1956), p. 43.
[72] *Ibid.*, pp. 44–5.

religious painting – that is, painting comparable as religious painting with the work of Renaissance and seventeenth-century artists, and comparable simply as painting with the work of the great painters of secular subjects, from Watteau to Renoir.

But music was different. Nearly all the great composers, from Handel through Haydn, Mozart and Beethoven to Verdi, Brahms and Fauré, poured some of their finest musical thought into masses, requiems and spiritual songs. It was not only the advantage which music had over painting, in that its exercise preserved something of the spirit of communal worship of an earlier, more orthodox age; it was its ability to create this spirit even when it was no longer clear what, if anything, was being worshipped.[73] It did not even matter very much whether this religious music used liturgical texts or not. Its impact was primarily on the emotions and it could accommodate any intellectual content. It could encompass Handel's astonishing fusion of Anglo-German Biblicism with an Italian and Baroque sense of drama just as easily as Mozart's masonic deism or the great paean to God the Creator of the world and of its order and harmony which is Haydn's *Creation*.

Later, in the nineteenth an early twentieth centuries, the Churches found it difficult to accept such works as church music. The author of the article on church music in the *Catholic Encyclopaedia* (1911) criticized particularly the church music of Haydn, Mozart and Beethoven and of the Protestant composers Bach and Handel. He distinguished, quite reasonably, between religious and church music and then stated categorically that these composers 'do not fulfil the requirements of the Church'.[74]

No one, however, demonstrated the capacity of music to create its own religious feelings more clearly than Beethoven. There is little doubt that when Beethoven wrote his *Mass in C*, Op. 86 (1806) and his *Missa Solemnis* (1819–23) he set out to write proper church music. He studied Gregorian chant, medieval hymns and Palestrina's masses with care, and

[73] The late Professor E. J. Dent realized this very clearly: 'It has often been maintained that the Church "inspired" the art of European music; it would be more true to say that music inspired the Church. The Church was the first great utilizer of music, and it sought to utilize it because, as we learn from St Augustine, it was afraid of music. The history of church music shows us plainly from the earliest days down to the *Motu proprio* of Pope Pius X that the so-called "hand-maid of the Church" very soon asserted herself, and continued to do so unabashed, as a *serva padrona*': Introduction to A. Yorke-Long, *Music at Court* (London, 1954), pp. xiii–xiv. I came across this passage after I had written the first draft of this essay. As far as I know, Dent never elaborated this point, which comes very near to the central thesis of this essay.

[74] G. Gietmann, 'Church Music', *The Catholic Encyclopaedia*, x, 650. Presumably, so as not to appear as a philistine, Gietmann added: 'The musical fame of these masters is thereby in nowise diminished.' In fairness, it should be pointed out that F. J. Molek, writing the equivalent article in the *New Catholic Encyclopaedia*, x (1967), is very much more perceptive about, and not in the least critical of, Haydn's and Mozart's church music.

incorporated elements of these styles in his work. But the work was clearly so far removed from the traditional mass and so individual in its conception that, during Beethoven's lifetime, only the *Kyrie, Credo* and *Agnus Dei* were performed, and this, moreover, in German translation, as *Drei grosse Hymnen* (Three Great Hymns), in order to avoid clerical censure.[75] But of its impact on the listener there has never been any question: 'Von Herzen – möge es zu Herzen gehen' (From the heart, may it go to the heart), as Beethoven wrote over the *Kyrie*.

But it was not just Beethoven's church music which has had this effect. It was the whole of his work. It seems that he himself believed that music, especially his own music, had transcendental qualities.

When I lift my eyes [he said] I must sigh; for what I see is contrary to my religion, and I must despise a world which does not perceive that music is a higher revelation than all wisdom and philosophy; it is the wine which rouses to new creations, and I am the Bacchus who presses this glorious wine for men and makes them spritually drunk; when they are sober again they will have fished up much which they can keep on dry land.

Thus Bettina Brentano reported her conversation with Beethoven to Goethe in 1810.[76] A few days later Beethoven elaborated his views to Bettina, especially for Goethe's benefit:

Talk to Goethe about me; tell him he should listen to my symphonies and he will agree with me that music is the only incorporeal entrance [*unverkörperte Eingang*] into a higher world of knowledge which encompasses man but which he cannot encompass . . . Thus art always represents the deity, and man's relation to art is religion . . .

As the seed needs the wet, soft electrical soil to grow, he continued, so music is the electrical soil in which the spirit lives, thinks and creates. Music gives the spirit its relationship to harmony and unity. All that is electrical stimulates the spirit to musical, pulsing, outflowing creation. 'I have an electrical nature', he exclaimed at the end – and then rushed Bettina off to a rehearsal. She wrote it all down, that night, and when she showed it to him the next morning he said: 'Did I say that? Well then I must have been in a trance [*Nun dann hab ich einen Raptus gehabt*].'[77]

The authenticity of Bettina's account has often been doubted, ever since she published it, in 1835, in her undoubtedly romanticized account of her friendship and correspondence with Goethe. But most modern scholars tend to accept that Beethoven did say something like

[75] G. Schuhmacher, 'Beethoven's geistliche Werke', Schallplatte und Kirche, Beiheft I zu *Musik und Kirche*, xxxvii (1967), 6.

[76] Bettina von Arnim (Brentano), *Goethes Briefwechsel mit einem Kinde*, ed. G. Konrad (Frechen-Köln, 1960), p. 246.

[77] *Ibid.*, pp. 247–9.

what she wrote. The very confusion of ideas, the faint echoes of Platonic harmony, the misunderstanding of contemporary scientific notions about electricity, all this seems highly likely for a man unused to finding words for his deepest thoughts about music. Goethe was evidently taken aback, but kept his Olympian calm.

It has been a great pleasure to me [he wrote in answer to Bettina's account] to receive this picture of a true genius without wanting to classify him . . . From what can be understood from these [i.e. Beethoven's] manifold utterances, I must confess that ordinary common sense might perhaps find contradiction in them: but what is uttered by one possessed by such a daemon must cause reverence in the layman . . . for here the gods are at work, sowing seeds for future understanding . . .[78]

Goethe's view of music was not a romantic one. Music could move him deeply. After a recital of Bach's *Well-tempered Clavier* he wrote: 'I said to myself: it is as if the eternal harmony was conversing with itself, as it might have happened in God's heart just before the creation'.[79] But principally he sought to understand music intellectually and to construct a theory of tones, in analogy to his theory of colours, involving both the mathematical elements and the psychological effects of music.[80] Characteristically, Bettina thought this a waste of time.[81] For her the matter was quite simple. 'Look out, Frau Rat', she claimed to have said to Goethe's mother, 'that the angels will not beat you about the head with their fiddlesticks until you have realized that heaven is music.'[82]

Bettina Brentano is important because her simple, romantic equation of music and the divine, and more especially of Beethoven's music and the Deity, was characteristic for much of the musical sensibility of the nineteenth and even twentieth centuries. It really mattered little what Beethoven himself had said or thought. His listeners felt themselves well able to interpret the master's meaning. It started in his lifetime, and before anyone but Goethe had read his conversation with Bettina. 'Even if you do not believe it, you are being glorified', a certain Hofrat Peters wrote into Beethoven's conversation book in 1823. 'You will rise with me from the dead and you will conduct the choirs while I pray.'[83] Beethoven's answer is not recorded.

After Beethoven's death, the minor Romantic poets celebrated his

[78] *Ibid.*, p. 250.
[79] Quoted in F. Blume, *Goethe und die Musik* (Kassel, 1948), p. 65.
[80] *Ibid.*, pp. 70ff. and *passim*.
[81] Bettina von Arnim, *Goethes Briefwechsel*, p. 142.
[82] *Ibid.*, p. 128.
[83] Quoted in A. Schmitz, 'Die Beethoven-Apotheose als Beispiel eines Säkularisierungsvorganges', *Festschrift Peter Wagner* (Leipzig, 1926), pp. 186–7.

divinity in reams of almost unbelievably bad verse. Nikolaus Lenau was, relatively, better than most:

> In der Symphonien rauschen,
> Heiligen Gewittergüssen,
> Seh ich Zeus auf Wolken nahn und
> Christi blut'ge Stirne küssen;
>
> Hört das Herz die grosse Liebe
> Alles in die Arme schliessen,
> Mit der alten Welt die neue
> In die ewige zerfliessen.[84]

Wagner, although he was sceptical of Bettina's account of her conversation with Beethoven, was completely uninhabited in his own interpretation of Beethoven's music. 'A deaf musician!' he exclaimed. 'Could one imagine a blind painter? But a blind seer we do know. Teiresias, who was shut off from the world of appearances but who is able to perceive the reason of all appearances with his inner eye – like him, the deaf musician listens to the harmonies of his inner being . . .' His inner light reflects on the world of appearances and gives it back its childlike innocence: '"Today thou wilt be with me in Paradise" – who does not hear this word of the Redeemer when he listens to the *Pastoral Symphony*?' Never has any art created anything so joyful. Wagner continues, as Beethoven's symphonies in A and F (i.e. No. 7 and No. 6, the *Pastoral*). Their effect on the hearer is that of freeing him from all guilt and their after-effect, when he returns to the world of appearances, is that of paradise lost. 'Thus these wonderful works preach repentance and penance in the deepest sense of a divine revelation.'[85]

The high point of the defication of Beethoven's music, and even of the composer himself, was reached in the Beethoven biographies of the early twentieth century. Paul Bekker wrote in 1912: 'Thus he regards himself as a vessel of supernatural revelation – as the hero, the conqueror who had suffered, had let himself be crucified, had descended to the dead and had risen and felt God awaken in himself.'[86]

---

[84] Quoted in L. Hirschberg, 'Beethoven und die Dichtung', *Die Musik*, x, 37 (1910–11), 350.

> In the surging of the symphonies,
> Holy thunderstorms,
> I see Zeus approach on clouds
> And kiss Christ's bloodstained forehead;
>
> My heart listens to the great love
> Embracing all,
> And to the old world and the new
> Dissolving into eternity.

[85] R. Wagner, 'Beethoven', *Gesammelte Schriften und Dichtungen*, ed. W. Golther (Berlin, n.d.) viii, 92–3.

[86] P. Bekker, *Beethoven*, 2nd ed. (Berlin, 1921), p. 89. Also quoted in Schmitz, 'Die Beethoven-Apotheose', p. 184.

Romain Rolland, in 1903, had put it more elegantly, but only a little less fancifully: 'Et à mesure qu'il était plus seul, veuf d'amitiés et d'amours, et qu'il s'acheminait vers le complet détachement de cette vie . . Dieu remplissait en lui tout l'espace: il épousait sa triple forme: la Force, l'Amour et la Lumière. Il s'identifiait avec la Toute-Puissance créatrice, en même temps qu'avec la tremblante humilité de la créature.'[87]

A German musicologist, A. Schmitz, has called this Beethoven-apotheosis an example of a process of secularization.[88] This seems to me true in so far as this phenomenon could occur only in an age of a rapid weakening of traditional religious feeling. But, essentially, the attitude of the Beethoven worshippers was not a secular one at all. It was, on the contrary, quite consciously religious and was expressed deliberately in religious language. It seems to me, therefore, that a kind of transference had occurred. Music and its emotional appeal, even the persons of the composers of music, had become identified with religion and were held to speak the language of religion, thus providing an emotional satisfaction which the traditional church service could no longer provide.

This becomes very clear from the persistent tendency, even in most recent time, for Beethoven's music to be interpreted in philosophical and religious terms. Aldous Huxley's comments, at the end of *Point Counterpoint*, on the slow movement of the Quartet, Op. 132, the *Holy Song of Praise of a Convalescent to the Deity*, are a typical literary example:

It was as though heaven had suddenly and impossibly become more heavenly, had passed from admired perfection into perfection yet deeper and more absolute. The ineffable peace persisted; but it was no longer the peace of convalescence and passivity. It quivered, it was alive, it seemed to grow and intensify itself, it became an active calm, an almost passionate serenity. The miraculous paradox of eternal repose was musically realized.[89]

Even Stravinsky, the composer who claimed that composing was the ordering of a certain number of tones in certain interval relationships,[90] wrote recently: 'These [Beethoven's last] quartets are my highest article of musical belief (which is a longer word for love, whatever else), as indispensable to the ways and meanings of art, as a musician of my era thinks of art and has tried to learn it, as temperature is to life. They are a triumph over temporality . . .'[91]

[87] R. Rolland, *Beethoven, Les Grandes Epoques Creatrices. Le Chant de la Resurrection* (Paris, 1937), p. 364.

[88] Schmitz, 'Die Beethoven-Apotheose', *passim*.

[89] A. Huxley, *Point Counter Point* (Harmondsworth, 1955; 1st ed., 1928), p. 433. It is irrelevant for my argument whether this passage represented Huxley's own feelings or whether he intended it only to represent those of a character in his novel.

[90] H. F. Redlich, 'Strawinsky', *Musik in Geschichte und Gegenwart*, xii (1965), col. 1,512.

[91] Review of J. Kerman, *The Beethoven Quartets*, *New York Review of Books*, xi, 5 (26 September, 1968), 4.

While no other composer has had quite such an effect on his hearers as Beethoven, the elevation of all music into a kind of religion was very much a part of the Romantic movement. It was given philosophical respectability by Schopenhauer. Ideas, Schopenhauer argued – that is, Platonic ideas – were the objectivization of the will, the basic principle of the world. It is the purpose of works of art to stimulate the recognition of these ideas by the representation of individual objects. Works of art therefore objectivize or mirror the will only indirectly, i.e. through the ideas. Music, however, differs from all the other arts in that it is not the image of ideas, but the image of the will itself; which explains the extraordinary effect of music, an effect much greater than that of any other art. Music is, moreover, independent of the world and could exist without it.[92]

Melody especially, Schopenhauer argues, expresses the manifold striving of the human will, from wish to satisfaction and then to a new wish; for just so melody meanders away from the keynote and through a series of dissonances, before returning to it. As the quick succession of desires and satisfactions constitutes happiness and well-being, so a quick melody is, in general, cheerful. Slow melodies, with painful dissonances analogous to delayed satisfaction, are sad. Thus 'the composer reveals the inmost being of the world and speaks its deepest wisdom in language which his reason does not understand'.[93] Music, Schopenhauer maintained, expresses in a very general language the essence of the world – it expresses joy or sorrow, jubilation or sadness, without anything contingent or particular attached to these 'abstract' emotions. Philosophy, however, is nothing else but a complete and correct repetition and expression of the nature (*Wesen*) of the world in general concepts. It therefore follows, always according to Schopenhauer, that a true explanation of music, i.e. a detailed repetition of what music expresses in concepts, would immediately be a sufficient repetition and explanation of the world, a real philosophy. Leibniz's epigram, 'Musica est exercitium arithmeticae occultum nescientes se numerare animi', should now really read 'Musica est exercitium metaphysices occultum nescientes se philosophari animi' (Music is a concealed practice of metaphysics by a soul that is not conscious of philosophizing).[94]

This was Platonism without tears; or, at least, without mathematics. For the theory of a mathematical equivalence or, at least, analogy between the structure of the universe and the nature of music (a theory which, rightly or wrongly and in however varying and attenuated forms, had constituted the hard core of the philosophy of music for some two thousand years), for this basically rational theory

[92] A. Schopenhauer, 'Die Welt als Wille und Vorstellung', *Sämtliche Werke*, i (Munich, 1911), 304.

[93] *Ibid.*, pp. 307f.

[94] *Ibid.*, pp. 308–13.

Schopenhauer substituted a deliberately non-rational and essentially romantic metaphysics of music. In detail, the results of Schopenhauer's views were inevitably arbitrary. Thus he quite seriously proposed an analogy between 'the four voices of all harmony, i.e. bass, tenor, alto and soprano, or keynote, third, fifth and octave' and the 'four gradations in the series of beings [*Wesen*], i.e. the mineral realm, flora, fauna and man'.[95]

Schopenhauer's metaphysics of music may have been philosophically shallow and musically naïve, but they managed very successfully to strike a certain mood of the nineteenth century. Never before had music been elevated so high above the other arts nor been identified so unequivocally with the self-expression of the Deity (Schopenhauer's 'will', at least as popularly understood). Wagner accepted Schopenhauer's philosophy with enthusiasm.[96] As a musician, and a very articulate one, he was, moreover, a great deal more specific than the philosopher: 'Just as Christianity arose in the international civilization of the Roman Empire, so music emerges out of the chaos of modern civilization. Both proclaim "Our kingdom is not of this world". And this means: we come from within, you from without; we derive from the essence, you from the appearance of things.'[97]

While Wagner had put music and Christianity on the same level, their relationship to each other remained somewhat confused in his thought. The music of the Greeks had 'intimately penetrated the world of appearances and had fused with its scientific and social laws'. But this paradise had been lost – presumably in the despised 'international civilization' of the Roman Empire. Then, however, 'it was the spirit of Christianity which revived music'.[98] This seems both orthodox and categorical. But immediately Wagner continues:

Church music was sung to the words of the concepts of dogma: in its effects it dissolved these words and the concepts of dogma contained in them to the point where their very perception disappears, so that it [music] now conveys their pure emotive content to the entranced emotions of the hearer. In this sense we have to recognize that music reveals the essence of the Christian religion with unrivalled definiteness . . .

In the painting of a Raphael Madonna, Wagner continues, we still have to say: *this means*. 'But music says to us: *this is* – because it abolishes the dichotomy between concept and feeling, and this through tonal form, a form which is wholly other than the world of appearances, yet one

---

[95]  *Ibid.*, ii, 509.

[96]  E.g. in his essay on Beethoven, pp. 66ff.

[97]  Article 'Musik', *Wagner Lexikon*, ed. C. Fr. Glasenapp and H. v. Stein (Stuttgart, 1883), p. 497.

[98]  *Ibid.*, p. 498.

which fills our soul as by grace and which is not comparable to anything real.'[99]

Here were St Augustine's and the theologians' fears of the powers of music not only fulfilled but actually made to triumph over the words of the dogma as mere 'concepts'. For Wagner the function of song was not to give greater effect to words. The human voice itself was simply one more musical instrument designed to serve the functions of music. He praised Bach for using his choirs with the flexibility of an orchestra and approvingly characterized the *Missa Solemnis* as 'a purely symphonic work of the truest Beethovenesque spirit'. The only reason why the words of great church music do not disturb us is because 'they do not stimulate rational concepts, but rather (and as, indeed, their ecclesiastical character requires) they touch us only with the impression of well-known symbolic formulas of faith'.[100] Even Zwingli, in his most pessimistic moments about church music, could hardly have foreseen such a reversal of values.

Seeing in Beethoven's symphonies a language of such power and subtlety as had never previously been spoken, Wagner asked himself why music should have reached such heights in his own century. The answer, he thought, must be found in the growing conventionality of the modern European languages which made the development of a completely new form of expression a 'metaphysical necessity'. The extraordinary popularity of even the most profound musical genres, the growing zeal in the introduction of music into the general system of education, all this showed the inner need of mankind for this new language.[101]

Let everyone experience for himself how the whole modern world of appearances [*die ganze moderne Erscheinungswelt*], which inexorably encompasses him on all sides to the point of desperation, suddenly vanishes into nothingness as soon as the first bars of these divine symphonies [i.e. Beethoven's] resound. How would it be possible to listen to such music with even a little devotion [*Andacht*] in our modern concert halls (where indeed Turks and Zouaves would feel comfortable!) if the optical perception of our surroundings did not vanish? But this is, in its most serious sense, the effect of music with regard to our whole civilization; music supersedes it as daylight supersedes artificial light.[102]

Wagner had observed a real phenomenon, even if he had assigned to it a wrong and unhistorical reason; for the splendours of nineteenth-century European literature make his theory of the growing

[99] *Ibid.*, pp. 498–9.
[100] Wagner, 'Beethoven', p. 103.
[101] *Wagner Lexikon*, p. 497.
[102] *Ibid.*

conventionality of the modern European languages quite unacceptable. The real reason for the extraordinary development of music must be sought rather in the decline of conventional religious beliefs and in the psychological inadequacy of the Churches in fulfilling the religious longings of large sections of the educated European public; for music was able to provide precisely these emotional satisfactions and, by a process of rationalization and justification, also, apparently, those eternal truths which the Churches used to provide. This explains Wagner's own consistent use of religious phraseology and metaphors when talking about music and musicians. After his famous interview with Rossini, in 1860, for instance, Wagner remarked: 'What might he not have produced if he had received a forceful and complete musical education? Especially if, less Italian and less sceptical, he had felt within him the *religion of his art*?'[103] It also explains the conception and history of the Wagner Theatre at Bayreuth and the passionate feelings, for and against, which it aroused and sometimes still arouses. For this was not the 'modern concert hall where Turks and Zouaves would feel comfortable' but, deliberately, the worthy place of pilgrimage for those who wished to listen to the master's music 'with devotion'. Here the performance of Wagner's operas attained to an almost liturgical status, and it was not until after the Second World War that Wagner's grandsons finally dared to break with the tradition of stage production established by the master himself.

If Wagner's was an extreme case, it was the extreme of a very widespread feeling in the nineteenth and early twentieth centuries. Richard Strauss, while a much more sober personality than Wagner, continued until the end of his life to speak of music in that mixture of Platonic and Schopenhauerian terms which had been so fashionable in his youth. 'Poetic inspiration', Strauss wrote in 1940, 'can still have a connection with the intelligence, because it must externalize itself through words – melodic inspiration is the absolute revelation of final mysteries . . .'[104] And again, in 1944, but this time with an admixture of Jungian concepts:

In Susanna's garden aria, in Belmonte's and Ferrando's A major and Octavio's G major aria, Eros himself sings in Mozart's melodies, Love in its most beautiful, purest forms speaks to our feelings . . . In the slow section of Donna Anna's so-called 'Letter' aria, in both arias of the Countess in *Figaro*, we have before us the creations of the Ideal which I can only compare with Plato's 'Ideas', the prototype of visions projected into real life . . . not to be recognized by the eye, not to be grasped by the understanding, but to be divined by consciousness as most godly which the ear is permitted to 'breath

---

[103] Quoted in H. Weinstock, *Rossini, a Biography* (New York, 1968), p. 297. My italics.

[104] *Composers on Music*, ed. S. Morgenstern, p. 338.

in'. Mozartean melody is detached from every earthy form – the 'thing in itself', like Plato's Eros, poised between heaven and earth, between the mortal and the immortal – liberated from the 'will', it embodies the deepest penetration of artistic imagination, of the unconscious, into the final mysteries, into the realm of the 'archetypes'.[105]

Characteristically for Strauss, and perhaps generally for the mid-twentieth century, the high point of musical expression is seen no longer in Beethoven, but in Mozart.

In such an atmosphere of musical emotion it is not surprising that someone should have taken the final logical step and formally proclaimed music as a religion. In 1905 Riccardo Canudo first published a book in Paris which, in 1913, appeared in England with the title *Music as a Religion of the Future*.[106] Canudo's arguments were neither original nor philosophically distinguished, and I do not think the book had any considerable impact. They summed up, however, a great deal of previous thinking and emotion about music. Canudo saw the secret of both art and religion in self-oblivion and he argued that music, alone among the arts, was capable of creating 'this indispensable condition of Oblivion which all Religions have bestowed on their faithful'.[107]

The ultimate step in the apotheosis of music, the *non plus ultra* of the claims for its powers, and for those of its composer, was made, not by a clever rationalist like Canudo, but by the Russian composer Alexander Scriabin. At the turn of the nineteenth century mystical and revolutionary ideas were fashionable in Russia.[108] Scriabin seems to have been receptive to all of them, from Marxist socialism to theosophy. By 1904 he was telling a friend in Geneva:

There will be a fusion of all the arts, but not a theatrical one like Wagner's. Art must unite with philosophy and religion in an indivisible whole to form a new gospel which will replace the old gospel we have outlived. I cherish the dream of creating such a 'mystery'. For it, it would be necessary to build a special temple – perhaps here, perhaps far away in India. But mankind is not yet ready for it. It must be preached to; it must be led along new paths. And I do preach. Once I even preached from a boat, like Christ. I have a little circle of people who understand me perfectly and follow me. Particularly one – a fisherman. He is simple, but a splendid fellow.[109]

More and more he wrote his music, and especially his orchestral works,

[105] *Ibid.*, p. 341.
[106] R. Canudo, *Music as a Religion of the Future*, tr. B. D. Conlan (London and Edinburgh, 1913).
[107] *Ibid*, pp. 15–24. Canudo's (or his translator's?) capitalization.
[108] M. Cooper, 'Scriabin's Mystical Beliefs', *Music and Letters*, 16 (1935), 110–15.
[109] Quoted by G. Abraham, 'Alexander Scriabin', in M. D. Calvocoressi and G. Abraham, *Masters of Russian Music* (New York, 1936), pp. 472–3.

as preliminaries for the great 'mystery'. The programme notes for Scriabin's orchestral work, *The Divine Poem*, written by his mistress, Tatiana Schlözer, speak of the evolution of the human spirit, emancipated from past beliefs and passing through pantheism to a 'joyous and intoxicated affirmation of its liberty and its unity with the universe, the divine Ego'.[110] In a later work for orchestra, *Prometheus: a Poem of Fire*, Scriabin developed his ideas of the conjunction of the different arts by introducing a *clavier à lumière* which was to throw coloured lights on to a screen during the performance of the work.

The nature of the final 'mystery' remained somewhat vague, both in theory and in the proposed details of its execution, although not, apparently, in the results it was meant to produce. Scriabin, it seems, saw the universe as dominated by an 'alternation of creative rhythms' or 'the breaths of Brahma'.[111] Two creative but opposite forces, evolution and involution, were to combine in an erotic act of love. This would result in a return to the primordial state of chaos and this, in its turn, would be followed by a new 'breath of Brahma'. Scriabin saw himself as the impressario or, rather, the creator of this great act which was to lift the world to a higher level. It was to take place in India, in a semi-spherical temple at the edge of a lake. Together with its reflection, this temple would then form the most perfect of all shapes, the sphere. Two thousand persons, all of them performers and none spectators, were to enact the 'supreme and final ecstasy' by means of all the known arts, music, dance, poetry and, even, light and scent. The artistic standards were to be superlative; for Scriabin considered the participation of Chaliapin and Karsavina, but rejected it, though, presumably, not for purely artistic reasons. Even so, this act seems to have been only the prologue, for which Scriabin actually wrote some of the poetry. It was to be followed by the 'mystery' itself, which was never clearly spelled out but which, Scriabin was convinced, would effect the end of the world as it existed and then initiate its transformation.[112]

It was characteristic of Scriabin's self-centred messianism that he actually welcomed the outbreak of the War of 1914–18 as a prelude to the great transformation. He died quietly in Moscow in 1915, while the outside world appeared to be nearing its end rather through wholesale slaughter than through the regenerative powers of his music and an ecstatic act of love. It is the final irony of Fate that Scriabin has remained alive as the composer of elegant short piano pieces while his grandiose orchestral works and his advanced theories of musical harmony have been forgotten, together with his mystical dreams.[113]

[110] *Ibid.*, p. 475.

[111] L. Sabaneyeff, *Modern Russian Composers*, tr. J. A. Joffe (New York, 1927), p. 48.

[112] *Ibid.*, pp. 59–60. G. Abraham, 'Alexander Scriabin', pp. 494–5.

[113] Since I wrote this sentence, about 15 years ago, there has been a certain revival of interest in both Scriabin's orchestral music and in his harmony.

It was only about the turn of the nineteenth century that the Churches finally reacted against this large-scale invasion of music into their own traditional fields of religion and religious emotion. The reason for this long delay, through practically the whole of the nineteenth century, was probably the essential ambiguity of the relations between music and religion; for they were never overtly hostile to each other and, as we have seen, nearly all the great composers of the century wrote superb and heartfelt religious music, even if it was mostly not strictly liturgical. In 1903, however, the recently elected Pope Pius X issued his famous *Motu proprio* with its call for a return to the traditions of Gregorian chant, its condemnation of secular elements in church music and its categorical declaration that music must remain 'the humble servant of the liturgy'.[114] About the same time there occurred a deliberate and self-conscious revival of Protestant church music, especially in Germany, which however looked for its models to the great period of Lutheran church music in the sixteenth and seventeenth centuries, rather than to Gregorian chant. In both the Catholic and the Protestant Churches, this seems to have been an attempt to rescue church music from absorption into secular music and to redraw sharp lines between them.[115]

It is not the function of this essay to evaluate the musical and religious results of these attempts. It is worth noting, however that in most recent years the lines between church and secular music are being deliberately blurred again, and this is happening just as it did in the seventeenth century, as part of an attempt to widen the appeal of church music. In contrast to the seventeenth century, however, the part played by church music in contemporary life has become quite small and, relatively, unimportant. The development of the psychological impact of music which we have traced was, up to the end of the nineteenth century, largely confined to the educated classes and to sophisticated, 'classical' music. But from about 1900 the decline of the religious appeal of the organized Churches began to spread to the mass of the uneducated or semi-educated population of Europe and America. The drastic decline of the figures for church attendance leave very little doubt of the reality of this phenomenon. Concurrently, it seems to me, there has occurred an enormous rise in the popularity and the sheer volume of performance, and through radio and gramophone in listening time, of all types of popular music. Is not the almost devout attendance of fans at jazz sessions comparable with the devout absorption of the mainly middle-class audiences at a Beethoven symphony concert? Is not the behaviour of a

[114] *Acta Sancta Sedis* (Rome, 1904), 36, 329–39.

[115] A. Adrio, 'Erneuerung und Wiederbelebung', ch. IV in Blume, *Kirchenmusik*. The difference in Catholic and Protestant attitudes was, however, not as great as it might appear; for the *Motu proprio* specifically singled out Palestrina's music as having attained 'the greatest perfection' in classical polyphony, the form of music which most clearly had the qualities that the Church demanded. *Acta Sancta Sedis*, xxxvi, 333.

teenage rock'n'roll audience remarkably similar to that of the congregation of a revivalist preacher?

I have deliberately left these observations as questions because it is notoriously difficult for a historian to see the events of his own age in a correct historical perspective. But some contemporary observers and enthusiasts have, in fact, made far-reaching claims, not only for the aesthetic, but also for the ethical and even religious significance of the best of modern popular music.[116] No doubt this is philosophy and religion for teenagers; but is it not part of the phenomenon which is the theme of this essay, the rise of music to a quasi-religious status and cult, as a psychological compensation for the decline of all forms of traditional religion? And do not young people feel the need for non-material values with special intensity?

What then of the second part of my original question, Max Weber's argument of the uniqueness of the development of European music, and my suggestion that this development was linked with the progressive secularization of European civilization? I do not think that such a link can be proved conclusively, even less so, perhaps, than Weber's own hypothesis of a link between the Protestant ethic and capitalism. Much, perhaps most, of the development of European music can and must be explained by its own laws of development, by a certain logic inherent in the art of composition and by the physical and physiological determinants of the art; above all, perhaps, by the genius of a long line of great composers and musicians. Moreover, if music was a psychological substitute for religion, it was not the only one: painting, poetry, the natural sciences, even politics and the quest for power have, at some time or other, been elevated to religious or quasi-religious status. But all these remained marginal, the beliefs of cranks or, at best, of relatively small groups of intellectuals. Music, however, was never marginal in European life and, as Wagner rightly saw, has shifted more and more into its centre. This centre had formerly been occupied by religion, as it was so occupied (and, in contrast to Europe, has continued to be so occupied, at least until very recently) in all non-European societies. The conclusion seems inescapable that here, indeed, there is a connection.

---

[116] Cf. B. DeMott, 'Rock as Salvation', *The New York Times Magazine*, 25 August 1968. Cf. also the 1968 Beatles film, *The Yellow Submarine*.

# 10

# Science and Religion in Early Modern Europe

Ever since Max Weber pointed to the development of modern science as one of the characteristic features of European civilization,[1] historians have proposed a variety of reasons for this phenomenon.[2] These proposals have included attempts to trace connections between certain Protestant religious doctrines and the 'scientific revolution' of the seventeenth century – in analogy to Weber's own attempts to derive the capitalist spirit from the Protestant ethic.[3] I do not intend to enter the controversies about these or other current theories but rather to propose a hitherto neglected aspect of the development of modern science. It is meant as an addition to a composite picture and not a criticism or rejection of any of its generally accepted or debated components.

Some years ago I attempted to show by a kind of inversion of Weber's approach that, as religious sensibilities declined in Europe from the Renaissance onward, there appeared a new psychological need, a kind of emotional void, which came to be filled primarily by music. This happened not so much by a direct opposition between music and religion, but rather through the longstanding alliance between them which allowed music to play an increasingly important and eventually preponderant emotional role in the European psyche. Non-European societies witnessed no similar decline of religious sensibilities, or at least not until much later. They missed one important psychological stimulus

An earlier version of this paper was read in German at the 32. Deutscher Historikertag in Hamburg on October 6, 1978. I would like to thank Peter Winch, Margaret C. Jacob, and Dorothy Koenigsberger for reading the typescript of this paper and for their helpful criticisms and suggestions.

[1] M. Weber, 'Die protestantische Ethik und der Geist des Kapitalismus', *Gesammelte Aufsätze zur Religionssoziologie*, vol. 1, (Tübingen, 1934), p. 2.

[2] P. M. Rattansi, 'The Social Interpretation of Science in the Seventeenth Century'. In P. Mathias (ed.), *Science and Society, 1600–1900* (Cambridge, 1972); A. R. Hall, 'On the Historical Singularity of the Scientific Revolution'. In J. H. Elliott and H. G. Koenigsberger (eds.), *The Diversity of History: Essays in Honour of Sir Herbert Butterfield* (London and Ithaca, 1970); and bibliographical references in these two articles.

[3] Cf. R. K. Merton, 'Science , Technology, and Society in Seventeenth-century England', *Osiris* 4 (1938); also as a book (New York, 1970); R. Hooykaas, *Religion and the Rise of Modern Science* (Edinburgh and London, 1972).

for the specifically elaborate development of music which Weber had detected in Europe.[4]

I want to argue a parallel case for religion and science. I shall take the phenomenon of secularization of European civilization for granted. This phenomenon started slowly in the later Middle Ages and the Renaissance and proceeded more and more rapidly and noticeably in the seventeenth century and from then onward. At that stage it was a phenomenon primarily of the educated classes, and much more than in the case of religion and music, we are here concerned with a small intellectual minority. This fact will allow us to take the role of theology in intellectual life as a rough measure of religious sensibilities. At least for intellectuals, secularization meant the emancipation of systematic thinking from the control of theology and theologians. This involved the gradual relegation of theology to a more or less exclusive concern with doctrine and morals. This happened simultaneously with a strong emotional and intellectual revulsion against the theologians' concentration on doctrinal controversies, for the bitter results of such controversies were only too apparent. Traditionally, young intellectuals in search of wisdom had chosen to be theologians, almost as a matter of course. Now it seemed to many of them that theology had become too narrow and sometimes even dangerous and destructive, while natural philosophy appeared as an intellectually more promising and emotionally more satisfying pursuit.

Historically, this shift in the choice of an intellectual career was somewhat masked by the available career structure for highly gifted young men. Jobs for pure scientists were few, and universities in both Catholic and Protestant countries continued to be controlled by the churches. It was often necessary to become a clergyman, whatever one's primary interests. There was no necessary contradiction. At least until the eighteenth century, very few of those interested in science were antireligious, but increasingly it was the pursuit of science which became the central interest of an important group of European intellectuals. For most of these men religion had not become unimportant, let alone an object of hostility. They approached religion by a long journey through natural philosophy, and this journey came to absorb more of their interests and energies. By the eighteenth and certainly the nineteenth century, natural philosophy had become for many of its most distinguished practitioners virtually self-justifying – a psychologically satisfying substitute for the former pursuit of religion, theology, and personal salvation – even while many scientists were unaware of this substitution and would not have admitted it. This phenomenon played an important part in that very distinctive European achievement – the development of modern science.

[4] H. G. Koenigsberger, 'Music and Religion in Modern European History'. In Elliott and Koenigsberger, *The Diversity of History*, and above, chapter 9.

In the later Middle Ages there was hardly any conflict between religion and natural science. Such conflict would have been almost unthinkable, for the most important religious and philosophical traditions of the time emphasized the basic harmony of the total created world, the world of ideas as well as the physical universe. This could be seen in different ways and with different emphases. From Plato came the argument that the world had to contain all possible kinds of things, and this later developed into the idea of a 'Great Chain of Being.'[5] From Aristotle came a coherent hierarchical model of the physical world. Both ideas had been Christianized without great difficulty, for they did not contradict the biblical teaching of God's creation of the world and everything in it.

A number of tricky philosophical and theological problems could arise when the implications of the different traditions were pursued. But the conflicts between different schools of philosophy and theology were not usually seen as arising out of any antithesis between a scientific and theological approach. Even the Ockhamists' denial of the possiblility of a rational understanding of divine creation did not produce such a conflict. On the contrary, the Ockhamists and Nominalists who believed in the validity of experience, as well as of revelation, were often the keenest students of the physical world. With very little exaggeration, the Platonist Nicholas of Cusa wrote in 1440: "All our greatest philosophers and theologians unanimously assert that the visible universe is a faithful reflection of the invisible, and that from creatures we can rise to a knowledge of the Creator, 'in a mirror and in a dark manner,' as it were."[6]

Cusa himself then went on to propound a revolutionary new view of the universe that contradicted the Aristotelian model in which the Earth was the fixed centre of the universe. While Cusa arrived at his conclusions partly by mathematical reasoning, he started not from systematic observation of natural phenomena, as a modern scientist would and as Aristotle had done, but from a theological premise: God is the absolute maximum and minimum, and this means that God is totality. He is the sum of all things, although not in their own form but in his. Thus, by analogy, the reality of line is in the dimensionless point, but the reality of motion is in rest, its absolute minimum, and this is parallel to the relationship between God and the Universe. In God all opposites coincide. In God the centre and circumference of a circle or sphere are identical. Therefore the Earth cannot be at the center of the universe nor can the universe be finite, because center and circumference can exist only in God. Equally, the Earth cannot be at rest, for only God can be at rest.

[5] A. O. Lovejoy, *The Great Chain of Being* (New York, 1960), pp. 50 *passim*.
[6] Nicolas Cusanus, *Of Learned Ignorance*, tr. G. Heron (London, 1954), bk. 1, ch. 11, p. 25.

Only at this point, having established his indefinite and essentially relativistic universe on theological principles, Cusa introduces observation into his argument to explain our apparently contradictory observational experience. How is it that we see the dome of the heavens above us, as we do, unless we stand at its center? We do, answers Cusa, but so would an observer standing on another planet or on a star or anywhere else in the universe.[7] As to the movement of the apparently stationary earth.

it is only by reference to something fixed that we detect the movement of anything. How would a person know that a ship was in movement, if, from the ship in the middle of the river, the banks were invisible to him and he was ignorant of the fact that water flows? Therein we have the reason why every man, whether he be on earth, in the sun, or on another planet, always has the impression that all other things are in movement whilst he himself is in a sort of immovable center; he will certainly always choose poles which will vary accordingly as his place of existence is the sun, the earth, the moon, Mars, etc. In consequence, there will be a *machina mundi* whose center, so to speak, is everywhere, whose circumference is nowhere, for God is its circumference and center and He is everywhere and nowhere.[8]

It is possible to see the origins of Cusa's concept of the crucial importance of the place of an observer in the contemporary development of the theory of perspective in drawing and of projection in cartography. Cusa was the first to apply the principles of artists and mapmakers to cosmology in conjunction with a theological approach.[9] It was a classic case of studying the "two books" in conjunction, the book of God's word – the Bible – and the book of nature – God's creation – and arriving at startling conclusions in both theology and cosmology. There is not the slightest hint of conflict. The idea that Cusa was a pantheist with heretical views derived from his scientific ideas was a complete misunderstanding. The Church never doubted his theological orthodoxy.

Cusa's cosmology was largely ignored, both by his contemporaries and for the next 150 years, until Giordano Bruno. The reason is probably that Cusa's argumentation was hard to follow and that, for all the esteem accorded to his theological and political work, his theory of the universe did not address itself to current intellectual problems. Even after Bruno, since cosmology was then set on a very different path, Cusa's view was regarded as something of a curiosity until the development of relativity theory led to a reappraisal of his astonishing argumentation.

[7] *Ibid.*, bk. 2, ch. 12, esp. p. 110.
[8] *Ibid.*, bk. 2, ch. 12, p. 111.
[9] For a detailed discussion of Cusanus and his epistemological and scientific thinking, see Dorothy Koenigsberger, *Renaissance Man and Creative Thinking: A History of Concepts of Harmony, 1400–1700* (Hassocks, 1979), ch. 3.

By the first half of the sixteenth century, large areas of traditional late-medieval scientific beliefs were coming under attack. Much of this was due to the discovery and publication of hitherto unknown texts of the ancients which contradicted Aristotle or Galen. Some of it was the result of a more critical attitude toward established authority, even a delight in cocking a snook at its great names, coupled with a typically Renaissance assurance of one's own merits. Paracelsus certainly had no doubts about these: 'What asses will you appear when Theophrastus [Paracelsus] will be the prince of this realm [of true knowledge]? How will it seem to you when you will have to accept my philosophy and you will shit on your Pliny and Aristotle and piss on your Albertus [Magnus], Thomas [Aquinas], Scotus, etc., and when you will say: they lie beautifully and subtly . . . How will it seem to you when I shall mess up your heaven and the [constellation of the] Dragon shall gobble up your Avicenna and your Galen?'[10] A physician had to be knowledgeable in three fields – philosophy, astronomy, and alchemy. The professors of the great medical schools of Paris, Montpellier, Salerno, Vienna, Wittenberg, knew nothing of any of these, for this profession depends not on the Holy Ghost but on 'the light of nature . . . The Holy Ghost teaches us faith, but natural matters belong to nature and therefore must be learnt from nature.'[11]

Setting up 'the light of nature' in opposition to the Holy Ghost was a significant shift in heuristic method, but for Paracelsus it meant neither a rejection of religious inspiration nor even the banishment of religion from the study of medicine. He drew no clear line between religion and science, astrology and astronomy, or between his religious and natural philosophy. His aim seems to have been to use the 'light of nature' to test and confirm his mystical religious beliefs.[12] His style was reminiscent of the contemporary religious reformers. Some called him the 'Medical Luther', although he rejected this clearly dangerous title. He was quite capable of inventing his own titles. But the enormous enthusiasm he evoked among his students was due, just as in Luther's case, not only to the attraction of his own teaching, but also to the eternal delight university students take in the deflation of pompous authority.

Scientists much less flamboyant than Paraclesus found themselves equally critical of established views backed by theological authority. The Belgian anatomist Vesalius was appalled by established theories of the brain propounded by scholastic philosophers:

If by accurate and painstaking examination of the parts of the brain and from an observation of the other parts of the body, the use of which is obvious even to

[10] *Theophrastus Paracelsus Werke*, ed. W. E. Peuckert, vol. 1 (Basel and Stuttgart, 1965), p. 501.
[11] *Ibid.*, p. 512.
[12] W. Pagel, *Paracelsus* (Basel and New York, 1958), pp. 349–50.

one little practised in dissection, some analogy were traceable, or if I could reach any probable conclusion I would set it out, if I could do so without injury to our Most Holy Religion. For who – Oh Immortal God – can fail to be astonished at the host of contemporary philosophers and even theologians who detract ridiculously from the divine and most wonderful contrivance (*admirabili machinae*) of man's brain. For they fabricate, like a Prometheus out of their own dreams – dreams blaspheming the Founder (*Conditor*) of the human fabric – some image of the brain, while they refuse to see that structure which the Maker of Nature has wrought, with incredible foresight, to accommodate it to the actions of the body. Putting before themselves the image which they have formed, little do they heed – oh shame! – the impiety into which they lure the tender minds which they instruct, when these, no longer mere students, yearn to search out Nature's craftsmanship, and many with their own hand pry into [the parts of] man and of other creatures which are handed into their power.

When he was a student at Louvain, Vesalius contined, the lecturer who taught Aristotle's *De Anima* was 'a theologian by profession and therefore, like the other instructors at that Academy, ready to mingle his own pious views with those of the philosophers' and taught that the brain was equipped with three ventricles each with specific functions. Not only was this an absurd view, Vesalius maintained, but it was likely to mislead those not yet confirmed in religion. It would lead them to ascribe 'every power of reason and even a rational soul' to animals, the structure of whose brains corresponded to that of the human brain. All this was the result of 'the inventions of those who never look into our Maker's ingenuity in the building of the human body.'[13]

There is nothing irreligious here; quite the contrary. But Vesalius, unlike Cusa and unlike his contemporary anatomist Servetus, does not start from theological propositions but, like Paracelsus, insists on the need for starting with the investigation of nature. This method, he maintains, will lead the young and inexperienced student to true religious belief. The reverse method, which was the traditional one and which 'mingled pious views with philosophy', was most likely to lead to false religious belief. It was not an approach which, as Vesalius was well aware, would recommend itself to the Church.

Yet the Church was slow to react to such views. It was more concerned with theological heresy. In this respect the Catholic church and the Protestant churches acted very similarly, as Servetus found to his cost. Paracelsus had a genius for offending the establishment as a whole and was outstanding even in an age which expected and appreciated academic invective. But the burning of a copy of Avicenna during a student's rag day, shocking as it was to the university authorities of Basel, did not have the same implications as Luther's burning of a papal bull of excommunication. Paracelsus, Vesalius, and

---

[13] *Vesalius on the Brain*, ed. and trans. C. Singer (Oxford, 1952), pp. 4–6; from A. Vesalius, *De humani corporis fabrica*, bk. 7, ch. 1.

other scientists with original ideas and methods were in trouble mainly with their enraged professional colleagues. They had no intention of breaking with the Church and were not regarded as having done so. By contrast, Servetus was accused of heresy, both by Catholic authorities and by Calvin, for his denial of the trinity and his rejection of infant baptism. His medical theory of the lesser circulation of the blood through the lungs was not mentioned in any of his indictments,[14] even though it was closely connected with his religious beliefs. Servetus identified man's rational soul with the animal spirits of the blood, spirits which were held to consist of an invisible but fine material substance. Such an identification was theologically unorthodox and, in Servetus's case, certainly heretrical,[15] but neither Catholic nor Protestant authorities were prepared to do anything about it.

Only from the last quarter of the sixteenth century were the implications of unorthodox scientific beliefs for religious orthodoxy being systematically thought out. This is not surprisng. Orthodox doctrine had seemingly now been definitely settled at the Council of Trent. Religious controversy had become full-scale confrontation. It had also become involved with all sorts of political and social ambitions, struggles, and fears. In France and in the Netherlands, it had escalated into civil wars with foreign intervention, fought *à outrance*. Every aspect of life and thought tended to become enmeshed with this all-pervading religious controversy. The churches, both Catholic and Protestant, could not afford to allow any field of human activity to escape from their influence, and thus perhaps become a centre for the opposing forces, which both sides equated with Satan and which were an objective threat to their survival. Where the churches differed was less in this basic attitude than in the powers of control they were able to wield either directly or through political authorities.

Many creative thinkers, artists, and musicians were perfectly willing to exercise their talents in the services of their own side and to allow all their activities to be judged by the criterion of religious orthodoxy, but not all were willing to go as far as they were asked. Painters, sculptors, and musicians, all had their brushes with church authorities, perhaps worst of all in some Calvinist parts of Europe. Inevitably, those who used words were most directly affected by this situation: philosophers, writers on politics and history, and scientists. They did not see their problem as one of divided loyalties, for most thought of themselves as good Catholics or Protestants. They saw it as a question of the autonomy of their own art or profession or, more precisely, of the

---

[14] R. H. Bainton, *Hunted Heretic: The Life and Death of Michael Servetus, 1511–53* (Boston, 1960), pp. 207–9.

[15] *Ibid.*, pp. 124–27. D. P. Walker, 'Francis Bacon and Spiritus'. In *Science, Medicine, and Society in the Renaissance: Essays in Honour of Walter Pagel*, ed. A. G. Debus, vol. 2 (New York, 1972).

autonomy of their own professional judgment as against the interference and misinterpretations of theologians. Often scientists rather than theologians were the first to raise the question of the religious implications of their work, to forestall accusations of unothodoxy. This they did by using one or both of two types of argument. The first was a straightforward defense of the orthodoxy of their views and the implications of their conclusions. This type of argument presented no problems for the Church. It could be judged in each individual case on its merits. The second type of argument turned out to be much more important. This was the attempt by the scientist to fence off altogether his work from interference by drawing dividing lines between the realm of religion and that of natural philosophy or knowledge of nature.

But was this possible? Was there not an inescapable overlap between these fields? And even if it were possible to draw a line, who was to draw it, the scientist or the theologian? To the theologians, Catholic and Protestant, the answer was clear. Religion was the ultimate measure of everything. Theology was the queen of the sciences and all others were her handmaidens. Scientists rarely disputed these views openly. But in practice, it was often only too clear that theologians did not know what they were talking about and that only scientists could draw the line. Gradually, they pushed this line outward, including increasing territory within the realm of science and even making alarming forays into the very core of the theological position, the study of the nature of God and his relation to creation. The very term by which such inquiries were described, *natural philosophy*, implied all the ambiguities of this changing balance.

Nowhere is this development clearer than in the history of astronomy and cosmology. There are good reaons for this. Many of the images and metaphors of the central doctrines of Christianity were astronomical and consmological. God, the Bible tells us, created the earth and the heavens and all that is in them. The heavens, the stars in their splendour and perfection, and ultimately God himself were above us. All that was below was of the earth, subject to change, decay, and sin but yet the centre of creation, for God had created man in his image and everything else for the sake of man.

When Copernicus displaced the Earth from the centre of the cosmos and reduced it to the status of one of six planets revolving around the Sun, he was fully aware of the shattering implications of what he was doing. Only at the end of his life was he finally persuaded to publish his theories. It is possible that Copernicus knew of Nicolas of Cusa's attack on traditional astronomy and of Greek views which posited the rotation of the Earth.[16] Whether he did or not, Copernicus had done something

[16] R. Klibansky, 'Copernic et Nicolas de Cues'. In *Léonard de Vinci et l'expérience scientifique au XVI^e siècle*, Colloques internationaux du Centre National de la Recherche Scientifique, Sciences Humaines. (Paris, 1953), pp. 230–31.

very different from Cusa. Cusa had shown that, logically, the Earth could not be at the centre of an infinite universe and that, since only God could be regarded as at rest, the Earth was bound to be in motion. But he had made no attempt to suggest, let alone calculate, what sort of motion this might be. This was precisely what Copernicus did, which made his theory a much more formidable problem for the churches than Cusa's apparently rather abstract speculations. It explains why Copernicus's Protestant theologian editor, Andreas Osiander, was so anxious to claim that Copernicus's theory was only a hypothesis, a mathematical model. It is now generally accepted that Copernicus fully believed that his heliocentric model represented reality. But although *De revolutionibus orbium coelestium* was widely read and even taught in some universities, both Catholic and Protestant, it did not at first stir up any serious opposition. The controversies started in the changed intellectual climate of the post-Tridentine church at a time when Tycho Brahe's observations were beginning to cast serious doubts on the Aristotelian model of the physical universe.

The first great open clash between religion and science owed a great deal to the personality of Galileo Galilei – just as the Reformation owed a great deal to the personality of Martin Luther. Kepler was as convinced a Copernican as his Italian colleague, and while he ran into plenty of opposition in Germany, he managed to avoid serious trouble with the churches. It was Kepler who urged Galileo to publish his Copernican arguments as early as 1597.[17] This is significant, for the educated European public was becoming passionately interested in astronomy and cosmology. When in January 1605 Galileo lectured on the *nova* of the previous year, his normal lecture room at the University of Padua proved too small, and he had to adjourn to the university's Great Hall.[18] His book *Sidereus Nuncius* (*The Message* [or *Messenger*] *of the Stars*), in which he published his first telescopic findings, was so eagerly awaited that Henry Wotton, the English ambassador in Venice, wrote about it to the Earl of Salisbury on the very day of its publication, 13 March 1610:

I send herewith unto his Majesty the strangest piece of news (as I may justly call it) that he hath ever yet received from any part of the world; which is the annexed book of the Mathematical Professor at Padua, who by the help of an optical instrument . . . hath discovered four new planets rolling about the sphere of Jupiter, etc. . . . So upon the whole subject he hath first overthrown all former astronomy . . . and next all astrology. For the virtue of these new planets must needs vary the judicial part, and why may there not be more? . . . By the next ship your Lordship shall receive from me one of the above instruments, as it is bettered by this man.[19]

[17] Kepler to Galileo, 13 October 1597. In *Johannes Kepler Gesammelte Werke*, ed. M. Caspar, vol. 13 (Munich, 1945), p. 145.

[18] M. Nicolson, *Science and Imagination* (Ithaca, 1956), p. 8.

[19] Logan Pearsall Smith, *Life and Letters of Sir Henry Wotton* (Oxford, 1907), vol. 1, pp. 487–88. Also quoted in M. Nicolson, *Science and Imagination*, pp. 35–36.

Galileo's book became an immediate best-seller in Europe, and it became fashionable to buy telescopes.

It was in this excited atmosphere that the theological implications of Copernicanism began to be debated and not only, as had been mainly the case hitherto, its radical destruction of the academically accepted Aristotelian world view and its apparent offense to common sense. Galileo himself was fully aware of these implications, more than church authorities who disapproved of the sniping against Galileo by individuals and uninformed clerics. The great debate was triggered neither by church authorities nor by Galileo himself, but by Benedetto Castelli, an enthusiastic pupil and follower of Galileo, defending his master at a dinner party at the Medici court at Florence against the needling of other learned guests and the doubts expressed by the pious mother of the grand duke, the Grand Duchess Christina. Castelli was convinced he had won the argument and reported triumphantly to Galileo:

Madame [the grand duchess] began, after some questons about myself, to argue the Holy Scripture against me. Thereupon, after having made suitable disclaimers, I commenced to play the theologian with such assurance and dignity that it would have done you good to hear me. Don Antonio [de Medici] assisted me, giving me such heart that instead of being dismayed by the majesty of Their Highnesses I carried things off like a paladin. I quite won over the Grand Duke and his Archduchess . . . Only Madame Christina remained against me, but from her manner I judged that she did this only to hear my replies. Professor Boscaglia [a philosopher who, earlier on at the dinner party, had raised doubts about the motion of the earth] said never a word.[20]

It was probably not just Castelli's indiscretion of 'playing the theologian' which now set the debate on the religious orthodoxy of the Copernican system in motion. The incident shows that such a debate was no longer avoidable. Certainly Galileo was now convinced of this. He wrote first a long letter to Castelli detailing his own views, and in 1615 he expanded and refined his arguments in the famous *Letter to Madame Christina of Lorraine Grand Duchess of Tuscany*. It was the most detailed and sophisticated statement yet of the relationship between natural sciences and the teachings of the Bible. Significantly, it was written by a devout Catholic who wished to preserve the Church from making the terrible blunder of linking its dogma to a mistaken theory of the physical world.

[20] Castelli to Galileo, 14 December 1613. In *Le Opere di Galileo Galilei*, vol. 11 (Florence, 1934), pp. 605–6. Trans. and quoted in Stillman Drake, *Discoveries and Opinions of Galileo* (Garden City, N.Y., 1957), pp. 151–52. The grand duke was Cosimo II (1609–21). His wife was the Archduchess Maria Maddalena of Austria (d. 1631).

Galileo started with an apologia. It was not he, he argued, who 'had placed these things in the sky with my own hands in order to upset nature and overturn the sciences'.[21] As to Copernicus, he did not discuss matters of faith but drew his conclusions from mathematical demonstrations based on exact observations. But these conclusions were condemned by people who quoted the Bible, the church fathers, and the councils.[22] The Bible Galileo said, could never speak untruth, but its true meaning must be understood and 'in discussions of physical problems, we ought to begin not from the authority of scriptural passages but from sense experiences and necessary demonstrations'.[23] Not only that, but 'having arrived at any certainties in physics, we ought to utilise these as the most appropriate aids in the true exposition of the Bible'.[24] Finally, and this was the longest part of his argument, Galileo tried to show that much of what the Bible said could not be interpreted literally. In the case quoted most often by anti-Copernicans, Joshua's bidding the sun to stand still, Galileo had some mathematical fun, demonstrating that in the Ptolemaic system this would have made the day shorter rather than longer.[25] Of course, the Holy Ghost who dictated the Bible did not get these things wrong, but it 'sometimes wished to veil itself under words of different meaning, whether for our exercise of for some purpose unknown to me'.[26]

Like Luther in his *Address to the Christian Nobility of the German Nation*, Galileo objected to the walls with which the Catholic church had surrounded itself to keep out free criticism. Where Luther relied on his reading of the Bible and on his God-given conscience, Galileo relied on his observation of nature and on his God-given reason. To the Church establishment and its conventional and traditionalist theologians, the two were almost equally objectionable, for both struck at the central tenet of the Church that it alone was the arbiter of truth. Unlike Luther, Galileo had no intention of reforming the church or its doctrine, except in the very specific matter of cosmology. He could not foresee that his path to truth would appear to later generations as a much surer path than the traditional religious path or, if not to ultimate truth, at least to an understanding of the universe and man's position in it. Here the Church had probably a surer instinct than Galileo. But it was an instinct rather than a fully reasoned position. Galileo's whole way of thinking and reasoning was different from religious thinking with which most churchmen were familiar. In the same year, 1615, in which Galileo wrote his letter to the Grand Duchess Christina, Cardinal

---

21 *Opere*, vol. 5, p. 309 (Drake, *Discoveries*, p. 175).
22 *Opere*, vol. 5, p. 314 (Drake, p. 179).
23 *Opere*, vol. 5, p. 316 (Drake, p. 182).
24 *Opere*, vol. 5, p. 317 (Drake, p. 183).
25 *Opere*, vol. 5, pp. 343–44 (Drake, pp. 211–12).
26 *Opere*, vol. 5, p. 332 (Drake, p. 199).

Bellarmine wrote *The Mind's Ascent to God by a Ladder of Created Things*. This was a work in a well-established tradition in which the author leads the soul upward in fifteen steps along the 'great chain of being', from the contemplation of the solid and immovable earth, 'the very first foundation of the whole world',[27] through the four elements, to the heavens, the sun, moon, and stars, and then to the angels and to God himself. Aristotelian cosmology and mystic contemplation reinforce each other: 'God, the Creator of all things, places his tabernacle in the sun, as being a most noble creature' and 'he willed that the heaven itself should be the palace of the sun in which it might freely take its course'.[28] Bellarmine saw God in physical as well as spiritual terms. But how were these physical terms to be described, apart from the use of epithets like 'great' and 'immense'? Bellarmine quotes the psalmist that the sun 'rejoiceth as a giant to run his course'.[29] This could be measured: 'I myself was once desirous of learning what space of time the sun would take in setting. At the beginning of its setting I began to read the psalm *"Misere mei Deus"*: and I had scarcely read it twice through when the whole sun had set.' Since the diameter of the Earth is 7,000 miles and the Sun is much larger than the Earth, 'it must traverse a distance much greater than 7,000 miles' and therefore 'every one but he who is stupid or a dunce must admire the infinite power of the Creator'.[30]

Bellarmine was perfectly happy to use scientific observations and arguments, and he shared with Copernicus and Kepler a view of the Sun derived most probably from hermetism. But the intellectual level of their, and Galileo's, scientific arguments was already a world apart from that of the cardinal. Of this difference, Bellarmine seems to have been quite unaware. To Paolo Antonio Foscarini, a theologian who had sent him a treatise supporting the Copernican view, he wrote courteously but half-dismissively: 'Since you ask for my opinion, I shall give it to you briefly, as you have little time for reading and I for writing' – and then proceeded to given an entirely conventional reply about the interpretations of the Bible by the common agreement of the Holy Fathers, the wisdom of Solomon, and the falseness of the argument that to an observer aboard a ship it appears that the beach moves away. The Copernican theory might well save appearances, but that 'is not the same thing as to demonstrate that in fact the sun is in the centre and the earth in the heavens'.[31] Bellarmine was still thinking in

---

[27] *Roberti Bellarmini De ascensione mentis in Deum per scalas rerum creatarum*, ed. F. X. Dieringer (Cologne, 1850), gradus tertius, ch. 1, p. 61.

[28] *Ibid.*, gr. sept., ch. 1, pp. 157–58.

[29] *Ibid.*, gr. sept., ch. 2, p. 161 (Psalm 19).

[30] 'Ego ipse volens curiose aliquando cognoscere, quanto temporis spatio sol totus occumberet in mari, coepi ad initium occasus ejus legere psalmum *Miserere mei Deus*; ex vix totum bis legeram, cum jam sol totus occubuisset'. *Ibid.*, pp. 162–63.

[31] Bellarmine to Foscarini, 12 April 1615. In G. Galilei, *Opere*, vol. 12, pp. 171–72 (Drake, *Discoveries*, pp. 162–64).

Aristotelian terms, for he imagined that Copernicus had simply interchanged the positions of the Sun and Earth and had therefore transplanted the latter into one of the celestial spheres. Just as in the case of Cardinal Cajetan's meeting with Luther in 1518, so a hundred years later the best minds in the Catholic Church were unwilling to spend the time and mental effort to try to understand the new views presented to them. They were content to leave this exercise to mediocre and self-serving pedants – with disastrous results for the Church.

Galileo had tried to draw a dividing line between religious knowledge and scientific investigation. He also claimed that a correct interpretation of the Bible (which he, not the professional theologians, provided) would confirm the basic unity of science and religion. Some of his contemporaries were prepared to go much further in dividing the two fields. Bacon held to the traditional belief that nature showed the power and wisdom of God. But he was emphatic that this was as far as one could go: 'If any man shall think, by view and inquiry into these sensible and material things, to attain to any light for the revealing of the nature or will of God, he shall dangerously abuse himself.'[32] The reverse was also true:

The corruption of philosophy by superstition and an admixture of theology is far more widely spread, and does the greatest harm . . . Yet in this vanity some of the moderns have with extreme levity indulged so far as to attempt to found a system of natural philosophy on the first chapter of Genesis, on the book of Job, and other parts of the sacred writings, seeking for the dead among the living: which also makes the inhibition or repression of it the more important, because from this unwholesome mixture of human and divine there arises not only a fantastic philosophy but also a heretical religion. Very meet it is therefore that we be sober-minded, and give to faith that only which is faith's.[33]

Such formulation swept aside both Galileo and Cardinal Bellarmine, and it is not surprising that it was published in a Protestant country, outside the reach of the Inquisition. Yet Bacon, like Bellarmine, was anxious to repress heresy, and his fear was of the radical reformers, those who judged everything by the special illumination they claimed to have received from the Holy Ghost.[34] We are still a long way from freedom of thought, even in England. Bacon's distinction between our possible knowledge of God and of nature was intended to safeguard the true religion, just as much as scientific inquiry, from dangerous attacks. It was also not always as categorical as he insisted it was. He maintained the traditional view of nature as the 'second book' in which to study the greatness of God, and he held that the end of such study was love and

---

[32] Bacon, *Works*, vol. 3, p. 218. Quoted in C. Hill, *Intellectual Origins of the English Revolution* (London, 1972), p. 91.

[33] Bacon, *Novum Organum*, 1, 65.

[34] Rattansi, 'The Social Interpretation of Science', p. 15.

charity and practical use.[35] Because he insisted on such pious ends for the study of nature, he gave it an enormous moral boost while shielding it from interference by theologians. It was not so much Bacon's contemporaries but the generation of the mid-seventeeth century that was to find Bacon's philosophy most congenial.

If Bacon had greatly contributed to the practical division between science and religion while proclaiming their common end, he had done so by turning his eyes away from the issues which had exercised Galileo and his opponents. This he was able to do, not least because he was not a mathematical scientist, in fact not a scientist at all. All he was putting forward was a method for the study of nature. He could therefore afford not to commit himself to a specific theory of cosmology or any other specific scientific theory. Yet the issues raised by Galileo, implied in scientific theories, would not simply go away by denying their existence, as Bacon had at least implicitly done. Inevitably they became a part of an even wider and more fundamental philosophical debate within an international scientific-philosophical community that was just beginning to emerge into self-consciousness in Western Europe.

The historical background of this emerging community was the religious wars and the revulsion they caused. The story is well known: the rise of political parties which placed political unity and stability above religious unity and orthodoxy, the spread of precepts of reason of state and neo-Stoicism, and above all, the growing attraction of a philosophical scepticism of which Montaigne was the most famous exponent. None of these was overtly and intentionally antireligious, but all in one way or another devalued religion as the principal criterion of political and intellectual activity.

The most fundamental breach with traditional religion and the authority and teaching of the Christian churches was made by a mathematician: Descartes, as he tells us in his *Discours de la méthode*, 'revered theology' and would not 'dare to submit it to the feebleness of my reasoning'.[36] Yet he rejected all received and established philosophy by carrying the doubts of the skeptics to the ultimate extreme of questioning the existence not only of the universe but of God. Claiming to use the methods of mathematicians of accepting as certainty only what was self-evident, he found such self-evident certainty only in his own consciousness, his activity of doubting everything and hence of thinking: *cogito ergo sum*. Only when Descartes had established his own 'being', he derived the existence of God and thence of the universe from a specific aspect of his consciousness, the recognition of a perfection which he did not possess and which a perfect being, God, must

---

[35] Hill, *Intellectual Origins*, pp. 91–92; R. McRae, *The Problem of the Unity of the Sciences: Bacon to Kant* (Toronto, 1961), p. 37.

[36] R. Descartes, *Discours de la méthode pour bien conduire sa raison et chercher la vérité dans les sciences* (Leiden, 1637/Manchester, 1941), p. 9.

therefore have given him.[37] In terms of human knowledge but not of creation, Descartes had established the priority of his own consciousness to the possibility of awareness of God's existence. Descartes had turned the tables on the atheists and skeptics and used their very doubts to establish God more firmly. He claimed he was constructing his new philosophy only for himself and did not advise everyone to follow his example. He would retain the religion in which, by the grace of God, he had been brought up.[38] He maintined that the laws of the material universe were established by God and that mathematical and other 'eternal' truths depended on God and could not exist without him.[39]

This was all very well, but it did not mask what had really happened. Descartes did expect to convince others of his views. If he hesitated before publishing them, it was not just because he was not convined of their correctness, but from a not unjustified fear of how the authorities, ecclesiastical and lay, would react to them. Their reaction was hostile. Descartes had not just drawn lines between scientific and religious knowledge as Galileo and, in a sense, Bacon had done. He had made an image of God and the soul of man, on the one hand, and of the material universe, on the other, which did not depend on the Scriptures and revelation. It is no wonder he found himself at odds, not only with the Catholic Church, but also with Calvinist authorities in Holland. Fortunately the latter did not dispose of the coercive powers of the Inquisition.

Both Bacon and Descartes had elevated God above the cosmological controversies with which the traditional Catholic world picture had encumbered religious belief. By doing so they had also placed him outside most principal intellectual and emotional endeavours.[40] These would now be increasingly concentrated on the investigation of nature, with the aim of controlling it for the benefit of mankind. On this worthy and Christian principle both Bacon and Descartes were agreed. Descartes, viewing the human body as a machine and passions as arising from the body, even argued that his physics would provide a 'certain foundation of morals'[41] and of the control of morality.

It was not long before Descartes' contemporaries realized that his 'clockwork universe' with its absolute division between mind and matter would open the door to atheism. This was not Descartes'

[37] *Ibid.*, pt. 4. A. J. Krailsheimer, *Studies in Self-Interest from Descartes to La Bruyère* (Oxford, 1962), pp. 38–39.

[38] Descartes, *Discours*, pt. 2, 3.

[39] Descartes to Mersenne, 15 April, 6 May 1630. In Descartes, *Oeuvres*, ed. Adam and Tannery, vol. 1, pp. 145, 149.

[40] I would like to thank Dorothy Koenigsberger for drawing my attention to this effect of both Bacon's and Descartes teachings.

[41] Descartes to Chanut, 15 June 1646. In *Oeuvres*, vol. 4, p. 441. Quoted in McRae, *Unity of the Sciences*, p. 59.

intention, nor did atheism necessarily follow from his philosophy. What did follow was a shift in interest among many of the most gifted minds in Europe. Bacon had excluded the Bible from scientists' arguments, and Descartes had gone further and excluded it from the arguments both of moralists and those looking for first causes. The full effects of this shift took time to work themselves out. But from then on the churches were on the defensive. They had lost the battle fought against Galileo and the Copernicans for the defense of their position as supreme arbiters of the validity of all human ideas about the universe. The basis of their arguments, the absolute validity of Scripture as the word of God and its interpretation through the traditional science of theology, had been sidestepped by argments which claimed an equally religious validity but which were based on the scientific investigation of the natural world.

The loss to theology was tremendous. Having been excluded from a vast intellectual field over which it had ruled benignly but autocratically for many centuries, it lost its attractiveness to young men wishing to embark on intellectual inquiry. The personal piety of most of these men is not in doubt, but natural philosophy had now become their primary interest. The religious and philosophical debates of the late seventeenth and early eighteenth centuries were concerned with the consequences of this new position.

Not everyone was prepared to go as far as Descartes in accepting the need to create a completely new metaphysical basis for the understanding of natural phenomena. Pierre Gassendi accepted a traditional religious metaphysics of the first causes of the world. But having allowed God to create atoms and the laws of their movement, he then excluded him from any further interference in, or influence on, the physical world. The task of physics was to determine the nature of the laws and movements of the atoms. This would allow the building of a coherent and systematic hypothesis on the nature of the universe. It was not the absolute truth which only God could comprehend, but it was the best man could in his limitation understand, and it did not conflict with God's truth.[42] For Gassendi the free philosophical study of nature lead to the greatest tranquility of the mind (*animi tranquilitas*) and hence to the greatest felicity (*summa foelicitas*).[43] The consolations of philosophy to the human mind was an old and, for Christians, entirely respectable topos. What was new in the seventeenth century was its exclusive interpretation in terms of the study of the natural sciences.

This happened even to some of those most anxious to uphold the primacy of religion. Nicolas Malebranche, youngest son of a distinguished robe family and destined for the church, found little to

[42] R. Tack, *Untersuchungen zum Philosophie-und Wissenschaftsbegriff bei Pierre Gassendi, (1592–1655)* (Meisenheim am Glan, 1974), pp. 108–10, 152, 155–56.
[43] *Ibid.*, p. 127, 140–41.

excite him in the traditional curriculum for Catholic intellectuals – the study of the Bible in its original languages, the history of the Church, and scholastic philosophy. At the age of twenty-six, if we are to believe Fontenelle's funeral oration, he came across Descartes' *Traité de l'homme* and 'was struck as if by a completely new light'.[44] From then on he set himself to harmonize Cartesian philosophy with Christianity in a system in which he equated God with reason.[45] 'Geometry and physics were the steps which led him to metaphysics and theology', says Fontenelle.[46] Malbranche had devoted followers, but there were many theologians whom he could not convince, and his life was a succession of controversies with such diverse and mutually inimical opponents as the Jesuits and the Jansenist theologian Antoine Arnauld. The Catholic Church, unable any longer to present a credible Aristotelian-Ptolemaic front, was equally unable to construct another generally acceptable view of the world which took account of the new scientific discoveries. Increasingly this intellectual initiative passed to scientists and natural philosophers.

It was this initiative which Leibniz took, to defend religion against atheism and to bring about a reunion of the churches on the basis of a true religion, which was to be a Christian faith based on scientific understanding of the harmony of the world which God in his divine goodness, omnipotence, and omniscience had created.[47] For this purpose (as well as dealing with the metaphysical problems involved in the Cartesian attempts to account for physical phenomena in purely mathematical terms), Leibniz reintroduced final causes, or metaphysics, into scientific investigations from which Cartesians had banished them. If, for instance, several bodies move with relation to each other, it is not possible by considering these bodies alone to determine to which one of them motion or rest can be attributed. What is needed is an investigation of force, a concept not found in the Cartesian categories of extension and motion. 'It appears more and more clear', Leibniz concluded,[48]

that although all the particular phenomena of nature can be explained mathematically or mechanically by those who understand them, yet nevertheless, the general principles of corporeal nature and even of mechanics are metaphysical rather than geometric, and belong rather to certain indivisible forms or natures as the causes of the appearances, than to the corporeal mass or

[44] B. de Fontenelle, 'Eloge du P. Malebranche'. In *Oeuvres*, vol. 1 (Paris, 1825), p. 321.

[45] E.g. in his *Entretiens sur la métaphysique*, 6. In *Oeuvres de Malebranche*, ed. A. Robinet, vol. 12 (Paris, 1965), pp. 145–56.

[46] Fontenelle, 'Eloge du P. Malebranche', p. 338.

[47] R. W. Meyer, *Leibnitz and the Seventeenth Century Revolution*, trans. J. P. Stern (Cambridge, 1952), p. 145.

[48] G. W. von Leibniz, *Discourse on Metaphysics*. In *Basic Writings*, trans. G. R. Montgomery (La Salle, Ill., 1962), p. 33.

to extension. This reflection is able to reconcile the mechanical philosophy of the moderns with the circumspection of those intelligent and well-meaning persons who, with a certain justice, fear that we are becoming too far removed from immaterial beings and that we are thus prejudicing piety.

What is this metaphysics? For Leibniz it was the laws of reason, and these had ultimate validity. Descartes had said that these laws were true because God had willed them so, Leibniz reversed this position: God willed these laws because they were true, because truth must be contained in God's nature, and he must therefore will it.[49] If the eternal laws depended on God's caprice, we could not be sure that he was not a demon or, indeed, the Devil. God's will is therefore identical with reason, and reason is, at least in principle, apprehensible by man.

This was an essentially Greek position, as against the Hebraic stress on God's inscrutable will, which was the basis of traditional Christian teaching. Since man must assume as a rational, as well as religious principle that God is good, it followed for Leibniz that the world God had created was bound to be the best possible world:

It follows from the supreme perfection of God that in producing the universe He chose the best possible plan, containing the greatest order, the best arranged situation, place and time; the greatest effect produced by the simplest means; the most power, the most knowledge, the most happiness and goodness in created things of which the universe admitted. For as all possible things have a claim to existence in the understanding of God in proportion to their perfection, the result of all these claims must be the most perfect actual world which is possible. Otherwise, it would not be possible to explain why things have happened as they have rather than otherwise.[50]

Perhaps not to offend orthodox Christains, Leibniz claimed that this choice among an infinite number of sets of possible worlds demonstrated God's freedom. It has been shown convincingly that, on Leibniz's premises, God could not have made a real choice but was bound to have chosen as he did by virtue of the eternal truths which did not depend on him.[51]

All this meant that even though man might not know all contingent truths, ultimately the universe was governed by reason and eternal truths accessible to him. The study of science and natural philosophy would become the basis of any valid theology. In the preface to his *Theodicée* Leibniz wrote: 'We see that Jesus-Christ . . . wanted God to be the object

[49] 'However, we must not imagine, as some do, that eternal truths, being dependent on God, are arbitrary and dependent on His will, as Descartes seems to have held.' *La Monadologie*, 46. In *Oeuvres Philosophiques de Leibniz*, p. 151, no. 421.

[50] Leibniz, *Principles of Nature and of Grace Founded on Reason* (1714), trans. M. Morris and G. H. R. Parkinson. In *Leibniz Philosophical Works*, ed. G. H. R. Parkinson, par. 10, p. 200. *Oeuvres*, 2, p. 613.

[51] Lovejoy, *The Great Chain of Being*, pp. 166 ff.

not only of our fear and of our veneration, but still more of our love and our tenderness . . . To love [Divinity], it is enough to envision its perfections, which is easily done because we find its ideas within ourselves.'[52]

It is not surprising that Arnauld, on first encountering Leibniz' ideas, reacted sharply: 'The Catholic Church would prohibit his entertaining them . . . Would it not be better for him to leave these metaphysical speculations which can be of utility neither to himself nor to others, in order to apply himself seriously to the most important matter he can ever undertake, namely to assure his salvation by entering into the Church.'[53] But almost at once Arnauld succumbed to the fascination of Leibniz' intellect and engaged in lengthy correspondence with him, although he could never quite get over his unease.[54] Voltaire was to make savage fun of Leibnizians in his *Micromegas* and in *Candide*.[55] But Leibniz' influence on his contemporaries was real enough and if it could not rival that of Descartes, it too tended to reinforce the role of scientific inquiry in both philosophical and religious speculation. Although the truth of nature could never indicate the whole truth of God, it still was the most accessible and certain pathway of human knowledge.

Leibniz had attempted to provide an intellectual escape from the religious passions of the century by the construction of a rational and scientific religious metaphysics. In England, where religious passions had flourished during the Civil War and Commonwealth period in great profusion and variety, many intellectuals turned to science and natural philosophy. The principles of Bacon's scientific method with their apparently clear-cut division between the study of God and the study of nature were particularly congenial to the founders of the Royal Society. Thomas Sprat, the historian of the Royal Society, is explicit on this question of motivation. Those who studied 'experimental philosophy' – science – could expect little material advantage from their studies.[56] However,

for such a candid and unpassionate company, as that was, and for such a gloomy season, what could have been a fitter subject to pitch upon, then [sic] *Natural Philosophy*? To have been always tossing about some *Theological question*, would have been, to have made that their private diversion, the excess of which they themselves dislik'd in the publick: To have been eternally musing on Civil business, and the distresses of their Country, was too melancholy a reflexion: It was *Nature* alone which could pleasantly entertain them, in that estate.

[52] Leibniz, *Essais de Théodicée. Oeuvres* (1866), 2, pp. 3–4.
[53] A. Arnaud to Ernst von Hessen-Rheinfels, 13 March 1686, *ibid.*, vol. 1, p. 581.
[54] Id., 31 August 1687, *ibid.*, p. 667.
[55] Voltaire, *Micromegas: Histoire Philosophique. Oeuvres complètes*, vol. 44 (Kehl, 1785), pp. 176 ff.
[56] T. Sprat, *The History of the Royal Society* (London, 1667), ed. J. I. Cope and H. W. Jones (St. Louis/London, 1959), p. 27.

In this contemplation of nature men could 'differ without animosity' and 'without any danger of a Civil War'.[57]

Here, as with Gassendi, the motivation for natural philosophy, especially in an age of social and political upheaval, anxiety, and passion was tranquility of mind. Where the medieval intellectual in similar circumstances had retreated into a monastery and studied theology and philosophy, the mid-seventeenth-century intellectual retreated into an 'invisible college' of like-minded men 'to assemble in a private house, to reason freely upon the works of nature: to pass Conjectures and propose problems, on any Mathematical, or Philosophical Matter, which comes in their way'.[58] It was, of course, a religious undertaking. Speaking of the help which the Royal Society would be prepared to give in setting up the *Académie des Sciences* in Paris, Sprat spoke of two common aims for similar institutions all over Europe: to fight the common enemy of Christendom, the Turk: 'The other also against powerful and barbarous Foes, that have not been fully subdu'd almost these six thousand years, *Ignorance and False Opinions*.'[59]

Membership in the Royal Society would not depend on religion or nationality, 'for they openly profess, not to lay the Foundation of an English, Scotch, Irish, Popish, or Protestant Philosophy; but a Philosophy of Mankind'.[60] The study of the works of God, the job of the natural philosopher, Sprat argued, is an excellent grounding for the contemplation of man's redemption. Work on man's body, especially the study of the spirits of the blood, will even lead to 'near-guesses' about the actions of man's soul'.[61] Yet the analogy of the retreat of the medieval monk must not be overdone. The founders of the Royal Society, for whom and with whose advice Sprat wrote his *History*, had very practical aims in mind, as well as the peace of mind to be achieved by the pursuit of natural philosophy. Like Bacon, they thought in terms of practical usefulness to mankind of scientific inquiry and of the moral and social value of such pursuits, keeping men from corrupting habits.[62] Henry Oldenburg, secretary of the Royal Society, wrote to his fellow John Winthrop, governor of the Massachusetts Bay Company: I doubt not but the savage Indians themselves, when they shall see the Christians addicted, as to piety and virtue, so to all sorts of ingenuities, pleasing Experiments, useful Inventions and Practices, will thereby insensibly and the more cheerfully subject themseves to you.'[63]

---

[57] *Ibid.*, pp. 55–56. Cf. also p. 344. Sprat's italics.
[58] *Ibid.*, p. 56.
[59] *Ibid.*, p. 57.
[60] *Ibid.*, p. 63.
[61] *Ibid.*, p. 83.
[62] *Ibid.*, pp. 342–45. J. R. Jacob, *Robert Boyle and the English Revolution* (New York, 1977), pp. 154–55.
[63] Quoted, *ibid.*, p. 155.

It was hoped that the religious tolerance which members of the Royal Society professed would benefit the Church of England. It would remain quite safe, Sprat claimed, in a 'Rational Age' and with the 'subversion of old opinions about Nature'. Both the Anglican church and the Royal Society derived from a reformation, 'the one having compass'd it in Religion, the other purposing it in Philosophy'.[64] There was even an element of millennnarianism in this attitude, which gave men an added incentive to pursue natural philosophy, for at some point, it was argued, God would give man complete mastery over nature. Naturally, this would be likely to happen in England where the true, rational Protestant religion, as believed by the latitudinarian wing of the Anglican Church, would triumph. For it was the latitudinarian Anglicans, as we now know, who were the leading spirits in the foundation of the Royal Society.[65]

The Royal Society represented, at least in the minds of many of its founders and early members, a deliberate attempt to reconstruct the unity of religion and science which Copernicanism had shattered. Characteristically, Robert Boyle held, just as Galileo had done, that the Bible and science did not contradict each other. Equally characteristically, he argued the need for careful biblical scholarship to make this evident.[66] Here was the key to the new attitude. The initiative had passed from the church and from theologians to scientists and scholars. It was by their efforts that God's providential design for man would be laid bare. It promised both material and spiritual satisfaction beyond even the individual felicity of the peaceful investigation of nature.[67]

It is in this context that we have to see the towering and still enigmatic and controversial figure of Isaac Newton.[68] At least since E. A. Burtt's classic *The Metaphysical Foundations of Modern Science* of 1924, it has become clear that Newton can no longer be simply regarded as the great early exponent of modern positivistic science, as was held in the nineteenth century.[69] On the contrary, the ultimate aim of his investigations seems to have been nothing less than a complete knowledge of God and his creation. This knowledge had been revealed and was known to the ancient Babylonians, Egyptians, and pre-Socratic Greeks and to Noah and Moses. But they or their successors had been corrupted and the knowledge had been lost. It was the task of

[64] Sprat, *Royal Society*, pp. 370–71.

[65] J. R. Jacob, *Robert Boyle*, pp. 154–59.

[66] *Ibid.*, p. 123.

[67] Cf. also Margaret C. Jacob, *The Newtonians and the English Revolution, 1689–1720* (Ithaca, 1976), pp. 135–37.

[68] For recent work on Newton, cf. C. R. S. Westfall, 'The Changing World of the Newtonian Industry', *Journal of the History of Ideas* 37 (March 1976).

[69] It seems as if Reiner Tack still sees Newton in this way. *Untersuchungen*, p. 226.

modern philosophers, and especially of Newton himself, to retrieve it.[70]

Newton set about doing this by his scientific investigations, which he conducted through mathematics and/or in the best Baconian tradition of inductive argument from observation and experiment. It was in this activity that he rejected metaphysical hypotheses. But equally important was unravelling the truths God had hidden, not in the physical universe, but in the more obscure parts of the Old Testament, the Revelation of St John, and in other ancient writings and prophesies. In Newton's eyes all these truths belonged together, were a part of God's providential design. No doubt this design was mysterious, but it was penetrable:

The main business of natural philosophy is to argue from phenomena without feigning hypotheses, and to deduce causes from effects, till we come to the very first cause, which certainly is not mechanical, and not only to unfold the mechanism of the world, but chiefly to resolve these and such like questions . . . and though every true step made in this philosophy brings us not immediately to the knowledge of the first cause, yet it brings us nearer to it, and on that account is to be highly valued.[71]

Thus Newton is his *Queries* to his *Opticks*. He made the same point in the *General Scholium* in the second edition of his *Principia*:

This Being [God] governs all things, not as a Soul of the World but as Lord over all. The Supreme God is a Being eternal, infinite, absolutely perfect; but a being, however perfect, without dominion, cannot be said to be Lord God . . . We know him only by his most wise and excellent contrivances of things, and final causes; we admire him for his perfections but we reverence and adore him on account of his dominion; for we adore him as his servants; and a God without dominion, providence, and final causes, is nothing else but Fate and Nature . . . And thus much concerning God; to discourse of whom from the appearances of things does certainly belong to natural philosophy.[72]

For Newton the universe was not only the creation of God, but it also constituted his true purpose, apprehensible by man through natural philosophy. Such a view, while theologically unorthodox, was not irreligious, nor did it oppose science to religion. God remained essential

[70] J. E. McGuire and P. M. Rattansi, 'Newton and the "Pipes of Pan"', *Notes and Records of the Royal Society of London* 21 (no. 2, December 1966), pp. 122–23 and *passim*. F. E. Manuel, *The Religion of Isaac Newton* (Oxford, 1974), pp. 42 ff.

[71] *Queries* to Newton's *Opticks*, pp. 334 ff, quoted in E. A. Burtt, *The Metaphysical Foundations of Modern Science*, 2nd ed. (Garden City, 1932), p. 260. Cf. also J. M. Keynes, 'Newton, the Man'. In *Essays in Biography*, ed. G. Keynes (New York, 1963), p. 314: 'He regarded the universe as a cryptogram set out by the Almighty – just as he himself wrapt the discovery of the calculus in a cryptogram when he communicated with Leibnitz.'

[72] Newton, *Mathematical Principles of Natural Philosophy*, 2nd ed., ed. F. Cajori (Berkeley, 1934), p. 545. Also quoted in Burtt, *Metaphysical Foundations*, p. 294.

to Newton's world view, not only as creator of the universe but as a constant replenisher and adjuster of its motive forces which, without such continual intervention, would have run down. Nevertheless, the balance between science and religion, in the common territory of the explanation of the physical universe, had now shifted still further in favour of science, or rather of natural philosophy.

In 1718 for instance, there appeared in London a translation of a Dutch defense of Christianity in which the author claimed he could convince the 'atheists and infidels', i.e. the Spinozists, of the authority of the Scripture by *'the right Use of the Contemplation of the Word'*. 'The Methods we have made use of to prove the same', he wrote, 'are only taken from the *modern Observations* and *probable Discoveries in Natural Philosophy*; without laying down any bare Hypotheses, since in the Things of natural knowledge, we have no farther Foundation for Arguments than we can produce Experiments.'[73] He went on to claim that 'the Manner of *proving the Divinity of the Holy Scripture from Natural Phenomena or Appearances'* was a totally new method.[74]

And so, at least in this formulation, it was. In traditional belief the study of 'the second book', i.e. nature, revealed to man the existence and greatness of God. But the first book, the Bible, had not depended on such study. The word of God had always stood by itself, without need of further proof. 'In the beginning was the Word, and the Word was with God and the Word was God' (St John I.1.). The most that Galileo had claimed was that the study of nature could, in certain specific cases, help in the interpretation of the true meaning of passages in the Scriptures which dealt with natural phenomena. But now, because the 'atheists' had thrown doubt on the divine nature of the Bible, it was claimed that the study of the 'second book', i.e. natural sciences, could provide the best proof of the divinity of the Scriptures. In this spirit the Newtonian propagandist Desagulier warmly welcomed the Dutch work. The translation would do even more good than the original, he wrote to the translator in a letter published in the English edition, for it had left out arguments the author drew 'from the Modern Philosophy for Reveal'd Religion; the weakness of which latter might give those Free-Thinkers occasion to triumph, who would be struck dumb by Convictions from the former'.[75]

The intellectuals of the Anglican Church were happy to use the Newtonian world picture with its emphasis on God's providence in a material universe composed of lifeless and inert matter, to fortify their own liberal Protestant theology and conservative social philosophy.[76]

[73] B. Nieuwentyt, *The Religious Philosopher*, trans. John Chamberlayne (London, 1718), vol. 1, p. 1. Nieuwentyt's italics. I wish to thank Margaret C. Jacob for drawing my attention to this source.

[74] *Ibid.*, p. II.

[75] *Ibid.* The pages of Desagulier's letter to John Chamberlayne are unnumbered.

[76] Jacob, *The Newtonians, passim.*

But Newtonianism was also used by the contemporary free thinker to support a materialist philosophy in which God and nature were equated and matter became the source of life and change and order. In this view Newton's concept of gravity became a force inherent in matter.[77] These were forerunners of the more famous eighteenth-century atheists La Mettrie and the Baron d'Holbach. But atheism was not the predominant belief of the Enlightenment. In general the alliance between science and religion held. Voltaire, the great apostle of Newtonianism , was convinced of its necessity. 'We know nothing of first principles', he wrote to Prince Frederick William of Prussia, in 1770.

It is surely very presumptuous to define God, the angels, spirits, and to pretend to know precisely why God made the world, when we do not know why we can move our arms at our pleasure. Doubt it not a pleasant condition, but certainty is an absurd one. What is most repellent in the *System of Nature [of d'Holbach]* – *after the recipe for making eels from flour* – *is the audacity with which it decides that there is no God, without even having tried to prove the impossibility . . . Si dieu n'existait pas, il faudrait l'inventer.* But all nature cries aloud that He does exist: that there *is* a supreme intelligence, an immense power, an admirable order, and everything teaches us our own dependence on it.[78]

Voltaire was a great deal more humble about man's ability to penetrate first causes, or God's purpose, than Newton or Leibniz had been. But while specific religious beliefs and the metaphysical bases of science were coming to seem increasingly doubtful, the positive laws of science itself, the practical results of scientific enquiry in a Newtonian universe assumed to be accessible to human reason appeared much more promising. 'Nothing is more necessary', d'Alembert wrote in his *Preliminary Discourse to the Encyclopedia of Diderot*, 'than a revealed religion, which may instruct us concerning so many diverse objects. Designed to serve as a supplement to natural knowledge, it shows us part of what was hidden, but it restricts itself to the things which are absolutely necessary for us to know. The rest is closed to us and apparently will be forever. A few truths to be believed, a small number of precepts to be practiced: such are the essentials to which revealed religion is reduced.'[29] The rest of his *Discourse* d'Alembert devoted to the sciences and the arts.

Some twenty-five years ago, the distinguished scientist and sinologist Joseph Needham suggested that one of the differences between the histories of science in Europe and in China was the

[77] Margaret C. Jacob, 'Newtonianism and the Origins of the Enlightenment', *Eighteenth Century Studies* 11 (no. 1, Fall 1977).

[78] *Voltaire's Correspondence*, ed. T. Besterman, vol. 77 (Geneva, 1962), pp. 119–20.

[79] D'Alembert, *Preliminary Discourse to the Encyclopedia of Diderot*, trans. R. N. Schwab (Indianapolis and New York, 1963), p .26.

development in Europe of the concept of the laws of nature.[80] This concept had appeared in rudimentary form among the Greeks and was fully developed during the sixteenth and seventeenth centuries. Its essence and importance in the history of science was its positing of a suprarational divine creator and law-giver whose creation was subject to law and hence discoverable and comprehensible by rational methods. In China the prevailing philosophical schools did not develop the analogy between human law and nature. 'Universal harmony', Needham writes, 'comes about not by the celestial fiat of some King of Kings, but by the spontaneous co-operation of all beings in the universe brought about by their following the internal necessities of their own natures . . . Nature shows a ceaselessness and regularity, yes, but it is not a commanded ceaselessness and regularity'.[81] The Chinese did not regard human reason and logic as capable of achieving a full understanding of nature. In the last two hundred years, Western philosophy of science has come closer to the Chinese view, with the laws of nature being regarded as statistical regularities rather than prescriptions imposed on matter by a creator. 'The problem', Needham says, 'is whether the recognition of such statistical regularities and their mathematical expression could have been reached by any other road than that which Western science actually travelled'.[82]

Granting the importance of the connection between Western religious and scientific thinking – was it not also the decline of religious sensibilities in the early modern period which gave scientific inquiry an added emotional attraction to European intellectuals? While such inquiry generally remained strictly Christian – whether Catholic or Protestant – it tended to expand into areas formerly the field of purely religious thought. In these areas it had great advantages over religion. It could give answers philosophically more satisfactory; it could promise results that would bring practical benefits to mankind; and, perhaps psychologically most important, its disputes could avoid the murderous consequences of theological disputes. Science, the handmaiden (*ancilla*) of theology and revealed religion, had not exactly asserted itself over its former mistress, but had set up house on its own. Many of Europe's most gifted intellects, while still paying occasional visits to the house of the old mistress, found the house of the new one more engrossing and came to spend most of their time and energy in it.

---

[80] J. Needham, 'Human Law and the Laws of Nature'. In *The Grand Titration: Science and Society in East and West* (London, 1969), pp. 299–331.

[81] *Ibid.*, p. 323.

[82] *Ibid.*, p. 330.

8. The Palace of Fame. The First Intermezzo from *Il Giudizio di Paride* with settings by Giulio Parigi. The play was performed in Florence in 1608 to celebrate the wedding of Cosimo de' Medici and Maria Maddalena of Austria.

Engraving by Remigio Cantagallina after Giulio Parigi.

# 11

# Republics and Courts in Italian and European Culture in the 16th and 17th Centuries*

It has long been recognized that creative human activities often occur in clusters and that the Italian Renaissance is an outstanding example of such a cluster. The reasons for this clustering are still a matter of debate; but most historians would probably agree that (in ways which they do not agree about) it had something to do with the pattern of life and traditions of the Italian city-states of the later middle ages and also with the patronage provided by the Italian courts.[1] There has, however, been much less debate about the reasons for the end of the Italian Renaissance, in so far as it is seen as the end of a clustering of creative activities and not just as a change in artistic and literary styles. Nor has there been much discussion about the nature of later clusters of creative activity or the conditions for their appearance. It is the purpose of this essay to suggest an approach to these problems for Italy and Europe in the sixteenth and seventeenth centuries.[2] For this purpose it will be necessary to make some overt value judgements – a practice frowned upon by some. But without it, no history of culture is possible at all; for the historian has to select those artists, writers, composers and others whom he chooses to consider, and I am here concerned, like nearly all

---

*An earlier version of this article was read at the Ninth Conference of the Istituto Internazionale di Storia Economica 'Franceso Datini' at Prato on 16 April 1977.

[1] For a recent summary of different views, together with a fascinating attempt to approach this problem from a sociological and statistical viewpoint, see Peter Burke, *Tradition and Innovation in Renaissance Italy: A Sociological Approach* (London, 1974).

[2] Some twenty years ago I reacted against the Crocean view of post-Renaissance Italy (which made the Counter-Reformation responsible for the supposed decadence of Italy during the age of the Baroque) by suggesting that what had really occurred was a shift of creative activity from the visual arts into music and scientific inquiry. I would not now like to defend all the arguments and details of this attempt; but I still think that the basic approach to the problem was in the right direction and that the concept of shift, which some other historians have accepted, is still a useful concept. B Croce, *Storia dell'età barocca in Italia* (Bari, 1929); H. G. Koenigsberger, 'Decadence or Shift?', *Trans. Roy. Hist. Soc.*, 5th ser., x (1960), pp. 1–18, repr. in H. G. Koenigsberger, *Estates and Revolutions: Essays in Early Modern European History* (Ithaca and London, 1971), pp. 278–97, from which subsequent references to the article are taken.

other writers on the Renaissance and the Baroque, with outstanding achievements.

To understand the end of the Italian Renaissance it is necessary first to understand some of its most important traditions. Most of the visual art of the Renaissance was public or, rather, communal art – that is, it was executed for the benefit not only of the actual patron, the person or institution who paid the artist, but also for the community, the city. Ecclesiastical authorities, gilds and other public bodies wanted their patronage to be publicly recognized and, hence, to be visible, whether in the building of churches with their frescoes and altar-pieces or in the public display of sculptures, as in the famous niches of the Or San Michele of Florence. From the point of view of this tradition it did not matter whether the aim and symbolism of such art was religious or political. In the *palazzo pubblico* of Siena, for instance, the frescoes of the council chamber represented a consistently republican symbolism for nearly two hundred years, from the commissions given to Lorenzetti, 1337–40, to those to Beccafumi, as late as 1529. *Amor patriae* and *amor communis* are contrasted with tyranny, *buon governo* with *mal governo*, and these civic virtues are shown to bring the blessings of justice and concord in their train.[3]

But religious paintings, too, could satisfy communal aspirations. Madonnas, angels and saints were, so to speak, public property. They belonged to the Christian community as patrons or protectors, and like the innumerable Venetian representations of St Mark and his winged lion, they signified its identity, authority and standing within the cosmic hierarchy of the Christian world. The *scuole grandi* of Venice, those magnificent charitable institutions which were run by commoners and which, it was argued in the sixteenth century, were deliberately designed by the Venetian aristocracy to keep the citizens content with their exclusion from political power, these civic religious institutions were also among the greatest patrons of the arts.[4]

At the same time, the practice of art, like that of most late medieval crafts, was essentially public. In the fifteenth century the master worked with his assistants and apprentices in an easily accessible workshop. Discriminating patrons therefore often specified that the most important parts of a ceiling decoration or an altar-piece were to be executed by the master himself, and not by his helpers.[5] As yet, only a

[3] N. Rubinstein, 'Political Ideas in Sienese Art', *Jl. Warburg and Courtauld Inst.* xxi (1958), pp. 179–207.

[4] O. Logan, *Culture and Society in Venice, 1470–1790* (London 1972), pp. 203 ff. See also B. S. Pullan, *Rich and Poor in Renaissance Venice: The Social Institutions of a Catholic State, to 1620* (Oxford, 1971), pt. I, *passim*.

[5] For example, the contract of Benozzo Gozzoli with the Company of the Purification, Florence, 1461; quoted in D. S. Chambers, *Patrons and Artists in the Italian Renaissance* (London, 1970), pp. 27–9. See also the discussion of this practice in M. Baxandall, *Painting and Experience in Fifteenth Century Italy* (Oxford, 1972), pp. 18–23.

very few artists – Uccello, Leonardo, Michelangelo – had private work-rooms or insisted on being alone.[6] The artists' work-shops were often the meeting-places of artists and philosophers, as was Verrocchio's where Nicholas of Cusa's friend, the mathematician Paolo Toscanelli, discussed and taught mathematics, and where Leonardo may well have learned the Cusan philosophy that became the basis of much of his scientific thinking.[7] Somewhat later we learn from Vasari of the workshop of Baccio d'Agnolo which was a meeting-place for Filippino Lippi, Sansovino, the brothers San Gallo, the young Raphael and even, on occasion, Michelangelo.[8]

Clearly, both activity and training of the Renaissance artist was centred in the urban workshop. So, inevitably, was much of the recruitment of artists. The decision to become a painter or a sculptor had to be taken early by a boy or his parents. Venice had a minimum age of twelve for admission to apprenticeship, but in other cities it was often earlier and Michelangelo, entering Ghirlandaio's studio at fourteen because of the earlier opposition of his father, was an unusually late starter.[9] Clearly also, the majority of these boys would come from the city itself, if only because they and their parents would know more about the workshops and the possible careers the boys might follow than those living in villages or small towns. Perhaps they would also prefer to keep their sons nearer home and many, of course, followed their fathers and grandfathers in these professions.[10]

The patronage of the Italian princes of the Renaissance fitted in well enough with these traditions, at any rate until the end of the fifteenth century. The Medici, who had to pretend to live as private citizens in a republic, were always anxious to exhibit their patronage of the arts as a public service.[11] They provided Donatello's *Judith*, in the Palazzo Medici Ricardi, with the unexceptionable republican-urban and anti-princely motto: 'Kingdoms fall through luxury; cities rise through virtue. Behold the proud neck felled by the arm of the humble'.[12] Even so, it is significant that the Medici spent far more money on their collection of antiques and engraved gems than they paid for

---

[6] M. Wackernagel, *Der Lebensraum des Künstlers in der florentinischen Renaissance* (Leipzig, 1938), p. 317.

[7] See Dorothy Koenigsberger, *Renaissance Man and Creative Thinking: A History of Concepts of Harmony, 1400–1700* (Hassocks, 1979), chs. 2–3.

[8] Quoted in Wackernagel, *op. cit.*, p. 359.

[9] *Ibid.*, p. 337.

[10] Wackernagel gives a fairly long list of Florentine artists whose family background is known. Of these, only Castagna was the son of a peasant. Wackernagel makes the suggestive point that the most original of the fifteenth-century Florentine artists did not come from artists' families, like Ghiberti, but were either first- or second-generation artists. *Ibid.*, pp. 336–7. See also Burke, *Tradition and Innovation in Renaissance Italy*, ch. 3, 'Artists and Writers'.

[11] E. H. Gombrich, 'The Early Medici as Patrons of Art', in his *Norm and Form* (London, 1966), pp. 35–57.

contemporary paintings.[13] Such collections were, of course, meant for private and not for public enjoyment; and the Florentines were not taken in by the spurious Medici republicanism. When they threw out Lorenzo the Magnificent's son, Piero, in 1494 they took care to transfer the Donatello *Judith* to a more public place, the outside of the Palazzo Vecchio, where it still stands with other forlorn symbols of former Florentine liberty.

The marquesses and dukes of Mantua or Ferrara did not, of course, pretend to be private citizens. But they were as anxious as the Medici to give their patronage of the arts a public aspect. Artists, writers and musicians were happy enough to accept such princely patronage. Some artists, like Mantegna or Cosimo Tura, spent most of their working lives at these courts. Yet there is a sense in which Mantua, Ferrara, Urbino and, even more, Rome itself, lived on the artistic potential of the great cities, above all of Florence and Venice. These cities, in their turn, were magnets for the creative talent of the whole of Italy but they impressed much of their own civic and artistic traditions on those who passed through their schools. Without this background the splendours of the Gonzaga or Este courts would have been inconceivable or, at any rate, much more short-lived than they actually were.

In the Netherlands and in south Germany there occurred in the fifteenth and early sixteenth centuries a clustering of creativity in the visual arts which was second only to that which occurred in Italy. Here too, we find the tradition of the artists' workshops in the great cities, in Bruges and Ghent, in Cologne and Nuremberg. Here, as in Italy, art was a public activity, designed for churches, town halls and market-places or, more ephemerally, for public festivals and triumphal entries of princes. Much more than in Italy, the drawings and designs of the greatest artists became public through the medium of woodcuts and engravings. It was as a woodcut designer and engraver, rather than as a painter, that Dürer gained his reputation in Germany and beyond.[14]

The great northern painters, from Van Eyck and Rogier van der Weiden to Dürer and Cranach, moved easily back and forth from their urban backgrounds to the courts of the dukes of Burgundy or the Emperor Maximilian and those German princes who wished to emulate them in the fashionable activity of public patronage of the arts.

[12] Gombrich's translation of 'regna cadunt luxu, surgunt virtutibus urbes, caesa vides humili colla superba manu'. E. H. Gombrich, *Meditations on a Hobby Horse* (London, 1963), p. 93.

[13] Gombrich, 'The Early Medici as Patrons of Art', p. 52, gives some startling figures: between 400 and 1,000 florins each for engraved gems, and as much as 10,000 florins for the antique cameo called the *Tazza Farnese*. Against this, Filippino Lippi, Botticelli or Pollaiuolo would get between 50 and 100 florins for an average-sized painting. Big fresco cycles were, of course, much more expensive, but might still be had for about 1,000 florins.

[14] E. Panofsky, *Albrecht Dürer*, 2nd edn., 2 vols (Princeton, 1945), i, pp. 3–4.

The northern Renaissance therefore developed on a basis similar to that of the Italian Renaissance, with a combination of urban-civic and courtly traditions.

But, just as in Italy, this clustering of creative activity did not last and, in Germany at least, the end came much more quickly and much more decisively than in Italy. It is to this problem that I now want to turn.

We can take Florence as the prototype for the history of the Italian Renaissance. Here we can trace most clearly the change from city republic to territorial monarchy; and since this change was bitterly fought over in a long drawn-out drama of several acts, it was also highly self-conscious. This is naturally most evident in Florentine historical and political writing. Here, too, we have the phenomenon of the clustering of creative activity and, in this case, it is easy enough to see why the social and political struggles of Florence should have sharpened men's perceptions and deepened their understanding of political problems. Nor is it surprising to find the greatest exponents of this school, Machiavelli and Guicciardini, imbued with a deep pessimism, both about human nature and about the possibility of the survival of a civic republicanism, a *vivere politico*, as Machiavelli called it.[15]

But for the historian an equally important phenomenon is the sudden collapse, or rather disappearance, of this school in the 1540s. By then it had become clear that a return to a republican form of government had ceased to be a political possibility.[16] Filippo Nerli summed up the situation in his *Commentarii*:

It no longer seems necessary to record Florentine politics. Because the city was reduced to the rule of such a prince, our citizens no longer have reason to contend among themselves about affairs of state and the government of the city. All matters are controlled by one prince, one signore.[17]

The intrigues of the Medici court could not interest the best minds. No one could take much pride in the inevitably low-key foreign policy of the dukes, nor their one departure from it, the disreputable conquest of the republic of Siena.

The influence of social and political changes on the arts was necessarily less direct than it was on the writing of politics and history. Thus it is possible to see the change from the classical Renaissance style to Mannerism as a largely formal development, arising naturally from

---

[15] For example, in his *Discorsi*, i, 55. See also above, chapter 2.

[16] L. von Albertini, *Das florentinische Staatsbewusstein im Übergang von der Republick zum Principat*(Berne, 1955), pp. 274 ff.

[17] Quoted in S. Berner, 'Florentine Political Thought in the late Cinquecento' *Il pensiero politico*, iii (1970), p. 184.

the attempts to solve certain formal artistic problems.[18] Yet it would be surprising if the visual arts had remained unaffected by the convulsions which affected every other aspect of Italian life.[19] For most artists the time was past for the painting of beautiful and serene madonnas enthroned in majestic repose over an orderly and harmonious world; for this world was now lost.

The reaction took several, often contradictory, forms. One was a rejection of traditional values. It is very clear in Machiavelli, and I think it is equally clear in the style of a new generation of younger artists, Parmigianino, Pontormo, Rosso Fiorentino and others. It was the great merit of these artists that, together with the older Michelangelo, they created a new style, Mannerism. It was a style that was deliberately anticlassical in form although not in iconographic content – and here again there is a striking parallel with Machiavelli, who found the exemplars of his revolutionary thinking in Roman history. It was a style that was often violent, sometimes downright ugly, a style which could play havoc with that most central of classical Renaissance achievements, the correct use of perspective. But it also produced subtle pictorial rhythms, the portrayal of strong emotions and a sheer technical virtuosity, all of which our present age has found more congenial than some intervening ages.

The second reaction, opposite but equally natural, was the quest for security. It led Guicciardini and the majority of the Florentine aristocracy to help restore the Medici and then support their monarchy. It led artists and theoreticians of art to emphasize the neo-Platonic view of the artist as an ideal personality, the perfect gentleman. In such a way is Raphael portrayed in Vasari's *Lives*, and a somewhat later theorist, G. P. Lomazzo, even managed to fit the notoriously difficult, withdrawn and ugly Michelangelo into this neo-Platonic pattern.[20]

For such a view of art and the artist, courts and court society would seem the ideal milieu, and the connection between court society and Mannerism has often been stressed.[21] But in the course of the sixteenth century these courts themselves were undergoing changes. Compared with their informal, open and, in the case of the Medici, even civic nature, the courts of the middle and latter part of the sixteenth century adopted Spanish etiquette and formality. Life at court became a matter of correct rules ·and maxims. Castiglione's courtier founded his behaviour on a philosophical view of life, on a wide appreciation of its cultural richness and on a sensitive recognition of the subtleties of

[18] This seems to be the view, for instance, of J. Shearman, *Mannerism* (Harmondsworth, 1967), p. 16, and *passim*.

[19] Cf. J. R. Hale, 'War and Public Opinion in Renaissance Italy', in E. F. Jacob (ed.), *Italian Renaissance Studies* (London, 1960), pp. 94–122.

[20] Quoted in R. and M. Wittkower, *Born under Saturn* (London, 1963), p. 93.

[21] M. Levey, *Painting at Court* (London 1971), p. 63, even characterizes the style of the fifteenth-century painters at the court of Ferrara, Tura and Pannonio, as Mannerist.

human relationships. Della Casa's gentleman, some forty years later, founded his behaviour on good table manners and on how to blow his nose genteelly. Castiglione's *Cortegiano* was put on the Index of Prohibited Books; Della Casa's *Galateo* became a best seller.[22] The artist, to be successful, now had to become a member of an academy, the formalized courtly successor of the free and easy gatherings of painters and philosophers in the workshops of Verrocchio and Baccio d'Agnolo. Inevitably and, in the long run, fatally, the academies began to impose their rules, to circumscribe the artist and to stifle his originality.

By the middle of the sixteenth century a real decline in Italian, and especially in Florentine, painting was becoming evident. Most of the first generation of Mannerists had died or, rather significantly, committed suicide, like Rosso Fiorentino. The ageing Bronzino, that most sensitive portrayer of the hidden tensions beneath the masks of court life but now no longer in favour with the grand duke, was reduced to writing a begging letter to Cosimo I which is astonishing even by the normal standards of fulsome adulation coupled with abject humility that had become the common currency of the period:

and although the Cavaliere Signor Tommaso de'Medici has told me that such salary is no longer due to me, still I hope that Your Illustrious Excellency will find occasion to make use of me for what little I am worth, that you will not cast me out from the number of your faithful servants and that you will reopen for me the door of your most holy house . . . and this I desire more than my life . . . and am not less desirous and ready to serve and adore you than ever.[23]

Competition for patronage was the normal condition of most artists' lives. But in court society, as it developed in sixteenth- and seventeenth-century Europe, it became part of men's life-style in the sense that everything else was subordinated to it and to its rules and patterns.[24]

[22] C. Dionisotti, 'La letterature italiana nell'età del Concilio', in *Il Concilio di Trento e la riforma tridentina. Atti del Convegno Storico Internazionale, Trent, 2–6settembre*, 1963, 2 vol. (Rome, 1965), i, p. 342, has observed a somewhat parallel development in Italian literature. At the turn of the fifteenth century the predominating subject matter was love; in the second half of the sixteenth century it was honour.

[23] *Carteggio inedito d'artisti dei secoli XIV, XV, XVI*. ed. G. Gaye, 3 vols. (Florence, 1839–40), iii, p. 134. My translation. This letter is also quoted in Levey, *op. cit.*, p. 105.

[24] See N. Elias, *Die höfische Gesellschaft* (Neuwied and Berlin, 1969), esp. p. 84. Cf. also the very perceptive passages on the effects of court life on literature by E. Mazzali in his introduction to Tasso, *Prose* (Milan, 1969), trans. in E. Cochrane pp. 135 ff. Goethe, the last great creative mind to spend most of his life at a small court, gives in his play *Torquato Tasso* a fascinating study of the tragic tensions between the explosive passions of a truly creative mind and a highly civilized, well-meaning, but inescapably narrow and formalized court society. The problem of the artist in society is, of course, a very wide one; but Goethe's choice of Tasso and the court of Ferrara in the 1570s for the discussion of this problem is highly significant.

To the artistic traditions of the Italian Renaissance these new conditions were highly antithetical. They coincided with the most restrictive period of the Counter-Reformation. Luigi Firpo has perceptively characterized the Counter-Reformation as a crisis of confidence in men's minds, a consequent distrust of social and political reforms and a need felt to concentrate on 'the necessity of acting on souls'.[25] The result was that artists and writers distrusted themselves and that the most creative were falling foul of authority and were persecuted for their real or supposed lack of orthodoxy. The sculptor Ammanati repented of having sculpted nudes. Tasso neurotically sought repeated reassurances of his orthodoxy from the inquisitors themselves. Those who would not conform could expect to spend their lives in prison like Campanella, to be burned at the stake like Giordano Bruno, kidnapped and murdered like the playwright Ferrante Pallavicino, or assassinated like the statesman, political writer and satirist, Boccalini.

Boccalini was assassinated in Venice, the state and city he admired above all others for the traditional civic freedom which it preserved. If the republic of St Mark could not prevent murder, it did, in general, manage to protect the freedom of its citizens and residents from outside interference. Veronese's brush with a pedantic inquisitor produced no greater penalty than the requirement of changing the title of his painting *The Feast in the House of Simon* (that is *The Last Supper*) to *Feast in the House of Levi*.[26] Just as Venice was self-consciously maintaining its republican traditions throughout the sixteenth century,[27] so it was maintaining the Renaissance traditions of the artist, not as a courtier but as a free citizen, treated as a friend and not as a servant by his aristocratic patrons and working as much for the public as for his employer.[28] Venice was the one city of Italy where the visual arts suffered no decline in the course of the sixteenth century, and (as I argued in my earlier article)[29] it is not far-fetched to relate this continued artistic vitality to the continued vitality of the Venetian city-state.

Nevertheless it was not courts and court society as such which made life difficult for the painter or sculptor. It was rather that, under certain historial circumstances, they could have a stifling effect on an artistic tradition which had developed in a very different milieu. About the turn of the sixteenth and seventeenth centuries some of these

[25] L. Firpo, *Lo stato ideale della Contrariforma* (Bara, 1957), pp. 241 ff.; quoted and trans. in Cochrane (ed.) *op. cit.*, pp. 149 ff.

[26] E. G. Holt (ed.), *Literary Sources of Art History* (Princeton, 1947), pp. 245–8.

[27] For example, Paolo Paruta, *Della perfettione della vita politica* (Venice, 1599), pp. 445–72; first published in 1579. For a general discussion of this topic, see W. J. Bouwsma, *Venice and the Defence of the Republican Liberty* (Berkeley and Los Angeles, 1968).

[28] Logan, *Culture and Society in Venice*, pp. 150–1, 190, and *passim*.

[29] Koenigsberger, 'Decadence or Shift?', pp. 287–9.

circumstances began to change. The small courts, it is true, remained as hispanically rigid as before; the Inquisition was as powerful and restrictive as ever.[30] But the artistic puritanism of the Counter-Reformation largely died with the generation of the churchmen of the Council of Trent. Mannerism gave way to the Baroque, a style which managed to combine the glorification of princes, popes and all established authorities with a most effective emotional appeal to the general public.

The Baroque style, like Mannerism, has been seen as a natural development of Renaissance style. But a purely stylistic development, however logical for the artist, does not explain its astonishing popularity; for it caught on in most of Europe and Latin America; it was favoured by Protestant, as well as Catholic, courts; and only France and, much less emphatically, England and Holland rejected it. The Baroque style provided exactly what courts, churches and the general public wanted at the time, an artistic and emotional bridging of the gulf between monarchies and their subjects, between the Church hierarchy and the Christian congregation, between court and bourgeois society. The Baroque artists achieved this result by emphasizing three specific elements in their art: first, the representation of a strongly personal type of religious emotion with which ordinary people could identify. This is already a characteristic feature of the paintings of the first of the great Baroque painters, Caravaggio. Secondly, they emphasized the grandeur and magnificence of churches, palaces and of great personages, lay or ecclesiastical; and this, of course, was what their patrons expected. Thirdly, they had a strong sense of the dramatic and of the theatrical in art and architecture; and this was popular with all classes in an age that saw the greatest efflorescence of the theatre since Athens in the fifth century B.C.[31] The French, especially during the reign of Louis XIV, managed to get similar results with their own, very different, classical style. This style, while much more restrained in its portrayal of religious emotions, was as magnificent and theatrical as that of the Baroque. But whereas in the Renaissance the relationship between art, artist and society had been, at least ideally, one of participation, in the Baroque, and in French classicism, it became a relationship of presentation, as in the presentation of a play to the non-participating audience in the theatre.

---

[30] Cf. Trevor-Roper's argument that these conditions led to the emigration of the economically most skilled and active 'Erasmian' capitalists from the Italian cities to north-western Europe: H. R. Trevor-Roper, *Religion and Social Change* (London, 1967), ch. 1.

[31] These three elements do not, of course, exhaust the characteristics of such a complex and varied phenomonon as the Baroque style. The quest for bringing together of different art-forms and for the 'total work of art' may well be regarded as equally significant, but I do not think it was as important as the other three in leading to the wide diffusion of the style.

And, in consequence, the courtly virtues of artificiality and virtuosity were as highly prized as they were in Mannerism.[32]

While Baroque churches, monasteries and palaces were now beginning to be built and decorated, from Poland to Portugal and from Sweden to Sicily, this cannot in itself be seen as the clustering of creative activities which were so characteristic of the Italian and the nothern Renaissance and which I am trying to investigate. Now, such clustering did still take place in Italy in the first half of the seventeenth century, but in only one place, in Rome.[33] The papal court was the only Italian court with resources comparable to those of the courts of France, England and Spain, and it enjoyed the great advantage of not having to spend its money on warfare or, at least, not more than the grudging subsidies given to some of the Catholic powers during the Thirty Years War. Added to this were the resources of the Roman aristocracy and of the religious orders, drawing funds from all over Catholic Europe and stimulated to spending on culture by the example of happily extravagant popes.

The Roman Baroque of the age of Urban VIII, Bernini and Borromini had many of the aspects of a court culture, but it was at the same time an urban culture dependent now no longer on a city republic but on a large capital city. Buying and selling of uncommissioned paintings had occurred in fifteenth-century Florence and sixteenth-century Venice. But it was only in seventeenth-century Rome that it became important. This was, in part, the result of the considerable number of people in seventeenth-century Rome who could afford to buy works of art – undoubtedly far more than ever in Florence and probably also more than in Venice. It was also the result of changing patterns of taste. During the Renaissance the habit of private enjoyment of works of art had been the privilege of princes and of a few rich courtiers and aristocrats. But this habit was now spreading to a much wider public, who could afford it at different levels of expenditure. Artists, while still for preference looking to the security of commissions, began to take notice of this market. In 1633 the painters' Academy of San Luca declared: 'It is serious, lamentable, indeed intolerable to everybody to see works destined for the decoration of sacred temples or the splendour of noble palaces exhibited in shops or in the streets like cheap goods for sale.'[34] But no amount of indignation by stuffy academicians could hold up the tide of economic and social

---

[32] Bernini made this point in his comedy, *Fontana di Trevi,* ed. C. d'Onofrio (Rome, 1963), p. 60. Speaking of a stage production one character says: 'Oh, what beautiful clouds do I see floating in the air. But, in fact, where there is naturalness there is artifice.' The point then continues to be discussed.

[33] For a general survey of the visual arts in Rome during this period, see F. Haskell, *Patrons and Painters* (New York, 1963).

[34] Quoted *ibid.,* p. 121.

change in an art world where even Velázquez exhibited his commissioned portrait of Innocent X at the annual art exhibition in the Pantheon.[35]

Not unnaturally, Barberini Rome attracted artists and collectors from all over Italy and, indeed, from much of Europe besides. Many of the greatest names of the period, such as Poussin, were foreigners and came from a stylistically very different tradition. The rest of Italy and its courts could no longer rival Rome as they had done in the Renaissance. The Medici, the Gonzaga and other dynasties were still anxious to act as patrons of the arts; but they could not compete financially with the papacy and with the courts of the great western monarchies. Their patronage, moreover, was too personal or dynastic, and hence too much subject to personal whims and to family vicissitudes. The failure of the Este dynasty in Ferrara in 1597 and of the Italian Gonzagas in Mantua in 1627 brought to an abrupt end two centuries of splendid, if somewhat patchy, art patronage.

The vulnerability of a purely court art was not only an Italian phenomenon. Perhaps no prince of the period was as successful in creating *de novo* the conditions for a many-sided court culture as the Emperor Rudolf II in Prague.[36] Yet it died with Rudolf's forced abdication, its artists leaving as quickly as they had come – more than ten years before Prague itself and its art collections were ruined by Calvinist puritanism, war, occupation, Habsburg revenge for its rebellion and, finally, a devastating sack by the Swedish army.

For the artists themselves a purely court atmosphere tended to become oppressive, even when they received as much patronage as they could wish for. Poussin claimed that he preferred 'some small corner from which he could comfortably watch the [human] comedy'. Rubens wrote of his 'horror courts', and even Van Dyck, that most courtly of court artists, grew tired of the English court and its insatiable demand for portraits.[37]

In Germany the decline of the visual arts from about 1540 onwards was much more catastrophic than in Italy. The German artists whom Rudolf II attracted to Prague were talented men, but there was no Dürer or Grünewald or Riemenschneider among them. The most gifted of the German painters of the period, Adam Elsheimer, went early to Rome and died young; and he, too, was no Dürer.

How much of an artistic wasteland Germany had become by the seventeenth century is painfully clear from the compilation of biographies of painters, sculptors and architects by Joachim von Sandrart, published in 1675. In his preface Sandrart defended himself

[35] *Ibid.*, p. 126.

[36] R. J. W. Evans, *Rudolf II and his World* (Oxford, 1973); H. R. Trevor-Roper, *Princes and Artists* (London, 1976), ch. 3.

[37] Levey, *Painting at Court*, pp. 133 ff.

against those who would think it strange that he had spent so much effort on matters generally held of little importance and that he would have been better occupied in writing about Marius, Sulla, Catiline and similar 'thirsters after human blood'. 'I do not think it is my job', he continued, 'to write heroes' tales dealing with the abomination of exploding saltpetre and thundering mortars, but rather to describe and present the delicate pen and brush strokes of the most distinguished artists.'[38] Neither Vasari nor Karel van Mander would have dreamed of needing such a justification in Italy or the Netherlands.

From Sandrart's book it is clear that in Germany the late-medieval and Renaissance tradition of the artists' workshops had effectively been broken. What remained was little more than craftsmen's workshops. Those few Germans with the talent and ambition to go beyond the level of mere craftmanship had to get their apprenticeship in the Netherlands or in Italy and pursued their careers in Rome. Even the memory of some of the great German Renaissance artists was lost. Sandrart writes that he heard of Grünewald only by chance as a boy from an old painter who had actually studied with Grünewald and collected many of the master's drawings. These drawings had then, characteristically, found their way into a private *Kunstkabinett* in Frankfurt where they remained to all intents and purposes buried.[39]

Modern German art historians have, of course, observed this artistic collapse, and perhaps the most interesting analysis of this phenomenon was produced by Georg Dehio, as early as 1913.[40] Dehio argued that Protestantism – and I think he must have meant especially Lutheranism – while not actually hostile to the visual arts contained nothing that actively demanded visual-artistic expression. Since much of German Renaissance art had been religious art this would certainly go a long way to explain artistic decline in the Protestant parts of Germany. It does not, however, explain why the decline occurred also in those parts of Germany which remained Catholic. Dehio therefore stressed the general economic decline of Germany and, more particularly, the ravages of the Thirty Years' War, and he also suggested a stylistic-psychological reason. He claimed that the spread of the Italian Renaissance style produced a break in the German artistic tradition which was basically non-classical. Dürer's epigones misunderstood the master's attempt to assimilate classicism to the northern tradition and 'confused form with formalism'. Only when Italian art ceased to be classical (that is, with the coming of the Baroque) could the Germans

[38] J. von Sandrart, *Academie der Bau-, Bild- und Malerei-Künste von 1675,* ed. A. R. Pelzer (Munich, 1925), p. 49.

[39] *Ibid.,* pp. 81–2.

[40] G. Dehio, 'Die Krisis der deutschen Kunst im XVI Jharhundert', in *Kunsthistorische Aufsätze* (Munich and Berlin, 1914).

understand the Italians again 'and make this foreign gift fruitful for themselves'.[41]

Allowing for a certain amount of nationalistic mysticism which was very common when he wrote, Dehio has provided a perceptive explanation of the phenomenon of German artistic collapse. I would, however, add some further reaons. It was precisely the big south German cities, Nuremberg, Augsburg, Strassburg and others, which became Protestant. At the same time they were under increasing economic and political pressure from the surrounding princes, already well before the outbreak of the Thirty Years' War. This would certainly help to explain the decline of the artistic workshops which, as in Italy and in the Netherlands, were of course situated mainly in the big cities. At the same time the courts of the German princes were also affected by Spanish (and later French) etiquette and formalism. Few of the German princes had the means to emulate Rudolf II, let alone compete with the court of Prague for scarce artistic talent. But, perhaps most important of all, the capitals of the German princes were nearly all relatively small towns. Courtly patronage was therefore as vulnerable as that of the smaller Italian principalities. German art could never have the advantage of the combination of a princely court and a large and rich metropolitan capital city, such as Rome, Paris, London or even Brussels. Only from the turn of the seventeenth and eighteenth centuries, following the successful defence of the city against the Turks, did Vienna become the site of a building boom of splendid Baroque churches and palaces. At the same time it saw the still modest beginnings of a clustering in musical activity. The really great age of Viennese music did not, however, begin until the last decades of the eighteenth century, when Vienna had become a relatively large city.

The relationship between courts and cities was equally important in the development of drama and particularly of grand tragedy. It has often been remarked that neither Italy nor Germany produced playwrights of the calibre of those of Spain, England, France and Holland. Recently the absence of important commercial theatres in Italy has been pointed to and the consequent sharp division between popular and aristocratic theatre, the latter remaining something of an 'amateur affair'.[42] This analysis would explain why Italy in the later sixteenth and in the seventeenth centuries produced a superb genre of popular comedy, the *commedia dell'arte*. Acted by professionals in market squares or palaces it had the advantages of realism, topicality and humour in recognizably human situations, together with a

---

[41] *Ibid.*, p. 43.

[42] P. Burke, 'Italian Literature and Society, 1350–1650', in D. Daiches and A. K. Thorlby (eds.), *The Old World: Discovery and Rebirth* (London, 1974), pp. 357 ff. The situation began to change after 1637 when several theatres and opera-houses began to be built in Venice.

flexibility which has allowed its characters and its modes to survive in the theatre, in opera and now in films right up to the present time. What the *commedia dell'arte* could not do was to explore the psychological depths of the comedies of Lope de Vega, Shakespeare or Molière; and what the court poets and learned humanist playwrights could not begin to produce was viable tragedy.

The reason for the absence of great commercial theatres in Italy and Germany lies, I believe, again in the situation of most of their courts in relatively small towns. Lope, Tirso de Molina and Calderón lived in Madrid; Marlowe, Shakespeare and Webster in London; Corneille, Molière and Racine in Paris; and Vondel in Amsterdam. This gave a dual patronage and audience, courtly and urban. In Germany this was quite impossible and in Italy it happened only rather late in Venice, which had no court, and it could elsewhere have happened only in Rome and, perhaps, in Naples. But in Rome the attitude of the papacy and of some of the most influential orders was too often altogether hostile towards the theatre, and even when it was not, the centre of Catholic Christendom was not the place to stimulate the presentation of the struggle of two divine powers or laws, or of the individual's relationship to society or fate, which are the essence of grand tragedy. At best there were the satirical comedies of Bernini, nearly all of which, however, have been lost.[43] Nor was the situation better in Naples. Its viceroys were foreigners. What patronage they would dispense or stimulate among the Neapolitan nobility was likely to change every three or six years with every new appointment. It is therefore not surprising that in Naples, as in Rome, patrons, audiences and playwrights preferred conventional comedy and, at most, conventional social satire, to a more profound analysis of the human condition. As to the theatre of the small courts, it preferred the nostalgia of the pastoral with its vision of a golden age, now lost. 'Oh beautiful golden age (*O bella età de l'oro*)' is the final chorus of Act I of Tasso's *Aminta*. Significantly the golden age came to an end because of the appearance of the 'tyrant honour'.

In my earlier paper I argued that in Italy and, even more dramatically, in Germany there occurred a shift of creative activity into music and into natural science (in Italy) and philosophy (in Germany). The reasons for this shift were, I suggested, that these activities were not as definitely linked with the specific urban communal traditions as were the Renaissance visual arts; that courts, even small and etiquette-ridden courts, could be effective patrons of music and science, and that, in both church music and opera, composers and musicians kept the vitalizing contact with the general public, so that music continued to

---

[43] See I. Lavin, review of Bernini, *Fontana di Trevi*, ed. d'Onofrio, *Art Bull*, xlvi (1964), pp. 568–72.

have aspects of a communal art which painting and sculpture had, to some extent, lost.[44]

For Germany Dehio had noticed such a shift and he ascribed it exclusively to the Protestant, and especially the Lutheran, ethos.[45] This is certainly right. To Luther and to generations of Lutheran pastors and cantors, music and theology were heavenly sisters. Through music the lay congregation could take an active part in the church serivce.[46] In hundreds, perhaps thousands, of Lutheran churches in north Germany music was loved and practised. There could hardly be more propitious conditions for the development of music. By contrast Switzerland, where the Zwinglian and Calvinist churches either banned music from church services altogether or severely restricted it, took little part in the great triumphs of German music, from the late sixteenth to the nineteenth centuries.

Yet religion cannot have been the only reason for the efflorescence of music in Germany, for it occurred also in the Catholic parts of Germany and, of course, in Catholic Italy; or rather, the relationship between religion and music was a complex and subtle one. In the long run, as I have tried to argue on a different occasion, it depended on the decline of religious sensibilities among the educated classes of Europe and the ability of music to fill the resulting emotional void.[47]

More immediately, in the later sixteenth and in the early seventeenth centuries it also depended on the nature of formal and philosophical thinking in and about music. It was here that Italy was in the forefront. The dominant medieval tradition in the idealistic theory of music had been the Pythagorean, which saw music as a reflection of the harmony of the universe. This tradition reached its highest point in the Netherlands contrapuntal style which dominated European musical life, including that of Italy,[48] in the early sixteenth century. It was in this context, and referring especially to Josquin des Prés, that Luther had said 'thus God preached the gospel also through music'.[49] Parallel with this religious concept of music there was another one, with equally respectable antecedents in both classical authors and in the Bible. This was the notion of the powers of music, its effects on the

[44] Koenigsberger, 'Decadence or Shift?'.

[45] Dehio, *op. cit.*, p. 156.

[46] F. Blume, 'Luther the Musician', in H. G. Koenigsberger (ed.), *Luther: A Profile* (New York and London, 1973), p. 222.

[47] See above, chapter 9.

[48] B. Castiglione, *Il libro del cortegiano*, ed. V. Cian, 4th edn. (Florence, 1947), pp. 190–1. Cf also A. Laszari, *La musica alla corte dei duchi di Ferrara* (Ferrara, 1929), p. iv: 'During the period when Italy really produced its immortal master-pieces in music – the art in which our country rightly considers itself to be outstanding – it was tutored by the Netherlanders . . .'

[49] Martin Luther, *Werke: Kritische Gesamtausgabe* (Weimar, 1883–, in progress), *Tischreden*, ii (Weimar, 1913), p. 11, no. 1258; quoted in F. Blume, *Geschichte der evangelischen Kirchenmusik,* 2nd edn. (Kassel, 1965), p. 7.

emotion or, as people said in the sixteenth and seventeenth centuries, the passions.

It is not really surprising that this aspect of music was pursued especially in Italy in the sixteenth century. What it needed was an educated lay society, for music devoted to affecting the passions was, in the first place, mainly secular music. To the churches and their theologians, both Catholic and Calvinist, this aspect of music was rather frightening.[50] Only in the seventeenth century, with the triumph of the Baroque, was the Catholic Church willing to accept such music.

Music which affected the passions we find first of all in the Italian madrigal and then in the *intermezzi* and other types of incidental music for festivals, processions and stage shows. Madrigals were upper-class entertainments, whether at court or in private houses. The *intermezzi* and processions appealed to all classes and were sponsored equally by the courts and by the republican authorities of Venice, just as they had been sponsored at the end of the fifteenth century by that arch-republican, Savonarola. It was in Venice, too, that there developed that particularly potent means of affecting the passions, the systematic use of instrumental music and its suggestive tone colours. In part, at least, this may be explained by the structure of the basilica of St Mark's itself, which almost imposed on its *maestri di cappella* the use of divided choirs and divided orchestras with the deliberate aim of producing dramatic musical effects. What was also necessary, however, was the circumstance that St Mark's and its music were under the control of the lay government of Venice and not of the church. This is a point I shall return to. Its importance in this context is that it preserved Venice from Tridentine puritanism in music and allowed the development of dramatic church music earlier than anywhere else.

Everything was therefore in favour of the development of music in Italy, and the social and political changes which had played such havoc with the visual arts tended to favour, rather than restrict, music. By 1600 Italy was as pre-eminent in Europe in music as the Netherlands had been in 1500. By contrast Italy had been pre-eminent in the visual arts in 1500, but after 1600 her claims were beginning to be disputed. Much of the development of music took place in a number of newly founded academies. It was the Academia Olimpica of Vicenza, in Venetian territory, which commissioned the building of the Teatro Olimpico by Palladio, himself one of the founder-members of the academy. It is characteristic of the state of Italian culture at the time that the 'Olimpians' were fully confident of their own and their contemporaries' ability to provide the theatre, the sets and the music for

---

[50] About this and other aspects of the development of dramatic music in Italy, see W. Osthoff, *Theatergesang und darstellende Musik in der Italienischen Renaissance* (Münchener Veröffentlichungen zur Musikgeschichte, xiv, Tutzing, 1969), pp. 326 ff., and *passim*. I would like to thank Dr. P. Petrobelli for drawing my attention to this work.

that most famous of dramatic 'happenings' of the sixteenth century, the inauguration of the theatre, in 1585 – everything, that is, except a great play. For this they chose Sophocles's *Oedipus*. Andrea Gabrieli's music for this occasion is generally regarded as one of the great dramatic achievements of composition before the invention of opera proper.[51]

This invention, as is well known, took place in another academy, a little more than a decade later, the famous Camerata of Florence. Nowhere is the shift of creative activity from the visual arts to music more striking than in Florence. For there is no question that by the 1590s Florence had become an artistic backwater.

Florentine opera undoubtedly began as an art-form for an élite of court society and private aristocrats. But from at least one important strand of its origins, that of the *intermezzi*, it had a popular appeal from the beginning. It was, in consequence, again in big cities that opera flourished most, and especially in capital cities such as Rome, somewhat later in Paris and, later still, in Vienna. Its earliest, and for the future history of opera perhaps its most crucial, triumph was in Venice. It was Venice which built the first public opera-house, in 1637, and soon it had many more. Their structure, which became the basic model for opera-houses all over the world until our own time, was quite deliberately designed to satisfy both the popular and the élite audience. Ordinary people occupied the stalls. Ladies and gentlemen sat in boxes. The boxes could be bought or hired for periods of time. They allowed their occupants to carry on conversations, to arrive late, above all to be seen in their fine clothes.[52] Contemporaries were well aware of the social and even political advantages of such an arrangement. At the same time it seems unlikely that these advantages were by themselves sufficient to explain the triumphant career of opera since the early seventeenth century, especially in Italy and Germany. Marco da Gagliano, one of the original Florentine composers of opera, claimed that the aim of the new genre was 'that both the mind and the most noble emotions should be enlivened by the most delightful arts the wit of man could invent'.[53] Opera, by attempting to represent words and emotions musically, gave them a dramatic and emotional depth which Shakespeare, Calderón and Racine were able to provide with their poetry but which the Italians and Germans, for reasons which I have tried to discuss, were unable to equal in their plays.[54] Socially, emotionally and artistically, opera came to play the role in Italy that

[51] *Ibid.*

[52] S.T.Worsthorne, *Venetian Opera in the Seventeeth Century* (Oxford, 1968), pp. 6 ff.

[53] *Ibid.*, p. 16 note 3. The original text, from the preface to Gagliano's opera *Dafne* (1608), is 'di maniera che, con l'intelletto, vien lusingato in uno stesso tempo ogni sentimento più nobile dalle più dilettevoli arti ch'abbia ritrovato l'ingegno umano'.

[54] Note, for instance, the importance which Monteverdi attached to writing music for human beings and their passions and not for talking stage winds:
'the winds are to sing, the zephyrs and the boreases; but how, my good Lord, can I imitate the
*continued*

Elizabethan and Jacobean drama played in England. And conversely, precisely because in Italy and Germany literary traditions and socio-political circumstances made it psychologically impossible to develop great drama, the dramatic instincts of both, the creative artists of these countries and their audiences, found their outlet and fulfilment in music drama – that is opera. For it was only in Italy and, somewhat later, in Germany that opera became both a highbrow and a popular art-form. Almost everywhere else, with the only very partial exceptions of Paris, and of London in the last twenty-five years, it remained, and is still now, an esoteric form of entertainment.

At about the same time that Italy became the pre-eminent centre of music in Europe, it was also becoming pre-eminent in the natural sciences, and this I would suggest, for very similar reasons. As in the case of music the traditions of Italian Renaissance science were not specifically linked to the city-state or communal life. At least until Galileo ran into trouble with the Inquisition, natural science or, more accurately, natural philosophy was a politically neutral subject, just as it was very consciously so regarded in mid-seventeenth-century England during the Civil War and Cromwellian period. It was not and could not be a subject of great popular appeal and its practitioners, then as now, were concerned almost exclusively with the esteem of their colleagues and students, or, at most, of a small educated élite. In the absence of industrial research, natural philosophers had to look for sponsorship and patronage to the universities and to governments, and from Florence to Copenhagen, courts were willing to spend money on attracting prestigious scientists. Moreoever the scientific societies and academics which were being founded, from the beginning of the seventeenth century, often by ruling princes or with their sponsorship, had a rather different effect on the development of science from that of the art academies on the development of art. For while the art academies tended to stifle originality, the scientific societies, by disseminating information and by forcing their members to explain their discoveries and prove their theories, tended to stimulate original work.

It is not possible in this context to discuss the socio-political development of science in detail. It is necessary, however, to return once more to the problem of court and of city patronage for both music and science. Fortunately it is here not necessary to work by inference;

*continued*
talking of the winds when they don't talk? and how could I in this way move the passions? Ariadne moves us because she is a woman, and Orpheus similarly moves us because he is a man and not a wind . . . The whole fable [that is, *The Marriage of Thetis*, for which Monteverdi was to write the *intermezzi*] . . . I can't feel that it moves me at all. Ariadne moves me to a true lament and Orpheus to a heartfelt prayer. But this fable – I don't know what it is meant to do. What would Your Illustrious Highness that music should do with it?'

Monteverdi to Alessandro Striggio, Venice, 9 Dec. 1616: Claudio Monteverdi, *Lettere, dediche e prefazioni*, ed. D. de'Paoli (Rome, 1973), p. 87. My translation.

for this precise problem was discussed in personal and urgent terms by the two greatest creative minds in Italy in the early seventeenth century.

Monteverdi had entered the service of the Gonzaga dukes of Mantua as a young man in 1570 and remained in it until 1612. It was a fruitful but difficult period of his life. He was overburdened with work and his advancement was slower than he thought he deserved. In 1608 his growing irritation boiled over in a famous letter to the duke's secretary. He had served the duke well and faithfully and often at great expense to himself, he wrote, but he had been badly rewarded and not been paid what he had been promised. His Highness had never thanked him by some public favour, 'although your Excellency knows that marks of favour shown by great princes to their servants are most needful to their honour and advantage, especially when foreigners are present.' What was particularly galling was the duke's much greater generosity to foreign musicians, such as Marco da Gagliano who, Monteverdi claimed not quite justifiably, had done nothing compared with himself.[55]

These were more than the sour grumblings of an ambitious man who felt the world was not giving him his due. In 1620, when Monteverdi had been in Venetian service for seven years as *maestro di cappella* of St. Mark's, the court of Mantua tried to rectify its blunder of 1612 of dismissing the most famous living composer by trying to get Monteverdi to return to Mantua. Monteverdi's reply spelt out why, for all the emotional attractions of service with the dukes of Mantua – and his remarks about this have the ring of more than just politeness – he preferred to stay in Venice. The republic, he argued was giving him four hundred *scudi* (florins) a year, double the salary it had paid to all his distinguished predecessors. Besides, he could easily earn an extra fifty *scudi* on commissions for a couple of vespers or a mass. The duke was not offering as much or, worse still, he had promised more but, when it came to the point, it turned out to be less, and some of it was money owed to Monteverdi for a long time anyway. He would still be getting less – and this was a complaint he had made before – than visiting foreigners or, worse, some of the singers. But, perhaps most important of all, he was greatly honoured in Venice, he had full control over appointments and dismissals of singers and instrumental players. 'There is no gentleman who does not esteem and honour me, and when I perform some chamber music or church music, I swear to Your Excellency that the whole city comes running to listen.' His position, he continued, was for life and was not terminated by the death of the *procuratori* of St. Mark's or of the doge, whereas in Mantua his employment would cease with the death of the prince or 'at his smallest whim (*a suo minimo disgusto*)'. In Venice he was paid regularly, and if he

---

[55] Monteverdi to Annibale Chieppo, Cremona, 2 Dec. 1608: Monteverdi, *Lettere, dediche e prefazioni*, pp. 33–7.

did not collect his salary himself, it would be sent to his house; but in Mantua he had:

had to go to the signor treasurer every day to entreat him to give me what is mine. God preserve me; I have not in my whole life suffered a greater mortification than when I had to go to the signor treasurer and ask him almost for the love of God to give me what belongs to me. I would rather go around begging than suffer such impertinence again.[56]

At just about the same time as Monteverdi was voicing his disenchantment with princely service and was beginning to look towards Venice, Galileo Galilei was considering the same problem the other way round. He had had his irritations and brushes with his professional colleagues but, unlike Monteverdi, he had no complaints against his employers, the university of Padua and, ultimately, the Venetian senate. However, he was irked by his routine duties. With all the considerable advantages of his position, he wrote to a friend in Florence, he did not have sufficient freedom:

for, at the request of various people, I have to give up several hours a day and often enough the best. It is not the custom to obtain a salary from a republic, however splendid and generous she may be, without service to the public; for to obtain something useful from the public one has to give satisfaction to the public . . . and as long as I am able to lecture and to serve, no one in a republic can exempt me from this duty while still leaving me my salary. In short, such benefits I can hope to obtain only from an absolute prince.

He did not, of course, want to be paid a salary without merit or work, he continued, but he wanted to have sufficient leisure to write three great works that he had in mind and to produce all sorts of useful inventions for his prince. 'As to daily work, I abhor only that vile servitude by which I have to present my efforts to the whims of every comer; but to serve a prince or a great lord . . . I would never abhor but always wish for.'[57] In Venice his salary was now a thousand *scudi* a year for life and it came from an 'immortal and immutable prince' – the same point that Monteverdi made about the payment of his salary, only Galileo's was well over double that of the *maestro di cappella* and that, as he told his correspondent, he could make as much again by private lessons and by taking into his house young gentlemen-scholars as paying guests. His duties, it now appeared, were not nearly as heavy as

[56] Monteverdi to Alessandro Striggio, Venice, 13 Mar. 1620: Monteverdi, *Lettere, dediche e prefazioni*, pp. 148–53.

[57] Galileo to S. Vesp, Padua, Fed. 1609: G. Galilei, *Le Opere*, 20 vols. (Florence, 1980–1909; repr. Florence, 1929–39), x, pp. 232 ff. Professor Stillman Drake has very kindly informed me that the identity of S. Vesp is not known and that this letter, which exists only in draft form, may well have never been sent. This latter point, however, does not affect my argument, for the draft still shows what Galileo had in mind.

he had suggested a year earlier when he was just angling for an invitation: 'not more than sixty half-hours per year, and this time not so strictly accounted that I could not, for any reason and without prejudice, take many days off. The rest of the time I am absolutely free and my own master.' He wanted, however, to be free from most of his pupils and from all public lectures, 'for in these one can lecture only about very elementary matters and there are many people who can do that'. Finally, he promised again to produce many useful inventions, but these could be accomplished only with the help of princes, 'for they wage wars, build and defend fortresses and through their royal diversions make huge expenditures such as neither I nor private gentlemen can make.'[58]

Galileo settled for a salary of one thousand *scudi*, the same as he had in Padua, and the titles of chief mathematician and philosopher to the grand duke.[59] He had got what he wanted and what many scientists have dreamed of ever since: a return to and recognition in his own *patria*, a very handsome salary for life with no teaching duties attached, and the prospect of generous funds for research. If there was also an element of snobbery in Galileo's attitude, this fitted in with the accepted attitudes of an arisocratically oriented society. Certainly it was not this which Galileo's aristocratic Venetian friends held against him. What alarmed Giovan Francesco Sagredo, the friend whom Galileo immortalized in his *Dialogue Concerning the Two Chief World Systems*, was precisely what induced Monteverdi to reject the invitation to return to Mantua: the insecurity of princely courts, compared with the security and liberty of a republic. 'Liberty and self-determination, where will you find it as in Venice? . . .', Sagredo wrote to Galileo in a remarkably candid letter.

You are now serving your natural prince, a great and virtuous young man, full of promise; but here you had command over those who command and govern others, and you had to serve no one but yourself, like a monarch of the universe . . . but who, in the tempestuous sea of the court, can hope to escape, I will not say being submerged but still being battered and troubled by the furious winds of envy? . . . Who knows what the infinite and incomprehensible accidents of the world may not do when they are abetted by the calumnies of evil and envious men who sow and raise in the minds of the prince some false and lying idea and make use precisely of his virtue and sense of justice to ruin a brave man? Princes will, for a while, delight in some curiosity; but then, when distracted by some matter of greater interest, they will turn their minds to other matters. I can well believe that the grand duke can amuse himself with looking at the city of Florence and its neighbourhood with one of your telescopes (*occhiali*). But when it becomes necessary for him

[58] Galileo to Belisario Vinta, Padua, 7 May 1610: Galilei, *Opere*, x pp. 348–50.

[59] *Discoveries and Opinions of Galileo*, ed. Stillman Drake (Garden City, N.Y., 1957), p. 65.

to look at the whole of Italy, at France, at Spain, at Germany and at the Levant, he will put your telescope aside. And although, with your skill, you may discover some other instrument for such a case, who can invent a telescope to distinguish the fools from the wise . . .?

Sagredo's final argument had an even more prophetic ring than the rest, although in fact it rested on recent Venetian experience. Was it safe, he asked, to go to a place where the Jesuits had so much influence as they did in Florence.[60]

In retrospect it is clear that Sagredo's judgement of the differences between a court and a republic was correct, just as was Monteverdi's similar judgment. It was not the fault of the individual princes. The Italian line of the Gonzaga dukes became extinct in 1627, and Mantua was overwhelmed by several years of war. Its role as a great centre for art and music was over long before it finally lost its independence to Austria, in 1707. The grand dukes of Tuscany did not withdraw their favour from Galileo. But, for political reasons, they could not defend their great philosopher from the Roman Inquisition as the Venetian republic undoubtedly could and would have done.[61]

It is now time to return to my original questions: what were the conditions of the clustering of creative activities, from the Italian Renaissance to the end of the seventeenth century, and how did such clustering come to an end, or, as a third possibility, how did it shift from one field, or group of fields, of creative activity to another? It may be useful to give my conclusions in schematic form while still trying not to do violence to the variety and richness of human experience and endeavour. For reasons of space I have had to forego any attempt to discuss England and Spain or to fit architecture into this account. Styles in building have generally been closely related to styles in the other visual arts; but actual building activity, in the early modern period just as now, was always commissioned, and depended on the resources of the patron, wherever he might have been living. Clusters of great architectural creativity are therefore even more directly related to the economic history of particular countries than those of other arts, especially as it has always been easy to import a foreign architect for a particular building, provided only the local craft skills are available. Yet it might still be

---

[60] G. F. Sagredo to Galileo, Venice, 13 Aug. 1611: Galilei, *Opere*, xi, pp. 171 ff. Sagredo's last point, about the Jesuits, was put obliquely and humorously: '. . . since this is in the place where the influence of friends of Berlinzone, as one might imagine, is very powerful, this troubles me very much.' Rocco Berlinzone appears to have been a Jesuit in Ferrara on whom Sagredo had played a trick, by writing him letters purporting to come from a rich widow asking the Jesuit fathers for advice on various matters. Apparently Berlinzone had been completely taken in, much to Sagredo's and Galileo's amusement. Cf. A. Favaro, *Galileo Galilei e lo studo di Padova*, 2 vols. (Florence, 1883), ii, p. 105.

[61] Cf. Stillman Drake's similar view: *Discoveries and Opinions of Galileo,* ed. Drake, p. 69.

considered significant that the two architectural styles which were to dominate most of Europe up to the eighteenth century, the Baroque and the Palladian, were first developed in Rome and Venice respectively.

1. The Italian Renaissance and *mutatis mutandis* the northern Renaissance produced remarkable clusters of the highest class of creative activity in all the visual arts and, in Italy at least, in poetry, classical scholarship and political and historical writing. This was made possible by a probably unique historical constellation: a long tradition of civic and communal art together with court patronage. This court patronage by and large accepted the civic and communal traditions but provided not only money and artistic opportunities for artists who were mostly city-trained but also a certain fruitful refinement of taste.

2. In the course of the first half of the sixteenth century this uniquely favourable constellation dissolved. Most of the remaining city republics lost their independence and/or much of their previous economic prosperity. The exponents of the visual arts, especially in Italy, tended to turn away from their previous traditions and created a new, essentially courtly style, Mannerism.

3. By the second half of the sixteenth century it became clear that this was too narrow a basis to maintain the cluster of creative activity in the visual arts at its previous level. The courts themselves had changed into much more rigid, etiquette-ridden societies in which many artists seem to have felt uncomfortable. The rigidity of this changed court society was reinforced by the now dominant ethos of the Counter-Reformation. In Italy, and especially in Florence, there was a marked decline in the quality of the visual arts, although not perhaps as much in sculpture as in painting. In Germany they collapsed altogether, a cultural catastrophe in which the indifference and even hostility of the different Protestant churches to the visual arts played a significant part. In both countries, therefore, the Renaissance clustering of the arts had come to an end, and this for reasons which cannot be explained satisfactorily from an analysis of style.

4. This conclusion is reinforced by the history of Venice, which runs counter to that of the rest of Italy. For in Venice the clustering of Renaissance art continued until the end of the sixteenth century and it did this even when Venetian artists had adopted and adapted for their own purposes the courtly style of the Florentine Mannerists. It seems reasonable to argue that the reason for this difference between Venice and the rest of Italy was the continued vitality of Venice as a city republic. This was certainly the reason given by many contemporaries.[62]

5. In the first half of the seventeenth century a new cluster of creative activity in the visual arts appeared in Rome. Its formal expression, the Baroque style, managed at one and the same time to glorify church,

[62] Some of these are quoted in my 'Decadence of Shift?', pp. 287 ff.

pope and princes and, largely because of its dramatic qualities, to have immense popular appeal. The gulf which had opened between the artist and the general public in the sixteenth century was therefore closed again. Nevertheless this cluster of creative activities was different from the Renaissance clusters. It depended not on a multiplicity of city-states and small courts but on a large metropolitan capital city and a very large court. These acted as a magnet for the rest of Italy and, indeed, for much of Europe. The only courts, which could compete with Rome – and even they were hampered by the Thirty Years' War – were those of Paris, Madrid, London and, to a lesser degree, Brussels. There was nothing like these courts in large cities in Germany.

6. The combination of a large court and a large capital city also provided fruitful conditions for the development of the theatre – drama and especially tragedy. We find characteristic clusters of high creative activity in this field in London, Madrid and Paris, where the theatres appealed to both court and urban society. Amsterdam, a large city without a court but with a wealthy patriciate, could also produce this, even though perhaps on a slightly lower level. Rome and Naples did not, mainly because the political and religious tone of their 'establishments' was unsympathetic to the adaptation of classical tragedy to modern sensibilities. Italy did, however, create a popular comic theatre in the *commedia dell'arte* which, for centuries, it exported over most of Europe.

7. The political, social and religious changes of the sixteenth century which had such profound effects on the visual arts, political thought and drama had far less effect on two other fields of creative activity, namely music and the natural sciences. Neither had been as closely linked with a civic tradition as the visual arts of the Renaissance. Churches, courts, town halls and the houses of private persons could all be, in their own way, excellent patrons of music. In Italy and in Germany music developed in all of them. It seems moreover that, precisely because of the problems encountered by the visual arts, there was an actual shift of creative talent into music in Italy and Germany. By this I mean that gifted young men and boys might well prefer to choose an apprenticeship in music rather than in painting or sculpture. Cellini still chose apprenticeship as a goldsmith but leaves us in no doubt that he might have, indeed did, become a superb musician. By the invention of the new genre of opera Italian and, later, German musicians created a dramatic form which was at once courtly and popular, and which gave an emotional dimension to Italian and German theatre which compensated for its absence in the 'straight' theatre.

8. By Contrast, scientists were, by the nature of their subject, largely indifferent to contact with a wide public. Therefore there seems to have also been a shift of creative talent into science, just as there was for music, although for opposite reasons.

9. Even in music and in natural science the differences between small courts and city republics remained important, and in the early seventeenth century were urgently discussed by the most distinguished exponents of these activities. Characteristically Descartes preferred republican Holland to monarchical France. Bruno's and Galileo's experiences with the Inquisition gave a religious dimension to this debate which had not previously been important.

10. From the early seventeenth century the terms of the problem of clustering of creative activities shifted. Small courts by themselves could still act as centres for such clusters. But more than ever they depended on attracting outsiders and usually their effectiveness as centres of patronage was limited both to a small group or even a single field of creative activity and to a relatively short period of time. Few of them managed to establish new traditions. Until the end of the eighteenth century cultural clusters tended to occur where there was a conjunction of courts and large capital cities, with a growing public who could afford to buy concert, theatre and opera tickets, and books and even paintings and *objets d'art*. Even the scientists were eventually happier in the big cities than in small courts or small university towns. The founders of the Royal Society preferred London to Oxford or Cambridge. Eventually the courts became irrelevant. Amsterdam in the seventeenth century was the home of a clustering of painting, drama and philosophy and scientific inquiry without the benefit of any court or court society. By the nineteenth century the former role of the courts in creative activity had been taken over by the capitalist urban market and by the political and military calculations of bureaucratic governments.

# Index

*Modern authors and editors in italics.*